D1367843

Behavior, Culture, and Conflict in World Politics

Behavior, Culture, and Conflict in World Politics

Edited by

William Zimmerman and Harold K. Jacobson

Ann Arbor

THE UNIVERSITY OF MICHIGAN PRESS

Copyright © by the University of Michigan 1993
All rights reserved
Published in the United States of America by
The University of Michigan Press
Manufactured in the United States of America

1996   1995   1994   1993   4   3   2   1

A CIP catalogue record for this book is available from the British Library.

Library of Congress Cataloging-in-Publication Data

Behavior, culture, and conflict in world politics / edited by William
    Zimmerman and Harold K. Jacobson.
        p.   cm.
    Includes bibliographical references (p.   ) and index.
    ISBN 0-472-10453-5 (alk. paper)
    1. International relations and culture.   2. Pacific settlement of
international disputes.   3. World politics—1989–   I. Zimmerman,
William, 1936–   .   II. Jacobson, Harold Karan.
JX1255.B42   1993
327.1'1—dc20   93-20921
                                                      CIP

Preface

The origins of this volume date to a conversation on the streets of Ann Arbor the editors had several years ago with Fritz Mosher of the Carnegie Corporation. All three of us, it turned out, thought there was a real need to encourage persons from a wide range of disciplines and areas of inquiry to provide an account of how they approached the study of conflict in order to ascertain whether these approaches might enrich the study of world politics. The University of Michigan seemed a particularly appropriate place to undertake such an effort in light of its great social and behavioral science tradition and its great strengths in area studies.

The editors benefited from the assistance of many people in putting this compendium together. We owe a special debt of gratitude to Dr. Mosher and to the Carnegie Corporation, which funded the research that made the substantive chapters in this volume possible, as well as to our colleagues, who remained generally patient as the volume went through what must have seemed on occasion an interminable gestation period. All the senior authors were at the time they prepared initial drafts members of the faculty of the University of Michigan, although Roman Szporluk has since relocated to another well-known institution on the East coast. Regina Baker in the early stages of the project and Linda Harvey and Patrick Dirker at later stages contributed their considerable organizational skills. Colin Day, the director of the University of Michigan Press, has been supportive throughout.

Contents

Introduction

William Zimmerman and Harold K. Jacobson

The post–World War II era has finally ended. Fundamental changes have occurred in the international system over the last several years that have altered, presumably forever, many of its defining features. To a considerable extent, the outlines of world politics in the 1990s remain uncertain. Minerva's owl flies at dusk; we are more clear about what is past than whether what is past is prologue. Gone certainly is the time when Soviet (or even Russian)–American relations defined the state of the international system: they are no longer, in Arnold Wolfers's terms, the locus of major tension or, as the Soviets used to express it, the main contradiction.

Gone, indeed, are the Soviet Union and that icon of the Cold War, the Berlin Wall. Eastern Europe—which always was a political concept—is now far more appropriately termed East Central Europe. What we thought were the givens of world politics in the aftermath of World War II have receded into the past. The Germanies have united. Western Europe is becoming increasingly integrated. By contrast, the Soviet Union has been replaced by several successor states bound together tenuously in a Commonwealth of Independent States, the capital of which will be located in Minsk, doubtless for the same reasons the capital of Illinois is Springfield and not Chicago and the capital of New York state is Albany and not New York City.

This book is written with these fundamental changes in mind. It is, however, neither an attempt to describe the changes that have occurred in the international system nor an effort to predict the future evolution of world politics. Rather, it represents an effort to encourage—the phrase, however hackneyed these days, is unavoidable in this context—new thinking about conflict in world politics. Our goal is to initiate a reassessment of the paradigms that have long governed the thinking of students of international politics by bringing together systematic research about conflict from a variety of disciplinary and cultural perspectives in a single volume. As it turns out, the disciplinary perspectives share much in common. Moreover, the differences among contemporary U.S., Russian, Chinese, and Japanese approaches to conflict are quite suggestive about ways to manage conflict in world politics, especially in a world in which the states of the Pacific rim will play an increasingly important role.

However much the twenty-first century differs from the twentieth, it will be a world of conflict, and so the task for policymakers and plain people alike will be to devise methods to manage that conflict, not to eliminate it. In this respect, state interactions parallel the interactions of hominids, other mammals, and primitive peoples. Bobbi S. Low's chapter, written from the perspective of an evolutionary biologist, is an edifying review of a vast literature in biology and anthropology on conflict. In that broad perspective, conflict for most animals is an inevitable consequence of the scarcity of resources—largely reproductive resources, i.e., mates or resources and status that contribute to reproductive success. Given scarce reproductive resources, she argues, "conflict is as old as life," and indeed "if evolutionary and behavioral ecological theory is correct, conflicts of interest, if not open aggression, are universal among living things."

The wild kingdom is really wild; "damaging aggression is surprisingly widespread." It is not, however, a realm of purposeless violence. Rather, both violence and conflict more generally occur systematically. Such conflict usually takes place when the stakes are high and is driven by sexual and kin selection. Open conflict most often occurs between "individuals of the same population, rather than between groups from different populations," and such conflict is "unlikely unless the actors are similar in status or power." A. F. K. Organski's power transition operates among animals; power differential and the direction of change in relative power contribute substantially to the prediction of the incidence of conflict.

The story is rather similar for relatively simple human societies. One of the most studied of such societies is that of the Yanomamo. Those among the Yanomamo who wage war benefit from that activity by siring substantially more children than do other males. The *unokai*—those who have killed on a war party—have on the average an additional wife and three more children than the non-*unokai*. Similar experiences are found among the Meru of Kenya, and the Blackfoot of North America. In preindustrial societies, warfare results in "increased direct access to reproductive females, and increased material resources useful for the lineage and in contracting marriages."

What relevance do the experiences of other animals and primitive peoples have for complex societies? Here Low is careful to avoid reductionist explanations or to engage in simple policy prescriptions. She does not think it likely, for instance, that reproductive success and the behavior of warriors correlate in modern societies. She does consider it likely, however, that some continuity exists between modern and premodern wars. The parallels show up more as mimicking traditional kinship emphasis and other proximate cues, rather than by the linking of reproductive rewards and overtly conflictual behavior. That linking has come "unhooked". What remains by way of continuity, she argues, is that the cleavages among groups that most frequently lead to lethal conflict are those over scarce local resources and involve ethnically defined social actors—i.e., are broadly kinship-based.

Scarcity-based explanations of conflict are also central to the analysis of economists, as John G. Cross explains in his chapter. At the same time, economists are, if anything, even more inclined than evolutionary biologists to emphasize that conflict is almost never completely zero-sum.[1] Rather, economists are concerned both with the creation of value and with the distribution or redistribution of resources as ways of managing conflict. One of the advantages, illustrated by the Cross chapter, of the kind of analysis economists do is that economists always see individual payoffs and focus on the interdependence of strategies. In particular, Cross shows formally how the presence of cost functions encourages parties to cooperate in the process of resolving a conflict, even under conditions of risk, if a durable agreement "yields continuing benefits to both parties."

In addition, Cross extends his analysis by introducing the notion of adaptive behavior. Social actors often do what worked before, even when the circumstances are radically different. Hence, it is possible that successful patterns of cooperation can be generalized even when there is no inherent reason why, on the merits of the particular case, the pattern of cooperation should transfer from one issue area where an "objective" basis for such cooperation may exist to one where no such basis exists. Moreover, Cross's chapter suggests a possible area of fruitful interdisciplinary research: with that kind of assumption as a starting point, the formal analysis of the economist could in some instances be blended with "softer" analysis of political cultures, schemas, and negotiating styles[2] to expand our ability to identify patterns of collaborative behavior between particular pairs of actors.

Robert M. Stern, also an economist, explores the possibilities of conflict and cooperation among states in the particular domain of international trade. It is well settled that free trade is not optimal for individual states except in specific circumstances. (The state must be a strict price taker over the goods it trades.) Optimal tariffs can be identified that increase the gains of the tariff-imposing state at the expense of other states and the world as a whole. In an imperfectly competitive world, moreover, the case for tariffs or other forms of

---

1. On cooperation and evolution see Low's chapter in this volume and especially Robert Axelrod, *The Evolution of Cooperation* (New York: Basic Books, 1984).

2. See the chapters by Munro, Campbell, Szporluk, and Burnstein, Abboushi, and Kitayama in this volume.

trade intervention becomes increasingly attractive; if only one state is going to defect, it is far preferable that it be my state.

Students of conflict in world politics will have immediately recognized the classic Prisoners' Dilemma. It turns out, however, Stern reports, that the more states believe that the imposition of a tariff will result in retaliation, the nearer the outcome of the bargaining process will approximate the optimality of free trade. Moreover, Stern enlarges our understanding of the conditions that might contribute to cooperation in international trade. He does this in two ways.

First, he develops a novel argument for the benefits of cooperation. It is not news that trade conflicts may result from trade measures or macro-economic policies adopted by a single state to safeguard some domestic constituency or in pursuit of some domestic objective such as higher employment. What is less obvious is that in some circumstances the reverse may also be true.

> There might be conditions when international harmony will be obtained by nations introducing macroeconomic policies that are targeted on domestic objectives . . . . [And] it may be desirable . . . for countries to attempt to cooperate by coordinating their policy actions rather than going it alone.

Second, he reports some results from a simulation model of the global trading system. That simulation was done employing the Michigan Model of World Production and Trade, designed initially to test the consequences of the GATT Tokyo Round. His results show that: (a) unilateral U.S. tariffs often do not benefit the United States because of the possibility of retaliation; (b) the preferred domestic safeguards policy is likely to be a "multilateral domestic production subsidy rather than a unilateral or multilateral import tariff or quota"; (c) cooperation in the GATT environment could create value for all parties through trade liberalization; and (d) "the United States would experience only comparatively minor employment shifts if trade in armaments were eliminated." Perhaps economics is not such a dismal science after all.

Economists are keenly attuned to the consequences of interdependence. Both the formal analysis by Cross and the quantitative simulations by Stern illustrate how, in long-term conflictual relationships, cooperation can be value-enhancing for both parties. Robert L. Kahn's chapter presents the perspective of an organization theorist to the mitigation of international conflict. For him, negotiation is essentially an attempt to manage interdependence. Such management, he avers, "is what organizations and organizational theory are about." Like an economist, Kahn is concerned with creating value, but he is somewhat more concerned with the remaining issue of dividing up the pie.

The division is likely to proceed most amicably in joint ventures of long standing, in which trust has been built over a substantial period of time rather than in "one-shot or episodic negotiations." He illustrates his point with two cases involving the United States and the former Soviet Union, the Antarctic treaty and the Standing Consultative Commission that was an outgrowth of SALT I. Perhaps the most important contribution of the chapter, however, is that Kahn imbeds the patterns of negotiations among states within a typology of organizations, the defining dimension of which is the degree of hierarchy among "cooperative antagonists." In this continuum of managed versus unmanaged interdependence, the joint venture, he argues, is particularly attractive as an organizational form in which successful negotiation can take place, inasmuch as it is itself a result of successful bargaining and it offers the institutional continuity likely to encourage continued success.

Structures matter in explaining conflict. Understanding those structures, whether they be an environment faced by primitive tribes or the rules of the game of GATT, enhances our understanding of the intensity of conflict and likelihood of cooperation among the relevant parties.

Structures have played a central role in the theorizing of specialists in world politics as well. For specialists in world politics, such explanations—what Kenneth Waltz, in *Man, State, and War* termed a third-image explanation (the first image being the nature of man, the second being the nature of the states in the system)—have been central to identifying the causes of war. Hence, it is not surprising that it is to structural explanations that the world politics specialists, J. David Singer and A. F. K. Organski, are drawn in their chapters.

One of Singer's central questions is whether the twenty-first century will more parallel the nineteenth or twentieth century. It is his conclusion, based on the multiyear Correlates of War project, that much that passed for received wisdom in the cold war does not withstand empirical scrutiny. Singer examines three pieces of conventional wisdom pertaining to the prevention of war that were widely accepted by American foreign policymakers for many years as being of relevance to dealing with the Soviet problem. These are (a) that acceptance of war encourages aggression; (b) that alliances deter war; and (c) that peace requires strength. His analysis of wars since 1815 does not find strong support for any of these notions as broad-gauge generalizations. Over that time period, prompt and vigorous aid of a victim of an armed attack made no difference in the likelihood that another war would follow. Likewise, he finds that, as a generalization, the notions of alliance involvement and prevention of war do not correlate. War entry and war avoidance occur with precisely the same frequency regardless of the level of alliance aggregation, though he finds that alliance aggregation did correlate with the relative absence of wars in the nineteenth century. Finally, he argues that an examination of the lessons of history since 1815 does not bear out the peace-through-strength proposition. "Relative capabilities do little to differentiate between war and nonwar distributions."

Singer's chapter is not limited to negative findings, and here is where a central theme of his chapter and his broader research becomes relevant, namely, the important differences between the behavior of states in the nineteenth and twentieth centuries. In the nineteeth century, higher alliance aggregation and greater system polarization were associated with the relative absence of war, whereas in the twentieth century, to the extent there was a trend either way, Singer finds that the situation was reversed.

If Singer is right, then an obvious question about the future presents itself. Will the twenty-first century be more like the twentieth or the nineteenth century? Singer speculates on this in his concluding remarks. There is, of course, an irony here. Should the world of the twenty-first century be more like the nineteenth than the twentieth century, there is an argument to be made that such realpolitik bromides as peace through strength and the advantages of alliances, the relevance of which for the twentieth century Singer vigorously challenges, may have a role in sensible strategies for conflict management in the context of twenty-first century world politics.

Similarly, Organski's and Marina Arbetman's initial intellectual thrust is an international-systemic one, although their central concern is with the structure of the international heirarchy rather than with system polarity. Theirs is a rather rosy prognosis about relations among the great states in the post–cold war era. Interestingly enough, however, they base that conclusion as much on a perception of the motives of the remaining superpower, the United States, and their perception of how the United States is perceived by the leaders of other key nations, as on the structure of the international system itself.

The link between the intensity of conflict, the intentions of the participants, and the likelihood of cooperation is emphasized by Helen R. Weingarten in her chapter. Drawing on the experience of families in conflict, Weingarten presents a five-level scheme—the Levels of Interpersonal Conflict Model—that nicely categorizes the major objectives of the participants, the motive or aim of the participants, the emotional climate in the dispute, and the empirically observed negotiation style.[3] The five levels in family conflicts are: problems to solve, disagreements, contests, fights, and war. Each level has its own characteristic attributes. Thus, in a level-I conflict (a problem to solve), the key assumption is, "We can work it out"; the climate is hopeful; and "open, direct, clear" communication between the parties takes place. By contrast, the object in a fight (level IV) is to hurt the other player, and the

---

3. Weingarten also includes the client's view of the practitioner and the key assumptions about the dispute entertained by the parties in the conflict.

conflict persists independent of the possibility of attaining identifiable goals. Antagonism and alienation are manifest. Words and deeds do not match, and perceptions clash. Life takes on attributes of the Japanese movie *Rashomon*. In a family war (level V), caricatured in the U.S. film *The War of the Roses*, the destruction of the enemy—usually the former spouse—becomes the main goal, force may be used, and the relevance of specific issues disappears. The dispute becomes one about the opponent's personality, and indeed the opponent is seen as "less human than [one]self."

Readers may take up the challenge presented by Weingartern's scheme and test for themselves the extent to which there is a one-to-one correspondence between the levels of conflict she identifies in family settings and the levels of conflict in world politics. Pending such an elaborate effort to extend the scheme to world politics, several inferences nevertheless emerge from a casual effort to analogize from her typology of family conflicts to world politics. First, the scheme brings home the point that, while conflict among families and between states is inevitable, it is important to differentiate between level I and II conflicts and level III, IV, and V conflicts in both settings. Second, the reader is likely to be struck once again, as in the chapters by Cross, Stern, and Kahn, by the interdependence of the behavior of the participants to a conflict. Families are systems. So are states. Third, intentions ("intentionality") matter, as does how people interpret reality.

How people interpret reality is an essential component of the chapter by Eugene Burnstein, Mark Abboushi, and Shinobu Kitayama. In their chapter, they ask how the mind preserves an image of the enemy. The answer is not encouraging. Like other hominids, humans differentiate themselves on the basis of group membership. Antagonism to the out-group is virtually automatic and "primordial." Three major hypotheses emerge from this study. Burnstein and colleagues find that stereotypic knowledge is "exceptionally coherent as well as categorical." They also conclude that "abstract issues will initially activate abstract knowledge, and concrete issues, concrete knowledge." Those who search memory exhaustively are likely to be less negative toward the out-group than those whose memory search is more casual. Finally, they find that when two groups have a long and intense relationship, a strong tendency exists to impart coherence to the acts of the other group. With only the slightest cues, members of the in-group ascribe a kind of consistency to out-group behavior that serves to deter the prospects of breaking down the distinction between groups. When groups are tagged Croats and Serbs and operate in the real world (rather than being named Tolo and Apat and drawn from introductory psych courses), the burden of the past contributes to preserving the image of the enemy.

The final section of this anthology compares the experience and conception of conflict by elites from four states key to the emerging world politics:

the United States, China, Russia, and Japan. Operating on the assumption that readers are most familiar with American understandings of conflict, Don Herzog contributes an intentionally provocative essay that attempts to complicate our understanding of American approaches to conflict in world politics. His is deliberately not an attempt to delineate "The American View of Conflict." He reminds us of points made many years ago by Arnold Wolfers, that national interest and national security are ambiguous symbols and that, Whose interest is the national? is always relevant. Neither U.S. publics nor U.S. elites are realists: "Appeals to morality have long played an important role in American foreign policy."

In addition, he identifies a number of other strands in American thought that need to be integrated into a composite picture of American thinking about war and conflict. One is the emphasis on U.S. purity, an offshoot in many respects from the long tradition of exceptionalism in U.S. culture. This finds expression in the notions that peace is pure and clean, that (paradoxically) war is purifying, and that the goals in a conflict are not subject to compromise.

Another strand in American thinking is the disposition to view the enemy of the moment as "having no standing"—"Indian killing" being an especially distasteful illustration. (As readers will have noted, this proclivity is not a distinctively American trait but rather an observed phenomenon, as Weingarten points out, that is characteristic of war as a form of conflict.)

As Herzog would be the first to emphasize, these are points about U.S. approaches to war, rather than an integrated and comprehensive inventory of U.S. approaches to war. He would think he had made his contribution should his points encourage "scholars of international politics . . . [to] pay more sustained attention to political culture, conceived not as a set of individual attitudes and behaviors but as a set of social concepts, categories and practices."

The last three chapters in the anthology illustrate the gains to be achieved by following Herzog's advice. There has been a dominant Chinese approach to conflict, which Donald J. Munro describes in his chapter. In Munro's careful reading, there is a unity to the Confucian and Maoist approach to conflict that renders these two alternative world views far more alike than dissimilar. Conflict in the Confucian perspective was avoided by virtue of the "uniform acceptance of the same ethical principles and of the practical rules of social conduct by which they are observed." This "one-mindedness" resulted in an ethic founded on social roles and ritualized rules of conduct. Maoism, Munro argues,[4] had many of the same attributes as Confucianism and was structurally similar. Roles are defined in class terms, rather than in family

---

4. For a similar conclusion from a quite different perspective see Charles Lindblom, *Politics and Markets* (New York: Basic Books, 1977).

terms, but the ethic remains one based on social roles; and ritual, especially ritualized discourse, occupies an analogously central role in controlling behavior and muting conflict. For both the Confucian and the Maoist, there was a grand unity fathomable to a specially trained elite.

In the post-Mao era, interestingly, this view has come under challenge in the People's Republic of China. In particular, the notion of a conflict-free society came under increasing scrutiny. In addition, some erosion of the use of "morally laden social categories" occurred. These two changes were linked: in order to legitimate conflict, it was necessary to challenge the idea that one social group could define reality for all others. Whether that view comes to prevail in China remains to be seen; much rides on that outcome, including to some extent how China and the Chinese will interact with foreign states and foreigners.

The monistic perspective on conflict had collapsed completely in the Soviet Union prior to the collapse of that country. Roman Szporluk describes the evolution of Soviet thinking about conflict and of interactions between governmental units both within the former Soviet Union and in the country's relations with states outside its borders. Much of this is well known such as Khrushchev's abandonment of the inevitability-of-war doctrine, and, the trend toward viewing the Soviet Union as a normal state.[5]

What Szporluk does in his chapter is to describe the gradual sea change in thinking about conflict *within* what was the Soviet Union, which may prove a harbinger of future relations among the successor states to the Soviet Union. Several points emerge. Increasingly in the late 1980s and in 1990, Soviet commentary both about the U.S.S.R.'s relations with its East European neighbors and relations within the Soviet Union paralleled Soviet descriptions of world politics generally. Remarkably, from the perspective of those who associate interstate relations with conflict, moreover, this turned out to be the good news rather than cause for alarm. It was, after all, in the realm of world politics that Soviet leaders first acknowledged that the operative norms ought to be those of mutual noninterference (peaceful coexistence). By contrast, traditionally, Moscow had always characterized Soviet-East European relations as ones governed by the norms of proletarian internationalism—i.e., the Soviet right to unilateral intervention—rather than peaceful coexistence.

In 1987, Gorbachev explicitly affirmed that peaceful coexistence applied to relations between *all* states, a statement that paved the way for the collapse of the socialist regimes in Eastern Europe. With the Soviet recognition of the Baltic states after the August 1991 coup attempt, it appeared that there was a growing inclination to think of relations within the former Soviet Union as

---

5. See William Zimmerman, "World Politics and Soviet Foreign Policy," *Journal of International Affairs* 44 (1): 125–39.

international relations and that Moscow—which now means Russia—will be increasingly disposed to forswear the use of force even in relation to the successor states to the U.S.S.R. The Alma Ata agreement signed on December 21, 1991,[6] by eleven of the former Soviet republics, refers to building relations on the basis of "respect for state sovereignty and sovereign equality, . . . principles of equality and non-interference in internal affairs, . . . a peaceful settlement of disputes, . . . a conscientious fulfillment of commitments and other generally recognized principles and standards of international law."

At the same time, the well-known rethinking of the role of conflict internationally was paralleled in the late 1980s and early 1990s with a re-evaluation of the role of some forms of conflict in domestic politics. "'Democracy is conflict'," Szporluk reports Soviet commentary as having said. The contrast with monistic perspectives—Stalin's monolithic unity or the Confucian-Maoist approach depicted by Munro—could scarcely be sharper. It is only a bit overdrawn to describe the evolution in Soviet thinking about conflict over the last forty years as entailing two major changes. There was an inversion of the traditional view that conflict internationally was both inevitable and desirable to a view that international conflict was both avoidable and dysfunctional. In addition, a parallel inversion with regard to internal politics took place. Increasingly, many scholars and politicians from the former Soviet Union have come to regard conflict domestically as both inevitable and desirable—the antithesis of traditional Leninist-Stalinist perspectives.

Likewise, John Creighton Campbell informs us, the Japanese accept the inevitability of conflict. He provides readers with a novel construction of the standard wisdom about Japanese attitudes toward conflict; to wit, that harmony is highly valued and decision making consequently advances by consensus. This is so, Campbell notes, but it does not follow from this that "Japanese are harmonious by nature . . . and therefore find it easy to cooperate." Not so. According to Campbell, harmony is valued precisely because Japanese view the nature of man as contentious and mean-spirited. Only with exceedingly careful attention to organization and to diplomatic niceties and details about form is it possible to achieve consensus; it is the very difficulty of achieving consensus that makes it of value.

The way the Japanese cope with conflict is observable in the sorts of organizations they construct and how those organizations deal with one another. Japanese are drawn to organizations that are neither rigidly hierarchical nor anarchic. For them, joint ventures[7] are a rarity. The modal organizational relationship for the Japanese is what Campbell terms the covenant—

---

6. *New York Times*, December 23, 1991.

7. For a discussion of joint ventures, see Kahn's chapter in this volume.

"institutionalized or regulated conflict"—rather than cooperation. Such mechanisms permit networks of relationships to evolve among people and firms as well as between firms and the government or ministries. In such organizational relationships, negotiation between a stable and small number of players over the nature of the interdependent relationship is a permanent feature. Moreover, such patterns of interaction presuppose the absence of universal principles; unlike the Confucian-Maoist perspective, Japanese are concerned with what is appropriate or proper in a particular context and nothing more. It's the ongoing, ever-shifting deal that matters in Japanese domestic politics and, Campbell speculates, such covenants—he notes the analogy to regimes in international relations—may serve as useful patterns for interstate relations as well.

This introduction began by noting that the post–World War II era in world politics had ended. Indeed, almost certainly historians will look back and say that, if the nineteenth century ended in 1914, the twentieth century ended in 1989. From that perspective, the twenty-first century is already well launched. The strands that link the chapters in this volume across a wide range of disciplines and permeate the visions of conflict from several cultures may help us begin to orient ourselves in the emerging world politics of the twenty-first century. Substantively, one strong theme is not just the inevitability of conflict but the widespread recognition that in some circumstances conflict is not only inevitable but desirable.

A second point that emerges from several chapters is an awareness of the consequences of interdependence with its logical implication of context-dependent propositions about the behavior of corporate actors, whether they be states or firms.

Third, many chapters, both by political scientists and by other social and behavioral scientists, share in common the notion that conditions in which the negative consequences of conflict may be mitigated occur as a result of the particular mix of attitudes held by key elites or particular internal organizational configurations within the states participant in the international system. The causes of conflict in world politics are largely structural—Waltz's third image. The factors that mitigate the least-attractive dimensions of conflict are often attitudinal (Waltz's first image) or pertain to the nature of the polities in the system (Waltz's second image).

A final realization that emerges from several chapters is how marginal the differences are between some relations between states and some relations within states. Partly, this is because of the proliferation of international and nongovernmental organizations globally such that anarchy seems a maladroit characterization for much of the emerging world politics. Partly, too, it is because the most violent conflicts are often those where ethnicity and kinship are key determinants. In Europe and North America, as a result, the prospects in the near term for violent conflict seem far more likely within states or former states than between them.

For students of conflict, moreover, this is a pedagogical point to be considered as well. We have deliberately chosen to consider this an anthology on conflict and world politics rather than war and international relations. Students of world politics have long emphasized the distinctiveness of relations *between* states. (Interestingly enough, at the beginning of the 1990s there were virtually no prospects for interstate war in Europe—if by "interstate" one meant states existing in 1989—in the near future.) The chapters in this volume provide something of a corrective to that perspective and suggest, instead, that conflicts within families, among primitive peoples and primates, within societies, and between states are sufficiently similar to hold forth the prospect that a general theory of conflict is a possibility. This volume is intended as an initial step in that direction.

An Evolutionary Perspective on War

Bobbi S. Low

> *Four things greater than all things are,—*
> *Women and Horses and Power and War.*
>
> —Rudyard Kipling

Conflict is as old as life. In fact, if evolutionary and behavioral ecological theory are correct, conflicts of interest, if not open aggression, are universal among living things. While some authors (e.g., Ferrill 1985) suggest that the origins of war are simply prehistoric, an evolutionary or behavioral ecologist would argue that by any functional definition, war—lethal conflict—is older than humanity itself. From an evolutionary perspective, two considerations have profound consequences: the reproductive effects for individuals of fighting and killing (including formal war), and the potential conflicts of interest among different individuals involved in conflict. To examine the evolution of war, I will begin not with complex and formal international military conflicts, but with much simpler conflict in nonhuman species, asking: Over evolutionary time, what has been the ecological context of conflict and killing in hominids and other mammals? Under what ecological circumstances are conflict and killing likely to occur, and what are the costs and benefits to the individuals involved? The functional nature of conflict may become clearer in these simpler cases; then more complex cases may be amenable to approach.

The Natural Selection Paradigm

The organisms we see today are the descendants of those that most successfully survived and reproduced in past environments; it is only half a joke

Numerous people were most helpful in discussion, providing useful challenges and thoughtful dialogue. In particular, Beverly Strassman, Carole Ember, Margo Wilson, Martin Daly, George Williams, Joseph Manson, Kenneth Lockridge, William McNeill, Leda Cosmides, John Tooby, Kenneth Organski, David Singer, Richard Wrangham, the members of the Carnegie International Peace and Security Seminar, and the participants in the Human Behavior and Evolution Program, have helped me enormously.

that the one thing we can say with assurance is that none of our ancestors was sterile. Strategies for survival and reproduction are all-important, though their appropriate analysis may be complicated. At its simplest, the analytic background derives from the differential survival and reproduction of individuals that use various strategies. This simple logic, first explicitly employed by Darwin (1859), gives rise to complex and profound effects. Even for relatively nonsocial animals, success is seldom achieved by the strategy "eat and reproduce all you can as quickly as you can." Successful reproduction does not necessarily involve producing the most offspring, or even the most surviving offspring.

Risky strategies like physical conflict seem at first likely to be selectively detrimental. In fact, Darwin treated such risky behaviors separately from natural selection, as sexual selection, because he was unable to see how risking one's neck could be reproductively advantageous. Yet as we will see, it can. Another nonobvious outcome of the action of selection is that cooperation can be an intensely competitive strategy. Reciprocity is common among individuals who spend time together, interacting repeatedly, rather than among strangers. When risks are high for behavior benefiting others, such behaviors are likely to occur only or primarily among kin. That is, if my potential cost for helping you is high, I am likely to defect unless you are a close relative (in which case, my genes may be assisted even if I die). In the evolution of warfare, this fact becomes central. Even among kin, of course, blind altruism is not predicted (e.g., Alexander 1979, 1987). Individuals have an array of variously related individuals with whom to interact, and, far from becoming blind altruists within their group, humans have become complex social strategists—judging costs and benefits, current and future, and behaving reciprocally as well as nepotistically (Alexander 1987, Humphrey 1983). Thus, for example, we see the use of kinship terms as a proximate device to promote xenophobia. Such manipulations of kinship terms (e.g., Johnson 1986, Johnson et al. 1987, Chagnon 1982), are important, but are unlikely to create and drive major conflicts consistently in the absence of strong selective advantages to major actors in the conflict.

Lethal conflict is a phenomenon like delayed reproduction, kin selection, direct and indirect reciprocity: all at first glance look as though they should decrease, rather than increase, reproduction, but in fact, each is found in specific, ecologically predictable, circumstances (e.g., see Cronk 1991a, Daly and Wilson 1983, 1988). In specific environments, the impact of these behaviors is increased net reproductive success, measured as inclusive fitness (Hamilton 1964). Were this not true, the behaviors would remain rare.[1]

---

1. A caveat is important. The fact that a trait exists, even if it currently has a positive effect on fitness, does *not* necessarily mean that it is an adaptation (Williams 1966). Biologists find it an

As in any behavioral analysis, it is important to distinguish *proximate cues,* or triggers, for behaviors from *ultimate adaptive causes.* If we ask, for example, why a bird migrates, one answer might be that changing daylength causes hormonal changes, triggering migration. This answer elucidates the proximate cue, but does not explain why individuals in some species but not others migrate, why, within species, some individuals migrate, and not others, and why daylength (as opposed to temperature, some other factor, or a combination of factors) has become the cue. The ultimate cause of migration is a seasonal better-versus-worse shift in (for example) foraging and nesting areas; individuals who follow the better areas, shifting seasonally, leave more descendants than those who remain in one area. When daylength is a reliable predictor of these seasonal shifts, individuals who use it as a cue will fare better than those using some other proximate cue or failing to leave as the environment deteriorates. The benefits and costs of migration may differ substantially for older, prime-age birds, compared to yearlings; in such cases, different categories of individuals are more or less likely to migrate.

Even in a simple example like migration, it should be clear that this is a behavioral ecological argument, based on individuals' relative reproductive costs and benefits, and does not require that a specific gene for migration be postulated. Similarly, we do not postulate some sort of gene for warfare; rather we ask under what environmental conditions warfare arises, who does it, and who benefits reproductively. Even in simple behaviors, selection has frequently operated on complexes of loci, many of which affect other behaviors, and which influence some part of the response system. External environment, development, and genes interact in a complex way. Just as many different environmental factors can be proximate cues triggering migration (whatever is the most reliable, predictable covariant with environmental quality is the trigger predicted), so can many different internal mechanisms be called upon to create complexes of behavior, including conflict behavior. While for many important behaviors we cannot specify the genetic loci involved (see Grafen 1984), we study trait-environment correlations and can often make powerful and unexpected predictions from them, using selection theory (see Cronk 1991a).

A final complication, extremely important in the case of lethal conflict, is that of evolutionary novelty. Imagine a reproductively advantageous behav-

---

onerous task to demonstrate that any trait is an evolved adaptation: we must show that the trait not only correlates with some environmental condition, but is effectively *designed in response to* that condition. Behavioral and evolutionary ecology focuses on the correlations among environmental circumstances, behavior, and inclusive fitness. We may see, particularly in complex systems, nonevolved effects of behavior that had originally an entirely different function. In such cases, we must distinguish between the questions: What is the evolutionary history of the trait? or Is it an adaptation? and What, in terms of fitness, is the current utility of the trait?

ior; if ecological conditions change, there is a possibility for that behavior to be driven by proximate cues (which in the past correlated with reproductive advantage), even when the proximate cues are currently unhinged from the (past) functional advantage. This is most common when environmental changes represent evolutionarily novel events, such as human technological changes.[2]

In the case of lethal conflict, we must examine not only whether it has ever created a selective advantage for those individuals engaging in it, and whether there is any current utility, but also, whether, as the character and scope of war have changed, any previous advantage has been disconnected from the proximate cues that have driven the conflict (comradeship, exhilaration in risky situations, pride in achievement). Thus, we need to ask: (1) was there previously reproductive advantage to engaging in lethal conflict; (2) is there currently reproductive advantage to engaging in lethal conflict; and (3) are the proximate triggers to conflict "unhooked" from any previous selective advantage?

Resources and Conflict: Predictions from Selection Theory

The argument above suggests that conflict is likely to center on items of real reproductive importance: mates, or status and resources when these contribute to reproductive success. Particularly when significant risks are involved, conflict over resources of little value is unlikely.

In nonhuman species, damaging aggression is surprisingly widespread. Typically, it arises from fights over mates or resources for getting mates, from infanticide, and from cannibalism (e.g., Huntingford and Turner 1987). The cost to an infanticidal killer (often a male taking over a harem and killing the offspring of his reproductive predecessor) is likely to be small, and infanticide

---

2. Sugar is a simple example of an evolutionary novelty. For omnivores, sampling new foods represents a risk. It is common in many species both to sample new foods at a low level and to use correlates in establishing preferences; if there are toxic effects, they will be likely to be minimal and simply unpleasant rather than lethal. Sweet foods are seldom harmful, and sour and bitter tastes are often correlated with the presence of harmful alkaloids. So a preference for sweet tastes has become widespread in omnivores. In natural situations, it is difficult to obtain sufficient sugar, without other nutrients and fiber, to create problems of obesity. Once we invented technologies for refining and concentrating sugar, we created foods that had enormous concentrations of sugar. Now the selective link has been broken between sweet taste (the proximate cue) and good food source (resulting in enhanced nutritional status). But there is no evidence that organisms evolve to have any awareness of ultimate selective relationships—proximate cues drive the system, and natural selection operates, like a passive sieve, through differential survival and reproduction. So, we retain a preference for sweet taste that is often currently counteradaptive (including health risks like obesity and dental caries, and perhaps sexual selection).

is more common than the killing of adults. Lethal fighting among individuals of similar age and status can be significant. In red deer, male mortality from sexual competition ranges from 13 percent to 29 percent of all adult male mortality (Clutton-Brock, Guinness, and Albon 1982). In nonhuman species, the resource over which conflict occurs is either a direct reproductive resource (territory, mates), or an indirect reproductive resource (elimination of competitors or competitors' offspring).

The ultimate costs and benefits are reproductive. Parker (1974, 1984) and Maynard Smith and Parker (1976) have used a game-theoretic approach to analyze adversarial relations. Combatants, they argue, assess each other's resource-holding power, and (Parker 1974, 223):

> the stake played for is infliction of loss of resource-holding power, and is determined by the fitness budgets of the opponents. . . . This defines a critical probability of winning . . . for each combatant, above which escalation (fighting) is the favorable strategy . . . and below which withdrawal is favorable.

Escalation, then, should occur only when the absolute probability of winning minus the critical probability of winning is positive for each combatant. Someone will always lose; if information were perfect, the loser-to-be would never attack, and would always withdraw if attacked. Depending on the costs, the stronger combatant may be expected to press an attack. Displays in many species involve deception and advertisements that make each potential participant appear bigger and stronger—advertising that an attack might prove costly (see also review by Huntingford and Turner 1987).

Open conflict in many species occurs primarily between individuals of the same population, rather than between groups from different populations; such individual conflict is unlikely unless the actors are similar in status or power (e.g., Parker 1974). In red deer, for example, subordinate stags are unlikely to escalate a confrontation—the risks of serious injury are too high. For an already dominant stag, escalation may incur cost for no additional gain. In some primate species, groups of varying size may separate from the main population on foraging trips. If they encounter smaller groups or lone individuals, groups may attack, exploiting the uneven balance of power (Manson and Wrangham 1991). Such group aggression is not qualitatively different (the context, benefits, and costs are similar) but is more complex, with cooperation among individuals.

Evolutionary theory predicts that potentially lethal conflict will occur when the possible reproductive (usually mating, not parental) rewards (mates, status, resources for mates) are high; and that, within mammals, males will more often be in a position to gain than females (see the next section of this chapter; also Manson and Wrangham 1991, Alexander 1987, Low 1992). Sexual selection (in competition over mates) and kin selection (in infanticide and intergroup conflicts) will be the driving forces. Intergroup, rather than interindividual, conflict will occur only in long-lived, social species. Several recent analyses reflect these predictions. Shaw (1985) and Shaw and Wong (1989) have argued that evolutionary explanations may be useful in analyzing warfare in complex nation-states. They focused primarily on kin-selection arguments as the background for xenophobia and ethnocentrism, major factors in promoting war (see also Johnson 1986 on the use of kinship terms by political leaders). Kin selection leads to the development of cohesive groups that are predisposed to intergroup conflict (though it does not predict the sex differences we see in most mammals). Ethnicity is the remnant of this process in modern societies. Kinship ties, as noted above, change the costs and benefits for individuals taking risks in potentially lethal combat.

Sexual Dimorphism: Why Women Warriors Are Rare

Mammalian aggression is sexually dimorphic. An analysis of coalitions in nonhumans makes it clear that, compared to females, males tend to form coalitions that are riskier, more aggressive, and more often among nonrelatives (see below, and Low 1990a, 1992). Because females' conflicts center on food or parental resources, while males' conflicts are likely to center on the acquisition of mates, the reproductive effect of conflict for male mammals may be many times greater than that for females (Low 1990a).

The return curve for reproductive success gained per unit of resources or status acquired differs for mating effort and parental effort. Mating effort, typical of mammalian males, has a large fixed cost; then the curve may rise steeply, for additional matings cost relatively little. For example, a male red deer, even to try for a first mating, must grow large (involving a cost of delayed maturation), grow antlers, and fight for dominance and control of good feeding grounds. The initial cost is great; the cost associated with each individual mating is small. For mammalian mothers, each offspring costs approximately as much parental effort as any other, and the maximum possible number of offspring is likely to be lower than for males.

Male mammals, while having the same average number of offspring as females, typically experience more variance in reproductive performance; more males than females in each generation fail to have any offspring in their lives, and the most successful males may have ten times as many offspring in their lives as the most successful female. Because males' variance is high, the stakes are higher. Great expenditure and risk may be profitable, so risky behavior and conflict are, in polygynous species, male endeavors. Thus sexual conflicts (more frequently male in mammals) seem more likely to escalate to lethal proportions than conflicts arising from other sorts of individual selection.

In humans, too, male reproductive variance exceeds female variance (see Low 1990a); thus it is not surprising that aggression is one of the most consistent sex differences across cultures (Ember 1981, Barry et al. 1976, Low 1989a), and homicides are principally a male endeavor (Daly and Wilson 1988). This difference in risks and returns, of course, is what prompted Darwin (1871) to treat sexual selection differently from "ordinary" natural selection, even though functionally it is identical. Ross's (1983) observation that women's politics and conflict over resources tend to be at the familial and neighborhood level, while men's conflicts tend to have broader scope, is therefore hardly surprising (Low 1990a, 1992); similarly, women warriors are predicted to be rare.

Women warriors, however, are not unknown. During the seventeenth, eighteenth, and nineteenth centuries, women occasionally passed themselves off as men and fought in the ranks of infantry and cavalry regiments (Holmes 1985, 102). From at least the time of Alexander (Keegan 1987), women traveled and sometimes fought with their men; children were legitimized in Alexander's time after the soldier completed his duties.

Cross-culturally, men can make enormous direct reproductive gains with access to power, status, and great amounts of resources, but it is not clear to what extent women can do so (Low 1990a, 1992); this parallels the reproductive ecology of resource control and status in other polygynous species. In the few societies in which women wield substantial public power, as opposed to informal influence, they evidence no clear reproductive gain. In fact, in some of the examples, it is apparent that there is a conflict between political and direct reproductive gain for women. In matrilineal and double descent systems, women's power appears to accrue to their sons, who may reap reproductive benefit (e.g., Trivers 1985, Clutton-Brock, Albon, and Guinness 1986, Low 1992). Through evolutionary history, men have been able to gain reproductively by warring behavior; women have almost never been able to do so.

It is important to distinguish this argument from others that might seem similar. This argument does not hinge on sexual size dimorphism in humans—the fact that men are generally bigger and stronger than women. Even in ungulate species like red deer, in which status and resource control are mediated through physical combat, and there is no evidence of reciprocal "political" alliances, size is not the only determinant of status (e.g., Clutton-Brock, Guinness, and Albon 1982). In primate species, and in human societies, the social complexities so far outweigh the effect of physical size that size alone is a poor predictor of success. Similarly, this argument does not reduce to an assertion that women are bound by the constraints of pregnancy, nursing, and child care. If that were true, sterile women and postmenopausal women might broadly be expected to engage in intergroup conflict; they do not.

Sexual dimorphism in use of resources and power in reproduction is the critical factor. Men appear to seek direct reproductive gain (wives, owed reciprocity) in intergroup conflict, while women, when they are (rarely) involved, seek resources for themselves and their offspring. Sometimes this is accomplished through indirect or informal influence and nepotistic gain. Most commonly, the amount of resources controlled by women is sufficient to support their family, but sometimes, particularly in matrilineal and duolineal societies (Low 1992), women may gain for their families. These societies, like the Cherokee and perhaps the Ashanti, are also those in which there is an occasional woman warrior.

Women have evolved to use resources differently from men in reproductive matters (Low 1990a, 1992), and this has had impact on their involvement in war. Further, patriliny with exogamy fosters men's, but not women's, confluences of reproductive interests in war, because related men—but not women—live together. Adams (1983) pointed out that under these conditions, women face a conflict of interest with their husbands (their husbands may be making war upon their fathers and brothers), and argued that the formal exclusion of women from warfare in so many societies may have its roots here.

War as Runaway Sexual Selection

Human war can become more complex and varied than intergroup aggression in other species, largely as a result of the development of technology (which itself is probably a product of intelligence, and probably a product specifically of Machiavellian intelligence; cf. Alexander 1971; Humphrey 1976, 1983; Byrne and Whiten 1988). The role of sexual selection in lethal conflict and the development of technology to currently lethal levels raise an important question: is war an example of runaway sexual selection, as described by Fisher (1958)?

Fisher noted that "remarkable consequences" follow if females exert a strong preference for particular traits in males. As Fisher pointed out, in sexual selection, two influences are important: initial, sometimes considerable, advantages not due to female preference (e.g., the advantage of large antlers in combat for red deer); and any additional advantage conferred by any female preference. The intensity of preference itself will continue to increase through sexual selection, so long as the sons of females exerting the preference have any advantage over other males. Fisher (1958, 152) noted, "The importance of this situation lies in the fact that the further development [of the favored trait] will still proceed, by reason of the advantage gained in sexual selection, even after it has passed the point in development at which its advantage in Natural Selection has ceased."

Thus, the immediate reproductive gains can be so great, and so powerfully selected for, that they outstrip the countering pressure of ordinary natural selection for survival, resulting in the development of lethal traits leading to extinction. When, as in the Yanomamo, warring skill results in a significant increase in the number of children produced (Chagnon 1988), sexual selection can be very powerful. Even in modern industrialized societies, in which participation in wars, and risk-taking behaviors may be "unhooked" from the advantages given by sexual preference, if sexual preference still exists for "war heroes" or if there are other proximate rewards, previously linked to selective advantage, the behavior may still be common.

Other Biological Approaches to Understanding War

One of the earliest and most influential biological approaches to understanding war was Konrad Lorenz's *On Aggression* (1966). Lorenz argued that aggression is an instinctive drive favored by selection. Although he specified that this did not make warfare unavoidable, others have inferred some sort of genetic basis (rather than a flexible response to ecological conditions, in which genetically identical individuals might act differently, depending on circumstances). Lorenz also argued that because humans lack lethal weapons in their simple physical makeup, relying on tools, humans also failed to evolve reliable inhibitions against killing each other. Variations of this argument are found in Eibl-Eibesfeldt (1979) and Ardrey (1966). The difficulty with such arguments is that they predict neither the occurrence of aggressive behavior—what conditions (e.g., reproductively important conflicts of interest) are most likely to precipitate aggression—nor the constraints (e.g., individual costs and benefits).

Perhaps in response to just such arguments, well-known and well-respected scientists, in a statement (May 16, 1986) for the International Society for Research on Aggression, argued from the fact that there is no evidence for a specific allele for aggression to an argument that warfare was "biologically possible, but . . . not inevitable, as evidenced by its variation in occurrence and nature over time and space." This view moves from patently true statements (e.g., the nonevidence for particular alleles for "warring behavior"), to generalizations that "biology does not condemn humanity to war, and that humanity can be freed from the bondage of biological pessimism and empowered with confidence. . . . Just as 'wars begin in the minds of men,' peace also begins in our minds. . . . The responsibility lies with each of us."

Such an approach is hopeful but fails to come to grips with the ecology of war, the circumstances in which aggression profits the individual or lineage genetically. It remains insufficiently specific or predictive.

Tooby and Cosmides (1988) argued that humans and chimpanzees have particular "Darwinian algorithms" that govern coalition formation and predispose both species to warfare. They argue that the psychologically imposed structure has certain characteristics: cheaters must be identified and excluded or punished; participants are rewarded or punished in proportion to the risks they take, and in proportion to their contribution to success. Each coalition member has impact on the coalition by regulating his own participation in the coalition and by the actions he takes to enforce the contract on other members. However, all that they specify seems likely to be true for numerous other coalitions (e.g., hunting, female lion parental; see Low 1990a), and their argument thus does not lead to the deduction that humans and chimpanzees are unique in having the appropriate algorithms for warfare. Further, although Tooby and Cosmides discuss allocation of rewards to participants (rewards may be unequal), they fail to address the fact that these payoffs must be compared to payoffs from other strategies (e.g., the dilemma of disenfranchised males). It is important to note, also, that Tooby and Cosmides's argument is not a true alternative to the argument I present here: that lethal conflict exists because individuals and families have profited from assuming the risks of lethal conflict under specific conditions, over evolutionary time. Theirs is an argument of psychological mechanisms, and mine is a behavioral ecological argument about ultimate causality; both may be true.

Ember and Ember (1992), in a major cross-cultural study of warfare, found some interesting ecological correlations with warfare. Ember and Ember found that societies went to war when particular sorts of resources became, or threatened to become, limiting. A major predictor was the threat of weather or pest disasters. When people perceive environmental threats, they are more likely to go to war. Given the difficulty of getting really sensitive measures on such a broad scale, their results are strong. Ember and Ember also found that societies which have more warfare also encourage boys to be more aggressive and tougher and to show more fortitude. This is consistent with the impact of sexual selection on warfare; Low (1989a) found that the greater the potential reproductive rewards for sons (the greater the degree of polygyny in unstratified societies), the more boys were taught to strive.

As we learn more about behavior, the importance of genes alone pales, particularly for complex conflict. Moore (1990) infers some sort of "warfare allele." If humans have evolved as complex social strategists, as Alexander and Humphrey argue, such an explanation is extremely unlikely. Dawkins (1986, 296 ff.) gives a useful analogy. Genetic coding is like a cake recipe, and in trying to decipher exactly how the cake (the phenotype, the individual) comes to be, it is a hopeless task to try and map any particular crumb of the cake, or any particular trait in the phenotype, to a particular word in the recipe. Thus, changing "350 degrees" to "450 degrees" changes many things subtly in concert. Perhaps there are a few exceptions—if I change "pecans" to "walnuts" I might find a match—but such cases are very rare.

Lethal aggression is most likely to be a function of the costs and benefits for the individual actors in any particular environment (see above; also Maynard Smith 1974, Maynard Smith and Price 1973). Societal complexity can generate situations in which wars could be escalated when escalation is clearly dysfunctional for some individuals, or even for the majority of the group. In complex societies, the interests of a soldier, a Pentagon general, and a State Department official are not identical; they may not even overlap. If humans have evolved, as Alexander and Humphrey argue, to assess the conditions around them, and to compete accordingly, there may arise situations in which, as part of an internal political competition, for example, troops are sent and resources committed to lethal conflict overseas. Thus the risk-taker, the front-line grunt, is paying a cost for the strategizing of an unrelated but powerful individual, as a result of a conflict of interests that may have little to do with his own interests. As Hackworth (*Newsweek*, 24 February 1992, 24) noted: "Not many men in the mud are connected in high places."

Bueno de Mesquita (1981) developed an expected utility model of warfare, but his model does not calculate separately the costs and benefits of the various actors. He never examines the actual goals of the opponents in his disputes, nor whether the winners achieve those goals. In complex societies, an evolutionary ecologist would want to know what happens to the distribution of goods within the society as a result of war, and whether this is related to the occurrence of repeated war. Parker (1974, 1984) and Maynard Smith and Parker (1976) have examined these patterns. Consider territory- or harem-holding ungulates such as red deer. Clearly subordinate males will not challenge, but as the breeding season (rut) progresses and dominant males pay the price of vigilance with decreased nutritional status and health, challengers, who have spent less on maintenance of status, become ever more likely to challenge; the risks of real injury or death are greatest when the males are at roughly equal condition, but on opposite trajectories. In this ungulate case, the situation is relatively simple; the rut is seasonally limited, and a male's loss of condition as a result of his exertions over the rut period become evident as he begins to metabolize muscle tissue, something other individuals can detect from the odor of his urine.

Resources and Reproduction in Nonhuman Species

If we postulate that aggression is usually related to acquisition of resources, we must define "resource." The significant aspect of a "resource" in evolutionary perspective is its influence on survival and reproduction. Thus some biologists (e.g., Alexander 1979) define as a resource anything giving relief from Darwin's "Hostile Forces of Nature"—climate, weather, food shortages, predators, parasites, and so on. In this broad view, not only physical resources such as food and shelter, but also status, coalition allies, and members of the opposite sex—potential mates—become resources. Though introducing complexity, this broad definition makes analytic sense, because the critical dependent variable is always differential survival (in order to reproduce) or reproduction. Because environments are complex, the focal resource will differ for different kinds of individuals (old, young, male, female, solitary or group-living). The job of specifying what resource is under consideration becomes critical.

Resources have repeatedly been shown to influence reproduction, even when only skill in resource acquisition, independent of social factors, is considered. For example, Ritchie (1990) demonstrated that optimally foraging ground squirrels have approximately six times as many offspring as nonoptimal foragers. For males of many species, there is a clear link between resource control or dominance status and reproductive success. The distribution (specifically economic defensibility), predictability, and richness of resources dictate the breeding system (e.g., Emlen and Oring 1977, Clutton-Brock and Harvey 1976). When resources are controllable by a single male, territorial systems are likely, and territorial males outreproduce "bachelor" disenfranchised males. In non-resource-controlling systems, while no physical resource of value may be controlled, more-dominant males tend to outreproduce less-dominant males (reviewed by Dewsbury 1982, Huntingford and Turner 1987, Cowlishaw and Dunbar 1991). Males may fight directly over mates, they may fight for dominance if females choose dominant males, or they may fight over territory if females choose good territories.[3]

---

3. Two of the best-documented examples of the behavioral ecology of reproduction, and the role of conflict and resources in reproduction, are Clutton-Brock, Guinness, and Albon's (1982, 1986) work on red deer, and Le Boeuf and Reiter's (1988) work on elephant seals. In elephant seals, males mature later than females, and grow to be much larger than females. Over 85 percent of all males ever born die without issue, but the most successful males may have over ninety offspring. Variance in reproductive success among males is extreme, whether measured seasonally or over lifetimes (Le Boeuf and Reiter 1988), and the reproductive stakes are much greater for male fighting than female. Approximately 60 percent of females ever born die without giving birth; the most successful females may have about ten offspring in their lifetimes. Males compete to control the sandy beaches on which females give birth, and fights can be severe. Seal pups are often injured and killed as males fight. Because females return to the same or nearby beaches every year, but male tenure changes, the probability that an infant killed is the offspring of the territorial male is difficult to determine.

In red deer, adult males may be bachelors, with no females, or they may control a harem of from one to more than twenty females (Clutton-Brock, Guinness, and Albon 1982). Harem-holders do virtually all of the breeding with the hinds in their harems. However, because the

Resources and Reproduction in Preindustrial Societies

What is the role of resources in human reproduction? As with other mammals, a sexual dimorphism exists in human resource use and reproduction. Males appear to be able to use large amounts of resources as mating effort to gain sometimes extraordinary numbers of wives and children (e.g., Low 1992; also Betzig 1986, who reviews despotic societies in which rulers may have thousands of wives and concubines). Females use smaller amounts of resources as parental effort, to raise a more limited number of healthy, thriving offspring.

Cross-culturally, men use resources to gain reproductively; in many societies men's increase in reproductive success is accomplished through polygyny—additional wives. The majority (85 percent; Murdock 1967) of societies for which there are data are polygynous. When resource differentials are great, men, like other mammalian males, can use resources to increase their lifetime fertility to a much greater extent than can women. As in other species, status, skill, dominance, and power can be "resources." Betzig's (1986) work shows definitively that in a number of societies, there are clear, formal reproductive rewards associated with status: high-ranking men have the right to more wives, and have significantly more children than others. White's (1988) data on the Standard Cross-Cultural Sample reflect the fact that in a number of societies there are explicit rules granting more wives to political leaders, skilled hunters, shamans, and so forth. Even in societies like

---

tenure of harem-holders is shorter than the breeding season, reproductive success of males does not vary so much as harem size. Variation in reproductive success among stags is a function of harem size, duration of harem-holding tenure, rutting area, fighting ability, and (less closely) life span. Stags achieve harem-holding status and matings through fights. Big, long-lived stags who are good fighters leave the most offspring. Among female red deer, variation in lifetime reproductive success is related to life span and calf mortality. Variation in fecundity is small, and less important than for stags. Thus, for stags, size and ability to gain dominance are crucial; for hinds, own and calf survivorship is important. The impact of different amounts of resources for the two sexes is quite different, and as is generally true, male red deer reproductive success varies more than female reproductive success. Both well and poorly invested hinds can be successful producing offspring; the reproductive effect of resources is far less for hinds than stags. There is a complication. Male calves that are born early in the season (with a long time to grow before their first winter) and at a high birth weight are more successful than those born "late and light." Not surprisingly, the sons of dominant hinds, in good condition, are more likely to be born heavy and early (Clutton-Brock, Albon, and Guinness 1986). Sons of dominant hinds have greater reproductive success than daughters of dominant hinds; daughters of lowstatus hinds have greater reproductive success than sons of lower-status hinds. Further, dominant hinds produced more sons than low-status hinds (Clutton-Brock, Albon, and Guinness 1986). Dominance in hinds is related to their own birth weight and their weight as adults. Thus, resources are not irrelevant for hinds' reproductive success, even though the effect is less than that on stags, and may be seen more strongly after a generation's lag, in the sons' success.

the Ache, in which there are no such formal rules, Hill and Kaplan (1988) found that skilled hunters have more wives, more children, and better-surviving children than other men.

In ten of twelve societies reviewed by Hill (1984), resource control clearly enhanced reproductive success. The two exceptions were large, densely settled societies with socially imposed monogamy. In most societies, the relationship was quite straightforward: in the Turkmen, for example, Irons (1979a, 1979b) found that richer men had more wives and more children than poorer men. Borgerhoff Mulder (1988, 1990) found that in the African Kipsigis, richer men married younger wives and produced more children than poorer men (although with the introduction of Western technology and medicine, differentials were reduced), and that women preferred to marry men with more land and no other wives. Among the pastoral Mukogodo of Kenya, Cronk (1991b) found that wealth enhances reproductive success for men; in his study he was able to show the direction of causality. Similarly, the Meru use livestock for bridewealth, and richer men can marry more wives (Fadiman 1982); cattle represent wealth, and wealth represents access to women and thus ultimately, reproductive success. In societies as diverse as the Hausa (Barkow 1977), Trinidadians (Flinn 1986), Micronesian islanders (Turke and Betzig 1985), and Mormons (Faux and Miller 1984, Mealey 1985), status and wealth correlate with male reproductive success. Even in societies such as the Yanomamo, in which few *physical* resources are owned, *social* resources (such as male kin available for coalitions, or women available as mates) are important, and men manipulate kinship terms in ways that maximize these resources for themselves (Chagnon 1982). Warrior status is directly related to reproductive success in the Yanomamo (see below), and reproductive success is uneven for men.

Even in nominally "monogamous" societies, monogamy may be far from absolute, and in fact, many are simply societies with limited polygyny. In the Kalahari Bushmen, for example, living in a resource-limited environment, 5 percent of the men manage to have two wives (Lee 1979). In nineteenth-century Sweden, certainly among the most egalitarian of states legally, resource-controlling men tended to outreproduce poorer men (Low 1989b, 1990b, 1991; Low and Clarke 1991, 1992). Voland (1990) found similar patterns in German villages, as did Hughes (1986) in England.

Thus, even in relatively modern times, in Western societies that are monogamous and attempt to be egalitarian, wealth differentials appear to promote fertility differentials (Low and Clarke 1991, 1992; Voland 1990; Turke 1989, 1990; Low 1989a, 1989b, 1990a, 1990b, 1991). When resources become constricted, (e.g., Low 1989a), family reproductive differentials are likely to disappear. Others also have found this generally to be true. Individual patterns in such important factors as age of marriage typically vary with resources (e.g., Wall 1984; Sharpe 1990; Cain 1985; McInnis 1977; Pfister

1989a, 1989b; Thompson and Britton 1980; Hayami 1980; Schultz 1982; Symons 1974). Families, depending on their own resource bases, may respond quite differently to such influences as market shifts (e.g., Galloway 1986; Schultz 1985), and treat their children quite differently (e.g., Mitterauer and Sieder 1982, 110). Even aggregate data tend to reflect resource influences, as individuals make decisions (e.g., Wrigley 1983a, 1983b). Vining (1986) has argued that no such trends (richer men reproducing more than poorer men) exist in Western society; however, he does not consider lifetime fertility, and his arguments are thus difficult to interpret. Vining and others (e.g., Wrong 1980, 1985) argue that we do not know why, during periods of population expansion, wealth and status differentials correlate with reproductive success, and why these correlations seem to disappear when population growth stops. However, in Western, technological, monogamous societies today, including Sweden and the United States, remarriage and second-family formation may be sex-biased (men remarry more than women, and have children in second marriages more than women). When this occurs, men's reproduction is more variable than women's, and the society is effectively polygynous (Essock-Vitale 1984, Daly and Wilson 1983, Hartung 1982).

Low and Clarke (1992) suggest several possibilities why studies such as Vining's may fail to find patterns which may nevertheless be true: First, census data are not designed to elucidate information about family lineages, but households (it is impossible to tell "own" children, from stepchildren, from other relatives living in the household, from nonrelatives living in the household); especially combined with inappropriate choice of measures, such data are highly unlikely to elucidate this relationship. In Vining's analyses, for example, (e.g., his tables 2–5) proxy measures like education are used, rather than resources, and lifetime fertility is not measured; thus they are difficult to interpret. When actual lineage data are examined (e.g., Mueller 1991), wealth and status are likely to be correlated with fertility for men even today.

In many studies from earlier times, wealth was men's wealth. Today, much household income is earned by women. In industrial market economies, the effort that women must expend to earn money in market economies often represents a real conflict—a woman cannot do child care at work. This represents a real shift from women's situation in traditional societies, in which women could do a variety of tasks while doing child care, and in which women could call on older daughters to help during much of the day (not after school) with child care (see Rank 1989, Low and Clarke 1992).

The ecology of infant survival, and of parental care effectiveness, also matters: when offspring must compete for limited resources, parental shifts from production of offspring to investment in offspring (MacArthur and Wilson 1967) will be favored. True parental investment, specific to particular offspring, must reduce the number of offspring, unless parental resources increase.

Finally, the existence of contraception is bound to complicate any relationship between wealth and fertility (Pérusse 1991). Thus, the link between men's resources and reproductive success may hold even today.

Conflict in Nonhuman Species

In most nonhuman species, conflict is liable to be among individuals in the same population: red deer stags, elephant seal bulls, mountain sheep males, and so on, fight over reproductively important resources. In primates, male-male coalitions may be elaborated, and approach the complexity of politics (de Waal 1982; Low 1990a, 1992). Conflict between groups of individuals from different local populations becomes important. In primates, defensive response to a behavioral challenge occurs in a number of species, in the contexts of territorial incursion, conflicts over a specific resource, including females (Manson and Wrangham 1991). It occurs in numerous group-living species. In chimpanzees, humans, and perhaps gorillas, there are regular cooperative raids by breeding adults against adults in neighboring groups. In chimpanzees, Manson and Wrangham argue that this is, first, low-cost because the social organization leads to variable-size parties (thus, one can hide when big parties are encountered, and attack smaller parties); and that males are the likelier sex when (as in chimpanzees) females change groups, leaving groups of related males behind. The complexity of such group raids may mean that their effectiveness is enhanced by intelligence (see Humphrey 1976, 1983, who argued that the evolution of intelligence has been largely shaped by the social, rather than the physical, world; also Byrne and Whiten 1988, for a review of such Machiavellian intelligence). For this analysis, the important questions are: Does group-versus-group lethal aggression occur in species other than humans? Are the contexts (reproductive competition, kin selection) different from those of intergroup aggression in humans?

Among social carnivores, three species show intergroup aggression. In wolves, family-based packs occasionally invade neighboring packs' territories, attacking residents; Mech (1977) found that intraspecific conflict accounted for 43 percent of wolf deaths not caused by humans. Among spotted hyenas, who, like wolves, live in family-based, territory-holding groups, intruders into a clan's territory are likely to be attacked and killed, and smaller clan subgroups patrol the territory boundaries, confronting other "patrols" (Kruuk 1972). In lions, which also live in groups (prides) based on a group of related females and one or more associated males, interpride encounters occur, but lethal injury is rare. When invading males are attempting to take over a pride, there may be lethal injuries, though once one male cedes reproductive rights, aggression typically stops. New males are likely to commit infanticide (Packer 1986).

Adult male chimpanzees make aggressive forays into the ranges of neighboring groups, sometimes fatally injuring conspecifics attacked during these invasions (Goodall 1986, Goodall et al. 1979, Nishida, Hiraiwa-Hasegawa, and Takahata 1985). Unlike lions, chimpanzees may not stop attacks once victory is apparent. Females are semisolitary, using a core area, but often traveling outside that area. Adult and subadult males are more gregarious and travel more widely (Goodall 1986, Nishida 1979). Total community size ranges from 20 to 110 individuals, but temporary groups range from 1 to 20 animals; group size fluctuates, and it is not predictable how many conspecifics a group might encounter. Further, in chimpanzees, it is more common for females to transfer from their natal group, while males are likely to remain among their relatives (Pusey and Packer 1987), thus changing the costs and benefits of risky fights (e.g., Goodall 1986, Manson and Wrangham 1991). Aggression occurs in a number of other primate species, including baboons, new world monkeys, lesser apes, and group-living prosimians (Cheney 1987).

Mountain gorillas live in small groups, with a single dominant male, and possibly one or more subordinate males. Both sexes may migrate from their natal group. Groups encounter each other often, and males with few or no females often "stalk" larger groups for several days. Harcourt (1978) reported that 50 percent of intergroup interactions in his study involved fights with physical contact. Severe injuries and death may result from such fights. Gorillas do not, apparently, attack cooperatively (though the challenged male may get assistance from his subordinate males), and fights are not escalated if the victim yields.

Male-male cooperation, and the benefits of risk-taking, may be enhanced by groups of related males living together (called "male-bonded" or "female transfer" in primates, and "patrilocal" in humans; e.g., see Chagnon 1988). This is, however, not a requirement. In lions, males leave the natal group, while female relatives remain—yet lions engage in male intergroup lethal conflict. In gorillas, both sexes may leave the natal group. In wild dogs, wolves, and mongooses, both sexes are involved in lethal intergroup aggression. Each of these last three species has a monogamous, extended-family structure in which male and female costs and benefits are more similar than in polygynous species. The basic reasons for male-male intergroup aggression, rather than intergroup aggression by both sexes, probably involve the different reproductive payoff curves for the two sexes in mammals (see above); the elaboration of this aggression is enhanced by conditions that result in related males living together.

In nonhuman vertebrates, then, most aggression, both interindividual and intergroup, has a reproductive cause. Male-male coalitions are frequently among relatives, but may be among nonrelatives. Males frequently come into open conflict over access to females, and control of resources useful in attracting females. Females may work in related coalitions to attack reproductive competitors, or the offspring of reproductive competitors (Wasser 1983, Silk and Boyd 1983). These situations typically involve harassment of subordinate females and infanticide, with little risk to the aggressors. Among primates, groups of males may fight in ways that resemble ambush attacks reported in preindustrial human societies.

Peace Making in Nonhuman Species

In most of the species reviewed here, gestures of submission decrease aggression by the attacker. In chimpanzees, attacks may continue in the face of submissive gestures (de Waal 1982, 1989). Males form coalitions, fight single-handedly and in groups, and reconcile using vocal and behavioral signals of submission and alliance-seeking (e.g., de Waal 1982, 1989). Males have a formal dominance hierarchy, with far more aggression and reconciliation than females. De Waal (1989, 53) suggests that the clear-cut dominance hierarchy provides a ritual format for reconciliation; reconciliations often follow a behavioral confirmation of formal status. Further (de Waal 1989, 53), "the unreliable, Machiavellian nature of the male power games implies that every friend is a potential foe, and vice versa. Males have good reason to restore disturbed relations; no male ever knows when he may need his strongest rival." Later (1989, 61–69), de Waal gives a striking and poignant example of how male-male power tensions, unresolved, can erupt with lethal consequences.

An important distinction between all nonhuman species and humans is the lack of elaborate mechanisms in other species for ending inter- (as opposed to intra-) group conflict. While the patterns of reassurance, even negotiation, are sometimes present, these occur in resolution of disputes within the group. Thus, participants all already know each other, and have a high likelihood of continuing to live together. This argues that intragroup conflicts have been more frequent and selectively more important in these species' evolutionary history than intergroup conflicts. New complexities are introduced by the need to resolve intergroup conflicts in humans—among groups of individuals who may have information (or misinformation) about each other, but who may not know each other or be able to predict reliability or probability of default.

Conflict in Preindustrial Societies

What are wars fought over in preindustrial societies? Durham (1976), Harris (1979), and Divale and Harris (1976), suggested that wars were fought to secure scarce animal protein from the hunting grounds accruing to the winning side. However, Chagnon and Hames (1979) and Chagnon (1979) argued that it was not the means of production, but the means of reproduction, that led to such serious escalation of competition (see also Ember and Ember 1992). In fact, what we call warfare in preindustrial societies is indistinguishable in context and function from much intergroup aggression seen in other species; it differs only in scope. Approximately 60 percent of the sample societies examined by Ross (1983) engaged in warfare frequently—at least yearly. Ember (1978) and Ember and Ember (1992), examining a similar and partially overlapping sample, also found that a high proportion of societies fought frequent wars. Warfare frequency was not related to subsistence type. Most attacks in foraging societies were ambush attacks, not always with numerical superiority, and often well coordinated to take advantage of the element of surprise.

Human societies are similar to other primate societies: individuals travel and work in small parties of varying sizes (Manson and Wrangham 1991). Thus, escalation by larger groups can be fairly low-cost. Further, patrilocal and patrilineal societies are more common than other types of societies, and these conditions, involving as they do the association of groups of related males, influence men's costs and benefits of warfare. Similar patterns emerge in otherwise divergent societies around the world.

Chagnon's (1988) detailed study of Yanomamo warfare suggests that there can be direct reproductive advantages to men who participate in revenge raids and ambushes, and reproductive costs to men who avoid warfare. Yanomamo men who have killed on a war party are accorded the title of *unokai*, and a man's performance in war parties affects him reproductively. War parties are small, from 2 to 20 men, and tend to comprise related men. Although there are mystical aspects, most war parties arise from disputes about reproductive matters. Men may choose to avoid any particular warring party, and war parties may turn back, often as the result of a prophetic dream. Nevertheless, if a man avoids several possible opportunities, or behaves in ways perceived as cowardly on the raids, he becomes the butt of jokes, and other men may begin to make sexual overtures to his wife. Once a man establishes himself as *unokai*, he is likely to average one more wife than non-*unokai*, and will average 4.5 children, compared to 1.6 for non-*unokai*. There are clear reproductive advantages in the Yanomamo for men who participate in war parties, and particularly for men who kill (Chagnon 1988). Likewise, among the Jivaro (e.g., Karsten 1923), though there is no stratification, and during times of peace no chieftainship, when wars erupt, older experienced men who have killed many men and captured many heads are chosen as war chiefs. No Jivaro can be chosen if he has not killed. Bloody feuds are frequently "for the sake of the women," and follow familial lines.

In North America, the Blackfoot Indians were known through the nineteenth century as formidable, aggressive warriors (e.g., Denig 1961). Blackfoot warfare was "aimed at neither the systematic extermination of enemy tribes nor the acquisition of their territory" (Ewers 1958, 126). Rather, numerous small raiding parties of volunteers banded together to capture horses from neighboring tribes; most parties comprised fewer than a dozen men (though Ewers cited a few raids comprising up to 50 men), for reasons of stealth. Horses were used as brideprice. Ewers (1958) found that many of the most active raiders were men from poor families "ambitious to better their lot" (126). Even sons of middle class families "needed more horses than their fathers could give them if they were to marry and set up their own household" (Ewers 1958, 126). Occasionally, a childless woman would accompany her husband on a raid. Horse-raiding parties were led by experienced men who were considered to have a good war record and good judgment. All participants were volunteers, and though the leader might be a mature man in his thirties, most of his followers were in their late teens or early twenties. The youngest were considered apprentices, and given jobs such as holding the first lot of horses outside an enemy camp as the raiders returned for more. Unless prior arrangements had been made (e.g., equal distribution), each man could claim the horses he had led out of camp, or the range stock he had captured. Bitter arguments could occur over ownership, and it was the leader's job to settle these. Some leaders gave horses they themselves had captured to men who could claim no horses. A leader's generosity helped him maintain a popular reputation, helping him to recruit future followers easily. Successful raiders gave horses to their relatives, most commonly to their fathers-in-law or brothers-in-law (Ewers 1958).[4]

Among the Meru of Kenya, geography fostered internecine conflict (Fadiman 1982). Livestock were used for brideprice; a man, to marry, must accumulate sufficient livestock (preferably cattle) to purchase a wife. Men fought to gain livestock and status. The military cycle followed the seasonal pastoral cycle. Negotiation of bridewealth was done by the families (principally male relatives; see Flinn and Low 1986) of the bride and groom, and interfamilial alliance was considered an important function. The father of the warrior transferred five specified items—a cow, a bull, a ram, a ewe, and a gourd of honey—to the father of the bride. Additional units of these and other items were negotiable, to sweeten the deal, but could not replace the basic five (Fadiman 1982, 43, 162). Additional symbolic gestures of alliance were involved (e.g., the warrior's father sending beer ahead of the actual brideprice, followed by the bride's father initiating a general beer-drinking to which the warrior's father was invited); however, a main point of the transaction was clearly economic. In fact, a portion of the bridewealth was often kept back by

---

4. It seems to be currently fashionable among some anthropologists to argue that cultural disruption (the introduction of horses) upset some balance and generated warfare. Yet the Blackfoot case is functionally identical to the Meru case (and many other pastoral societies), in which no such "disruption" could be postulated.

the warrior's family, often for years (Fadiman 1982, 44). War was the principal method of gaining livestock, and warriors were expected to earn bridewealth as well as ever-increasing familial wealth and status. Rules and traditions of warfare among the Meru, in fact, facilitated rather than limited cattle stealing. In individual conflict between warriors, for example, a warrior could save his life by declaring that his opponent could take his cattle; this was accepted as a declaration of surrender (Fadiman 1982, 46). All captives, female and warrior, were redeemable for livestock. Married female captives could be kept as concubines or wives; unmarried and uncircumcised females were taken as "daughters," and later traded for brideprice (Fadiman 1982, 44). Among the Meru, as among the Yanomamo, men clearly gained reproductively by establishing themselves as successful warriors.

The broad cross-cultural data are consistent with data from the Yanomamo, the Jivaro, the Blackfoot, and the Meru.[5] Ember and Ember (1992) found that 75 to 80 percent of wars involved land, clearly useful in establishing a family. Divale (1973), although not quantifying the data or emphasizing the functional point of reproductive competition, found that among most groups it was adultery and wife-stealing that caused wars. Similarly, in the full Standard Sample, women are captured in 66/158 societies (White 1988), and in the vast majority of these cases, women are married or kept as concubines by their captors. In other societies, like the Maori, in which there is no direct association between warfare and women or resources directly used to acquire women, the warfare patterns still reflect conflict over resources directly useful for the family line (e.g., Vayda 1960). Even in our own Judeo-Christian heritage, women were a valued profit from warfare (Hartung 1992). The benefits of warfare to men in preindustrial societies thus include increased direct access to reproductive females, and increased material resources useful for the lineage and in contracting marriages (individual [including sexual] and kin selection). The communal location of related males (kin selection) appears to enhance warring behavior.

Transition in the Evolutionary Ecology of War: Societal Complexity

Many social behaviors show a clearer functional pattern in smaller, simple societies than in large, politically complex societies; the same appears to be

---

5. In the seventy-five societies analyzed by Manson and Wrangham (1991), reproductive matters were at the root of most wars. Women (abductions, failure to deliver a bride) were causes of warfare in thirty-four (45 percent) societies (Manson and Wrangham, personal communication). Material resources specified as useful in obtaining a bride were causal in another twenty-nine (39 percent), and in nine of these, ethnographies specified that richer men obtained more wives than poorer men. In only twelve societies (16 percent) was there no immediately obvious connection between warfare and men's direct reproductive striving.

true of lethal conflict. Let us follow, then, the trends in the ecology of warfare. Among preindustrial societies, ambush warfare by raiding parties of varying size (almost indistinguishable from ambushes in other primates), appears to have been the common pattern. The rewards, as in other species, were reproductive: women as mates, and resources to purchase women as mates. The transition from such warfare to the complex, multinational warfare discussed in treatises on military history seems almost unfathomable, but must be examined if we are to understand whether there has been any change in the function of war.

The costs and benefits of warfare in traditional societies can vary. Among the Yanomamo, for example, a man's reproductive prospects are influenced by several things: his personal qualities, his ability to manipulate kinship terms (allying himself with powerful groups, making otherwise unavailable women nominally available as mates), the size of his kin group (male allies), and his prowess as an *unokai*, or revenge killer (above). Yanomamo society is not stratified, and aside from the size of his kin group, a man's chances for success may be largely under his own control. Individual men are rewarded in similar ways for similar war performances, and ferocity and leadership lead to reproductive gain.

Keegan's (1987) description of Alexander the Great suggests that even in large, hierarchical armies during Philip's and Alexander's rule in Macedonia, personal characteristics, kin-group size, and ability to inspire loyal reciprocity still were crucial to success in warfare. The Macedonian kingship was elective; Alexander had claim to the succession, as the eldest son of the king's acknowledged wife, but, had he not been bold and eager for battle, he would have found it hard to press his claim. The period postdated the "cavalry revolution" between the twelfth and fourth centuries. Macedonia was an imperial power, and the Macedonian army was large and hierarchical, comprising a cavalry, the Foot Companions, light cavalry, light infantry, and specialized troops, including archers, siege artillerymen, engineers, surveyors, and supply/transport specialists. The soldiers were neither a tribal war band, as in the Yanomamo, nor were they conscripts. They were recruited from a variety of social classes. Nonetheless, central to the army was the inner core of warriors, the Companions, whose relationship to the leader was close, and often a blood relationship (Keegan 1987, 34). It was important that Alexander consistently led his men, fighting by their sides, and performing dramatic feats of courage and leadership. Thus, while courage mattered among tribal societies like the Yanomamo (simply to avoid losing a wife, for example), in other cultures and by Macedonian times, heroism became a prerequisite for leadership of vast and complex organizations.

Similarly, the transition to the state of modern Nepal, accomplished by Prithvinarayan Shah, owed much to his ability to reward individual interests.

What is now Nepal comprised several small kingdoms; geographical constraints divided the area into small, self-contained units. Peasants' lives were hard. All land belonged to the state; those who worked the land typically paid half of the harvest to the state as well (Stiller 1973), as well as compulsory unpaid labor (*jhara*), even though few of the valleys were very fertile, with thin soils and poor harvests. Gaining a freehold was the only escape from this situation; it could be accomplished in three ways: a *jagir* grant (valid during the term of service), for services to the state; a *birta* grant (for a particular service, valid until revoked); or reclamation of waste land (Stiller 1973, 17–18). With only perhaps 8,000 to 10,000 men (Stiller 1973, 88), in the face of serious logistic problems, Prithvinarayan Shah drew men of the hill tribes, notoriously pragmatic and unlikely to follow others' dreams, into his ambitions, offering *jagir* grants for services as a way for followers to break out of the cycle of agricultural poverty that bound so many. Stiller (1973, 94) argued that Prithvinarayan Shah spelled out in concrete terms the advantages for his soldiers individually, and drew them on to seeing the advantages of a farther-reaching group goal—true leadership. In addition, throughout the long campaign, in negotiating with his enemies, he offered substantial rewards for converting to his views—and was often successful. No other individual had been able to overcome the fragmentary relationships and forge a modern nation from the region's tribes.

Leaders in war, then, had more likelihood of becoming leaders in peace. War has been proposed as a mechanism involved in the very formation of states. For example, Carniero (1970) argued that warfare was a necessary, if not sufficient, condition for the formation of states. Strate (1982) found a clear association between degree of central political organization and success in warfare. Otterbein (1970) also found correlations between the level of political complexity and the degree of military sophistication.

Warfare requires individual strife, and as noted above, strife is likely to be centered about matters of reproductive importance. Warfare further, at all levels above the simplest ambushes, involves organization and opportunities for gain through leadership; successful war leaders are likely to be good manipulators of others, and they accumulate an armed following. The path from leadership in war to political leadership may be short. The risks of political leadership, too, are sometimes less lethal than those of war leadership. Thus, the distinction between "preheroic" and heroic leadership (e.g., Keegan 1987) may be a matter of scale rather than function. Recognition of the importance of reproductive interests in the evolution of lethal conflict, as I propose here, makes trivial some apparent discrepancies among earlier models of warfare and the rise of states. Thus, if competition can be driven to lethal levels by reproductive conflicts, it is no longer important whether population growth (e.g., Carniero 1970 vs. Wright 1977, Webster 1975) is demonstrated to precede warfare. Reproductive competition is a major, evolutionarily important selective force underlying lethal conflict; warfare is a principal mechanism, and may be waged in the name of women, revenge, agricultural lands, new territory, or any devised reason.

In hierarchical armies, the interests of the actors may diverge considerably, depending on their roles in warfare in more complex societies: the state leaders, the military leaders, support personnel, and the grunt on the front line. As societies become more complex, so does the scope of the problem. Axelrod and Dion (1988) have shown formally that increasing the number of actors makes cooperation more difficult; and "noise" (misperceptions, incorrect information) can invite exploitation. In fact, no strategy is evolutionarily stable if the "shadow of the future" is long enough, for we all discount what might happen to us in the uncertain future.

It is not selectively irrelevant that, in all warfare involving hierarchies of power (i.e., rank and specialization; probably all but tribal ambush warfare), risk is correlated with prior status and/or rank. From at least the middle ages, it has been disenfranchised or low-status males who go to war in positions of greatest risk. Boone (1988) noted that sons of Portuguese nobles took three-week crusades to nearby, relatively safe locations, while sons of poor families went to Jerusalem, often dying there. Similarly, Dickemann (1979) found that it was disenfranchised males who went to war. And Moore (1990) found that among the Cheyenne, men who controlled more resources and had greater familial networks became peace chiefs; such men tended not to assume the risks of war. Instead, men who had no relatives, often simply orphans, became war chiefs; they could achieve some status, but remained unmarried. These war chiefs could gain the proximate rewards of status, but could not turn status into reproductive gain. The Cheyenne case appears to be an example of intragroup conflict of interest, between peace chiefs and war chiefs, with kinship and power on the side of peace chiefs. It would be extremely interesting to learn the history of the Cheyenne condition: were the first peace chiefs (political leaders) originally successful war chiefs who then discovered how to avoid the risks of leading war parties without losing status? Only when an individual's other options are severely constrained, or he becomes convinced of some overwhelming benefit, should such extreme behavior be seen. Thus, the suicide missions of some Japanese in World War II and the extreme risks taken in jihads in the Middle East should correlate either with the otherwise very low status of the men, or with otherwise unmatched promises of gain.

Shaw and Wong (1989) have argued persuasively that kin selection still drives much conflict today. They argue that when societies become very large and comprise diverse groups, intragroup or ethnic conflict (once again) becomes important; thus, civil war is today more common than international war. If, as I have argued above, lethal conflict arose in the evolutionary context of reproductive striving, international wars are likely to be simply epiphenomena—although national leaders may use tactics of referring to proximate cues important in evolutionary time (e.g., familial terms to promote patriotism). Real strife over local resources seems most likely to escalate into lethal conflict; thus, it is not surprising that even today civil war and ethnic strife are far more common in nation-states than international war (see below; also Brogan 1990, Keegan and Wheatcroft 1986, Dunnigan and Bay 1986).

Greek Hoplites: Early "Western" Warriors?

Hanson (1989) argues that classical Greek warfare has "left us with what is now a burdensome legacy in the West: a presumption that battle under any guise other than a no-nonsense, head-to-head confrontation between sober enemies is or should be unpalatable" and that the Greeks provided the first real shift, in the West, at least, away from small-band, guerrilla ambush attacks (the usual pattern in preindustrial societies). Indeed, the Greek situation shares some characteristics with modern war, but it also shows some important, and perhaps underappreciated, differences.

The rise of the hoplite—a heavily armed and armored infantryman—in warfare during the second half of the seventh, and the sixth, centuries B.C., had important political as well as military consequences (McNeill 1963). Hoplites fought in phalanxes, and each man's life depended "upon the stalwart behavior of his neighbor in the battle line" (McNeill 1963, 198). For the most part, hoplites were small farmers, and the agricultural constraints of vineyards, olive groves, and grainfields meant that battles were fought during the summers by local farmers to gain or protect local property (Hanson 1989). In most city-states (except Sparta), there was little combat specialization and very limited drill (Hanson 1989, 120). Men were vulnerable to the draft in any summer from their eighteenth to their sixtieth year, and in any battle, the majority of men were likely to be over thirty (Hanson 1989, 90). Men of rank fought as ordinary hoplites among their less noble neighbors, and men fought with others of their tribal affiliation. When columns were decimated, they were not immediately reconstituted, but men simply moved over to take the places of men killed—usually friends, relatives, or neighbors (Hanson 1989, 122). Thus, the survivors of a battle were likely to know all of those killed. Men testified to the numbers of battles others fought, a sort of mutual recommendation system that Hanson (1989, 123) characterized as a "rather intensive mutual interest." Men fought, then, with their kindred and their neighbors, with whom they held many interdependent relationships. Strong bonds were reinforced. Even the famous homosexual bonds of Spartans and the Sacred Band of Thebes had military impact (e.g., Hanson 1989, 124).

Thus, while these conflicts (like others of the times) involved trained warriors in organized combat, rather than tribal ambushes, individual men were still fighting to protect (or gain) their own land resources, and they fought with their families, tribes, and neighbors. Shared interests were immediate, local, and often kin-based. Commanders fought in the front lines with their men, suffering almost certain death if defeated, and, perhaps surprisingly, a relatively high proportion of victorious generals died. Hanson (1989) suggests that these patterns result from the crucial importance to troop morale of a general fighting at the front, being among the first to face the spears of the enemy. In contrast, in most modern wars (e.g., Keegan 1987), commanders have moved further from the front lines and share fewer risks with their troops (with some notable exceptions in the U.S. Civil War).

The Evolutionary Ecology of Renaissance War

War in the Middle Ages, up until the mid–fifteenth century, involved many small-scale territorial wars, and local powerful men—a sort of "violent housekeeping" (Hale 1985, 13). Knights, up until perhaps 1450, fought largely as individuals and small coalitions (Hackett 1983, 28). Typical causes included revival of old family claims to previously lost estates: "political Europe was like an estate map, and war was a socially acceptable form of property acquisition" (Hale 1985, 22). While particular causes differed, familial economic interests were clearly present. Noblemen, landed gentry, had strong vested interests in waging warfare, not only for reasons of territory defense or acquisition, but for the spoils and riches gained from plunder or ransom. Later-born sons, with lower access to resources and titles than their elder brothers, tended to end up in high-risk warfare (Boone 1988). In Europe, from Roman times until Charles the Bold's military ordinance of 1473, differentiation by insignia in larger armies reflected social status (Vale 1981, 148).

Kinship-mimicry was also used: military adventurers often became *fratres jurati*, sworn brothers. When William the Conqueror invaded England, Robert de Oily and Roger de Ivery were *fratres jurati*. Receiving honors for battle, Robert gave Roger one as his sworn brother. Fifteenth-century *compagnies d'ordonnance* (Hale 1985, 92) engaged the monarch's personal interest, provided a route to high administrative office, confirmed disputed titles, and paved the way for handsome plunder or ransom profits.

The introduction of guns permanently changed the nature of war, its conduct and conditions. At some level, of course, it is fair to say this of any technological development, any new war tool, such as horses (Newark 1979) or crossbows (McNeill 1982). But gunpowder may have had an unforeseen effect that fed back into the nature of selection on warfare. Gunpowder led to larger and more costly armies, with more support personnel (e.g., masons to make balls of stone if the iron ones ran out). It led to longer-lasting conflicts (previously limited by an individual's ability to exert sustained physical effort). It changed the nature of confrontation (guns could be poked through holes in fortifications). Sieges became more common. Perhaps most important, it changed the requirements for soldiers: it took far less skill or resources to fire a musket than to train as a longbowman or cavalryman. This separated the risk bearers from those who could profit from warfare. Further, a new group emerged: weapons makers, with complex skills and political power, who could profit from lethal conflict without the risk of engaging in it (see McNeill 1982).

Increased costs were passed on to the population in the form of higher taxes, and in "voracious" recruiting, although field armies probably never drew on more than 5 percent of the population (Hale 1985, 75; taxes become an important issue in all but the most local wars; see also Miller 1975, and Elton 1975). Mercenaries became prominent. Efforts to intensify the involvement of the landed gentry were not too successful, for predictable reasons: percentage quotas, rather than individuals (except in the case of personal indentures; Hale 1985, 77) were drafted, and those who could buy or litigate their way out of the draft passed the burden on to those with fewer resources. Early in the period, substitutes were liable to be younger sons of nobility, but later substitutes were those without skills, poor, and hungry, even on the run from criminal proceedings. Hale (1985, 109) quotes the Venetian commander Giulio Savorgnan in 1572, regarding why his troops had enlisted: "To escape from being craftsmen, working in a shop; to avoid a criminal sentence; to see new things; to pursue honour—but these are very few. The rest join in the hope of having enough to live on and a bit over for shoes or some other trifle that will make life supportable." Similarly, in 1600, Thomas Wilson assessed English forces (Hale 1985, 125) as comprising chiefly cottagers and copyholders, but also those who are "poore, and lyve cheefly upon labor, workeing by the day for meat and drinke and some small wages."

Renaissance wars, then, were fought by mercenaries; the standing army came into being after the Renaissance (Chamberlin 1965, 143). The power held by those possessing desired skills passed largely to others, who did not fight. Further, mercenaries had impact on civilians during peacetime: unlike knights, who were likely to return home, or paid soldiers, responsible to their employers, mercenaries during peacetime were "the responsibility of no man and they consequently became bandits" (Chamberlin 1965, 151).

Over time, then, the potential individual reproductive gain of warfare fostered technological innovation, and then the technology of war changed the nature of warfare itself. The balance of benefits seems to have shifted, for most actors, from a familial, resource- or status-building strategy, as in the

Yanomamo, the Meru, and Europe of the early Middle Ages, to a more stratified situation in which the poor and disenfranchised began to shoulder the risks and costs of warfare—as in the Cherokee, Portuguese nobles, and even Vietnam. A shift occurred, in which more expertise was required for the manufacture than the use of common weapons, further separating the risk and the costs for warriors. Of course, it's hardly so simple; rewards and booty remained important resource advantages for some men. Even today, it would be difficult to disprove an accusation that individual fortunes and family empires are sometime built from war, but the range of variation in advantages available for warriors appears to have increased, and nonwarriors have entered the equation.

The Evolutionary Ecology of Modern War

It is almost certainly true that past correlations between warriors' behavior and reproductive success no longer hold; certainly the necessary data, with appropriate controls, are lacking. Nonetheless, several aspects of men's behavior in wars, and of the organization of fighting forces, suggest that *proximate* correlates of reproductive success due to risky and aggressive behavior still exist in modern wars, and successful leaders organize field units in ways that play on the past kinship structure of warring groups.

Training

Many features of the training of young men for warfare mimic the proximate cues of both kin groups and close reciprocity. It is common for new recruits in many armies to undergo forced transformation to uniformity (GI haircuts, uniforms; e.g., Holmes 1985). Their training emphasizes communal values, often by using kinship terms. Training is aimed not only at obvious skills; as the sheer size and complexity of warring groups increases, training aims at ensuring cohesion, inciting hostility, enforcing obedience, and suppressing mutiny (e.g., Holmes 1985, Dixon 1976). Recruits are likely to be called "son," "boy," or "lad." As Holmes (1985, 46) notes, this paternalistic language goes far beyond basic training, and has done so for centuries. The "sworn brothers" fighting together in the Middle Ages also represented reciprocity bolstered by mimicking kinship.

Hackworth (1989, 633–35) argued that a significant portion of the combat failures in Vietnam arose directly from a limited number of causes, including poor training that broke the pattern Holmes reviews. Instruction was done by returned short-timers who had not wanted to go to Vietnam in the first place; dissatisfaction often led to war stories rather than training when supervision was absent. Perhaps most significant, men were not trained and put into combat in units, with their mimic of familial structure and their strongly developed reciprocity. Rather, men were sent individually into combat. In a strange land (the finishing preparation for this jungle war was done on snow-covered fields), without the required skills (e.g., none of Hackworth's trainees could answer what to do when the gun jammed), and dependent on strangers, many died.

Prebattle Exhortation

Successful commanders from time immemorial have played upon the major themes of gain: not only economic, but reciprocity and the powerful pull of kinship and sexual selection. Thus Du Guesclin, a French knight of the mid-fourteenth century, mixed penitential motives with profit, when he urged his recruits (cited in Gies 1984, 157): "If we search our hearts, we have done enough to damn our souls . . . . For God's sake, let us march on the pagans! . . . I will make you all rich if you [follow me]!" Interestingly, Hugh of Caveley, an English knight fighting with him, responded by invoking kinship and reciprocity: "Bertrand, fair brother and comrade, mirror of chivalry, because of your loyalty and your valor, I am yours, I and all these here." Shakespeare captured the essence of this strategy, when he had Henry V, before Agincourt, first recite a litany of famous and powerful names, then exhort his ragtag collection of men, calling them brothers even while highlighting their class diversity. The folks at home are sometimes similarly exhorted. In the news headlines of the Middle East conflict, headlines reinforced kinship images: "Shipmates become like brothers in Gulf pressure-cooker" (*Detroit News and Free Press*, February 10, 1991).

Resistance to Interrogation

Watson (1978; see also Hackworth 1989) makes an important point about the importance of group structure and intragroup reciprocity; he notes, for example (1978, 298; also Schein 1957) that during the Korean war, the most successful North Korean interrogations followed breakdown of the prisoners' group structure. Thus reliable group structure—the presence of dependable comrades-in-arms—contributes not only to desired behavior in battle but to increased ability to resist interrogation after capture.

The Role of the Disadvantaged

War has changed. From the engagement of relatively few (often related) men in individual combat over resources directly related to their lineage's success, armies have grown and become hierarchical, with increasing divergence among the actors' interests. From related men who might squabble over this bride or those cows, we now have administrative groups sending others to fight.

Maintaining discipline and loyalty in the face of unequal payoffs can be tricky. Alexander (1979) argued that this problem lies at the very root of the transformation of societies from often highly polygynous states to (at least relatively and prescriptively) monogamous states. In polygynous societies engaged in large-army warfare and conquest, formal reproductive and re-source distribution schemes are common.

As warfare technology changed and armies became larger, status differentials increased. No longer, as among the Yanomamo, were the spoils of war a relatively simple reflection of individual courage and skill. More high-status men opted out of conflict, and more low-status men were recruited or drafted. These men, from at least medieval times (Boone 1988) to the Vietnam war (Hackworth 1989, 634) suffered higher casualties than their richer competitors.

Hackworth (1989, 634) called the failure to mimic the familial structure of preindustrial warfare (which resulted in high casualties and an increasing need for replacements, followed by a lowering of induction requirements) "the most blatant example of the use and misuse of the poor and disadvantaged in America's wars." These men, the Project 100,000 soldiers, were those who had (or would have) previously failed the armed services' physical or mental requirements; they proceeded through the Army "as they proceed through life, walking wounded in the center of a monstrous joke, forced to struggle with basic training as they are forced to struggle with everything else" (Just 1970, 62). The Vietnam example may simply be the most recent and extreme case; Watson (1978, 34) reviews a 1960 PRB Technical report showing that the more intelligent, able soldiers, the better fighters, cluster in the safer jobs, away from the front line; Watson calls this "Catch 23."

Yet the fate of disadvantaged men is not so simple; if it were, the only question would be why any ever serve. Just as, for any individual, the costs and benefits of living in a group must be weighed against the costs and benefits of living alone or in another kind of group (e.g., Alexander 1974), the question must be asked: Did these men, on average, fare better or worse than if they had remained civilians? No data exist. For those who survived, it is possible that they did in fact fare better than if they had not served, through the status of wearing a uniform (see Holmes 1985, 93).

Insurgency and Terrorism

In evolutionary terms, individuals and groups should engage in potentially lethal conflict only when the net reproductive outcomes are likely to be positive. Gunpowder is one example of a technological change with great effect on these costs and benefits for the primary actors—warriors. Technology has another effect: as the lethality of weapons increases, a small number of people can threaten the stability or lives of large numbers of people (e.g., Wilkinson 1986). As major powers shy away from escalation of international conflicts most likely to lead to nuclear engagement, local, usually ethnic, conflicts become more important, and as the technology available to small groups increases in sophistication (surface-to-air and heat-seeking missiles have been captured), the danger posed by small groups increases.

Reviews of contemporary terrorism (e.g., Gutteridge 1986) and low-intensity conflict (e.g., Klare and Kornbluh 1988) suggest that, despite exceptions like the Red Brigade, most conflicts in fact originate as local ethnic or religious conflicts of interest—e.g., the Basque struggle, Northern Ireland, the West Bank. Conflicts like these are probably intensified by the sorts of pressures prevalent throughout the evolutionary history of warfare: genetic lineages in conflict, expanded to become regional conflicts (see Shaw and Wong 1989 for good discussion of several such conflicts). It is probably not irrelevant that in many successful (long-lasting) terrorist groups, the leader assumes a paternalistic role, and the group structure mimics that of families (e.g., Aston 1986). However, as Wilkinson (1986) points out, a major "growth" area in terrorist activity is the expansion, allowed by technological advances, of basically local ethnic and religious conflict to international scale. Some patterns are evident: kidnappings are more likely on "home" territories, barricades and hostage taking elsewhere (Aston 1986). In Western Europe, there is an ethnic bias to kidnappings (Aston 1986). Even a review of larger-scale conflicts suggests that ethnic and racial components are still important after World War II—far more important than ideology or nationalism (e.g., Brogan 1990, Keegan and Wheatcroft 1986, Dunnigan and Bay 1986). Current tensions in the Middle East and the former Yugoslavia speak clearly to this point.

The real danger is probably that small, originally local conflicts, because of technological advances, can wreak international havoc, and major powers can then be drawn into the fray. For example, Goose (1988) notes that U.S. funding for Special Operations Forces, typically involved in low-intensity interventions in local conflicts, increased 100 percent during the 1980s. There is real potential for major powers to be drawn into confrontation through (originally) local conflicts (Maechling 1988), and balancing such conflicts can impose high costs and real risks (Barnet 1988).

Deception and Warfare

In other species, aggression is accompanied by advertisements that exaggerate an individual's prowess (e.g., Alexander 1987). In human conflicts, there are probably not qualitative differences, but it may be that there are important quantitative differences, compared to conflicts of other species. We may be capable of more subtle deception; this may in fact make conflict more, not less, likely, because conflict is more likely when at least one contestant's information is faulty (Parker 1974, Alexander 1987, 239; also see above). In human arms races, Alexander (1987, 239) argues, secrecy, deception, and misinformation are necessary; otherwise there would be unpredictable occasions when the stronger party might simply use its force (that there exist examples of precisely this tactic merely shows that bluff doesn't always work). The outcome of this requirement for secrecy and misdirection, argues Alexander, is that policymakers and government officials must often oppose citizen concerns. This situation is complicated by the fact that leaders and their advisors play a double game, both laterally, with other national leaders, and vertically, with the public, and the influence of the public on leaders' policies is maximized only periodically (in the United States, every four years), and the public has imperfect, manipulated information.

War and Reproduction

In preindustrial societies like the Yanomamo and the Meru, a man's lifetime reproductive success was likely to be closely correlated with his performance in war. Nor are these two examples atypical; in many societies, reproductive rewards for valor were standard (e.g., the Comanche, Cabello y Robles 1961, 178; the Natchez, Swanton 1911, 104). Both direct reproductive rewards and status or privilege before the law were common rewards for leadership and success in war (e.g., Betzig 1986).

As armies became larger and more stratified, and as direct formal reproductive rewards for performance disappeared, the situation became far less clear. The origins of this shift appear in Renaissance warfare. For many, there are obvious risks, but no longer obvious reproductive rewards. For disenfranchised men, with little or no chance of success in peacetime environments, there is possibly a correlation (see above; Holmes 1985), but it is hard to measure.

Proximate and Ultimate Causes of War: Evolutionary Novelty

Warfare evolves to be common only in circumstances in which the net fitness of warriors has been enhanced. Reproductive costs and benefits, and conflicts of interest, are central. In an evolutionary sense, the ultimate causes of war, as of all lethal conflict, are sexual selection and kin selection. Throughout the animal kingdom, lethal risks are taken only when the reproductive stakes are high. Individuals and groups of related individuals, principally males, fight over mates and resources important to reproduction. Groups of chimpanzee males attack each other in ambushes very similar to those in preindustrial societies. Sexual selection and kin selection are the driving forces creating the reproductive rewards that make the risk of death worthwhile; kinship and reciprocity are the principal binding forces among those who fight together.

Throughout the evolution of conflict, in humans as well as other species, there have been reproductive profits associated with the risks of lethal conflict. With the elaboration of war, and the increased pace of weapons development, selective outcomes have become less tied to individual actions and characteristics. Those with the most to gain from warfare came frequently to suffer lower risks than those with little to gain. We may well have unhooked the reproductive rewards from the behavior, so that lethal conflict is now counterselective and driven only by proximate cues. Now, perhaps, though there are no data, war may not profit anyone directly involved in the conflict—but the driving cues remain.

With this in mind, let us review very briefly some of the proximate causes of warfare assigned in modern conflicts. This subject is far too broad for a detailed analysis here; the specific causes are multifarious; others (e.g., Singer 1980, 1989; Huth 1988) deal with it in more detail. There are, however, some major patterns uncovered by others that may be well worth reviewing briefly here. Consider for a moment some of the causes and correlates of war: number of contiguous neighbors (Richardson 1960), economic conflicts (approximately 29 percent of the wars from 1820 to 1949; Richardson 1960), territory disputes (Richardson 1960), ideological differences (Winter 1989), and misperception or distortion of information (wars in this century; Stoessinger 1982). Pacifying influences include shared ethnicity (Shaw and Wong 1989, Richardson 1960), common government (Richardson 1960), recent alliance (Richardson 1960), and extended deterrence when military strength is sufficient in the short term (Huth 1988). Stoessinger (1982) and Winter (1989) note the important potential influence of leaders' personalities. Even in the huge number of specific causes of wars in modern times, the "ecological" categories are still rather limited: conflicts arise over resources (economic or territorial), and are less likely the longer and deeper are common bonds (kinship or reciprocity); open conflict is often precipitated by faulty information.

There is, however, a behavioral ecology of war in our evolutionary past. The multiplicity of proximate correlates in modern warfare does not mute the importance of the ethnic (and perhaps male competitive) forces. Brogan (1990) counts at least eightly wars since 1945, resulting in fifteen to thirty million deaths. The vast majority of these, he finds, are between peoples and races; few are international or ideological. A review of other recent atlases of war (e.g., Dunnigan and Bay 1986, Keegan and Wheatcroft 1986) reinforces the importance of essentially tribal conflicts of interest.

Can Evolutionary Theory Help Avert Arms Races?

If potentially lethal conflict has very old evolutionary and ecological roots, can learning about these roots help us avert arms races? It is difficult to tell, but perhaps a knowledge of evolutionary theory can help us mitigate and control them. Understanding the evolutionary background of lethal conflict and arms races may simply help us to understand that costs and benefits, deception and misperception, may involve currencies other than the immediate and obvious ones (cf. Stoessinger 1982).

Shaw and Wong (1989, 204–8), in their analysis, review both the hope held out by evolutionary theory and the barriers to its usefulness. Sadly, after the eloquent analysis of their entire work, they are reduced (1989, 208) to calling for "some form of world government, some management force that might stabilize the most immediate threat to humanity—nuclear destruction." Their entire work, however, is an acknowledgment that the power of in-group amity and out-group enmity would likely force any such world government to be a conquest state, a chilling prospect. There are suggestions, however (e.g., Keohane 1984, Oye 1986), that even in the absence of power hierarchies or hegemony, certain costs and benefits may promote cooperation.

If the data reviewed here are correct, warfare evolved in circumstances in which mating and thus fitness benefits were worth lethal risks. We now have largely broken that link, but we, like other organisms, have not evolved to "calculate" ultimate (lineage) results, but to respond to proximate cues. Now, the reproductive profits may be largely gone, but the proximate cues remain. Writing of just such problems, Alexander (1987, 240), found that "it seems to place me in a camp of those who see mutual deterrence as the basis for peace, even though I doubt that either self-extinction or massive destruction can be prevented indefinitely by deterrence alone." He then suggested that, given our finely honed social and predictive ("scenario-building") intellect, several partial brakes on arms races may exist—e.g., if sufficiently numerous and powerful individuals and groups perceive that no matter who wins the confrontation, we all will lose, their power in internal social and political coalitions may allow them to force some solutions. The difficulty is that the brakes are weakened by the dilemma a biologist would call the "levels of selection" problem: because natural selection works in the genetically selfish ways described above, long-term costs and benefits to groups are discounted compared to immediate, short-term costs and benefits to the individual. The larger and less-related the group, or the farther in the future that costs and benefits must be calculated, the greater will be the discount. Thus, given a short-term gain in status or tax base for a local constituency versus an unspecifiable risk of nuclear warfare some time in the future, we do not predict restraint. However, the levels of selection problem has a positive side. Internal war (war among factions in a society) is more common when there are participatory institutions—but these same institutions, by including more individuals in the decision-making process, make external war (war against outside groups) less likely (Ember, Ember and Russett, 1992). The more "democratic" or participatory the system of governance, the less likely is warfare, even cross-culturally among small societies. Thus, perhaps encouraging participation in governance, as an independent endeavor, can have some moderating effect on warfare frequency.

Any attempt to foster peaceful behavior must change individual costs and benefits in the proximate sense (e.g., Goldstein 1989, Keohane 1984, Oye 1986); as Groebel and Hinde (1989) note, currently many social institutions and rewards mediate strong status pressure on individuals to enter into wars. This sounds simple enough, and has parallels in economic approaches, but the following difficulties are serious: (1) unlike small-scale societies, there are no longer simply a few easily identified, powerful groups or coalitions with focused costs and benefits, so it is hard to figure out how to direct any such proposed manipulations; (2) now, to an extent previously unknown, small groups of individuals can control highly destructive devices. When these individuals are unaffected by the sorts of costs and rewards humans have evolved to recognize, we call them terrorists. Our technology is sufficiently advanced that even such small groups can wreak havoc, killing great numbers of people.

REFERENCES

Adams, D. B. 1983. "Why There Are So Few Women Warriors." *Behavioral Science Research* 18 (3): 196–212.
Alexander, R. D. 1971. "The Search for an Evolutionary Philosophy of Man." *Proceedings of the Royal Society of Victoria* (Melbourne) 84: 99–120.
———. 1974. "The Evolution of Social Behavior." *Annual Review of Ecology and Systematics* 5: 325–83.
———. 1979. *Darwinism and Human Affairs.* Seattle: University of Washington Press.
———. 1987. *The Biology of Moral Systems.* New York: Aldine De Gruyter.
Ardrey, R. 1966. *The Territorial Imperative.* New York: Atheneum.
Aston, C. C. 1986. "Political Hostage-Taking in Western Europe." In *Contemporary Terrorism*, edited by W. Gutteridge, 57–83. New York: Facts on File Publications.
Axelrod, R., and D. Dion. 1988. "The Further Evolution of Cooperation." *Science* 242: 1385–90.
Barkow, J. H. 1977. "Conformity to Ethos and Reproductive Success in Two Hausa Communities: An Empirical Evaluation." *Ethos* 5: 409–25.

Barnet, R. J. 1988. "The Costs and Perils of Intervention." In *Low-Intensity Warfare: Counterinsurgency, Proinsurgency, and Anti-Terrorism in the Eighties,* edited by M. T. Klare and P. Kornbluh, 207–21. New York: Pantheon.

Barry III, H., L. Josephson, E. Lauer, and C. Marshall. 1976. "Traits Inculcated in Childhood. 5. Cross-Cultural Codes." *Ethnology* 15: 83–114.

Betzig, L. L. 1986. *Despotism and Differential Reproduction: A Darwinian View of History.* New York: Aldine.

Boone, J. L. 1988. "Parental Investment, Social Subordination and Population Processes among the 15th and 16th Century Portuguese Nobility." In *Human Reproductive Behaviour: A Darwinian Perspective*, edited by L. Betzig, M. Borgerhoff Mulder, and P. Turke, 201–19. Cambridge: Cambridge University Press.

Borgerhoff Mulder, M. 1988. "Kipsigis Bridewealth Payments." In *Human Reproductive Behaviour: A Darwinian Perspective,* edited by L. Betzig, M. Borgerhoff Mulder, and P. Turke, 65–82. Cambridge: Cambridge University Press.

———. 1990. "Kipsigis Women's Preferences for Wealthy Men: Evidence for Female Choice in Mammals?" *Behavioral Ecology and Sociobiology* 27: 255–64.

Brogan, P. 1990. *The Fighting Never Stopped: A Comprehensive Guide to World Conflict since 1945.* New York: Vintage Books.

Bueno de Mesquita, B. 1981. *The War Trap.* New Haven: Yale University Press.

Byrne, R., and A. Whiten. 1988. *Machiavellian Intelligence: Social Expertise and the Evolution of Intellect in Monkeys, Apes, and Humans.* Oxford: Clarendon Press.

Cabello y Robles, D. 1961. "A Description of the Comanche Indians in 1786 by the Governor of Texas." *West Texas Historical Association Yearbook* 37: 177–82.

Cain, M. 1985. "On the Relationship between Landholding and Fertility." *Population Studies* 39: 5–15.

Carniero, R. L. 1970. "A Theory of the Origin of the State." *Science* 169: 733–38.

Chagnon, N. 1979. "Is Reproductive Success Equal in Egalitarian Societies?" In *Evolutionary Biology and Human Social Behavior: An Anthropological Perspective*, edited by N. A. Chagnon and W. Irons, 374–401. North Scituate, MA: Duxbury Press.

———. 1982. "Sociodemographic Attributes of Nepotism in Tribal Populations: Man the Rule-Breaker." In *Current Problems in Sociobiology*, edited by King's College Sociobiology Group. Cambridge: Cambridge University Press.

———. 1988. "Life Histories, Blood Revenge, and Warfare in a Tribal Population." *Science* 239: 985–92.

Chagnon, N. A., and R. Hames. 1979. "Protein Deficiency and Tribal Warfare in Amazonia: New Data." *Science* 203: 910–13.

Chamberlin, E. R. 1965. *Everyday Life in Renaissance Times.* London: B. T. Batsford, Ltd.

Cheney, D. 1987. "Interactions and Relationships between Groups." In *Primate Societies*, edited by B. B. Smuts, D. L. Cheney, R. M. Seyfarth, R. W. Wrangham, and T. T. Struhsaker, 267–81. Chicago: University of Chicago Press.

Clutton-Brock, T., S. Albon, and F. Guinness. 1986. "Great Expectations: Dominance, Breeding Success and Offspring Sex Ratio in Red Deer." *Animal Behavior* 34: 460–71.

Clutton-Brock, T., F. Guinness, and S. Albon. 1982. *Red Deer: Behavior and Ecology of Two Sexes.* Chicago: University of Chicago Press.

Clutton-Brock, T., and P. Harvey. 1976. "Evolutionary Rules and Primate Societies." In *Growing Points in Ethology*, edited by P. P. G. Bateson, and R. A. Hinde, 195–237. Cambridge: Cambridge University Press.

Cowlishaw, G., and R. I. Dunbar. 1991. "Dominance Rank and Mating Success in Male Primates." *Animal Behavior* 41: 1045–56.

Cronk, Lee. 1991a. "Human Behavioral Ecology." *Annual Review of Anthropology* 20: 25–53.

———. 1991b. "Wealth, Status, and Reproductive Success among the Mukogodo of Kenya." *American Anthropologist* 93 (2): 345–60.

Daly, M., and M. Wilson. 1983. *Sex, Evolution, and Behavior*, 2d ed. Boston: Willard Grant.

———. 1988. *Homicide*. Hawthorn, NY: Aldine De Gruyter.

Darwin, C. 1859. *On the Origin of Species by Means of Natural Selection.* Facsimile of the first edition, with an introduction by E. Mayr, published 1987. Cambridge, MA: Harvard University Press.

———. 1871. *The Descent of Man and Selection in Relation to Sex.* 2 vols. London: John Murray.

Dawkins, R. 1986. *The Blind Watchmaker.* New York: W. W. Norton.

Denig, E. T. 1961. *Five Indian Tribes of the Upper Missouri: Sioux, Arickaras, Assiniboines, Cree, Crows.* Edited and with an introduction by John C. Ewers. Norman: University of Oklahoma Press.

Dewsbury, D. A. 1982. "Dominance Rank, Copulatory Behavior, and Differential Reproduction." *Quarterly Review of Biology* 57: 135–59.

Dickemann, M. 1979. "The Reproductive Structure of Stratified Societies: A Preliminary Model." In *Evolutionary Biology and Human Social Organization: An Anthropological Perspective*, edited by N. A. Chagnon and W. Irons, 331–67. North Scituate, MA: Duxbury Press.

Divale, W. 1973. *Warfare in Primitive Societies: A Bibliography.* Santa Barbara: American Bibliographic Center Clio, Inc.

Divale, W., and M. Harris. 1976. "Population, Warfare, and the Male Supremacist Complex." *American Anthropologist* 80 (1): 21–41.

Dixon, N. F. 1976. *On the Psychology of Military Incompetence.* London: Cape.

Dunnigan, J. F., and A. Bay. 1986. *A Quick and Dirty Guide to War: Briefings on Present and Potential Wars.* Updated ed. New York: Quill/William Morrow.

Durham, W. H. 1976. "Resource Competition and Human Aggression. Part 1. A Review of Primitive War." *Quarterly Review of Biology* 51: 385–415.

Elton, G. R. 1975. "Taxation for War and Peace in Early-Tudor England." In *War and Economics in Development*, edited by J. M. Winter. Cambridge: Cambridge University Press.

Eibl-Eibesfeldt, I. 1979. *The Biology of Peace and War.* London: Viking Press.

Ember, C. R. 1978. "Myths about Hunter-Gatherers." *Ethnology* 17: 439–48.

———. 1981. "A Cross-Cultural Perspective on Sex Differences." In *Handbook of Cross-Cultural Human Development*, edited by R. H. Monroe, R. L. Monroe, and B. B. Whiting, 531–80. New York: Garland.

Ember, C. R., and M. Ember. 1992. "Resource Unpredictability, Mistrust, and War: A Cross-Cultural Study." *Journal of Conflict Resolution* 36 (2): 242–62.

Ember, C. R., M. Ember, and B. Russett. 1992. "Peace between Participatory Polities: A Test of the 'Democracies Rarely Fight Each Other' Hypothesis." *World Politics* 44: 573–99.

Emlen, S. T., and L. W. Oring. 1977. "Ecology, Sexual Selection, and the Evolution of Mating Systems." *Science* 197: 215–23.

Essock-Vitale, S. M. 1984. "The Reproductive Success of Wealthy Americans." *Ethology and Sociobiology* 5: 45–49.

Ewers, J. C. 1958. *The Blackfeet*. Norman: University of Oklahoma Press.

Fadiman, J. A. 1982. *An Oral History of Tribal Warfare: The Meru of Mt. Kenya*. Athens, OH: Ohio University Press.

Faux, S. F., and H. L. Miller. 1984. "Evolutionary Speculations on the Oligarchic Development of Mormon Polygyny." *Ethology and Sociobiology* 5: 15–31.

Ferrill, A. 1985. *The Origins of War*. London: Thames and Hudson.

Fisher, R. A. 1958. *The Genetical Theory of Natural Selection*. New York: Dover Books.

Flinn, M. V. 1986. "Correlates of Reproductive Success in a Caribbean Village." *Human Ecology* 14: 225–43.

Flinn, M. V., and B. S. Low. 1986. "Resource Distribution, Social Competition, and Mating Patterns in Human Societies." In *Ecological Aspects of Social Evolution*, edited by D. Rubenstein and R. Wrangham, 217–43. Princeton: Princeton University Press.

Galloway, P. R. 1986. "Differentials in Demographic Responses to Annual Price Variations in Pre-Revolutionary France: A Comparison of Rich and Poor Areas in Rouen, 1681–1787." *European Journal of Population* 2: 269–305.

Gies, F. 1984. *The Knight in History*. New York: Harper & Row.

Goldstein, A. P. 1989. "Aggression Reduction: Some Vital Steps." In *Aggression and War: Their Biological and Social Bases*, edited by J. Groebel and R. A. Hinde, 112–31. Cambridge: Cambridge University Press.

Goodall, J. 1986. *The Chimpanzees of Gombe: Patterns of Behavior*. Cambridge: Harvard University Press.

Goodall, J., A. Bandora, E. Bergmann, C. Busse, H. Matama, E. Mpongo, A. Pierce, and D. Riss. 1979. "Intercommunity Interactions in the Chimpanzee Population of the Gombe National Park." In *The Great Apes*, edited by D. A. Hamburg and E. R. McCown. Menlo Park, CA: Benjamin Cummings.

Goose, S. D. 1988. "Low-Intensity Warfare: The Warriors and their Weapons." In *Low Intensity Warfare: Counterinsurgency, Proinsurgency, and Anti-Terrorism in the Eighties*, edited by M. T. Klare and P. Kornbluh, 80–111. New York: Pantheon.

Grafen, A. 1984. "Natural Selection, Kin Selection, and Group Selection." In *Behavioural Ecology: An Evolutionary Approach*, 2d ed., edited by J. R. Krebs and N. B. Davies, 62–64. Oxford: Blackwell Scientific.

Groebel, J., and R. A. Hinde. 1989. "A Multi-Level Approach to the Problems of Aggression and War." In *Aggression and War: Their Biological and Social Bases*, edited by J. Groebel and R. A. Hinde, 223–29. Cambridge: Cambridge University Press.

Gutteridge, W. 1986. *Contemporary Terrorism*. New York: Facts on File Publications.

Hackett, J. 1983. *The Profession of Arms*. New York: Macmillan.

Hackworth, D. H., with J. Sherman. 1989. *About Face: The Odyssey of an American Warrior*. New York: Simon and Schuster.

Hale, J. R. 1985. *War and Society in Renaissance Europe, 1450–1620*. New York: St. Martin's Press.

Hamilton, W. D. 1964. "The Genetical Evolution of Social Behaviour. I, II." *Journal of Theoretical Biology* 7: 1–52.

Hanson, V. D. 1989. *The Western Way of War: Infantry Battle in Ancient Greece*. Oxford: Oxford University Press.

Harcourt, A. H. 1978. "Strategies of Emigration and Transfer by Primates, with Particular Reference to Gorillas." *Zeitschrift Tierpsychologie* 48: 401–20.

Harris, M. 1979. *Cultural Materialism*. New York: Random House.

Hartung, J. 1982. "Polygyny and the Inheritance of Wealth." *Current Anthropology* 23: 1–12.

———. 1992. "Getting Real about Rape." *Behavioral and Brain Sciences* 15 (2): 390–92.

Hayami, A. 1980. "Class Differences in Marriage and Fertility among Tokugawa Villagers in Mino Province." *Keio Economic Studies* 17 (1): 1–16.

Hill, J. 1984. "Prestige and Reproductive Success in Man." *Ethology and Sociobiology* 5: 77–95.

Hill, K., and H. Kaplan. 1988. "Tradeoffs in Male and Female Reproductive Strategies among the Ache. Part I." In *Human Reproductive Behaviour: A Darwinian Perspective*, edited by L. Betzig, M. Borgerhoff Mulder, and P. Turke, 277–89. Cambridge: Cambridge University Press.

Holmes, R. 1985. *Acts of War: The Behavior of Men in Battle*. New York: Free Press.

Hughes, A. 1986. "Reproductive Success and Occupational Class in Eighteenth-Century Lancashire, England." *Social Biology* 33: 109–15.

Humphrey, N. K. 1976. "The Social Function of Intellect." In *Growing Points in Ethology*, edited by P. P. G. Bateson and R. A. Hinde. London: Cambridge University Press.

———. 1983. *Consciousness Regained: Chapters in the Development of Mind*. Oxford: Oxford University Press.

Huntingford, F., and A. Turner. 1987. *Animal Conflict*. London: Chapman and Hall.

Huth, P. K. 1988. *Extended Deterrence and the Prevention of War*. New Haven: Yale University Press.

Irons, W. 1979a. "Natural Selection, Adaptation, and Human Social Behavior." In *Evolutionary Biology and Human Social Behavior: An Anthropological Perspective*, edited by N. A. Chagnon and W. Irons. North Scituate, MA: Duxbury Press.

———. 1979b. "Emic and Reproductive Success." In *Evolutionary Biology and Human Social Behavior: An Anthropological Perspective*, edited by N. A. Chagnon and W. Irons. North Scituate, MA: Duxbury Press.

Johnson, G. 1986. "Kin Selection, Socialization, and Patriotism: An Integrating Theory." *Politics and the Life Sciences* 4: 128–39.

Johnson, G., S. H. Ratwik, and T. J. Sawyer. 1987. "The Evocative Significance of Kin Terms in Patriotic Speech." In *The Sociobiology of Ethnocentrism: Evolu-*

tionary Dimensions of Xenophobia, Discrimination, Racism, and Nationalism, edited by V. Reynolds, V. Falger, and I. Vine. London: Croom Helm.

Just, W. 1970. *Military Men*. New York: Knopf.

Karsten, R. 1923. *Blood Revenge, War, and Victory Feasts among the Jibaro Indians of Eastern Ecuador*. Bulletin 79. Smithsonian Institution, Bureau of American Ethnology.

Keegan, J. 1987. *The Mask of Command*. London: Jonathan Cape.

Keegan, J., and A. Wheatcroft. 1986. *Zones of Conflict: An Atlas of Future Wars*. New York: Simon and Schuster.

Keohane, R. O. 1984. *After Hegemony: Cooperation and Discord in the World Political Economy*. Princeton: Princeton University Press.

Klare, M. T., and P. Kornbluh, eds. 1988. *Low-Intensity Warfare: Counterinsurgency, Proinsurgency, and Anti-Terrorism in the Eighties*. New York: Pantheon.

Kruuk, H. 1972. *The Spotted Hyena: A Study of Predation and Social Behavior*. Chicago: University of Chicago Press.

Le Boeuf, B., and J. Reiter. 1988. "Lifetime Reproductive Success in Northern Elephant Seals." In *Reproductive Success: Studies of Individual Variation in Contrasting Breeding Systems*, edited by T. H. Clutton-Brock, 344–83. Chicago: University of Chicago Press.

Lee, R. B. 1979. *The !Kung San*. London: Cambridge University Press.

Lorenz, K. 1966. *On Aggression*. New York: Harcourt Brace Jovanovich.

Low, B. S. 1989a. "Cross-Cultural Patterns in the Training of Children: An Evolutionary Perspective." *Journal of Comparative Psychology* 103: 311–19.

———. 1989b. "Occupational Status and Reproductive Behavior in 19th Century Sweden: Locknevi Parish." *Social Biology* 36: 82–101.

———. 1990a. "Sex, Power, and Resources: Ecological and Social Correlates of Sex Differences." *Journal of Contemporary Sociology* 27: 45–71.

———. 1990b. "Land Ownership, Occupational Status, and Reproductive Behavior in 19th Century Sweden: Tuna Parish." *American Anthropologist* 92 (2): 457–68.

———. 1991. "Reproductive Life in Nineteenth Century Sweden: An Evolutionary Perspective on Demographic Phenomena." *Ethology and Sociobiology* 12: 411–48.

———. 1992. "Sex, Coalitions, and Politics in Preindustrial Societies." *Politics and the Life Sciences* 11 (1): 63–80.

Low, B. S., and A. L. Clarke. 1991. "Occupational Status, Land Ownership, Migration, and Family Patterns in 19th Century Sweden." *Journal of Family History* 16 (2): 117–38.

———. 1992. "Resources and the Life Course: Patterns in the Demographic Transition." *Ethology and Sociobiology* 13: 463–94.

MacArthur, R. H., and E. O. Wilson. 1967. *The Theory of Island Biogeography*. Princeton: Princeton University Press.

Maechling, Jr., C. 1988. "Counterinsurgency: The First Ordeal by Fire." In *Low Intensity Warfare: Counterinsurgency, Proinsurgency, and Anti-Terrorism in the Eighties*, edited by M. T. Klare and P. Kornbluh, 21–48. New York: Pantheon.

Manson, J., and R. Wrangham. 1991. "Intergroup Aggression in Chimpanzees and Humans." *Current Anthropology* 32: 369–90.

Maynard Smith, J. 1974. "The Theory of Games and the Evolution of Animal Conflict." *Journal of Theoretical Biology* 47: 209–21.

Maynard Smith, J., and G. A. Parker. 1976. "The Logic of Asymmetrical Contests." *Animal Behavior* 24: 159–75.

Maynard Smith, J., and G. R. Price. 1973. "The Logic of Animal Conflicts." *Nature* 246: 15–18.

McInnis, R. M. 1977. "Childbearing and Land Availability: Some Evidence from Individual Household Data." In *Population Patterns in the Past*, edited by R. Lee, 201–27. New York: Academic Press.

McNeill, W. H. 1963. *The Rise of the West: A History of the Human Community.* Chicago: University of Chicago Press.

———. 1982. *The Pursuit of Power: Technology, Armed Force, and Society since A.D. 1000.* Chicago: University of Chicago Press.

Mech, D. 1977. "Productivity, Mortality, and Population Trends of Wolves in Northeastern Minnesota." *Journal of Mammalogy* 58: 559–74.

Miller, E. 1975. "War, Taxation, and the English Economy in the Late 13th and Early 14th Centuries." In *War and Economics in Development*, edited by J. M. Winter. Cambridge: Cambridge University Press.

Mitterauer, M., and R. Sieder. 1982. *The European Family.* Oxford: Blackwell.

Moore, J. H. 1990. "The Reproductive Success of Cheyenne War Chiefs: A Counter Example to Chagnon." *Current Anthropology* 31: 169–73.

Mueller, U. 1991. "Social and Reproductive Success. Theoretical Considerations and a Case Study of the West Point Class of 1950." *ZUMA: Zentrum für Umfragen, Methoden und Analysen.*

Murdock, G. P. 1967. *Ethnographic Atlas.* Pittsburgh: University of Pittsburgh Press.

Newark, T. 1979. *Medieval Warfare.* London: Bloomsbury Books.

Nishida, T. 1979. "The Social Structure of Chimpanzees of the Mahale Mountains." In *The Great Apes*, edited by D. A. Hamburg and E. R. McCown, 73–122. Menlo Park, CA: Benjamin Cummings.

Nishida, T., M. Hiraiwa-Hasegawa, and Y. Takahata. 1985. "Group Extinction and Female Transfer in Wild Chimpanzees in the Mahale Mountains." *Zeitschrift Tierpsychologie* 67: 284–301.

Otterbein, K. F. 1970. *The Evolution of War: A Cross-Cultural Study.* Cambridge: HRAF Press.

Oye, K. A. 1986. *Cooperation under Anarchy.* Princeton: Princeton University Press.

Packer, C. 1986. "The Ecology of Sociality in Felids." In *Ecological Aspects of Social Evolution*, edited by D. I. Rubenstein and R. W. Wrangham, 429–51. Princeton: Princeton University Press.

Parker, G. A. 1974. "Assessment Strategy and the Evolution of Fighting Behaviour." *Journal of Theoretical Biology* 47: 223–43.

———. 1984. "Evolutionarily Stable Strategies." In *Behavioral Ecology*, edited by J. R. Krebs and N. B. Davies, 30–61. Oxford: Blackwell Scientific.

Pérusse, D. 1991. "Cultural and Reproductive Success in Industrial Societies: Testing the Relationship at Proximate and Ultimate Levels." Paper presented at the 1991 International Human Behavior and Evolution Meetings, Hamilton, Ontario, August 22–25.

Pfister, U. 1989a. "Proto-Industrialization and Demographic Change: The Canton of Zurich Revisited." *Journal of Economic History* 18: 629–62.

———. 1989b. "Work Roles and Family Structure in Proto-Industrial Zurich." *Journal of Interdisciplinary History* 20: 83–105.

Pusey, A. E., and C. Packer. 1987. "Dispersal and Philopatry." In *Primate Societies*, edited by B. B. Smuts, D. L. Cheney, R. M. Seyfarth, R. W. Wrangham, and T. T. Struhsaker, 250–66. Chicago: University of Chicago Press.

Rank, M. A. 1989. "Fertility among Women on Welfare: Incidence and Determinants." *American Sociological Review* 54: 296–304.

Richardson, L. 1960. *Statistics of Deadly Quarrels.* Pittsburgh: Boxwood Press.

Ritchie, M. 1990. "Optimal Foraging and Fitness in Columbian Ground Squirrels." *Oecologia* 82: 56–67.

Ross, M. H. 1983. "Political Decision Making and Conflict: Additional Cross-Cultural Codes and Scales." *Ethnology* 22: 169–92.

Schein, E. 1957. "Distinguishing Characteristics of Collaborators and Resisters among American POWs." *Journal of Abnormal and Social Psychology* 55: 197–201.

Schultz, T. P. 1982. "Family Composition and Income Inequality." Paper #25. Yale University, Economic Growth Center.

———. 1985. "Changing World Prices, Women's Wages, and the Fertility Transition: Sweden, 1860–1910." *Journal of Political Economy* 93 (6): 1126–54.

Sharpe, P. 1990. "The Total Reconstitution Method: A Tool for Class-Specific Study?" *Local Population Studies* 44: 41–51.

Shaw, R. P. 1985. "Humanity's Propensity for Warfare: A Sociobiological Perspective." *Anthropology* 22: 159–83.

Shaw, R. P., and Y. Wong. 1989. *The Genetic Seeds of Warfare: Evolution, Nationalism, and Patriotism.* Boston: Unwin Hyman.

Silk, J. B., and R. Boyd. 1983. "Cooperation, Competition, and Mate Choice in Matrilineal Macaque Groups." In *Social Behavior of Female Vertebrates*, edited by S. Wasser. New York: Academic Press.

Singer, J. D. 1980. "Accounting for International War." *Annual Review of Sociology*, 349–76.

———. 1989. "The Political Origins of International War." In *Aggression and War: Their Biological and Social Bases*, edited by J. Groebel and R. A. Hinde, 202–20. Cambridge: Cambridge University Press.

Stiller, L. F. 1973. *The Rise of the House of Gorkha: A Study in the Unification of Nepal 1768–1816.* New Delhi: Manjusri Publishing House.

Stoessinger, J. G. 1982. *Why Nations Go to War.* New York: St. Martin's Press.

Strate, J. 1982. "Warfare and Political Evolution: A Cross-Cultural Test." Ph.D. dissertation, University of Michigan.

Swanton, J. R. 1911. *Indian Tribes of the Lower Mississippi Valley.* #43. Bureau of American Ethnology. Washington, D.C.

Symons, J. 1974. *The Effects of Income on Fertility.* Monograph #19. Chapel Hill, NC: Carolina Population Center.

Thompson, J., and M. Britton. 1980. "Some Socioeconomic Differentials in Fertility in England and Wales." In *Demographic Patterns in Developed Societies*, edited by R. W. Hiorus, 1–10. London: Taylor and Franci.

Tooby, J., and L. Cosmides. 1988. "The Evolution of War and Its Cognitive Foundations." Technical Report 88-1. Institute for Evolutionary Studies.

Trivers, R. L. 1985. *Social Evolution*. Menlo Park, CA: Benjamin Cummings.

Turke, P. W. 1989. "Evolution and the Demand for Children." *Population and Development Review* 15 (1): 61–90.

Turke, P.W., and L. Betzig. 1985. "Those Who Can Do: Wealth, Status, and Reproductive Success on Ifaluk." *Ethology and Sociobiology* 6: 79–87.

Vale, M. 1981. *War and Chivalry: Warfare and Aristocratic Culture in England, France, and Burgundy at the End of the Middle Ages*. Athens: University of Georgia Press.

Vayda, A. P. 1960. *Maori Warfare*. Polynesian Society, Maori Monographs No. 2.

Vining, D. R. 1986. "Social Versus Reproductive Success: The Central Theoretical Problem of Human Sociobiology." *Behavioral and Brain Sciences* 9: 167–87.

Voland, E. 1990. "Differential Reproductive Success within the Krummhörn Population (Germany, 18th and 19th Centuries)." *Behavioral Ecology and Sociobiology* 26: 65–72.

de Waal, F. 1982. *Chimpanzee Politics*. London: Jonathan Cape.

———. 1989. *Peacemaking among Primates*. Cambridge: Harvard University Press.

Wall, R. 1984. "Real Property, Marriage, and Children: The Evidence from Four Preindustrial Communities." In *Land, Kinship, and the Life-Cycle*, edited by R. M. Smith, 443–79. Cambridge: Cambridge University Press.

Wasser, S. 1983. "Reproductive Competition and Cooperation among Female Yellow Baboons." In *Social Behavior of Female Vertebrates*, edited by S. Wasser. New York: Academic Press.

Watson, P. 1978. *War on the Mind*. New York: Basic Books.

Webster, D. 1975. "Warfare and the Evolution of the State: A Reconsideration." *American Antiquity* 40 (4): 464–70.

White, D. R. 1988. "Rethinking Polygyny: Co-Wives, Codes and Cultural Systems." *Current Anthropology* 29 (4): 529–58.

Wilkinson, P. 1986. "Terrorism: International Dimensions." In *Contemporary Terrorism*, edited by W. Gutteridge, 29–56. New York: Facts on File Publications.

Williams, G. C. 1966. *Adaptation and Natural Selection*. Princeton: Princeton University Press.

Winter, J. M. 1989. "Causes of War." In *Aggression and War: Their Biological and Social Bases*, edited by J. Groebel and R. A. Hinde, 194–201. Cambridge: Cambridge University Press.

Wright, H. T. 1977. "Recent Research on the Origin of the State." *Annual Review of Anthropology* 6: 379–97.

Wrigley, E. A. 1983a. "The Growth of Population in Eighteenth-Century England: A Conundrum Resolved." *Past and Present* 98: 121–50.

———. 1983b. "Malthus's Model of a Pre-industrial Economy." In *Malthus Past and Present*, edited by J. Dupâquier, A. Fauve-Chamoux, and E. Grebenik, 111–24. New York: Academic Press.

Wrong, D. 1980. *Class Fertility Trends in Western Nations*. New York: Arno Press.

———. 1985. "Trends in Class Fertility in Western Nations." *Canadian Journal of Economics and Political Science* 24: 216–19.

Some Economics of International Relations

John G. Cross

An image of two nations engaged in pure conflict has never provided a good case for economic modeling because the economist's conception of social processes incorporates the creation of value into the same model as its distribution, so that the outright conflict that is inherent in zero-sum views of social interaction never has seemed entirely appropriate.[1] It is perhaps for this reason that the Prisoners' Dilemma, with its emphasis on aggregate value, had such a powerful influence in disciplines that do focus on zero-sum conflict, while economists were more likely to see it as a neat pedagogical description of models and theories that had been in existence for years.

The limitation in economic modeling arises in a different area—that of the definition and specification of value itself. A political scientist might see conflict arising from the values and objectives of individuals and nations, and investigate changes in those values and objectives as means for avoiding conflict. An economist is more likely to take values and objectives to be parameters of the problem, and attribute conflict to structural features of the environment; in that view, changes in international relations come about because of properties of that structure rather than because of changes in attitudes or values.

This chapter provides examples of the reasoning from which these conclusions are drawn. It begins with a simple model of conflict, then describes one set of problems inherent in the structure of international relations (those associated with risk and uncertainty), and, finally, introduces an adaptive view of interactive processes that is a little broader than what is usually found in the economics literature.

Two-Person Interdependence

Conflicts are indexed by variables that are defined by circumstances. Examples are levels of military expenditures in arms races, tariff barriers in the

---

1. Zero-sum descriptions of interpersonal relations arise in economics only in the relatively narrow context of multiple equilibria in which alternative solutions have implications for the distribution of value across participants.

cases of trade wars, and levels of diplomatic conflict. It is important to distinguish the objects of choice (the arms or the tariffs) from the costs of their use, because the variables and their costs enter into economic models in different ways. For example, X_1 might be used to describe the armament level of one country, and X_2 the armament level of another, but cost functions $C_1(X_1)$ and $C_2(X_2)$ reflect the total burdens imposed on the two countries by their expenditures on these arms.

It is the cost variables that are distinctive to the economic model. The X variables are related to the conflict itself—they may even be entirely offsetting, in the sense that who "wins" a conflict depends on the difference $X_1 - X_2$ rather than on the absolute magnitude of either one. The costs, of course, do not offset one another, but are cumulative, and represent a loss to both sides.

Simple models treat the parties as having consistent preferences over possible outcomes. These preferences are represented by means of "utility" functions ϕ and ψ with the following properties:

$$U_1 = \phi(X_1, X_2, C_1)$$

$$U_2 = \psi(X_1, X_2, C_2)$$

$$\phi_1 > 0, \qquad \phi_2 < 0, \qquad \phi_c < 0$$

$$\psi_1 < 0, \qquad \psi_2 > 0, \qquad \psi_c < 0 \tag{1}$$

That is, U_1, for example, increases with X_1, and decreases with increases in cost and X_2.

Because C_1 is really a function of X_1, and C_2 is really a function of X_2, the utilities could be made functions of X_1 and X_2 alone, but it is helpful to retain the functions in their existing form in order to keep a clear distinction between the conflict component and the cost component.

The X variables reflect pure conflict. In the most elementary formulations, they may be completely offsetting—in utilities as well as in outcomes. That is, the utilities of the outcomes are proportional to the outcomes themselves as represented by the difference $X_1 - X_2$. In such a case, the functions also satisfy the condition:

$$\psi_1 = -\phi_1, \qquad \psi_2 = -\phi_2 \tag{2}$$

This description presumes that the utility functions have been adjusted so as to make the zero-sum aspect of the conflict transparent, and it is this presumption that makes possible the condition in (2).

It is useful to construct indifference curves—combinations of X_1 and X_2

that will leave the utility levels of the parties unaffected. In the case of the first party, for example, the slope of the indifference curve is obtained by differentiating ϕ with respect to X_1 and X_2 such that U_1 is constant:

$$\frac{dX_2}{dX_1} = -\frac{\phi_1 + \phi_c C_1'}{\phi_2} \tag{3}$$

where C_1' is the slope of the cost function $C_1(X_1)$, and naturally $C_1' > 0$.

Suppose, for example, that the conflict variables referred to levels of military armament. At small levels of X_1, $\phi_c C_1'$ is small in magnitude because the resource costs of increases to X_1 will be small. Moreover, at small levels of X_2, ϕ_1 will be large because it is easy to overcome small resistance. Given the sign of ϕ_2, therefore, the slope dX_2/dX_1 will be positive at small values of X_1, X_2.

At high levels of X_1, X_2, these conditions would be reversed. As X_2 grows large, it becomes increasingly difficult to achieve parity, not to say a margin of superiority, and so ϕ_1 tends to become small. As X_1 grows large, the economic costs of the arms become much heavier, the parties become increasingly unwilling to bear additional costs, and therefore the product $\phi_c C_1'$ becomes large. Because this term has a negative sign, the slope defined by (3) is eventually reversed in sign so that $dX_2/dX_1 < 0$. Indeed, it is quite possible that for very large levels of X_2, this slope is negative throughout: Small levels of expenditure on X_1 would be ineffective (and thus useless), while levels that would be adequate to challenge the opponent would incur unbearably high costs. This is just a formal way of saying that it would be pointless for a very small country to arm itself for the sole purpose of challenging a great power. Its citizens would be much better off eschewing arms altogether and spending their resources on other things.

This specification of the nature of the indifference curves guarantees that, corresponding to any value of X_2, there exists some optimal value of X_1 for the first party. Formally, this is the value of X_1 that maximizes U_1 given X_2. This value is obtained by solving the first-order conditions for a maximum of U_1, or simply by choosing the value of X_1 that makes $dX_2/dX_1 = 0$:

$$\phi_1 + \phi_c C_1' = 0 \tag{4}$$

A similar and symmetric analysis is developed from the perspective of the other party.

It is at this point in the analysis that economic models sometimes diverge from one another. The most common model adheres to a "Nash Equilibrium" (or "Cournot") concept, under which each party seeks to satisfy an equation of the form of (4). That is, each attempts to maximize its own level of well-being, given the expenditure on X chosen by its opponent.[2] Alternative approaches produce different sets of implications regarding the nature of the interaction. Because of the introduction of the cost functions, however, none of them would envisage any sort of unlimited conflict—"arms races" that continue indefinitely, or unlimited trade wars.

Bargaining

The analysis does not end with the specification of the "solution" defined by equations of the form of (4). The presence of the cost functions provides the two parties with an incentive to engage in cooperative efforts to reduce the elements of conflict in their relationship—that is, to reduce the values of the variables X.

Suppose that, beginning at the static "solution" (described by equation 4), the two parties consider simultaneous downward shifts in X_1 and X_2. Call S the value of the proposed $\frac{\Delta X_2}{\Delta X_1}$. The first party will be made better off by this reduction whenever S is greater than the slope of its indifference curve at the current values of X, that is, whenever:

$$S > \frac{\phi_1 + \phi_c C_1'}{-\phi_2},$$

and the second party will be made better-off by this reduction whenever S is smaller than the slope of its indifference curve at the current values of X:

$$S < \frac{-\psi_1}{\psi_2 + \psi_c C_2'}.$$

It follows that whatever the current level of conflict may be, there is a possibility for negotiated reduction whenever there exists some slope S that meets both of these conditions simultaneously, and such a slope exists whenever:

$$\frac{\phi_1 + \phi_c C_1'}{-\phi_2} < \frac{-\psi_1}{\psi_2 + \psi_c C_2'} \tag{5}$$

The sign conditions in (1) guarantee that this condition is satisfied for *any* positive values of X_1 and X_2. (Replacing $-\psi_1$ with ϕ_1 and ψ_2 with $-\phi_2$, the

---

2. Many other interpretations are possible. For example, a "Stackleberg" approach would postulate that one party seeks to maximize its self-interest subject to the *reaction curve* of the other. Even more sophisticated models would have each party manipulating its own reaction curve so as to modify the behavior of the other.

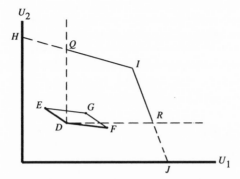

Fig. 1. Available utilities for the two parties

sign conditions make the numerator on the left of (5) smaller than the numerator on the right, while the denominator on the right of (5) is smaller than the denominator on the left.) Thus, it makes no difference what theory is used to describe the countries' choices of X, because apart from points on the axes, no matter where they start, there exist reductions in X_1 and X_2 that are beneficial to both sides. Indeed, there is no point in stopping these reductions until $X_1 = 0$, $X_2 = 0$, or both.

This argument is traditionally described with a diagram such as that given in figure 1. The point D in figure 1 describes the two parties' utility levels at the "individually rational" equilibrium point, i.e., both parties are solving conditions such as equation (4). A unilateral reduction in X_1 is represented as a movement to some point such as E: the situation of the second party is improved at the expense of the first. The slope of the ray $\overline{DE}$ is equal to:

$$\frac{\psi_1}{\phi_1 + \phi_c C_1'}.$$

Similarly, a unilateral reduction by the second party is represented as a movement to some point such as F, along a ray with slope:

$$\frac{\psi_2 + \psi_c C_2'}{\phi_2}.$$

It is clear from the geometry of the figure that a unilateral reduction in the value of X_1 would be detrimental to the individual welfare of the first party, while a unilateral reduction in the value of X_2 would operate to the disadvantage of the second. Nevertheless, if these reductions could be combined into a *joint* reduction (such as a movement to point G), it would be possible to achieve an outcome both sides would prefer to D. The condition for this to be possible is that the slope $\overline{DE}$ must be steeper than the slope $\overline{DF}$, and it is easy to show that this reduces to satisfaction of condition (5).

A series of reductions such as $\overline{DG}$ would eventually lead to the outer frontier corresponding to disarmament. The point H in figure 1 corresponds to an "optimal" level of X_2 if $X_1 = 0$, the point I corresponds to the point $X_1 = 0$, $X_2 = 0$, and the point J corresponds to an "optimal" level of X_1 when $X_2 = 0$. The actual outcome of the mutual reductions must lie on the frontier between points Q and R. Points outside of this range would be inferior to D from the point of view of one side or the other, and voluntary reductions would not lead to such outcomes.

The formulation of a conventional negotiation problem is straightforward. Two parties recognize the potential for mutual gain, such as a movement to a point on the frontier $Q - I - R$, but they must agree on its division (the specific point on the frontier) before the gain can be realized. There are a number of alternative models that describe bargaining processes and bargaining outcomes, but there is no need to go into them in detail here. They all share a presumption that negotiations are eventually settled, however complex and time-consuming the bargaining may be, because even though there may be disagreements among the parties as to how the fruits of cooperation are to be distributed, it is pointless to forego those fruits indefinitely by engaging in endless bargaining. There are settlement points that are better than the status quo, and it is this fact that ultimately drives negotiations to agreement, no matter how far apart the parties may be initially.

The logic of this conclusion is compelling, and although the model just described is defined in relatively technical terms, the conclusion does not depend on any particular behavioral model or institutional structure. It is a simple consequence of the fact that there are costs linked to stratagems associated with conflict. One is faced, nevertheless, with the irrefutable fact that international negotiations have often proved to be almost impossible to bring to successful conclusions. It is easy to demonstrate the existence of substantial potential mutual gains from a realignment of tariff and trade barriers, from steps toward international arms reduction and control, and even from petroleum price maintenance (from the point of view of members of the cartel); all the same, effective negotiations over these issues have proven to be extraordinarily difficult to conclude successfully. The well-publicized recent disintegration of US-USSR modes of conflict demonstrate how easy the elimination of conflict ought to be, but that demonstration seems to be lost on the participants in current tariff negotiations, or on the participants in the conflicts of the Middle East.

There are a number of possible explanations for this difficulty, and several of these stress the distinction between international negotiations and the smaller-scale bargains that individuals strike every day. The most prominent among these are:

1. The possibility that there exists no simple "preference" ordering that can guide international negotiators in choosing among alternatives. There is no analytically satisfactory way to describe "utility" functions for groups, and collective decisions are not necessarily even transitive. If preference functions cannot be defined, then "optimization" cannot be defined either, and we are left with no general theory of organizational behavior. The ambiguity inherent in group decision processes means that stated objectives of political, international, and social organizations are usually stated in loose or ambiguous terms. As a result, there is no unique objective that can be used to align all members to identical purposes. Thus, the application of traditional optimization theory seems to be impossible from the very start.

2. The fact that international negotiations are conducted by agents rather than their principals, so that the "wrong" preferences may be represented at the bargaining table. Most large organizations, and even many individuals, do not carry out negotiations directly, but employ agents to do it for them. This brings up the question as to how much the selection of a specific individual to represent one at the table might influence the outcome. There is a particular danger that if one must use bargaining agents whose specialized knowledge enables them to deal with the enormously complex issues that arise in international negotiations, then one must at the same time introduce bargaining agents whose personal preferences may be inconsistent with the outcome goals of the wider society. Arms-control negotiations may be dominated by people with associations with the military or the arms industries and who may personally profit from arms expenditures. Trade negotiations may be dominated by individuals from industries that are most directly affected. The negotiating agents may well settle at some agreement point that is mutually beneficial from their own private perspective, but the resulting trade agreements will permit higher tariffs than are appropriate, and the arms "settlements" will permit unduly high levels of armament.

3. The absence of any superordinate authority that is in a position to enforce contracts, in effect making it impossible to establish long-term commitments or commitments that will be honored even when circumstances make those commitments no longer consistent with the interests of one of the parties. From a selfish viewpoint, it is not always desirable to keep one's promises; on the other hand, long-term agreements are only possible if one's word is good. If borrowers could, with no adverse consequences, default on their loans, then they would have great difficulty borrowing money, because lenders would, with reason, be suspicious of the likelihood that the money would ever be repaid. For this reason, economists attach great importance to the

enforceability of contracts as mechanisms for guaranteeing that actions will be taken in the face of an opposing self-interest. The single most important distinction between negotiations that are carried out between nations and those between individuals or groups within nations is the absence of any fully satisfactory means for enforcing international contracts. What this means is that the scope of possible international agreements is sharply reduced because it must assure *continuing* mutual benefits. An international agreement that must be sustained without any contract requires that both parties benefit under every conceivable circumstance, not just under the aggregation (or expectation) of circumstances. Only a tiny fraction of the domestic agreements that are struck routinely would meet this condition.

4. The presence of substantial uncertainty in the specification of the situation, imposing on the negotiators extreme caution and unwillingness to face risk. This aspect of the problem is the focus of the next section.

Risk

In one sense, the introduction of cooperative agreements has the effect of reducing risk. An obvious example is the fact that a mutual reduction in military forces might also reduce the risk of unintended conflict. Negotiated settlements may also introduce an atmosphere of cooperation under which events that at one time might have led to outbreaks of conflict can now be settled peacefully.

In another sense, however, the establishment of cooperative agreements may actually increase risk. This is the case partly because it makes each party more dependent on the actions (or political whims) of the other. In a Prisoners' Dilemma, the only way for one party to signal a willingness to cooperate is to choose a strategy that exposes him or her to increased losses if the opponent does not respond. Empirical studies of Prisoners' Dilemma behavior have uncovered a number of personal traits that are associated with the ability of experimental subjects to break out of noncooperative situations, and many of these are associated with willingness to face risks: it is joint risk takers that are most likely to achieve stable cooperative play quickly.

There are quite a number of aspects of international relations that can contribute to an increase in risk in negotiated agreements. Among these are the following:

1. It is hard to guarantee that promises will be kept. The absence of an effective means for enforcing contracts takes on added significance in an environment of risk. The existence of contracts makes it pos-

sible for domestic negotiations to lead to stable and enforceable agreements—in the international arena, the only inhibition to unilateral defection is the existence of other parallel agreements whose existence would be jeopardized by the threat of retaliation.

2. There is a great risk of failure in political decision making. The political dimension of national leadership inevitably interferes with effective and coordinated management of policy. If a government feels little obligation to honor the obligations of its predecessors or has no power to obligate its political successors, then its agreements can last no longer than it does itself, subjecting any agreement to the same political risk that is attached to the leadership of the nation.

3. Domestic commercial negotiations rarely move into uncharted territory. When labor and management agree on a new contract, they are in fact settling on a state that is not very different from the status quo. If there is uncertainty concerning future market or working conditions, the parties can negotiate relatively short contracts, so that their continuing relationship can be made responsive to changes in circumstances. The environments in which international agreements must be struck are neither so stable nor so well understood. International negotiations usually involve enormously complex military or economic relationships that are barely understood at current levels, much less under some newly negotiated circumstances. They invariably involve forecasts by experts, many of whom disagree, and who frequently are proven wrong by experience.

Cooperation itself may be associated with risk if an agreement takes the two parties into new and unexplored circumstances—in which it is much harder to define "equitable," "balanced," or "stable" outcomes. The circumstances under which international negotiations take place are always subject to a considerable amount of uncertainty. Rapid changes in military technology can introduce military imbalances into a settlement that appeared to have equal effects only a few years earlier. Changes in economic conditions may prove to give one country a marked trade advantage over another despite a carefully reasoned and developed trade bargain.

In principle, if cooperation is accompanied by increases in risk, the benefits from cooperation still remain. Formally, it is not difficult to adapt the model already described to treat this more general situation. Suppose that one were to identify a series of possible political and technological "states" of the world, and suppose further that one could attach probabilities to each of these states so that state i can occur with a probability p_i. The "utility" functions of the two countries then depend on the state that is realized, so that we have to write them in the form:

$$U_1 = \Phi_i(X_1, X_2, C_1)$$

$$U_2 = \Psi_i(X_1, X_2, C_2).$$

(6)

Using the p_i's, one can determine expected utilities:

$$E[U_1] = \sum_{i=1}^{n} \Phi_i(X_1, X_2, C_1) p_i$$

(7)

$$E[U_2] = \sum_{i=1}^{n} \Psi_i(X_1, X_2, C_2) p_i.$$

So long as the probabilities remain fixed, these expected utility functions depend only on X_1, X_2, and the costs, and they may therefore take the place of the original functions $\phi(\cdot)$ and $\psi(\cdot)$. They will continue to meet the sign conditions in (1), and, from this point on, the argument is parallel to that described in figure 1, including the conclusion that if the two parties continue to make independent decisions, they will invest in significant but stable levels of X_1 and X_2, and that the resulting costs will be high enough to make mutual reductions beneficial. So long as the two parties accept the same values for the probabilities (that is, both parties see the likelihood of event i as equal to a given p_i), then the conclusion that the optimal frontier entails a value of $X_1 = 0$, $X_2 = 0$, or both still applies.

The situation is quite different if the increase in cooperation leads at the same time to an increase in risk. An example of the possibility is given in figure 2. Suppose that outcomes are valued in proportion to the difference $X_1 - X_2$ as before, and use the variable Y to represent that difference from the point of view of the first party. Increases in Y then lead to increases in utility for that party. If some cooperative agreement comes about that decreases cost from C_0 to C', then utility is higher for every possible value of Y. Suppose, however, that the situation is characterized by uncertainty, and that, in the original state, the range of possible outcomes runs from a low of Y_1 to a high of Y_2, with an expectation of $\overline{Y}$. The negotiated agreement may expand the range of outcomes to Y_1' to Y_2' and still be entirely neutral in the sense that it leaves $\overline{Y}$ unchanged. The expected utility of the agreement, however, is U' rather than U_0, and this represents a *reduction* in payoff value. Thus, it is possible for an agreement to be neutral in its effect on expected outcomes, and beneficial in the sense that it reduces costs, but still represent a value loss to both parties.

Figure 2 describes how an agreement that maintains a "balance" between

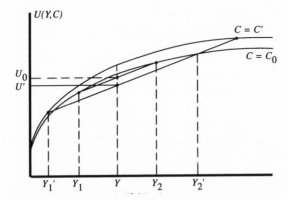

Fig. 2. Consequences of a change in costs and risk

two parties and that reduces cost can nevertheless reduce the perceived welfare of a negotiating party. This loss is attributable to risk aversion—the fact that gains and losses are not symmetric in value. The prospect of coming out the victor in a military confrontation may be appealing, but that gain pales in the face of the fear of coming out the loser. Thus symmetric outcomes are given asymmetric values. In principle, this sort of risk is *insurable*. Ordinary commercial insurance markets arise whenever there are conditions that produce random asymmetric payoffs among similar risk-averse individuals. The same needs can arise internationally: Each country would happily sacrifice the potential gain from some unexpected advantage if in return it could receive a guarantee that it would never suffer loss from some unexpected disadvantage. Ideally, the two countries could come to some negotiated agreement never to use unexpected advantages, but how would they enforce such an agreement? The lack of some superordinate authority that can enforce international contracts means that the only durable agreements must be those that yield continuing benefits to both parties; no country can irrevocably commit itself to transactions whose benefits are asymmetric over time or that are subject to the sort of risk inherent in military competition.

Cooperative Behavior

Negotiations in practice are linked, even though the simple models characteristic of economics treat each negotiation as though it were a freestanding event. "Linkages" among international negotiations are a constant source of speculation in journalistic circles, however much they may be denied in formal diplomatic statements.

Even when explicit links are hard to find, there is clear parallelism in international behavior. A "climate" becomes more friendly, for example, and multiple agreements begin to develop in economic and political areas in which no progress had been made for years before. This is not an easy phenomenon to address with formal models, but it is worth considering the possibility that cooperative negotiation is as much a behavioral phenomenon as it is a formal one, and that behaviors that arise in one context are easily transferred to another, even though the logical structures of the two situations are unrelated.

Economists are increasingly interested in convergent models of adaptive behavior. The idea is that, although choices are conditioned by the outcomes that they govern, the mechanism is less one of direct logical calculus than one of experience. One does not make a choice because it will bring some desired outcome about, one makes it because it has seemed to work in the past. Under simple static circumstances, it is often easy to show that such adaptive models converge on outcomes that are similar to those predicted by traditional optimization paradigms.

An important consequence of this new view is that it implies that behaviors are generalized from one set of circumstances to another. A strategy that has worked once may be used again, even though, by any objective measure, the second situation may be quite different from the first. In this sense, international negotiations are closely linked—not because the economic, military, or social problems that they address have direct interdependence, but because the negotiating styles that are found to be successful in one tend to be generalized to the others. In this sense, it is possible for cooperation to "break out" across a whole range of disparate issues.

This is a broader view than one that limits behavioral learning over the course of a single negotiation. During the play of a repeated Prisoners' Dilemma game, for example, one might learn to be cooperative or not, or one might discover strategies that induce an opponent to behave in a more cooperative fashion. In this sort of case, the adaptation occurs within the framework of one game. On the other hand, one might enter a negotiation with an established plan of action (a "strategy"), adhere to that plan throughout the course of the game, and then evaluate and revise the plan for future use in the light of the overall experience. Both of these forms of adjustment could be called "learning" or "adaptation," and it is easy to blur the distinction between them, but they are clearly not the same thing, and they can have quite different implications for the definition of equilibrium states.

The broader interpretation proposes that behavioral adjustments take place *between* encounters rather than *during* them. Instead of adapting to circumstances over the course of a relationship, negotiators develop styles of behavior that are maintained throughout each encounter, and only after an interaction is completed is a style evaluated and perhaps modified (or eliminated). This property makes possible much more farsighted modes of behavior than simple learning would allow, and it is this new dimension that introduces the possibility of evolutionarily based altruism or cooperation that is found in modern sociobiological writing.

Most of the work in this area is framed in a context of perfect information. After the fact, each party to a interaction "knows" with certainty what choice was made by the other. It is easy to see, for example, that the "optimality" of the tit-for-tat strategy in a Prisoners' Dilemma game depends on this assumption—if one party makes an error in identifying which alternative the other chose, the tit-for-tat strategy can quickly lock two ostensibly "cooperative" parties into long phases of hostile behavior.

The issue is whether adaptation in this sense can lead to a climate of cooperation wherein "cooperative" strategies come to be used as a matter of course, even in situations in which individual rationality appears to be incompatible with fully cooperative behavior. Axelrod (1984) has discussed this problem at length in the case of the Prisoners' Dilemma. In the following section, a formal model is developed that applies to the question in general.

A Formal Model

Suppose that there is a large population of potential "negotiators." From time to time, these individuals encounter one another in two-person, non–zero sum game situations. These encounters may include "repeated" games. The population is large enough so that the likelihood of the same two individuals engaging in more than one game interaction is small. There may be a variety of different games, but the model here will be restricted to one set of indistinguishable ones. Games are allowed to be different in that they may have different payoffs, so long as they are not otherwise distinguishable by the players. Finally, the payoffs may be subject to random elements in the environment so that payoff information from a small number of plays may not be sufficient to indicate to one party either what strategy is being chosen by the other or even what game is being played. Of course, if these are repeated games, then the participants may make choices that are designed to extract interim payoff information that might reveal more about the nature of the situation.

Attention in this elementary model is confined to situations involving identical agents. Interactions between distinguishable participants—models of predators and prey, or cases in which dissimilar organisms mate in some way to produce a common benefit—might be developed along the same lines at the cost of somewhat more complex notation.

Each member of the population has available a finite set of alternative strategies $S_1,\ldots,S_n$, These may contain conditional elements (as does the tit-for-tat strategy). In principle, this list might include both "pure" and "mixed" strategies—the former being lists of actions and conditional actions, and the latter being lists of probabilities that are attached to the pure strategies so that a random device must be used to make an actual strategy choice. In practice, the structure of many situations may not readily admit to the use of mixed strategies, and so one should leave open the possibility that they are not allowed. If mixed strategies do exist, then (from Nash 1951) there exists at least one equilibrium strategy pair, S_1, S_2 for any pair of players 1, 2, and these have the property that neither party can benefit from unilateral deviation from the given strategy. There is no assurance that there is only one Nash equilibrium pair.[3] Because the individuals in the population are indistinguishable, they must have identical strategy options. It does not follow, of course, that an equilibrium strategy pair has the property that $S_1 = S_2$, but it does follow that if $S_1 \neq S_2$, where party 1 has chosen S_i and party 2 has chosen S_j, then there must exist a symmetric equilibrium strategy pair $\tilde{S}_1$, $\tilde{S}_2$ where $\tilde{S}_1 = S_j$ and $\tilde{S}_2 = S_i$.

Use a_{ij} to describe the (expected) payoff to strategy S_i when it encounters strategy S_j, and a square matrix A to contain all the payoff coefficients: $A = \{a_{ij}\}$. In general, a_{ij} is not equal to a_{ji} when i is not equal to j, because the payoff to S_i is not necessarily equal to the payoff to S_j when the two are played against one another. Most of the games that have attracted the attention of game theorists have this property for at least some strategy pairs.

Games in which $a_{ij} = a_{ji}$ for all i,j are symmetric in the sense that the matrix A is equal to its transpose A'. Games of this sort are generally not very interesting, because any strategy change that one player found to be to his or her own benefit would provide an equivalent benefit to the other player, and this would leave no competitive element in the game. Such games go beyond elementary maximization problems only to the extent that coordination is a problem for the parties. For example, suppose $a_{ij} = 5$ when i is not equal to j, and $a_{ij} = 10$ if $i = j$; in this case, the interests of the players are coincident, but the achievement of a maximal payoff is still not a trivial problem.

Use the fraction p_i to describe the proportion of the population using the strategy S_i, and use the (column) vector $P = [p_1,...,p_n]$ to describe the frequencies with which each of the n strategies are used.

Suppose a new individual were to enter the population. This new member must select a strategy from the set $S_1,...,S_n$, but this selection cannot be conditioned upon whom the player faces in any encounter because the players are indistinguishable. The expected return to the new entrant from the strategy S_i is then given by the ith element of the vector AP. The expected *contribution*

---

3. If the strategy sets are to include mixed strategies, and if there should happen to be an infinite number of equilibrium mixed-strategy pairs, then in order to implement the model in this paper, some finite subset of these would have to be chosen in order to keep the number of alternative strategies finite.

by this new member to others is given by the ith element of the vector $(P'A)'$, which by the rule of transposes is equal to $A'P$. It is possible that at the current value of P these two vectors are equal, so that the expected return to the new member is equal to the contribution made by that member to everyone else, but in general that is not true except in the symmetric case in which $A = A'$.

In a finite population, a new entrant would alter expected payoffs to everyone else by adding probability weight to whichever strategy she or he selected. By restricting attention to a very large population, the significance of this effect is eliminated. Under this assumption, AP is the vector of expected returns to each strategy type, and $A'P$ is the contribution made by each strategy type to everyone else. The product $P'AP$ is the mean expected payoff per individual, and V will be used to describe this value.

Equilibrium

Define an "evolutionary mechanism" to be an adjustment process with the property that strategies that receive greater-than-average expected payoff become more predominant in the population while those with less-than-average expected payoff tend to decrease in frequency. This mechanism may either be embodied in a process that increases the survival probabilities of individuals who use strategies that generate above-average payoffs, or reflect a learning process whereby some individuals discover the existence of strategies superior to those they have been using and switch to them. Whatever the form of its operation, such a mechanism will tend to alter the values of P whenever there exists at least one i with $(AP)_i > V$.

An equilibrium for an evolutionary mechanism (occasionally called an "evolutionary equilibrium"), is characterized by a vector P^* where:

$$p_i^*[(AP^*)_i - V^*] = 0 \qquad \text{for all} \quad i. \tag{8}$$

This condition generally assures that for all i with $(AP^*)_i < V^*$, the corresponding p_i^* must equal 0, while those alternatives with $p_i^* > 0$ all receive the same (maximal) payoff. It may be a bit surprising that equation (8) allows for an equilibrium with $(AP^*)_i > V^*$ for some i so long as $p_i^* = 0$. That is, there may be an equilibrium in which superior alternatives are not chosen. This property is characteristic of evolutionary (as well as psychological-learning) models. Experience-driven mechanisms can lead to increases in the selection likelihoods of only those alternatives that already have nonzero selection probabilities; if some choice is never taken, there is no way for simple adaptation to introduce it into a set of likely behaviors. General theories of evolution or learning always incorporate some form of mutation or spontaneous choice as means for introducing new alternatives outside of the elementary evolutionary process. An alternative device is to define an evolutionary mechanism that never permits elements of P to converge all the way to zero in finite time, and to start with an initial P vector that has all positive elements. This chapter is concerned primarily with the properties of equilibrium points, and so it is presumed that all elements of P are at least potentially positive.

It is easy to show that there exists at least one equilibrium of the form given by (8). Note, however, that at an equilibrium that satisfies (8), it does not follow that $p_i^*[(A'P^*)_i - V^*] = 0$: Although each strategy type will receive the same expected payoff, each strategy type does not necessarily *contribute* the same amount to the welfare of others.

The analogy between this equilibrium and a Nash equilibrium is very close. If one were to invent a symmetric, two-person, bimatrix game with the same payoff structure as that given by the matrix A, then any vector P would describe a mixed strategy and P^* would be a Nash equilibrium for that game. Insofar as the original games do not possess unique Nash equilibria, P^* will not be unique either.

The solution vector P^* can be given two alternative interpretations corresponding to two alternative descriptions of the relevant strategy options. If mixed strategies are included in the set $S_1,...,S_n$, then there must be at least one pair of strategies that already constitute a Nash equilibrium. It follows that P^*, as a weighted average of strategies and as a Nash equilibrium itself, could not do more than duplicate such an equilibrium. Attention can then legitimately be confined to P^* vectors that are on the vertices of the simplex—that is, vectors with one element equal to 1 and all the rest zero.

It is much more interesting to confine the set $S_1,...,S_n$ to pure strategies. In this case, no individual in the population uses random elements in its strategy of play, but different individuals do choose different strategies. The solution P^* then describes an equilibrium mix of *types* of individual, and if one were to take a random sample from this population, and tabulate their strategy choices, one would encounter strategy frequencies that correspond to a mixed-strategy Nash equilibrium. In effect, it is possible for mixed strategies to determine equilibria in social settings even though no individual ever uses one.

The expected payoff to any individual in the population is the same in either of these models. This is an important fact because there are many situations in which mixed strategies are not very practical. Traditional models of genetic evolution, for example, have focused largely on physical characteristics that are not easily randomized by one individual. Eye color, height, and physical strength are not natural candidates for inclusion in mixed strategies. Thus, these models are necessarily examples of the second type. *Behav-*

ioral characteristics may be more easily introduced into mixed strategies, but it is not clear that most individuals are sophisticated enough to use such devices, so that even here, the second model may be the right one to use.[4]

Optimality

Nash equilibria are not necessarily optimal (as the single-play Prisoners' Dilemma equilibrium is not), and thus P^* is not necessarily optimal either. If the distribution of strategy choices in the population is given by some vector P, then the mean payoff per player is $P'AP$. Define the "optimal" distribution P_m to be that vector of strategies that maximizes average payoff. That is, P_m satisfies the problem:

$$\max_{P} P' AP \qquad \text{subject to}$$

$$\sum_{k=1}^{n} p_k = 1 \qquad \text{and} \qquad P \geq 0. \tag{9}$$

In evolutionary models with stationary environments, it is easy to propose adaptation mechanisms that move systems toward equilibria that are also optima: perturbations away from optima generate forces that tend to drive the system back. The same is not true of interdependent evolutionary systems. This is not merely a consequence of the fact that equilibria such as P^* are not necessarily optima: the equilibria themselves may not be the foci of any convergent dynamic system. It is easy to propose plausible adjustment processes that systematically increase the likelihoods of those strategies with the highest payoffs, and reduce the likelihoods of those with low payoffs. Unfortunately, the identities of the best and worst strategies may change during the course of adjustment because of changes in the mix of strategies that one is playing against, so that the dynamic system may become cyclic and never converge at all.

In principle, an adaptive mechanism is a continuous process that produces a rate of change in P, designated as $\dot{P}$, and which satisfies the condition:

$$\dot{p}_i[(AP)_i - V] > 0 \qquad \text{for all} \quad i \quad \text{with} \quad p_i > 0 \tag{10}$$

Equation (10) is a general representation of what are called "replicator equations" in the biological literature. (See, for example, Sigmund 1986.) These

---

4. If individuals use only pure strategies, then the assumption that individuals are a priori indistinguishable is essential to equilibrium.

are usually written as adjustment equations in the form: $\dot{p}_i = p_i(F_i(P) - \Phi)$, where $F(P)$ is some simple (often linear) function. Such simplifications greatly increase the analytical tractability of models, and they also ensure that no element p_i ever converges all the way to zero during the course of adjustment (which could lead to an equilibrium in which some maximizing alternative never occurred). Even in these forms, it is possible that the adaptive process might not converge; this possibility is often avoided in biological applications of replicator equations by choosing specific functional forms that limit the range of dynamic behaviors that must be considered.

Even if there exist both a unique group optimum, and a unique equilibrium that is the focus of a global evolutionary process, it is not necessarily true that they are the same. Indeed, in spite of the uniqueness of P^* and P_m, these two points generally differ.

An Example

It turns out that the condition for adaptation toward a (mixed-strategy) equilibrium and the second-order conditions for a group maximum are the same, but aside from this, the two stationary points have little in common. Except for the special symmetric case, there is no guarantee that evolutionary mechanisms will lead toward efficient group outcomes.

This conclusion may be illustrated with a few numerical examples. Suppose that the individuals in the population engage in iterated, two-person Prisoners' Dilemma games. These games have the form as in Matrix 1:

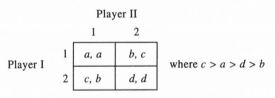

Matrix 1

Here 1 is the group-optimal ("cooperative") choice, and 2 is the dominant (uncooperative or "defecting") choice. The value-laden terms "cooperation" and "defection" have acquired an unfortunate currency in the literature, but as there is no denying their expressiveness in the construction of examples, they are used here. Suppose the game to be repeated exactly n times, and consider three strategies: Always Cooperate (C), Always Defect (D), and Tit-for-Tat (T). This (intentionally) restricts the problem to a rather artificial example in that it is easy to find strategies that would dominate Tit-for-Tat in this finite-play game, but this will make the mathematics much simpler. The elements in the matrix A are now as in Matrix 2:

Player II

		C	D	T
	C	*na*	*nb*	*na*
Player I	D	*nc*	*nd*	$c + (n - 1)d$
	T	*na*	$b + (n - 1)d$	*na*

Matrix 2

The strategy C never does better than T, and does worse everywhere except in an equilibrium involving either C or T. If, during the adjustment process, the strategy D ever carries positive weight, then the dynamic adjustment defined by (10) will always favor T relative to C. Therefore, C will not be found in the equilibrium of any system that does not begin in equilibrium. It does not greatly weaken the example, then, to consider only the two alternative strategies D and T. Now, the matrix becomes Matrix 3:

Player II

		D	T
	D	*nd*	$c + (n - 1)d$
Player I	T	$b + (n - 1)d$	*na*

Matrix 3

Call K the value of the determinant of 3×3 matrix defined by constructing a bordered hessian matrix from this matrix A. Expanding:

$$K = (c - d) - n(a - d) - (d - b) \tag{11}$$

The second-order condition for the optimality of P_m requires $K > 0$. If this condition is not satisfied, then in this simple 2×2 example, it is certain that all evolutionary equilibria are at boundaries, as is the global optimum. Call p the probability attached to T, so that $1 - p$ is the probability attached to D. Now, equilibrium in this model may be summarized as below, while the dynamic adjustment paths are shown in figure 3.

• If $K > 0$, then the first order conditions specify a global optimum at

$$p = \frac{K + n(a - d)}{2K}. \tag{12}$$

This point lies within the simplex (i.e., p is in the interval $(0,1)$) so long as $K - n(a - d) > 0$. The path followed by $P'AP$ is described by the arrows on curve I in the figure. Even though the group optimum occurs at an interior point, this outcome is not stable, and all evolutionary processes will go to the point $p = 0$.

- If $K > 0$ but $K - n(a - d) < 0$, the global optimum lies on the boundary of the simplex at $p = 1$ (That is, Tit-for-Tat is the optimal strategy pair). This outcome is not stable either, and all evolutionary processes will lead to the point $p = 0$, as described by curve II in the figure.

- If $K < 0$, then $p = 1$ is still the global optimum, but if $K + n(a - d) < 0$, then $p = 0$ is a local optimum as well. (That is, the stationary point in (12) would minimize the group payoff.) Curve III describes the case $K < 0$, $K + n(a - d) > 0$. Here, the only group optimum is at $p = 1$, and this point is also the stable outcome of an evolutionary process. However, it is not the only stable outcome point. If a fraction $\bar{p}$ of the population are using the Tit-for-Tat strategy, while the rest use D, then the system will converge toward $p = 1$ if $\bar{p} > -(d - b)/K$. Otherwise, it will converge toward $p = 0$. Thus, the larger is the value of K, the more "likely" it is that "cooperation" will evolve. In particular, if n is large (meaning that the game is repeated many times), then $\bar{p}$ may be quite small. (Conditions of this kind are discussed extensively by Axelrod 1984.) Note that $\bar{p}$ is always positive unless $n(a - d) < (c - d)$. If this should be the case, then the strategy D always dominates T, and $p = 0$ is the only possible equilibrium. Curve IV describes the case $K + n(a - d) < 0$. Here, both $p = 0$ and $p = 1$ are local group optima, although $p = 1$ is still the global optimum. These outcomes are both evolutionarily stable, and again, which of them comes about will depend on the initial value of $\bar{p}$.

- The boundary point $p = 0$ is stable whenever $d - b > 0$. Since this is always true, the strategy pair D,D is always a possible endpoint for the evolutionary process, regardless of the value of K.

- If $(c - d) - n(a - d) < 0$, then the boundary point $p = 1$ is stable. That is, Tit-for-Tat may be the outcome of an evolutionary process.

Summary and Conclusions

The patterns described in figure 3 are similar to those allowed by Axelrod (1984); nevertheless, within the framework of the model, the prospects for spontaneous cooperation are still not especially bright. Many parameter values still lead to noncooperative equilibrium behavior, and even those that are consistent with cooperative equilibria only converge to one if the initial

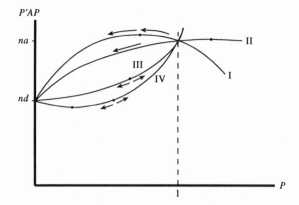

Fig. 3. Four cases of group optima and evolutionary trends

conditions are suitable. If the negotiators start in a noncooperative stance (as most empirical evidence suggests that they do), the prospects for an evolutionary cooperative equilibrium are bleak.

Indeed, given that noncooperation is always a stable equilibrium in this example, the phenomenon of cooperation has not been explained. The fact that subjects in Prisoners' Dilemma experiments usually succeed ultimately in establishing group-optimal behaviors suggests that human subjects are typically able to rise above the mechanical forces described by our simple models in order to reap mutually recognized benefits. They do so, in my view, by taking risks—by exposing themselves to significant losses in order to move the system ahead. The introduction of risk taking in a model of interdependent behavior is certainly possible, but it would introduce complexities substantially beyond the scope of this chapter.

On the other hand, the adaptive model does indicate that cooperative behavior is often compatible with a dynamically stable equilibrium. In cases III and IV in the example, cooperative modes of behavior are sustainable indefinitely. This is an important result because of the principle that behaviors may generalize from one setting to another. This is indeed a model of a "climate of cooperation" rather than an instance of one successful negotiation.

The original purpose of this chapter was to describe the approach taken by economic models in order to facilitate comparison with alternative approaches. To that end, the chapter began with an observation that economic models typically take preferences and values as fixed parameters, focusing on the structural details of interdependence to generate interesting results. That has been the approach here—using the relationship between values and behavior to produce a model in which both cooperation and noncooperation are possible equilibria, and in which rapid wholesale shifts from one state to the other are possible.

An alternative explanatory approach might be to note that a "climate of cooperation" could come about because a change in values took place that made cooperative negotiation a dominant strategy. If that were the mechanism, the appropriate explanatory approach would be quite different—it would entail an investigation into values themselves rather than the mechanisms that transform values into action. This is a different dimension of the problem, and for this reason does not really reflect a competitive theory of reality; it is rather a complementary part of the same problem. A complete analysis of cooperative behavior would surely have to deal with both of them.

REFERENCES

Axelrod, R. 1984. *The Evolution of Cooperation*. New York: Basic Books.

Chiang, A. C. 1974. *Fundamental Methods of Mathematical Economics, 2d ed.* New York: McGraw Hill.

Cournot, A. 1897. *Researches into the Mathematical Principles of the Theory of Wealth*. New York: Macmillan.

Cross, J. G. 1983. *A Theory of Adaptive Economic Behavior*. New York: Cambridge University Press.

Hamilton, W. D. 1972. "Altruism and Related Phenomena, Mainly in Social Insects." *Annual Review of Ecology and Systematics* 3.

Intriligator, M. D. 1976. *Mathematical Optimization and Economic Theory*. Englewood Cliffs, N.J.: Prentice-Hall.

Nash, J. F. 1951. "Non-Cooperative Games." *Annals of Mathematics* 54.

Sigmund, K. 1986. "A Survey of Replicator Equations." Institute of Mathematics, University of Vienna, Vienna, Austria.

Smith, J. M. 1978. "The Evolution of Behavior." *Scientific American* 239.

Conflict Research, the Security Dilemma, and Learning from History

J. David Singer

With the advent of nuclear weapons and ballistic missile delivery systems in the years following World War II, some social scientists in the West began to consider seriously whether they might now have a more useful role to play. It was appreciated that war over the past few centuries had been increasingly destructive, but now we were confronted with the possibility of devastation so massive and so swift as to make even the havoc of the two world wars modest by comparison. Could social scientists shed much light on the conditions and events that might make nuclear war more—or less—likely, and more to the point, could their research make a difference?

By the mid-1950s, we began to see a modest coming together of those who hoped to respond to this unprecedented challenge. They came not only from history and political science but from psychology, sociology, economics, and anthropology as well, and 1957 saw the establishment—at the University of Michigan—of both the *Journal of Conflict Resolution* and the Center for Research on Conflict Resolution. While some of these scholars turned to the results of laboratory and field research, a fair number of us looked to history as a source of lessons that might shed some light on the strategies of conflict management and war avoidance. And, despite some suspicions and intimations to the contrary, appeasement and capitulation were not the strategies of choice that either shaped or emerged from these early essays into peace and conflict research. While we shared a general repugnance of war, neither the naïveté of peace-through-strength nor that of peace-through-weakness was particularly evident. Put differently, we were as interested in the implications of deterrence as with the implications of disarmament; illustrative is the title of one of the first books to come out of the Michigan center: *Deterrence, Arms Control, and Disarmament* (Singer 1962).

In any event, those of us who chose to look to international history for the relevant lessons were not especially blessed with a solid set of scholarly precedents that might serve as a point of departure. To be sure, people such as

Buckle (1885), Condorcet, and Bagehot had pondered the possibility of bringing scientific method and history together, and more recently we could turn to the pioneering efforts of Bloch (1899), Richardson (1939), and Wright (1942), but there certainly was no sustained body of work, nor even a shared norm that history—political, diplomatic, or military—might be treated in the scientific style. To the contrary, the dominant tradition was that of "ransacking history" in pursuit of those particular cases that might illuminate a problem, or worse yet, support a given contention. Despite the above pioneers, most political scientists continued on the one hand to cite Santayana (to the effect that those who fail to learn the lessons of history are doomed to repeat it) while at the same time acting as if history were merely "one damned thing after another."

Be that as it may, a good many of us have decided that history *is* the most promising source of such knowledge as may help understand, and avoid, the processes that culminate in war. That choice is not, however, as obvious as it might appear; other sources of insight are indeed available. First, there are other empirical settings to which we might turn for analogies to international conflict—and it should not be forgotten that the international system of the past is also no more than an analogy of the system of today and tomorrow. Among these might be the economic marketplace, labor-management relations, preindustrial social systems, animal societies, municipalities, traffic jams, large organizations, the galaxy, and meteorological configurations, to mention some of the more evident possibilities.

Second, there are social science experiments, carried out in moderately controlled environments, with individuals and groups acting as nations, factions, government ministries, diplomats, and so forth. While often used for teaching purposes in recent years, these social psychology experiments have also shed appreciable light on decision making and attitude formation.

Third is the computerized simulation, whose value can be considerable, especially when it rests on well-documented empirical generalizations. Even in the absence of the latter, the simulation provides a powerful exercise in logical consistency as well as a potentially rich source of hypothesis and insight. Fourth, and closely related, is formal modeling, based on such abstract schemes as game theory. While far removed from the complexities of real human behavior, modeling can also offer both a test of one's logic and an unconventional source of hunch and hypothesis. Other strategies come to mind, but my intention here is to concentrate on the prospects—and pitfalls—of learning from history.

Some Essential Criteria

Choosing history as our potential source of knowledge concerning the dynamics of war and peace is more than merely turning to History. Without that discipline and its gifted practitioners, the social scientist could hardly begin to ply her or his trade; historians have done, and continue to do, an impressive job in sorting out the empirical facts, evaluating assertions, and tracking down the elusive, the ambiguous, and the disputed. They also offer up a rich, and often dizzying, variety of interpretations, all of which are essential grist for the social science mill. But, with only a few bold exceptions, they shy away from any explicit search for generalizations, preferring rather to give us a rich, textured, subtle, and thorough analysis of a given episode, era, or locale. Nor would we get far down the scientific road with *Thinking in Time* as our guide; the standards and criteria are rather more complex than Neustadt and May (1986) suggest, but in no sense arcane.

To begin, the relevant geographical-temporal domain must be specified, and second, *all* relevant cases from that domain must be examined. Third, the cases or situations must be compared with one another in a rigorous fashion, and in terms of characteristics that are both precisely defined and clearly germane to the case at hand. To illustrate, when the American foreign secretary Dean Rusk asserted that the "lessons of Munich" were applicable to the Indochina confrontation in 1967, journalists, members of Congress, and citizens should have posed the following questions: "Along which dimensions were these two cases similar? How similar? Along which dimensions were they different? How different? How many cases of this type do we find since, let us say, the Congress of Vienna? In which cases were which policies pursued? Which cases turned out which way? In sum, Mr. Secretary, please tell us about Fashoda, Agadir, Constantinople, and Sarajevo, as well as about the one case that you happen to like!" Rusk was, of course, neither the first nor the last of those diplomats who frequently "fell into a habit which can be neither cured nor pardoned: making history into the proof of their theories" (Acton 1909).

This same principle would seem to apply to the question of military preparedness: under which circumstances are various levels of preparedness most successful in enhancing a nation's security? Could it be more complicated than it appears to both the overarmers and to the underarmers? More specifically, can a nation jeopardize its security by overarming as well as by underarming? Obviously, no two situations are perfectly identical, but neither are any two situations totally different. Nations differ, but have many characteristics in common. Military strategies differ, but rest upon remarkably similar premises. Historical periods are marked by change, but also by an impressive degree of continuity. Thus, despite the variation across time, place, and circumstance, and the dangers of interpreting historical lessons *too* literally, it would be irresponsible *not* to turn to the historical record for policy guidance.

As already suggested, we cannot expect to learn much from history if we merely use the past as a grab bag from which we select the cases that support our views of the moment, while putting back into the bag those cases that contradict these prejudices. Only a well-defined total population of cases, or a carefully and explicitly drawn sample of that population, can serve as a legitimate basis for generalization; a biased or distorted population or sample of cases will inevitably give us distorted results.

But that is not the only requirement for discovering the lessons of history. A second requirement is that each of the phenomena about which we seek to generalize must be converted into very clear verbal forms (that is, a variable) and thence into unamibiguous quantitative forms that can serve as an indicator of the variable. This is achieved by "operationalizing" the variable, on the basis of one or the other processes of quantification (Singer 1982). The most obvious type of quantification is that of *measurement*: height in centimeters, temperature in degrees, earthquake severity in the logarithmic Richter scale units, velocity in kilometers per hour; many physical phenomena are operationally quantified by measuring them against a scientifically accepted scale. Less obvious, but equally familiar, is quantification by *enumeration*: the percentage of women in a parliamentary body, the number of bottles in a case of wine, the fraction of the work force that is unemployed, the number of tanks in an armored division; many physical and social phenomena are operationally quantified by enumeration, or counting.

However, accurate counting requires unambiguous classification, and that is easier when it comes to women, bottles, workers, or tanks than when it comes to less easily defined phenomena like crises, manic-depressives, small businesses, political radicals, great musicians, effective teachers, or economic depressions. The criteria for inclusion and exclusion of our cases in or out of these categories are often not sufficiently clear and operational, and even if they are, there may well be some disagreement over the classification criteria or "coding rules." Thus, when it comes to events or conditions that are not ordinarily treated as quantifiable—such as national security or military preparedness—we need first to articulate our coding rules.

If most of the specialists in a given area of competence agree on these coding rules and how to apply them, so much the better. That seldom happens at the beginning, and it often takes years or decades before they come to general agreement on how to identify a genius, a delinquent, and a typhoon, or how to measure the hardness of a steel alloy, the viscosity of a liquid, the permeability of a membrane, the severity of a war, the culpability of a criminal's accomplice, and the duration of a business cycle. Eventually, however, certain conventions emerge, and general agreement is reached on the procedures for inclusion-exclusion and measurement, permitting us to produce scientifically useful sets of data. Hence, in the field of international politics today, we find a rather clear consensus on how to identify sovereign states, major powers, militarized disputes, civil wars, and international wars, and on how to measure national capabilities, diplomatic importance, and the severity and magnitude of a war. (Small and Singer 1982; Gochman and Maoz 1984;

and Singer and Diehl 1991.) This is, unfortunately, not yet true of some of the concepts and variables that are used in the study at hand, but that need not be a source of paralysis; most of those listed above were also ignored or regarded skeptically when they were originally devised and applied.

There is, finally, a third major requirement to be satisfied if we are to learn from history. We must not only operationalize our concepts and examine all of the relevant cases; we must also statistically analyze the resulting sets of data in such a fashion that our expectations or preferences do not pre-determine the results of the investigation. Our analysis must not be allowed to "load the dice" in favor of, or against, a given theoretical position, and we must look not only at those patterns that point in the hypothesized direction, but also at those that point in other directions as well. In the same vein, our statistics must tell us how probable it is that the observed patterns could have occurred by chance alone, so as to distinguish between historical accident and randomness on the one hand and robust empirical findings on the other.

Historical Reality Testing

Having considered both the relevance of international history, and some of the criteria to be kept in mind if we hope to draw accurate generalizations from the historical record, let me now put some of these principles to work. There would seem to be two major uses that can be made of observed regularities in the relevant past. One is essentially scholarly, driven primarily by the hope of adding to our knowledge via the testing of hypotheses or the construction of a theory or both. In that application, we ask whether a given pattern is repeated over and over, how frequently it occurs, and whether it rises or falls over time or whether it is cyclical. Further, we ask the extent to which certain variables rise and fall together, whether that relationship holds only in some regions or some decades or is more general in time and space. Of course, with Bernard de Voto (1952), we recognize that "history abhors determinism," but unlike him, recognize that it can indeed "tolerate chance." The occasional naive critic to the contrary, then, we rarely expect, and even more rarely find, that the same relationship between or among variables will obtain in every case or every spatial-temporal context. As noted earlier, we generate data in an opera-tional way to ascertain what happens when, where, and under what condi-tions, and we analyze those data statistically to measure the regularity of a given pattern and its likelihood of having occurred by chance alone.

Shifting from theory to practice (and in this case the expression is used literally), a second use is to build our policies on a more solid foundation than provided by those cases that were most recent, most dramatic, most success-ful, most disastrous, or most easily remembered. Rather, the hope is to examine *all* relevant cases, and while relevance may be open to a range of interpretations, there *are* explicit criteria such as those mentioned above in connection with U.S. policy vis-à-vis the Vietnam War; others will be noted in the substantive sections below.

The idea here is to generate what might be called a "contingent forecast," by which we mean that the historical evidence permits us to say that "if we do this, under these circumstances, the most likely result is such and such." That is, by examining all the cases since perhaps the Congress of Vienna or World War I involving disputes between, let us say, two major powers of approximately equal strength, the record can show which moves and countermoves culminated in which types of outcome with given frequencies. To be sure, there is no certainty in such a forecast, given the tentative and incomplete nature of our knowledge base, the possibility of faulty classification (assigning the case at hand to an inappropriate class of cases), and, of course, the fact that the international system—like all social and biological systems—is a developing one in which the relationships between variables do not remain constant over time.

Worth noting here is the intimate connection between the theoretical and the practical; as the cliché has it, "there is nothing as practical as a good theory." Whereas a fair amount of competent scientific research can indeed generate the findings on which to base an impressive array of contingent forecasts, these remain in the realm of correlational knowledge—useful as far as they go. But if the right kinds of research are combined with creative speculation in a recurrent and iterative fashion, we might come up with a reasonably coherent theory for the explanation of different (and as yet unknown) types of international war. At present, there is no such theory, even though we have a great deal of speculation, from vague to precise, a small portion of it operational and testable, and even less of it already tested. Much of this is, pretentiously, called "theory," but if we use that precious word more carefully, to describe a body of coherent explanatory knowledge, much of it verified against the historical evidence, then it can be said that we have no theory.

As and when we approach that advanced stage of thoughtful research, the policy payoff could be impressive, inasmuch as it will provide strong clues as to the factors that account for those confounding changes in the relationships between and among variables. That is, because we will have a better sense of *why* these shifts occur across time, and in response to which conditions, we should be able to predict more solidly the results of given policy moves. In the interim, and as that research effort goes forward, we are not exactly bereft. Thus, we return now to the sorts of policy-relevant contingent forecasts that are now possible, thanks to the correlational knowledge generated to date by the University of Michigan Correlates of War team and other colleagues working from the same methodological perspective (Singer 1980, Gochman and Sabrosky 1990, and Vasquez and Henehan 1992).

Before turning to some of these contingent forecasts that might serve as indicators of early warning or timely assurance, there is a prior sort of role that this type of quantitative history can play. Reference is to "reality testing" in the sense that people in the policy community often assert that "history teaches us" some lesson or other, when history may indeed *not* teach us that, or might even—if studied systematically—teach us quite the opposite. Quite clearly, when such general assumptions are widely shared, it is essential that they be well grounded in the historical facts; otherwise, the likelihood of disaster becomes all too high.

Let me illustrate by reference to a veritable bible of cold war aphorisms found, not in the little red book of Chairman Mao or the green book of General Khadaffi, but in the "State of the World" reports produced in the United States during the Nixon administration. While these self-evident historical truths were not usually stated in precise and disconfirmable terms, we were careful to operationalize and then examine them in several possible forms, giving them the benefit of the statistical doubt. Three will be examined here.

Acceptance of War Encourages Aggression

In the first example, we find the statement that "the resort to military solutions, if accepted, would only tempt other nations . . . to try the same." We compared this generalization to the historical evidence in ten different versions, with perhaps the most accurate translation being: if other states did not come to the aid of a victim of an armed attack promptly and vigorously, there would be another act of aggression within two years. Looking at the fifty interstate wars between 1816 and 1965, we found that only thirteen of the target nations were promptly joined, while thirty-seven of them were left to fight alone. Since 46 percent of the former wars and 41 percent of the latter were also soon followed by another, coming to target nations' aid made little future difference. Another translation would be one in which the initiators were allowed to emerge victorious, and here we found that of the thirty-four cases in which the initiator won the war, 35 percent were quickly followed by a subsequent war. But in those sixteen in which the initiator *lost*, 56 percent were followed by war; while not a statistically significant difference ($Q = .40$; $x^2 = 1.96$), it comes alarmingly close to suggesting that peace is best preserved by permitting the *initiator* to be successful in its aggressive behavior!

Alliances Deter War

In the post-1945 period, U.S. foreign policy was heavily influenced by the historical doctrine that "we must build an alliance strong enough to deter those who might threaten war." This was reflected in the establishment of the North Atlantic Treaty Organization, Central European Treaty Organization, Southeast Asia Treaty Organization, and Australia–New Zealand–United States Tripartite Security Treaty, as well as a number of bilateral defense pacts. Without judging the success of that doctrine in the case at hand, let us examine its performance in the period since the Napoleonic War.

Once more, the notion can be interpreted in several ways. The most general is that the incidence of war in the international system is lowest during and shortly after periods of highest alliance aggregation; while this pattern indeed holds for a variety of alliance types in the nineteenth century, the evidence is to the contrary in this century, albeit weakly. Another version might posit that, for each of the major powers, those years in which it was in one or more formal alliances would be followed in the next three years by little or no war, whereas, years without alliance partnerships would be followed by one or more war entries. We found that of the 648 major-power alliance-membership-years, only 18 percent were followed by war entry while the remaining 82 percent were not. But to paraphrase the reference to the opera and the fat lady's singing, the analysis is not over until all four cells of the matrix are examined. Thus, when we looked at the 239 nation-years *not* marked by alliance involvement, we found the identical percentages: 18 percent followed by war entry and 82 percent not. Alliance membership by itself historically does nothing to affect the war-proneness of the major powers.

Yet another interpretation of the deterrent effect of alliances is to examine the consequences of *entering into*, rather than already *being in* a formal alliance. Here the doctrine does even less well vis-à-vis the historical facts: of the 135 major-power alliance-entry-years, 23 percent were followed by war involvement while 77 percent were not. Moreover, of the 752 no-alliance-formation years, only 17 percent were followed by war entry, while 83 percent saw no war entries in the following three years. In sum, the alliance is a slim reed if war avoidance is the objective.

Peace Requires Strength

This generalization not only "stands to reason" but is perhaps the most universally accepted bromide within both the scholarly and the policy communities, resting on the comfortable premise that *we* are peace-loving but *they* only understand force. It is nicely captured in the U.S. State of the World message of 1971: "Peace requires strength. So long as there are those who would threaten our vital interests and those of our allies with military force, we must be strong." Does this lesson of history fare any better than those discussed above, bearing in mind the crucial distinction between military strength and political power?

At first blush, it would seem so. That is, of the total fifty-nine major-power entries into war, thirty-four occurred when the combatant state was *below* the major power average on capabilities as reflected in military, industrial, and demographic strengths; and only twenty-five occurred when *above* the average. Shifting from the static score to the direction of change, however, this difference disappears, with thirty of the war entries occurring under conditions of relative decline and twenty-nine when holding steady or rising. But since it is one thing to participate in interstate war, and quite another to be compelled to do so in response to an enemy's initiation, we look next at the capabilities of the major powers since 1816 when they were the targets in wars initiated by others, major or minor powers. While there were only nine such occasions, five took place when the target was above average in capabilities and four when it was below; similarly, five were steady or rising vis-à-vis the rest of the major powers and four were declining. The differences are quite negligible.

Of course, the Administration's lesson from history might be more fairly tested by comparing the war-entering major power's capabilities to those of its specific opponent, rather than to *all* the majors. Looking only at the nine major-versus-major wars, it turns out that the victim of attack was indeed weaker more often, but only in five of the nine cases, and that all of the four that were stronger than their opponents were nevertheless declining in relative capabilities. Put in its most positive form, there were no cases of a major power being attacked when it was both stronger than, and rising, vis-à-vis the potential attacker.

But when we examine those cases in which war did *not* occur, we find that relative capabilities do little to differentiate between war and nonwar distributions. For example, we look at each major-power half-decade to see which of these powers was above or below the average capabilities score, and then whether it experienced war or peace in the subsequent half-decade. We see that 94 of those *below* average went to war, as opposed to the 84 *above*-average nation-periods that did, but when we examine the no-war outcome, it turns out that the *weaker* major-power half-decades were followed by 126 no-war half-decades while the *stronger* ones were followed by only 52 no-war periods. With a Q value of only .19 and x^2 of 1.37, the pattern certainly questions the utility of military strength, but is remarkably close to random; the same is true if we measure, not high versus low capabilities, but rising versus declining ones as well.

These three examples, then, serve a rather practical purpose. They show that, with close attention to all the relevant cases, the development of operational or quantitative indicators (or both) of the key variables, and intelligent translation of the verbal policy problem into a careful statistical analysis, we can more accurately estimate the lessons of history. This approach makes it less likely that we will either drift into acceptance of some generalizations whose major virtue is their plausibility, or go along with forceful assertions of those generalizations that fit the preconceptions of those at the center of the decision process.

Early Warning and Timely Assurance

In addition to providing a basis for evaluating alleged lessons of history, there is a second policy application of the results of systematic and statistical research of this sort. This is the development of indicators that can serve to provide both early warning and timely assurance.

Looking first at early warning, several analogies come to mind. For a motorist, signs indicating some sort of dangerous condition ahead can help to avoid a grisly demise: sharp curves, steep hills, narrow bridges, loose gravel, and icy surfaces, are more prudently navigated when the impending difficulty is anticipated. Similarly, advance warning, on the basis of systematic prior research, that a tornado, hurricane, blizzard, or earthquake lies ahead can lead to a number of lifesaving responses. Perhaps a close analogy rests not so much upon notification of dangers in impending environmental conditions as upon those inherent in one's behavior. Whether it is driving too fast, drinking before driving, heavy gambling, sustained drug consumption, and other addictive behavior, we can predict—on the basis of competent prior research— that disaster may well lie ahead.

Solid research can also provide harbingers of *good* news in the form of timely assurance. We can usually expect that moderate rainfall in the spring will lead to good crops, as will proper cultivation and choice of seed, that a rising barometer promises blizzard-free ski touring, and that an offshore breeze will typically blow away the traffic smog. Again, there are not only ecological but behavioral indicators of assurance: a light meal will enhance our endurance in the upcoming match, attentive reading will lead to better performance on an examination, and leaving for the train station promptly will reduce the need for a desperate and hurried search for parking.

Of course, most of these indicators of trouble or success rest on more solid evidence and greater experience than we can expect to find in international politics, but this is not necessarily due only to less-complex causal processes; more and better research over a longer period of time also helps considerably. Had scholars in our field turned to more rigorous research methods as early as engineers, agronomists, meteorologists, and biologists did, we would be markedly further along in our ability to generalize and forecast. Despite our tragically tardy initiatives—and it was less than three decades ago that the first explicitly scientific research got under way—some modest gains have nevertheless been registered. Let me illustrate by reference to a few of the nearly five hundred studies reported in two volumes devoted to brief abstracts of virtually every data-based historical analysis published over these three decades (Jones and Singer 1972; Gibbs and Singer, forthcoming).

When Is the System More Dangerous?

One question that national-security elites seldom ask, but should ask more frequently, is whether disputes are more likely to escalate to war under varying systemic conditions. The global system, or one of its regional or functional (e.g., major powers) subsystems may for example be sharply bipolar, multipolar, or, less frequently, quite diffuse in its clusterings. Further, such configurations can be a function of bonds reflecting formal alliances, diplomatic representation, shared memberships in international organizations, or trade; they may rest on only one set of links or several such. In addition, these sets of bonds and links can be strongly isomorphic and reinforcing, or quite different from one another and thus tending to cancel one another out.

Shifting from configurations on the horizontal dimension—the way the nations are connected to one another—to those on the vertical dimension, we have in mind the way the nations fall on one or another hierarchical scale. Here we look at military capabilities, industrial strength, demographic mass, diplomatic importance, global trade, and so forth. There are, in addition, certain structural properties of the system that reflect combinations of horizontal and vertical arrangements, as well as, of course, rates of change in any of these.

Let us, then, look at a few studies that might be used as predictors, or more accurately, contingent forecasts. By the latter phrase, we mean if-then statements: if we do this, under this general set of conditions, vis-à-vis another nation of certain attributes, that nation is most likely to respond as follows, or, somewhat more generally, if we do this under these conditions, these are the most likely results. That is, to the extent that we are working from research results that not only do a competent scientific job of historical generalization, but also are responsive to those secular trends or cyclical patterns that generate those all-too-familiar changing relationships among our variables over time, we can begin to make policy-relevant contingent forecasts of increasingly high accuracy.

Alliance Configurations

Social scientists have, in recent decades, given a fair amount of attention to what has been called the "ecological fallacy" (Robinson 1950) or the "level of analysis/aggregation" problem (Singer 1961), by which they mean, inter alia, that we need to specify the level of social aggregation at which we intend to generalize. Just because there is, for example, a high and positive correlation between worldwide military expenditures and the amount of war in the total system, it need not follow that this is true at the regional, dyadic, or national levels of aggregation. The big spenders may not be fighting wars, but exporting weapons at low prices to nations in other regions where the wars occur, or the high military allocators may be successful in mutual deterrence whereas the low allocators may not—for reasons quite independent of relative capabilities.

Bearing this consideration in mind, we reexamine the alliance-war relationship, but this time at the system level, on the assumption that it might serve the purpose of warning or assurance. Given the centrality of alliance arrangements in the realpolitik approach, we first asked whether the system itself would experience less war when there were higher levels of alliance aggregation; the latter indicates very simply the fraction of the system's member nations involved in one or more formal alliances in a given year. Interestingly enough, for the entire period under examination by the project—from 1816 up through the extent of the data base at the time of the study, in this case, 1945—we found a very weak, but positive correlation; that is, when alliance levels were high, so were war levels in the years immediately following. On reexamination of the nineteenth- and twentieth-century patterns separately, we found that the realpolitik hypothesis was indeed borne out by the nineteenth-century data, but in the first half of the current century, higher alliance-aggregation scores were followed by *higher* frequencies and magnitudes of war. Given the powerful effects of the first and second World Wars, we ran our analyses without those two time periods and still found the positive relationship.

In that same study, we next looked at the relationship between bipolarity among the major powers and fluctuations in the onset of international war. Not too surprisingly, the results are quite similar. That is, all else being equal, we would expect that the more the number of nations in defense, neutrality, and entente commitments, the more polarized the system will be. Thus, in the nineteenth century, the more clearly the major powers and their allies are aggregated into opposing camps, the less war there is in the ensuing several (one, three, and five) years, but in our century, contrary to the realpolitik expectation, this approximate "balance" of the powers is associated with *increases* in the incidence of war.

The policy implications of these findings are modest, but suggestive. They merely alert us to the fact that—all else being equal, which is rarely true—the world in this century is more dangerous during periods of high alliance involvement and high polarity. Thus, the prudent policymaker would do well to avoid escalatory behavior under such systemic conditions, and better still, stay away from politics that lead to polarization around opposing camps.

This finding and its implications immediately raise a follow-on question: are those nations that belong to alliances specifically more war-prone, or is it a more general danger? And, as indicated in the previous section, we discover that the systemic-level generalization does indeed hold at the national level, especially for the major powers. That is, while alliance membership depressed the propensity to get into war in the nineteenth century, the "effect" of such involvements in this century has been to increase the frequency and magnitude of national war experience. Worth noting once more is that the premises of the realpolitik approach were borne out in an earlier epoch but essentially refuted by more contemporary experience.

One possible explanation of this counterintuitive finding is suggested by yet another investigation into the alliance-war relationship. In looking at the performance of alliance partners when their cosignatories approach—and cross over—the brink of war, we find a surprisingly low fraction of cases in which allies did indeed fight alongside their partners (Sabrosky 1980). Between 1816 and 1965, barely one-quarter (27 percent) of the opportunities to honor alliance commitments were so honored, although the performance level was slightly better in the nineteenth century. Worse yet for the reliability— and hence the possible deterrent effect—of alliances, alliance partners not only stood aside in 61 percent of the 108 opportunities to aid an ally, but in 12 percent of those cases (21 times up through 1965), they actually went to war *against* the formal alliance partner. Thus, one partial explanation for the deleterious effect of alliance membership on national war involvement is the "placebo effect"; believing in the reliability of the commitment, a national-security elite is more willing to go to the brink of war on the assumption that the apparent solidarity of its coalition will lead the adversary to back down.

The policy implications of these modest studies should be clear. As Deutsch and Singer (1964) argued deductively, alliances hinder the more or less salutary effect of pluralistic and cross-cutting ties in any system that is essentially anarchistic. If that system is weak in both its cultural norms and its structural institutions, conflict may be more frequent—but far less violent—if the "invisible hand" is allowed to generate an incessant level of low-intensity and multilateral pushing and hauling. Alliances, in the age of the welfare state, are no longer made and unmade with alacrity, and thus rigidify and amplify conflicts that might otherwise peter out in a self-correcting fashion or be overtaken by new and apparently more pressing concerns. The dynamics are, of course, considerably more complex (Gulick 1967, Riker 1962), but a prudent policymaker would certainly do well to attend to alliance formation and the potential of contagion as a useful indicator of early warning.

Capability Distributions

This part of the chapter noted, in opening, that system structure may be described on both a horizontal and a vertical dimension and then went on to summarize a few studies that addressed formal alliances as one example of the horizontal dimension of system structure. Shifting now from such internation bonds and links to capability rankings as an example of the vertical dimension of system structure, we look at the extent to which these configurations may be useful for early warning, assurance, or both.

One of the earliest investigations of the link between capability patterns and war is found in a pioneering anthology assembled by Russett (1972). In that study, Singer, Bremer, and Stuckey (1972) developed several indicators of the extent to which material capabilities were either equally distributed among the major powers since 1816 or highly concentrated. Using each nation's percentage share of six different indicators of military, industrial, and demographic capabilities within the major-power subsystem, we devised three different indicators. One of these reflected the concentration score for each of the twenty-eight half-decades from the Congress of Vienna through 1965, another tapped the change in that score over each half-decade, and the third was designed to capture the total redistribution of capability shares in each period, regardless of whether it led to any change in the rank orderings.

What did we find? To a large extent, the realpolitik model was supported for the nineteenth century and essentially refuted for the twentieth century. That model (appropriate to an epoch in which foreign policy was more the "sport of kings" than an extension of domestic politics) holds that the more equal—and fluid—the distribution of strength, the more readily the "invisible hand" could play its self-correcting role. Thus, in the last century, there was a dramatic correlation of .81 between concentration and the incidence of war in the next five years. In this century, however, that relationship was reversed, but at a more modest figure of $-.23$; high concentrations did indeed "make for" more war in the earlier period, but for less war in the more-contemporary period. Furthermore, when all three indicators were used in the statistical analyses, the effects were quite clear, with equality of capabilities as well as fluidity in their redistribution predicting lower levels of war in the 1816 to 1899 era, but higher levels of war from 1900 through 1965.

As suggested earlier, it can be very useful to examine the effects of any set of factors at different levels of social aggregation, and this certainly applies to capabilities and their distribution. Thus, we now shift from the systemic to the *dyadic* level and examine certain widely accepted propositions as to the efficacy of military preparedness in the pursuit of national security. In one such study (Wayman, Singer, and Goertz 1983), we found that it is indeed true for the period from 1816 to 1976 that military superiority is positively associated with victory in war, but it also turns out that industrial superiority accounts for more of the variance in victory. In addition, prevailing over the adversary in a dispute that is militarized, but short of war, is *inversely* related to capabilities; not dramatic, but nevertheless surprising, is that the weaker party in terms of both military personnel and expenditures comes off more successfully with greater frequency than the stronger one.

Looking now at military-allocation ratios—reflecting the fraction of a state's industrial or demographic resources allocated to the military—the conventional wisdom is refuted by the historical facts. While higher *armed forces* allocations contribute to victory in war, higher *military expenditure*-to-industry ratios are associated with defeat. Perhaps more interesting is that the low allocators consistently prevail over the high allocators in disputes, while the high allocators are significantly more likely to get into militarized disputes and wars than the low allocators, casting considerable doubt on the deterrent effects of high levels of military preparedness.

Looking Ahead, Pessimistically

As we move through this final and dramatic decade of the twentieth century, what do our findings suggest for the next century? I begin, of course, with a reiteration of the proposition alluded to earlier: scientific research in the macro-social sciences does not assume continuity of prior trends, nor does it assume that observed regularities, patterns, and correlations will continue into the future. The intercentury differences reported here should make that clear, and this is why a solid, data-based, and dynamic theory will always serve as a more reliable basis of prediction than simple extrapolation, or the postdiction to prediction strategy.

Be that as it may, in response to our editors' urgings, let me venture three forecasts: first, what the international system will look like in the early twenty-first century; second, how warlike it might be; and third, how well the nineteenth- and twentieth-century models will fit the war patterns of the twenty-first century. As to the first, we are already well into a process that can only be understood as system transformation. Perhaps most dramatic is the Soviet Union's demise as a superpower, the liberation of the East European states, and the consequent unification of the two Germanies. This may not imply the end of major-power rivalries, but the international system has already begun to take on the more familiar multipolar configurations that obtained from the Congress of Vienna through World War II. Along with this mixed blessing, the next century will be characterized by several other challenges and opportunities: an acceleration of environmental degradation; rising population pressure and higher rates of migration; advances in weapons technology and its proliferation; continuing economic stagnation outside the central system, coupled with a worldwide increase in economic interdependence; the disintegration of familiar political entities and the creation of new centers of power, both smaller and larger; and, perhaps most significant, a clear upsurge in popular assertiveness worldwide.

As to conflict and war, the outlook is not especially promising. The political entities, as noted, will remain territorial well into the century, despite increasing incentives toward nonterritorial association based on commerce, education, research, and ideological affinities—all facilitated by major advances in the technologies of communication, transport, and miniaturization. In somewhat the same vein, weapons technology *could* make armed conflict less likely, but probably will not. That is, we seem to be well into a long period in which the offense enjoys a superiority over the defense in inflicting devastation, but quite the opposite when it comes to holding territory against an invader. Earlier transitions in weaponry *should* have led to a decline in war, but did not; and this time, the grounds for war will be more diverse and compelling. Despite incremental growth in supranational institutions, the new world order will remain essentially anarchistic, nor will the norms of civil responsibility soon extend beyond the boundaries between we and they. By midcentury, and plenty of disaster—largely manmade—the institutions and norms may begin to catch up with the imperatives, but the auguries are far from reassuring for the next two generations. Thomas Hobbes would find it all too familiar.

Finally, what effect might these dismal predictions have on the correlates of war, and to what extent are we likely to find the statistical patterns of the past two centuries repeated? If our children and grandchildren are fortunate, the nineteenth-century patterns will reappear. Even though they rest largely on a Eurocentric state system, they could be resurrected if the emerging international system turns out to contain a fairly large number of territorial entities of approximate parity, with relatively weak and fluid spheres of influence for the more powerful actors. Such a state of affairs could permit the "invisible hand" of the separate parochial interests to exercise a restraining and rationality-inducing influence, in which case the old-fashioned, multipolar balance-of-power mechanism might be reasonably effective. Then, armed conflict might be fairly frequent but of limited severity, in response to the tendencies of polarization and capability concentration that typically generated war between the Napoleonic War and World War I. Conversely, and equally probable, the next century could look a lot like Orwell's *1984*, with a handful of powerful actors, governed by the Big Brother mentality, anticipated by Lasswell's (1941) Garrison State, and equipped with the technologies that permit and encourage oppression within and militarism abroad. Which of these directions will typify the next century remains an open question, but it seems safe to say that the intellectual and epistemological issues raised in the conclusion below will count as much as the anticipated changes in our physical environment or any likely tendencies toward a moral-ethical rebirth.

Conclusion

Needless to say, not all of these studies were conducted for policy purposes in general, or to generate predictive indicators of warning or assurance. To the contrary, most derive from more academic considerations in pursuit of codified knowledge about international politics, and with an eye to the development of theory. And while this is surely a sufficient basis for devoting considerable time, energy, and material resources to systematic research, there are several more immediate implications; one might refer, rather lightly, to the "socially redeeming value" of such data-based research.

First, as suggested in the opening section of this chapter, the results can often provide a more solid basis for believing or questioning the "lessons of history" that are often invoked by foreign-policy elites, their supporters, and their tormentors. Whether to legitimize or to debunk, it is always valuable to evaluate ad hoc or opportunistic generalizations against reasonably solid evidence. Second, as noted here, research results can provide a basis for inferring certain predictive regularities: under these specified conditions, such and such behavior is likely to culminate in this particular outcome.

Third, and perhaps more useful in the longer run, is that such research should, in due course, contribute to the development and verification of more complex and more comprehensive theories. And while many of us agree with the earlier comment that "there is nothing as practical as a good theory," we rarely ask why this might be so. As suggested, there are no solid theories in the field of international politics at this date, if we define a theory as a coherent body of explanatory knowledge, rather than an interesting surmise, a set of reasonable hunches, or even a nicely mathematized cluster of hypotheses. But, as our research progresses—and it will progress if we try to build upon one another's work and utilize reproducible methods—we can expect to come up with some fairly compelling theories before too long.

A major practical value will be to the marked enhancement of the reliability of our predictions. That is, while explanation and prediction are not the same, and the former is (despite the folklore) a more demanding task, explanatory theories can carry us beyond observed, recurrent patterns of covariation. Recognizing that the international system is in a continuous state of flux, and that the relationship between and among key factors will also vary over time, we can appreciate that few patterns hold over and over, forever and ever. A solid theory will not only rest on and offer an explanation for such change in the past, but will also aid us in predicting the ways in which certain factors will vary with one another in the future. To put it another way, the postdiction-to-prediction strategy is better than mere surmise, but a data-based and coherent theory will be far more powerful and reliable than either of these, or both of them together.

Shifting from the *generation* of knowledge to the question of *application*, we need to remember that the results of solid scholarship are not automatically translated into public policy, or even noticed by those who make such policy. Hence, we need to consider, inter alia, our several audiences. Needless to say, the results of research such as that summarized here are not restricted only to the political elites who deal with the foreign-policy and national-security problems of their respective societies. Given their well-demonstrated proclivities for using research findings for their own purposes—not all of which are identical to those of the nation in general, not to mention the world community at large—we should note that such findings may be of equal interest to the counterelites. That is, those who are out of power or out of favor can make equal, or better, use of our work, especially when the elites invoke (as they often do) the "lessons of history" to buttress their arguments and policies of the moment. The same holds, of course, for people in the media who presumably have no particular policy axe to grind, but whose responsibility might be expanded to report not merely what the elites and counterelites are saying, but also what systematic researchers have discovered. I say this with some trepidation, given the tendency to give front-page coverage to the musings of a Kissinger or a Brzezinski, typically resting on some mix of folklore, selective recall, and self-serving motivation, while ignoring the results of a careful, thorough, and scientifically competent team of political scientists and historians.

These considerations are, of course, rather premature, for several reasons. One, it should be reiterated, is that compared to such more advanced disciplines as physics, chemistry, biology, and even psychology, the scientific study of international politics is in its infancy. One indicator of that is the recency of the practise, another is the dearth of universities and institutions in which the scientific method is used and taught, leading in turn not only to a modest handful of such scholars, but to a virtual absence of same in government, consulting firms, and the media. With depressing regularity, furthermore, when these well-educated scholars take up employment in government or the media, not to mention the more prescientific academic departments in the United States and abroad, the prevailing methodological norms quickly discourage them from continuing their research and teaching in that mode. Within a few years, one sees them regress to the more traditional methods in response to peer pressure, the relative lack of funding, the recalcitrance of their students, and perhaps also the fact that writing an interesting essay is far easier than formalizing one's model, operationalizing one's hypotheses, generating a credible data base, and mastering and staying on top of the most appropriate statistical and mathematical methods. One might add that even in the absence of all these disincentives, there remains the problem of publication; of the scores of American journals in our field, there are only four that consistently publish data-based research: the *Journal of Conflict Resolution* since 1957, and more recently, *International Studies Quarterly*, *International Interactions*, and *Conflict Management and Peace Science*.

Given the purposes of this volume, it might not be amiss to urge those foundations with a commitment to serious research that might bear on matters of war and peace, as well as other aspects of international affairs, to reexamine their priorities. Without denying for a moment the value of research that leads to new insights and alternative perspectives, all of which is necessary, such writing remains far from sufficient. Work that is to be relevant to the issues of war, peace, and international security needs to be numerate as well as literate, and when it is both it can provide the sort of knowledge that may well guide the nations away from policies that range from costly to catastrophic, and toward those that increase the likelihood of making the global village safe for human habitation and conducive to human survival.

REFERENCES

Acton, Baron, J. E. 1909. *The History of Freedom and Other Essays*. London: Macmillan and Co.
Bloch, J. de. 1899. *The Future of War*. New York: Doubleday and McClure.
Buckle, H. T. 1885. *History of Civilization in England*. London: Longmans, Green.
Deutsch, K. W., and J. D. Singer. 1964. "Multipolar Power Systems and International Stability." *World Politics* 16(3): 390–406.
de Voto, B. 1952. *The Course of Empire*. Boston: Houghton Mifflin.
Gibbs, B. and J. D. Singer. Forthcoming. *Empirical Findings on World Politics*. Greenwich, CT: Greenwood Books.
Gochman, C., and A. Sabrosky, eds. 1990. *Prisoners of War?* Lexington: Lexington Books.
Gochman, C., and Z. Maoz. 1984. "Militarized Interstate Disputes, 1816–1976." *Journal of Conflict Resolution* 28: 585–615.
Gulick, E. V. 1967. *Europe's Classical Balance of Power*. New York: Norton.
Jones, S., and J. D. Singer. 1972. *Beyond Conjecture in International Politics*. Itasca, IL: Peacock.
Lasswell, H. 1941. "The Garrison State." *American Journal of Sociology* 46: 455–68.
Neustadt, R. E., and E. R. May. 1986. *Thinking in Time: The Uses of History for Decision-Makers*. New York: Free Press.
Richardson, L. F. 1939. "Generalized Foreign Politics." *British Journal of Psychology* (June): 1–89.
Riker, W. 1962. *The Theory of Political Coalitions*. New Haven: Yale.

Robinson, W. S. 1950. "Ecological Correlations and the Behavior of Individuals." *American Sociological Review* 15: 351–56.

Russett, B. M., ed. 1972. *Peace, War, and Numbers*. Beverly Hills, CA: Sage.

Sabrosky, A. 1980. "Interstate Alliances: Their Reliability and the Expansion of War." *The Correlates of War II: Testing Some Realpolitik Models*, edited by J. D. Singer, 161–98. New York: Free Press.

Singer, J. D. 1961. "The Level of Analysis Problem in International Relations." *World Politics* 14(1): 77–92.

———. 1962. *Deterrence, Arms Control, and Disarmament*. Columbus: Ohio State University Press.

———, ed. 1980. *The Correlates of War II: Testing Some Realpolitik Models*. New York: Free Press.

———. 1982. "Variables, Indicators, and Data: The Measurement Problem in Macro-Political Research." *Social Science History* 6(2): 181–217.

Singer, J. D., S. Bremer, and J. Stuckey. 1972. "Capability Distribution, Uncertainty, and Major Power War, 1820–1965." In *Peace, War, and Numbers*, edited by B. M. Russett, 19–48. Beverly Hills, CA: Sage.

Singer, J. D., and P. Diehl. 1991. *Measuring the Correlates of War*. Ann Arbor: University of Michigan Press.

Small, M., and J. D. Singer. 1982. *Resort to Arms*. Beverly Hills, CA: Sage.

Vasquez, J., and M. Henehan. 1992. *The Scientific Study of Peace and War*. New York: Lexington Books.

Wayman, F., J. D. Singer, and G. Goertz. 1983. "Capabilities, Allocations, and Success in Militarized Disputes and War, 1816–1976." *International Studies Quarterly* 27: 497–515.

Wright, Q. 1942. *Study of War*. Chicago: University of Chicago Press.

The Second American Century:
The New International Order

A. F. K. Organski and Marina Arbetman

This chapter presents a set of hypotheses about the structure of the present international order. Accompanying the propositions presented here are explanations of why the hypotheses are plausible, cohesive, and worthy of further investigation.[1]

The central propositions of this chapter suggest that the power distribution underpinning the current general vision of world order is not a reversal but a strengthening of the past structure of power in world affairs; the present worldwide perceptions of U.S. dominance are congruent with realities on which the international order rests; major players show no incentive to change the U.S. role and status in world affairs; players that might wish for change in the international order are, for now, impotent. The international system is in equilibrium.

Far more significant than changes in power distributions have been changes in "perceptions," which have finally come to join long-standing international realities. The acceptance of U.S. leadership improves the opportunities for conflict resolution in international relations. It was the Soviet acceptance of U.S. preeminence in the Gorbachev era that forced universal recognition of the *unipolarity* that had characterized the international order since the end of World War II. Defining the system as a new world order to point out the change in *perceptions* was in part misleading, for it obscured the fact that realities (i.e., the distribution of power) during much of the Gorbachev era had not changed very much from what they had been during the long decades of the cold war.

However, changes are incubating now that will affect future power distributions in international affairs, and the international order those distributions

The appendixes to this chapter are a slightly modified version of the appendix to Organski 1992. They have been translated into Italian for a paper in *Storia d'Europa*, vol. 1, ed. Perry Anderson, Maurice Aymard, Paul Bairoch, Walter Barberis, and Carlo Ginzburg (Turin: Giulio Einaudi, 1993). The formulation of the model presented here has been developed by Marina Arbetman (Arbetman 1990).

1. I would like to thank Mr. David A. Singer for his help in putting the successive drafts of this manuscript together.

will be expected to support. These changes, importantly, do not involve the replacement of U.S. dominance over world order. *Rebus sic stantibus*, rivals that can pose a realistic challenge to U.S. dominance appear to be still below the horizon.

To provide a tracing of the changes that have occurred, or should be expected, we shall review the power distribution among the members of the great power system at four different points. The great power system includes those countries that are key to the stability and workability of the system of international relations. As we shall see, given the skewedness in the distribution of international power, the set of countries in question is inevitably small. In each of these comparisons the questions will be the same: What share of the economic and power resources in the system does each player have? What inferences can one legitimately draw from such distributions?

Our first comparison is in 1988. The cold war is clearly in remission. 1988 is also the last year of the "old" international order.

Second, we address the question, to what extent is the distribution in the last year of the "old order" representative of past distributions? The comparison presents a series of the distributions of power and economic resources among the great powers throughout the twentieth century.

Third, we seek to provide a glimpse of the power structure supporting the system at the present time and for the immediate future.

Our last comparison is the most difficult of all. We shall seek to gain an insight of the shape of the future international order. Some of the assumptions made will seem heroic.

A Primer on the Conditions for the Working of a World Order

As in all political systems, the authority structure of the international system rests on the distribution of power that underpins the relations of its members. The essential conditions for international order to come into being and survive were first presented in the Power Transition theory in 1956 and can be represented graphically, as in figure 1.

As figure 1A indicates, the international order is hierarchical, much like the domestic political order of national societies. Two factors determine the structure of this hierarchy. One is the share of power of each member of the order in relation to all others, and the other is the degree of "satisfaction" of each member with its position in the order and the rules of international intercourse. Figure 1B points to the ratio between power and satisfaction that makes the system work. The figure indicates that a large set of the members of the international order are probably "not satisfied" with their position and the rules of the system. Such dissatisfaction need not affect, however, the functioning and stability of the system.

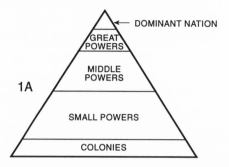

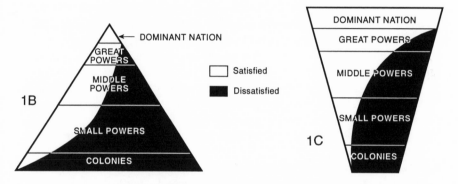

Fig. 1. The ingredients of world order: power and satisfaction

Power and satisfaction may compensate for one another to maintain the stability of the international order. As figure 1C seeks to show, most of the powerful must be satisfied if the order is to be workable and stable. The dissatisfaction of the weak states will make little difference as long as they can do little about their grievances.

Two critical conditions can be deduced from the state of affairs we have just described, as shown in Matrix 1. The necessary, though not sufficient, conditions for conflicts and potential changes in the structure of the international order are that nations are both powerful and dissatisfied.

Thus, the rule for peace and war affecting the structure of the international system can be written as follows:

1. Essential but not sufficient conditions for *major instability or wars* are present when there is an equal distribution of power among contestants, and the situation is particularly threatening when the nations involved are leaders of the international order and any potential challengers.

	Satisfied	Not Satisfied
Powerful	Peace	War, conflict
Weak	Peace	Peace

Matrix 1. Conditions for International Stability and Instability. *Note:*
Power and satisfaction, shown here as dichotomous, are in reality continuous variables and should be so treated.

2. The necessary, but not sufficient, conditions for *peace* are present whenever there is a vast power difference between the dominant nation, the leader of the international order, and any nation that has the aspirations and the resource potential to create a challenge. The venerable Balance of Power theory has it precisely backwards (Morgenthau 1948).

Contrary to conventional wisdom and much scholarly writing (Morgenthau 1948), asymmetries in power provide conditions for peace and security for all members; power equilibria (particularly between potential challengers and the dominant nation) have the effect of dislodging the foundations on which the great power system rests and create the conditions for major international political shifts often punctuated by devastating wars. It should be added that gains or losses of leadership of the international order are much more a function of rates of growth of the members' own domestic political and socioeconomic development—these changes produce the resources that are the source of power, and are not easily manipulable—than the result of international maneuvering and diplomatic manipulation.

The connection between domestic development generating changes in the distribution of international power and the stability and peace of international relations is the key to understanding how the international system changes. The phenomenon of the Power Transition connects differences in the rates of economic and political growth and resulting shifts in the distribution of power. That very destructive conflicts fought over the leadership of the international order resulted from such differences was recognized[2] by Simon Kuznets (1971, 37), in a trenchant passage:

---

2. Changes in the distribution are, at the core, a function of rates of national, political, economic, and demographic development. The major determinants of national power are population size, political efficiency, and economic development. (See the appendixes to this chapter.)

The significance of this association between high average growth rates, the wide absolute differences that can be generated, and rapid shifts in economic magnitude among nations lies in the possible connection between the shifts and strain-producing attempts to modify political relations to correspond to the changed relations in economic magnitude, and hence possibly in economic and military power. The acceleration in the aggregate growth rates that produces acceleration of shifts in relative magnitude among nations may therefore cause acceleration in political adjustments and strains and under some conditions, in the frequency in conflicts in response to recognized but disputed shifts in economic power.

Comparisons of economic magnitudes, of course, do not suffice for our purpose here. The problem is to measure not only economic wealth but national power, and for that one needs to capture both the dimension of the human and material resources possessed by a society and, importantly, the capacity of its government to mobilize such resources (Organski and Kugler 1980, Organski 1992, Organski et al. 1985; Kugler and Domke 1986). For a brief description of the measures of relative political capacity used herein, see the appendixes to this chapter.

The First Comparison: The End of the "Old" Order

The last good point at which to take stock of the great power system in the "old" international order appears to be 1988.[3] It is the last year when Gorbachev was in power with the Soviet Union still intact and its empire in Eastern Europe still attached. The important change in the Gorbachev era, so far as international relations were concerned, was Gorbachev's signaling of

---

These changes are interrelated. Because development has spread differentially across regions, and across nations within regions of the world, one should expect great shifts in national power and major changes in the world distribution of power. Large states that are latecomers to development can grow very rapidly. If they are large enough, and can sustain faster rates of growth for a longer period than potential rivals, they can catch up with and overtake nations that had preceded them in the developmental trajectory and that, because of the power gained due to their earlier start, had become leaders of the international order. When an overtaking is threatened or takes place, a potential challenger may be resisted. In this case, major conflicts result somewhere around the point where the trajectories of the countries intersect.

The theory was first stated in Organski, *World Politics* (1958, chap. 12). A good deal of subsequent research proved the fundamental hypotheses of the Power Transition theory to be valid (Morrow and Kim, in preparation; Bueno de Mesquita and Lalman 1992; Organski and Kugler 1980, chap. 1; J. Kugler and A.F.K. Organski 1989). The theory generated a large literature. A very similar theory was presented in 1981 (Gilpin 1981).

3. The critical characteristic of the "old order" was that the realities of the international power structure diverged substantially from perceptions of how power was distributed.

his acceptance of the subordinate position of the Soviet Union within the international order. By then the Soviet Union had transformed itself from a "dissatisfied" to a "satisfied" power. In the case of the Soviet Union, acting on the illusion that the U.S.S.R. could realistically compete with the United States carried with it the high costs of building the Potemkin villages that made it appear plausible that the Soviet Union and the United States were competing. This illusion was in fact ruinous to Soviet life. Remember Gorbachev's first words to Shevardnadze on assuming power: "all is corrupt." Fantasies, if acted out, do corrupt.

The public recognition by the Soviet Union that its challenge to the United States could not be won, and that the U.S.S.R. would remain, at best, a distant second in the world, did not mean that the old order had changed. Rather, the vision of world order had returned to its Rooseveltian formulation after the end of World War II. The Big Three would manage the peace and security of the world. But the managing would be based on U.S. dominance, with the Soviet Union a distant second, and the United Kingdom a very distant third. Neither the U.S.S.R. nor the United Kingdom liked that ordering, and the Soviet Union fought it in vain for forty years. The acceptance of the U.S. international preeminence by Gorbachev, followed by the liberation of Eastern Europe, signaled a return to the agreements reached at Yalta. The Soviet Union moved from the position of "preeminent challenger" to the position of great power "satisfied" with the rules of the system and pleading for admission. The change led observers to argue that a *new* order had been created.

One should add that, Gorbachev's admission, through actions rather than words, that the Soviet Union could not stay abreast of nor overtake the United States was an act of great statesmanship. As a result of this Soviet policy, the United States remained very protective of Soviet superpower status and abandoned that endeavor only when the U.S.S.R. disintegrated. Gorbachev's policy is, in some sense, comparable to Churchill's acquiescence to the U.S. takeover of international leadership more than forty years earlier. Under Churchill also, the United Kingdom carefully avoided public tests of will with the United States that would have revealed the weakness of the United Kingdom. Avoidance of such tests protected the image of the United Kingdom as a great power. Less wise Englishmen and Frenchmen did test the realities of that power distribution in the Suez crisis and were badly punished by the United States for their pains.

Let us turn to our comparison of great power capabilities. The numbers in table 1 indicate the distribution of economic and power resources among all major powers at the end of the cold war. In 1988, clearly the United States was towering in both dimensions over all other major powers. If one accepts the CIA estimate (Central Intelligence Agency 1989), the United States had a pool of economic and power resources about twice that of the Soviet stock, and two and one-half times the Soviet pool, if revised estimates of Soviet gross national product are accepted. The U.S. advantage over Japan, the third country on the power ladder, is slightly larger. The ratios between the United States and the United Kingdom and France are between four and five to one, respectively.

Clearly the critical piece of information in table 1 is the difference in economic resources and in power between the United States and the Soviet Union. That interval was roughly three to one. That interval existed *before* the Soviet Union began to falter, *before* the Soviet Union withdrew from Eastern Europe, and *before* the centrifugal forces within that society succeeded in tearing it apart.

Why the Soviet Union chose to change course when it did, and not ten years before or after, is a fascinating question to be answered by Soviet specialists. In that regard, we would simply warn against facile explanations that the Soviet Union went broke as a result of the military competition with the United States. To be sure, Soviet arms stockpiling was part of the illusion that the Soviet Union and the United States were equal in power. And military investments and expenditure were terribly wasteful and expensive. But, contrary to so many accounts, the Soviet Union was not "broke" when Gorbachev came

TABLE 1. Percentage Share of Economic and Power Capabilities among the Great Powers, 1988

	GNP (1)	Percentage of Economic Resources (2)	Percentage of Economic Resources (3)	Power Capability (4)	Percentage of Power Capability (5)	Percentage of Power Capability (6)
(1) U.S.	4,862	39	41	4,183	42	44
(2) Japan	1,840	15	16	1,364	12	13
(3) W. Ger.	1,120	9	10	1,006	9	9
(4) U.K.	758	6	6	796	7	7
(5) France	939	8	8	761	7	7
(6) U.S.S.R.	2,500[a]	2		2,250	22	
(7) U.S.S.R.	1,875[b]		16	1,668		17
(8) China	350	3	3	270	2	2

Source: GNPs are from the Central Intelligence Agency 1989.

[a]There have been long-standing questions as to the correct estimate of the Soviet GNP. Economists have suggested that CIA estimates inflated actual values between 25 percent and 30 percent (Bergson 1991).

Row 6 presents Soviet GNP (and the derived calculations) as estimated by the Central Intelligence Agency. Row 7 presents Soviet GNP decreased by 25 percent.

Columns 2 and 5 present the Soviet percentage shares of economic and power resources of the total great power pool if one accepts CIA estimates; columns 3 and 6 represent results if one reduces CIA estimates by 25 percent.

[b]The data in column 4 are calculated by adjusting GNPs with a measure of political capacity. For a summary explanation of such measures see the appendixes to this chapter.

to power. Between 1971 and 1986 Soviet real growth was reported as averaging 2.5 percent, between 1976 and 1986 real growth was 2.2 percent, and in 1986 Soviet growth was reported as 3.8 percent. Growth fell by more than two percentage points *in subsequent years* (Central Intelligence Agency 1988).

The massive U.S. advantage in national capabilities augurs well for stability and order in international affairs in the coming decades, for it offers hope that any challenger or plausible combination of challengers would think again before initiating aggression. Indeed, given the structure of power underpinning the international order at this time, one should expect that the end of the twentieth century and much of the twenty-first century will be an era of peace and order among the great powers, similar in many respects to the situation in most of the nineteenth century, when *Pax Britannica* ruled the day, and, at least in part, for the same reasons. Disputes will not disappear, and force can be expected to be threatened and to be used. Yet the strife will represent the jostling and adjustments of members *within* the order and will not threaten the order itself.

The Second Comparison: The Power Distribution and the Cold War

Before we move on in our discussion to the present and the future, we should make a very important observation about the past. The distribution of international power underpinning the present international order is nothing new. In general outline that distribution has been in place, as tables 2 and 3 quite clearly suggest, from the end of World War II.

The data in table 2 tell one important part of the story. In economic resources, the United States far surpassed each other major power in the first

TABLE 2. Percentage Distribution of GNP among the Great Powers, 1900–1980

	U.S.	Japan	(West) Germany	U.K.	U.S.S.R.	France
1900	30.6	5.3	16.4	17.8	17.1	12.8
1913	36.0	5.5	17.0	14.3	16.9	10.3
1925	42.5	8.0	12.2	12.6	15.1	9.6
1938	36.3	9.2	15.0	11.7	20.8	7.0
1950	50.0	5.0	7.1	10.6	20.1	7.2
1960	45.2	7.5	9.9	9.7	20.5	7.4
1970	40.4	13.1	9.6	7.8	21.7	7.4
1980	39.2	14.6	9.1	6.9	22.5	7.7

Source: From Kugler and Organski 1988.

Note: The reasons for the omissions of China from this table are discussed later in this chapter.

part of the century as well as in the second. There is remarkable consistency in the U.S. share of economic capabilities through the eight decades covered in the table. The series reflects the rise in importance of Japan in the 1970s and 1980s, while Soviet data are probably inflated. The series also shows the much-discussed U.S. decrease since the end of World War II (1950–80.) The decrease was largely a result of the distortion caused by the fact that, immediately after World War II, the United States had the only functioning industrial economy in the world and that all other industrial nations had been devastated by a five-year war. Again, it is important to note, as one thinks of challenges then and now, that the proportion of combined resources of Germany and Japan, just before World War II and at present, are just slightly over the share of power resources available to the Soviet Union through the cold war period. Most important of all, however, in the first half of the twentieth century, the economic capabilities of the United States did not convert into power. Clearly the governmental allocation between foreign and domestic affairs of the human and material resources of a national society is a critical determinant in the role the nation plays in international politics.

But it is the distribution of national capabilities or power resources, as presented in table 3 that tells the more important story. The numbers suggest what is the "same" and what is "new" in the international order and give us critical hints about how the international order works.

Two very important points emerge from table 3. Those who draw conclusions about national capabilities from purely economic data—e.g., trade trends and capital flows and exchange rates—are engaged in an iffy business. Power resources and economic resources are clearly related but are not the same; indeed, they may vary substantially one from the other. As noted, the United States in the first half of the century had a pool of economic resources substantially larger than that of the European powers. But the economic

TABLE 3. Percentage Distribution of National Capabilities among the Great Powers, 1900–1980

	U.S.	Japan	(West) Germany	U.K.	U.S.S.R.	France
1900	24.6	3.8	29.0	25.4	10.0	7.8
1913	25.6	11.0	17.7	14.2	20.4	11.0
1938	21.2	18.0	23.1	12.5	19.6	5.5
1950	43.1	5.0	8.4	13.3	25.2	5.0
1960	46.4	6.7	9.8	9.7	20.6	6.8
1970	42.8	10.8	9.1	8.6	22.4	6.3
1980	42.9	11.2	9.0	6.8	24.1	6.0

Source: Data from Kugler and Organski 1988.

advantage did not convert to an equivalent advantage in power terms. The differences in U.S. power in the first and second halves of the century present an interesting example of the importance that governmental capability plays in the international power game. Governmental performance only recently has yielded to rigorous measurement, and a good index of governmental capability is now available. (See the appendixes to this chapter.)

Table 3 also clarifies the power distributions through the whole period of the cold war, and here what the table tells us is very startling. *The U.S. towered over every other major country through the period of the cold war.* The advantage has never been less than four to one in the case of Japan, almost four and one-half to one in the case of Germany, in the case of Britain almost five to one, France seven to one, and, finally, in the case of the Soviet Union, almost two and probably even three to one.

Here we must raise what appears to me an obvious and very important point. The beliefs and perceptions about the power relationship between the United States and the Soviet Union were completely spurious. Yet the leaders of both countries and countless students of international politics and security matters propagated the view. Clearly, mass publics everywhere believed it. It is a fascinating puzzle why such an error could have continued for so long. In the words of Oleg Bogomolov, the Soviet Academician, how could a country (the U.S.S.R.) that had a gross national product one-third or one-fourth of that of another country (the United States) believe itself as strong as its opponent? It was a profound question that was key in the occurrence of the cold war and represents a welcome challenge to Soviet specialists to answer how such an error could have been made.

The other side of the issue is also important. One must repeat the same question in the case of the United States. How could a country whose gross product was three times that of another country believe that its rival was as strong as it was and could be a serious threat to its security (Organski, In preparation)? As is their wont, the army of security experts that were responsible for the estimates in the first place turned their backs on the problem.

It is perhaps easier to understand why European political leaders erred in regard to Soviet power. When one looks at the percentage distribution of national capabilities across countries, and specifically the two-to-one and three-to-one advantages that the Soviet Union had over Europe's other great powers, one understands immediately why the Europeans were frightened, at least at the beginning of the cold war, and why they were tempted to inflate their estimate of the Soviet danger. After all, if Soviet strength had been portrayed as the estimates in table 3 indicate, Americans might have become convinced that the Europeans could care for themselves, particularly if they chose to unite as they are doing now. Were that to have happened, the coalition of U.S. elites, who continued to fight to bring U.S. troops home from Europe and decrease U.S. military and political expenditures there might have carried the day.

Some have argued that it was nuclear stockpiles that made the United States and Soviet Union equal in power. The argument is flawed. Soviet nuclear forces designed to deter the United States would have added to the power of the Soviet Union *if* the United States had wanted to attack, but the United States did not wish to do so because of Soviet retaliatory capabilities. We have evidence that the United States did not intend to attack because it did not attack when it had a nuclear monopoly. It also did not attack when it had an overwhelming advantage over Soviet nuclear power, and this advantage lasted for half of the period of the cold war. If we accept the argument that mutual nuclear deterrence was the mechanism that kept the peace, how does one account for the fact that when the Soviet Union did not possess a deterrent, the United States did not attack? If Soviet nuclear capabilities served solely to deter U.S. aggression and the United States did not want to attack, the Soviet nuclear stockpile was for naught. We do not have the same kind of evidence the other way around, for there was no period when the U.S.S.R. had nuclear weapons and the United States did not. Nevertheless the evidence we have of U.S. behavior clearly violates a fundamental assumption of mutual-nuclear-deterrence theory. It is at least plausible to advance the hypothesis that nuclear stockpiles may not have kept the peace, and that peace was kept because neither country wanted to commit direct aggression against the other.

Our main point comes down to the fact that the power advantage of the United States over the Soviet Union, discovered in the Gorbachev era, is not new. It has existed since 1945 when World War II ended. It is only now that *perceptions* and *realities* coincide. The last doubters finally fell in step when further sharp declines in the Soviet power position occurred at the very end of Gorbachev's turbulent last years. World order is now recognized as very hierarchical, indeed as unipolar. Arguments that the structure of international politics was or is bipolar or multipolar, or that the international system is in a state of anarchy, was just talk, often self-serving, always misleading and misled.

It is also our hypothesis that, although this power reality may have been missed by the academic and governmental research communities, it was well understood at the leadership level of the two countries. The relevant Soviet elites knew, through Malenkov, Khrushchev, Brezhnev, and Gorbachev, that the U.S.S.R. was far behind the United States in power. Given its weakness, acting out a challenge to the United States would end in ruin. There is ample evidence of this knowledge. The implicit Soviet acknowledgment of U.S.

superiority came *before* the August 1991 coup hastened the disintegration of the Soviet Union. The U.S. leadership could not help but know, and knew that the Russians knew they knew.

Our estimates that the United States had over 40 percent of the power resources in the great power system throughout the period of the cold war, and that its share remained almost unchanged, stand in sharp contrast with arguments made in the 1980s that the United States was declining (Keohane 1980, 1984; Gilpin 1981; Kennedy 1987). Clearly, were such judgments correct, the U.S. fraction of power resources in the great power system would have decreased substantially.

Contextual evidence supports the view that U.S. dominance over the international order, if anything, increased through the years of the cold war. Consider the fact that the U.S. reach in the world was, in fact, most restricted immediately after World War II. It expanded massively through the sixties, seventies, eighties, and nineties. At the end of World War II, U.S. influence could effectively be felt over North and South America, Western Europe, and Japan. One-third of the rest of the world was in Communist hands, while the remaining 25 percent was held in captivity as colonial possessions by European powers. The United States was excluded from both. Soon, however, European empires were swept aside with U.S. help, and U.S. political, economic, and military power penetrated the excolonial world.

The Communist world held out. Until roughly 1987, U.S. and Western influence could not penetrate communist territory in Europe and Asia. But after the mid-1980s, with the Soviet demand for détente intensifying, U.S. political penetration inevitably increased. The retreat of the Soviet Union and liberation of Eastern Europe extended massively U.S. influence and opened the way also to economic penetration. One can appreciate how much of a change had in fact occurred when one recalls that it was the iron curtain, i.e., the exclusion of U.S. (and Western) political and economic influence from the Soviet-controlled world, that set off the cold war.

The expansion of U.S. influence is continuing. In 1991 it began in earnest in the Middle East, where Iraqi aggression made clear to the elites of oil-producing states that their wealth was not only insufficient to protect them from their real enemies, the radical states, but very nearly the opposite. American penetration of the Middle East should prove a long and halting process, but the logic of events will push in the direction of an institutionalized increase of U.S. influence in the region. The American order has expanded and solidified. Only the Asian Communist world is still closed to American penetration.

In short, the power realities in the cold war era fit closely the classic conditions for international peace and security laid down by the theory of the Power Transition.

The Third Comparison: The Present International Order

Two changes in the roster of great powers signaled the beginning of the present period. Within two months of the August 1991 coup, the Soviet Union fragmented. The understudy for the international role of the U.S.S.R. was to be the Commonwealth of Independent States. Few have taken this substitution seriously, however. Russia, almost immediately, took the place of the former Soviet Union in international affairs. It seems a plausible guess that, in power terms, Russian domination of the other republics in the Commonwealth, again *if* and *when* recovery is under way, is a political, economic, and demographic fact of life. It makes sense to use in this inquiry the estimates for Russia.

A second change in the great-power roster is the unification of Germany. A united Germany represents a substantial 15 percent increase in both economic and power terms over the pool of resources represented by West Germany. From a regional perspective, this unification only reinforces the advantage Germany already had over the other three major European powers. On the world power scale, however, the German position (with 10 percent of the economic and power resources in the system of great powers) remains a distant third from the top. German reunification may, eventually, have greater world significance in that a united Germany—with a 33 percent advantage in power resources over the United Kingdom, a 36 percent advantage over France, and a 50 percent advantage over Italy—bodes well to dominate the European community. One should note that a united Germany holds 28 percent of the total resources of the European Community, and in alliance with any one of the other three big European powers, would hold only slightly less than half of the resources in the system. It was the conventional wisdom before German unification that Western European nations, particularly France, pressed for unification because they thought that a Germany tied to the Community would be controllable. Our own data suggest that the influence may move the other way, and that it will be the European Community that will be more easily controllable by a united Germany.

One cannot refrain from making the point that Germany achieved peacefully what it had failed to do through very costly wars. Its winning strategy, since its defeat in the cold war, was subordination to the United States and passivity in foreign policy. It confirms the suspicion that the national power of the contestants, before, during, and after the cold war has been, and shall continue to be, rooted in the socioeconomic and demographic resources of each of the countries in question. Military power was considered essential, then as now, to run the order, but much of the military investment on both sides (in the case of the United States, perhaps as much as one-third to one-half of the military budget, and in the case of the Soviet Union, one-half to two-thirds) represented "excesses" of spending permitted by a political coalition that found fighting phantasms convenient for its domestic and international rule. Among great powers, a hint of the proper relationship between socioeconomic and political resources on the one hand, and military resources on the other, as the assets out of which national power is derived can be gleaned from the following proposition. In the long run, those who cannot overtake rivals in the race for power resources without war, cannot overtake them in the long term with war, while those who can do not need to fight (Organski and Kugler 1977, 1980.) How the "leaders" and "followers," "survivors," "victors," and "vanquished" of World War II fared in the cold war and beyond should give us food for thought.

From an international perspective, key questions in regard to the Community's unification are, in the end: How unified will Europe be? What fraction of the resources of each of the members will be put in the common pool? How long will "unification" take? The answers to these questions are not obvious.

The two changes in the roster of great powers introduced in the comparisons in table 4 provide a glimpse of the present structure of power in the great-power system. This comparison shows clearly the extent of U.S. dominance in the world. The U.S. advantage over Japan, the nation that has the second-largest pool of resources of all major powers, is over two and one-half to one in economic resources, with a three-to-one advantage in power resources. If our trace of the international distribution of power does in fact capture the international power reality, the current perceived threat of Japan is unfounded. One Japanese official remarked, "Americans should not be so discouraged.

TABLE 4. Percentage Share of Economic and Power Capabilities among the Great Powers, 1990

	GNP (Billion US$)	Percentage of Economic Resources[a]	Power Resources[b]	Percentage of Power Resources
U.S.	5,465	42	5,410	46
Japan	2,115	16	1,808	15
Germany	1,327	10	1,227	10
Russia	1,050	8	945	8
U.K.	858	7	901	8
Italy	845	7	634	5
France	844	7	620	5
China	413	4	318	3

Source: CIA 1990.

[a]do not add up to 100 because of rounding.

[b]The power estimates result from the adjustment of GNP or GDP by the index of the capacity of the political system to mobilize resources. (See the appendixes to this chapter.)

They are really much stronger than they think." It should be noted that the Japanese pool of economic and power resources is very similar in size to the Soviet pool in the period of the cold war. That is the major reason the shape of the distribution of power in the system is as it has been for fifty years.

As far as Germany is concerned, the U.S. advantage over that largest of European countries is a shade more than four to one in economic terms and four and one-half to one in power terms. The advantage over Russia is over five to one in economic resources and almost six to one in power resources. The ratios in question suggest that *the United States is now more advantaged in terms of economic and power resources than it was at the end of World War II*. The differences in capabilities between the United States and all other countries suggest that in the short run (ten to twenty years) and even, perhaps, in the longer run (thirty to forty years), one should expect no state or group of states in the international system with the capability to threaten the U.S. position of dominance.

If anything, the comparison above distorts the power reality in the great-power system by the inclusion among the great powers of nations that belong really in the middle rank, states with less than sixty million people and less than a trillion dollars in their gross national products. It can be argued justifiably that such nations represent pools of resources too small to permit their governments to play a decisive role on the world scale. If one addresses this concern and limits the number of nations to the United States and the three other greatest powers, one obtains the results in table 5. The United States has more economic resources and more power resources than Japan, Germany, and Russia combined. Looking at the numbers in table 5, one can only conclude that it takes strange vision to believe that Germany and or Japan will overtake the United States, or that the United States is declining (Keohane 1980, 1984; Gilpin 1981; Kennedy 1987).

TABLE 5.   Percentage Share of Economic and Power Capabilities among the Greatest Powers, 1990

	GNP (Billion US$)	Percentage of Economic Resources	Power Resources[a]	Percentage of Power Resources
U.S.	5,465	54	5,410	58
Japan	2,115	21	1,808	15
Germany	1,327	13	1,227	13
Russia	1,050	11	945	10

Source: CIA 1990.

[a]The power estimates result from the adjustment of GNP or GDP by the index of the capacity of the political system to mobilize resources. (See the appendixes to this chapter.)

Changes in the Great-Powers System:
The Future International Order

The massive U.S. power advantages characteristic of the present period will not hold. Changes are incubating that, in due course, should lead to massive shifts in the distributions of international power and in the structure of the international order those distributions will need to sustain. One change is the unification of the European Community. (The discussion of European unification is based on Organski 1992.) The other is the U.S. pooling of North American resources. Both of these changes have only started.

The estimation of the pool of economic and power resources that these two entities should be expected to possess fifteen or twenty years hence is a problematic undertaking. I assumed that present growth rates of North American and European collectivities would remain unchanged, and I approximated the collective strength of these new international entities by adding up the resources for each collectivity. The data used were for 1990, the most current and easily accessible data available.

Much the same was done with power resources. It should be noted that this procedure is less satisfactory in attempts to calculate power than economic aggregates. Estimates of power (see the appendixes to this chapter) are obtained by adjusting total product figures by a measure of the capacity of central governments to mobilize resources. However, neither the European Community nor the North American Region (Canada, Mexico, and the United States) has a central government. What was done, therefore, was to add together the "power values" for each nation in the two regions. One assumed that the total value would give a hint of what the estimates would be if central governments existed for the European Community and the North American Region, and there were two unified pools of resources.

This is not entirely satisfactory, but it is the best that can be done. In the case of Europe, this approach should create more of a distortion than in the case of North America. In Europe, the pooling of resources should be expected to be more heavily dependent on the development of central political institutions than in North America, where the distribution of power among the members of the regions is severely skewed. The pooling of resources should be far more difficult in the European Community, given the greater number of actors and the more egalitarian distribution of power. In North America, the sharp asymmetry in power renders the unification of the region less dependent on central political institutions. The American elite can, and probably will, act as the leadership echelon for the United States and for the region.

The European Community will fall far short of economic unification, in fact, at least for the foreseeable future. Moreover, European political unification is very much a question mark at present.[4] Although one should expect that there will be major efforts in that direction, unification is just beginning and will likely take decades. During that period the situation presented in table 4 will reflect the reality of the international power structure. In the medium term, therefore, the crushing U.S. advantage over the European Community will remain. Moreover, the United States should undoubtedly be expected to be an important player in the European process to unify.

For over forty years, the United States has clearly been a force in European critical decisions. In security decisions and in economic, cultural, and social arenas, U.S. penetration of European life has been very extensive. The North Atlantic Treaty Organization has been a central conduit channeling U.S. influence to Europe. NATO was created to deter or to repel Soviet aggression. In the 1940s, many argued that Western European nations were too small to cope with the Soviet threat if it ever materialized, and U.S. presence and subsidy was essential to compensate for their deficits. What was not highlighted was that if European nations had unified, they would have been more than well-situated to deal with their own collective security needs. As is the case with all subsidies, the U.S. subsidy through NATO made it unnecessary for European elites to do the kind of reorganization that, in a world dominated by giant states, would have made the populations of Western Europe competitive.

That reorganization, of course, would have meant that West European national elites would have seen their power and privileges, derived from their countries' sovereignty, diminished. NATO was the optimal solution. It permitted the United States the control over European decisions that was so important to the U.S. international order, and permitted European elites to husband the power and privilege they had. Since the U.S.S.R. never attacked Europe, the net effect of NATO on Europe's existence during the cold war was to derail or postpone any drive for unity that might have developed. Now that such a move has started, the threat to U.S. influence in the region is a matter of U.S. concern.

The United States should prove unwilling to relinquish its influence over Western Europe. It is in U.S. interests to have a European common market to which the United States can have access. On the other hand, if one assumes

---

4. The commentary that has accompanied the process of European unification makes up a vast literature stretching over decades. Some recent works and older classics that have influenced my thinking on the present European process would include: Galtung 1973; Pinder 1991; Bueno de Mesquita and Stokman, in preparation; Garrett 1992; Hoffman 1982; Ornstein and Perlman 1991; Sbragia 1992; Wallace 1991. The list is only a sprinkling of recent reading. Of major importance in establishing my angle of vision on the problem have been some classic works: Haas 1964; Mitrany 1966; Organski 1965; Tilly 1975, chaps. 2, 3, 4.

that U.S. leaders are seeking to maximize U.S. utility, it is not in the interest of the United States to have a politically unified Europe, which would be far more difficult to deal with than the relatively weak, smaller countries that make up the European Community today. If this proposition is correct, one should expect that the United States will work for, or, at least, not oppose further economic unification but lobby against political unification.

In this regard, the issue of a European army is revealing. There is reason to believe that at the core of any attempt to sparkplug a new international entity is the formation of an army. A European military force may be essential for any political union. The French and German plan for a nucleus that could become a common European army met considerable resistance.

Not surprisingly, the reaction of the U.S. government to this plan has been quite negative. For example, at the October 1991 NATO meeting in Rome, President Bush, after private discussion with U.K. Prime Minister Major, faced down the French and German leaders and bluntly confronted them with a choice: if the Western European nations wanted to go it alone in the field of security they were, of course, welcome to do so, but they should inform the United States now. The European leaders backed down. NATO with U.S. influence in it would remain central, at least for the time being. Given dissension among European nations and U.S. opposition, Western European political unification should be expected to experience very rough going, though the major proponents in the drama, France and Germany, should also be expected to persevere.

One has the impression that, since the end of World War II, the United States has been successful in riding the waves of intra-European political competition for supremacy in Western Europe. Competition among the Western European nations for primacy over continental Europe was in evidence in the protected environment the United States provided Europe during the cold war. England sought to gain preeminence in Europe through its special relationship with the United States, France sought to exclude the United States and achieve preeminence through a special relationship with a truncated Germany that could not tower over France and the U.K. and was, therefore, less threatening than a united Germany. Franco-British jockeying for position as leader, or co-leader, in Western Europe appeared vain when Europe saw itself as dependent for security on the United States. Now that the two Germanies have been reunited, French and English competition over position appears equally vain. One wonders at French leaders insisting on German acknowledgments of French "political equality" when Germany is more than one and one-half times France's size and power. (This was precisely the ratio in 1940, at the beginning of World War II.) Be this as it may, non-German members of the European Community pursued unity in the hope of holding Germany in check. Germany in its pursuit of unity could not be unaware that it would dominate the Community.

But Western Europe is not the only group of nations seeking to pool their resources. The United States, too, is seeking to pool the resources of North America through the creation of a Free Trade Area, though the nature of the pooling is quite different from that of the European experience.

Our last comparison of actors in the great-power system will include both the European Community and the North American Free Trade Area.

Table 6 suggests that *if* and *when* the European Community unifies, it will be a bit shy of the power level of the United States. If Europe unifies, the subordinate and frequently submissive behavior of "Europe" toward the United States should be expected to give way to a new assertiveness. A rivalry with the United States in the decades to come is therefore entirely possible. Such a state of affairs has been speculated about often enough, and the speculation is very probably correct.

However, *rebus sic stantibus*, this is a rivalry the European Community appears destined to lose, though clearly at this point the U.S. advantage over the Community is 6 percent in economic resources and 9 percent in power terms. This calculation assumes that the Community would reach full unification, while the reality over the medium term will fall far short of such expectations. The United States is advantaged over the European Community in economic productivity. If one uses per capita product as a readily available, though admittedly very imperfect indication of economic productivity, it is clear that U.S. productivity is more than a third higher than the average in the European Community. The advantage of the European Community over

TABLE 6. Percentage Share of Economic and Power Capabilities among New Great-Power Units, 1990

	GNP (Billions US$)	First Percentage	Second Percentage[a]	Power Resources[b]	First Percentage	Second Percentage[a]
N.A.R.[c]	6,217	42		6,120	45	
U.S.	5,465		39	5,410		42
E.C.[d]	4,786	32	34	4,254	31	33
Japan	2,115	14	15	1,808	13	14
Russia	1,050	7	8	945	7	8
China	413	3	3	318	3	3

Source: Economic data from Central Intelligence Agency 1991.

[a]The second percentage is calculated counting the U.S. and excluding the N.A.R.

[b]The power estimates result from the adjustment of GNP or GDP by the index of the capacity of the political system to mobilize resources. (See the appendixes to this chapter.)

[c]North American Region includes Canada, Mexico, and the United States.

[d]Includes all twelve members of the European Community.

the United States, on the other hand, is about 120 million more people. The fundamental question in seeking to guess the future of this possible rivalry is to speculate which entity can overcome the other's advantage.

Clearly, were Western Europe's average productivity to catch up with U.S. productivity, Europe could overtake the United States. This would require huge increases in the productivity of most members of the European Community, and such changes could not be achieved without the payment of serious socioeconomic and political costs. It is almost certain that it cannot be done quickly, and whether it can be done at all remains an open question.

On the other hand, if the United States increased its present population to equal that of the European Community, that would erase the core advantage of the Community. It is clearly unlikely that the United States could admit that number of new people into its borders. On the other hand, the United States, could, for limited purposes, unite with other countries as the European Community is doing. The population of Mexico and Canada is now a shade less than the difference in population between the United States and the European Community. Mexico is roughly 90 million people, and Canada is about 26 million. For reasons adumbrated earlier, it should prove easier for the United States to pool the human and material resources of the North American Region than it will be for the Economic Community to catch up with U.S. levels of economic productivity. The United States, therefore, can have the clear advantage. Military strength, however, is likely to play a negligible role.

The numbers in table 6 support the conclusion that the European Community, as presently constituted, does not have the resources to overtake the United States. Particularly because unification in Europe will be a slow and imperfect affair, the United States will remain even more comfortably ahead if the North American Free Trade Area is successfully extended to Mexico and the United States thus manages to pool the resources of North America.

Some Important Data Problems: A Footnote

There is a pressing problem on the research agenda for the immediate future. The estimates for the People's Republic of China's total product and power presented in this chapter may well be a severe underestimation, distorting profoundly the overall picture of the power structure undergirding the present world order. There is an ongoing, wide-ranging debate over different procedures for the estimation of Chinese per capita product. Resulting estimates from these approaches are very far apart from one another and range from a low of $400, the value used in this chapter, to $1,900 (international dollars) (Maddison 1989; CIA 1991). If the larger numbers are accepted and the 1.1 billion-person Chinese population is taken into account, China's GNP, inevitably, balloons into very large numbers, indeed a size larger than the GNP of Japan and second (though a distant second) only to the United States.

The issue has now broken into the elite press. (*New York Times*, February 15, 1993). But the international and domestic political implications of these new economic numbers for China have not really begun to be addressed. When they are, U.S. reactions are quite likely to be sharp. History may well repeat itself. The rise of China to the position of a credible challenger may well start the domestic debate over raising again the U.S. investment in political ties and military resources that had been lowered in the post–cold war period. It is highly likely that there will be again an intra-elite struggle over who will control these resources. If the new estimates are anywhere near correct, it is clear that the error in the U.S. strategy toward China all along has been the opposite of the error made in the case of the Soviet challenge. In the case of the U.S.S.R. the error was one of a massive overestimation, in the face of all evidence, of Soviet power. In regard to China the error (if the new estimates prove correct) was the other way, with Chinese power vastly under-estimated. It is also likely that the cold war experience will be repeated in that U.S. policy will be predicated on the belief that arming will be the best way to confront the problem. After all, U.S. military security policy was said to have brought the Soviets to their knees. What such a policy would overlook is the critical difference between the U.S.S.R. and China as challengers. The Soviet Union did not have the capability to pass the United States in power. On the other hand, *if* China develops economically and keeps its political system in working order there is no international strategy that can deflect it from over-taking the United States.

Be that as it may, which of the evaluations capture reality most accu-rately is a complicated question, beyond the scope of this chapter. The impor-tance of this problem, however, should be obvious. As Kuznets's (1971) observation quoted earlier makes clear, given its vast population, even rela-tively small changes in the Chinese per capita product have inevitably very substantial effects on the magnitude of Chinese totals. The upper estimates are understandably controversial. However, even if they are partially correct, it should be noted that profound ongoing changes in the international system that have remained almost unnoticed dwarf the expected changes that we have discussed. In the long run, the distribution of power between the United States and Europe and Japan would no longer be the main event. One is reminded of the end of the nineteenth century, when Germany and the United Kingdom were competing for leadership of the international order, only to be overtaken by the United States. The question is being treated elsewhere (Organski, In preparation), but it is of such importance for the future of the international order that it should be noted here.

Conclusion

It is definitely true of the world order, that it has not been so much the power realities that have changed—though there have been important changes in the set of great powers over the last half century—as it is perceptions of these realities that have changed profoundly in recent years. The world now recognizes the preeminent power position of the United States. One should expect the misleading conceptions of a "bipolar" and a "multipolar" world to fall into disuse. The international order appears new to those who did not realize or did not wish to admit what the power realities always were.

The peaceful nature of major shifts in the set of great powers has been largely due to the fact that none of the alterations in question has threatened the leadership of the dominant nation. Indeed, all confirmed that leadership position. Credible challengers and challenges to U.S. dominance are still in the wings.

But U.S. preeminence was a fact of life during the cold war as well. Why such preeminence was not recognized before—people seemed not to want to see—demands an answer. The fact that the U.S. advantage over all major powers, including specifically the Soviet Union, has been as massive as our data show, raises fundamental doubts about the validity of hypotheses that have been central to the way in which experts have accounted for the cold war over these last fifty years. Clearly, such explanations and the data presented here are mutually exclusive. Either or neither may be valid, but they cannot both be true. Revisions of the history of the cold war are indicated.

We have indicated the changes in the distribution of power that have occurred. The two major losers of World War II, Germany and Japan, have clearly overtaken three of the major European winners of World War II, the United Kingdom, France, and the U.S.S.R. Japan and Germany are now positioned second and third on the power ladder, but considerably behind the dominant nation in the system. Indeed, the U.S. advantage over Japan, the present number-two country in the world order, is roughly the same as the advantage the United States held over the Soviet Union all through the cold war period. Moreover, Japan, as the Soviet Union before it, cannot be a successful challenger to the United States. The Soviet Union lacked the capacity to mobilize the human and material resources it possessed to the extent required; Japan has the capacity but not the human and material resources it requires for such a challenge. The reunification of Germany has confirmed and deepened German ascendancy over Western Europe. This unification could become significant at the world level *if* a united Germany were to come to dominate a united Europe.

The dismemberment of the U.S.S.R. at the hands of its own elites has led to a major change in the ranking of great powers, with Russia substituting for the Soviet Union and occupying a distant fourth place on the power scale. The decline of the U. K. and France are an old story in international politics; these two are now at the bottom of the great-power ladder, if they have not in fact slipped from the bottom rungs altogether. The resulting changes in the distribution of power and in the rankings of great powers have strengthened the existing order and U.S. dominance of it.

The distribution of power in the great-power system will be altered significantly if the present European Community succeeds, in fact, in unifying politically and economically. The resulting pool of economic and demographic resources would be sufficiently close to the size of the U.S. pool to stimulate a rivalry between the Community and the United States. A truly united Western Europe would be a power the United States would need to reckon with. It certainly would not be an illusory contender as was the Soviet Union. I have written elsewhere,

> It is an ironic twist of U.S. fate that in the end of the Cold War, the U.S. should find that Western Europeans, the very allies and nations NATO permitted the U.S. to defend and control, have the capacity to be the real rivals to its leadership . . . and this after discovering that the challenge to its leadership on the part of the Soviet Union, a challenge the U.S. has made such ruinous investments to exorcise, was found to have been all along one part reality and more than two parts illusion, a classic case of Potemkin's villages. (Organski 1993)

It seems highly unlikely, however, that the European Community will displace the United States from its premier position for two reasons. Western European unification will be at best a lengthy and very imperfect affair. To assume, as we have for our calculations, that the European Community will succeed in unifying fully is extreme. Reality will fall far short of such a goal. Moreover, as things stand now, European resources are smaller than those of the United States alone, and the pooling of North American resources would lengthen the U.S. advantage. We do not mean to imply that U.S. dominance cannot be shaken, or that the present order will not give way to another. There is no reason why the United States should always rule. It rules now because, in terms of power, it is by far the biggest kid on the block. But if a bigger kid were to appear, the present dominant nation could and most probably would be replaced. Empires are not forever. In this regard, the major unknown is the estimate of the pool of resources of the People's Republic of China. Has China grown as much as some believe? And even if it has, can it continue growing at the rates of the last ten years?

American dominance is rooted in social, economic, and political changes begun at the end of the nineteenth century and stretched over the last one hundred years. The beginning of the next millennium augurs to be a second American century.

At the end of the World War II, many advocated one world and world government. Our brief discussion at the beginning of this chapter of the power distributions required for an effective world authority structure that maximizes order and stability and, therefore, approximates world "order" leads one to the conclusion that the present *Pax Americana* comes as close to those requirements as we are likely to see. Many of those who have dreamt of world government and world order, now that they have to confront the realistic rendition of their dream, do not really like what they see. It is enough to weary Job! Remember the Italian saying *"Hai voluto la bicicletta? Pedala!"* Realities always differ from fantasies in that they include the costs to reach one's goal. Those observers and ideologues who remain committed to a vision of world peace, stability, and order that comes about *not* as a result of the U.S. power advantage, believe in magic.

Appendix A

The yardstick of national capabilities used in this work combines gross national product or gross domestic product, used as an indicator of the total basket of human and material resources a "nation-state" represents, and the capacity of governments to mobilize such resources, into an overall measure of national capabilities (Organski and Kugler 1980, Organski et al. 1985, Kugler and Organski 1988, Arbetman 1990, Kugler and Arbetman 1989, Kugler and Domke 1986, Rouyer 1987). The national-power equation can be expressed as the interaction between the size of the productive population, its level of productivity, and the capability of the government in mobilizing such resources.

$$\text{National Power} = \text{Population} \times \frac{\text{GNP}}{\text{Population}} \times \text{Political Capacity}$$

In this formulation, total population reflects the size of the population of working and fighting ages, and per capita product implies their productivity level. The interaction of components assumes a proportional weighting system. Fluctuations in productivity affect the importance of populations, upward or downward. A given population twice as productive as another implies that two individual workers in the less-productive economy are required to perform the labor of one in the more-productive. The use of the total products to evaluate the pool of human and material resources contained by a national society is straightforward.

The key to the problem of the development of an index of national capabilities is a measure that captures the capacity of the government to mobilize the resources imbedded in the national society.

The index that has been developed is a relative measure, estimating the capacity of any one country relative to that of every other country in the set. The procedure is based on the following logic. All governmental performance rests on the ability of government to obtain the resources essential for its policies. Such an ability is rooted in the capacity of the government to penetrate the civil society and obtain from it the necessary resources. It is these two dimensions, governmental penetration and extraction, that need to be measured. Relative political penetration (RPP) and relative political extraction (RPE) vary and interact and provide the overall measure of political capacity.

Each of the components RPE and RPP has been found to have direct effects and also interactive effects. Therefore, the full equation of the model would be as follows:

$$RPC = \alpha_0 + \alpha_1(RPE) + \alpha_2(RPP) + \alpha_3(RPP * RPE)$$

where:

RPC = Relative Political Capacity
RPP = Relative Political Penetration
RPE = Relative Political Extraction

Each component of the model is described in more detail in appendixes B and C.

Appendix B: Political Penetration

Different methods are used to estimate the size of the labor force in the informal sector. These approaches intend to capture underemployment or disguised employment.

One model analyzes the structure of labor supply in major developing regions and assesses changes in underemployment and employment. When the index is greater than one, the rate of growth of the demand for labor exceeds the rate of growth of the labor supply. In this situation the structural conditions for unemployment and underemployment are more likely to be absent. Conversely, when the index is less than one, the population is more likely to take jobs outside the formal labor market.

Bruno Contini (1979, 1981) proposed that the fall in the activity rates was really not as high as the official estimates showed. A large portion of the population officially registered as "inactive" was employed and unreported. The difference between the two captured the undeclared labor force (see, for example, Contini 1987).

Contini estimated the informal labor force as a residual in the following way:

$$FLT = OT + OA + U_1 + U_2$$

where:

FLT = Potential Labor Force from Surveys
OT = Permanent Employment in Industry (more than thirty-two hours a week
OA = Permanent Employment in Agriculture
U_1 = Industrial Unemployment
U_2 = "Marginal" Labor Force

U_2 is a "catch-all indicator that includes most of the informal industrial labor force, marginal and irregular workers of all sectors, including the underemployed seasonal worker, part-timers, as well as the "discouraged" fraction of the population in working age excluded from the official count of the labor force" (Arbetman 1990). The informal activity, U_2, cannot be calculated from the official statistics alone because they underestimate the supply of labor; therefore, Contini uses surveys of the unofficial workers to interpolate the midyears to obtain an estimate of the Potential Labor Force. Then, U_2 is estimated as the residual.

Finally, Paolo Pettenati set an alternative way of gauging the size of the informal sector (see also Fua 1976). He asserted that the difference between the average proportion of active population in countries with similar levels of development and the actual active population in each specific country can be attributed, ceteris paribus, to the informal labor sector. This approach is very appealing. The unexplained differences in the active population among similar economic structures are probably due to differences in the supply side of labor, rather than to differences in the output side since the average active population corresponds to similar levels of product. Under these assumptions, Pettenati estimates a simple index to determine the share of full-time or part-time employment that is not officially recorded.

To control for levels of development, different averages of active population are calculated. When the index is more than one, it means that the conditions for disguised labor activity probably do not exist because there seems to be an excess demand of labor compared to other countries with similar levels of development; when the index is less than one, the possibility of concealed labor is present because an excess supply of labor exists. It is this index that we use to estimate levels of political penetration.

The reliability of this indicator has been ascertained by comparing Political Penetration to other models (i.e., Tokman 1985, Gaetani-D'Aragona 1981). The results show that the Political Penetration measured along Pettenati's line provides a parsimonious indicator yielding similar results to the more complex ones (see Arbetman 1990). This measure can be considered to have been validated by its ability to account for political-economy issues, such as exchange rate fluctuations, and for demographic changes (see Arbetman 1990, Kugler and Organski 1989).

Appendix C: Relative Political Extraction

The RPE measure is quite similar to the measure of penetration, and it is based on government's performance in raising revenues. The measure of relative political extraction (RPE) is the ratio between actual revenues and the levels of revenue one would expect that the nation would obtain given the average revenue performance of all other countries with a similar tax base (Organski and Kugler 1980; Arbetman 1990; Kugler and Domke 1986; Snider 1988; Organski et al. 1985; Rouyer 1987).

The problem of making the tax ratio comparable across time and across countries was tackled primarily by economists, who focused on the concept of tax effort. Tax effort is measured as the ratio between actual tax collections— which include tax revenues and exclude social security because, in the case of the latter, the government acts merely as a conduit in the transfer of resources— and estimated tax collection, which is the average taxes that countries under similar structural conditions should extract (Bahl 1971, Lotz and Morse 1967). The tax-effort formulation requires economic controls: exports, imports, mining, agriculture, literacy and per capita GDP (Chelliah 1971, Chelliah et al. 1975), because these factors aid or obstruct the government in its efforts to tax its population. For example, the government's attempt to collect taxes on foreign trade, oil, or diamond production is relatively easy. The reverse is true for agriculture because, in subsistence economies, the population can more effectively resist the attempts of central elites to tax them. As for the controls for level of individual wealth and literacy, the argument is that the higher the level of productivity in a society, the broader the tax base.

Alternative tax-effort models are provided by Jorgen Lotz and Elliot Morse (1967) and Roy Bahl (1971). Lotz and Morse cover seventy-two countries, developed and developing, for the period from 1963 to 1965. The tax comparison of expected and actual tax extraction by countries with similar economic bases provides us with a way to index the effectiveness of government performance.

Tax Effort as Political Measures

The model of political extraction needs to take into account the different economic and political circumstances of the developing and developed worlds.

Developing Countries

The main idea behind the RPE is that the political variables affecting extraction are to be found in the residuals from the regression of tax-effort equations. In the final model used in political analyses, the explanatory variables chosen to set the equation to determine the average tax capacity for developing countries were three: agricultural production as a percentage of GNP, exports as a percentage of GNP, and mineral production as a percentage of GNP. The results are as follows:

Model 1: Estimation of predicted political extraction in developing nations controlling for mining, agriculture, and exports.

$$\text{Tax/GDP} = \beta_0 + \beta_1(\text{Time}) + \beta_2(\text{Mining/GDP}) - \beta_3(\text{Agr/GDP})$$

$$+ \beta_4(\text{Exports/GNP})$$

The models were first tested by using them to adjust the overall national capabilities of governments faced with total international conflict. Efficient governments acted as multipliers of their own economic resources and assistance received from other countries; the reverse is true for inefficient governments (Organski and Kugler 1977, 1980; Kugler and Arbetman 1989; Kugler and Domke 1986).

Developed Societies

In developing countries, governments are driven to extract as much as their economic structures permit, while in developed societies, the political values of the society define the level of extraction. For example, Sweden chooses to provide education and health in the public sector, while in Japan these services are provided in the private sector. The lower level of taxation in Japan is not due to the inability of the government to extract more, but to societal preferences. Thus, for developed countries, the model is adjusted for expenditures as well as for revenues. Organski and Kugler (1977) experimented with several controls to account for differences in the tax ratio due to the different levels of public services provided by governments; the final model chose education, health, and defense expenditures as controls. See Organski and Kugler (1977) for details.

Model 2: Estimation of predicted political extraction for developed nations controlling for mining, productivity, exports, and health expenditures.

$$\text{Tax/GDP} = \beta_0 + \beta_1 (\text{Time}) + \beta_2(\text{Mining/GDP}) + \beta_3(\text{GDP/capita})$$

$$+ \beta_4(\text{Exports/GNP}) + \beta_5(\text{Health/GNP})$$

In addition, a number of models, each with different controls, were developed for tests that permitted one to observe how the measures performed when governments were (or were not) under stress and, also, dealing with the very special case of oil-producing countries.

The testing of models seeking to measure performance of government systems under great stress used, as independent variables, central government revenue, including "uncommitted" resources, and GNP/capita. Time was added to the model to indicate an increasing trend in the public sector (Kugler and Domke 1986, 49).

Political-capacity indices were developed to measure performance of governments under no stress. The most extensive tests were constructed in the critical policy areas of demography. The first test was built on the proposition that, if one controls for socioeconomic influences, the growth of political capacity should be found to have a substantial effect (downward) on vital rates. Socioeconomic models account for some 30 percent of the variance in the "demographic transition." Taking into account the effects of politics permitted to account for 50 percent of the variance (Organski et al. 1985). A test more immediately relevant to policy-making explored the effects of capacity of governments in Indian states on family planning programs. A strong connection was found between political capacity and success of family planning programs (Rouyer 1987).

A third model (Snider 1988) was developed to deal with oil producers. Vast deposits of oil greatly affect the task of rentier states in obtaining revenue. When oil production is the overwhelming source of government income, that fact must take this into account. This model seeks to set oil producers apart through three interactive terms: (1) a first-term multiplier, a dichotomous variable, high-income oil-exporting countries, multiplied by mineral production as a percentage of their GDP; (2) a dichotomous variable that captures members of the Gulf Cooperation Council (small Arab emirates and sheikdoms) by their mineral production as a percentage of GDP; and (3) a third term that singles out net oil-exporting governments less dependent on oil revenues for their income.

REFERENCES

Arbetman, M. 1990. "The Political Economy of Exchange Rate Fluctuations." Ph.D. Dissertation, Vanderbilt University.
Arbetman, M., and J. Kugler. 1989. "Exploring the Phoenix Factor with a Collective Goods Perspective." *Journal of Conflict Resolution*, 84–112.
Bahl, R.W. 1971. "A Regression Approach to Tax Effort and Tax Ratio Analysis." *IMF Staff Papers* 18 (November): 570–610.
Bergson, A. 1991. "The U.S.S.R. Before the Fall: How Poor and Why." *Journal of Economic Perspectives* 5 (4): 29–44.
Bueno de Mesquita, B., and D. Lalman. 1992. *War and Reason: Domestic and International Imperatives*. New Haven: Yale University Press.
Bueno de Mesquita, B., and F. Stokman, eds. In preparation. *From Twelve to One: Models of Policymaking in the European Community*.
Central Intelligence Agency. 1987, 1988, 1989, 1990, 1991. *The World Fact Book*. CIA.
———. 1991. "The Chinese Economy in 1990 and 1991: Uncertain Recovery." June. CIA.
Chelliah, R. J. 1971. "Trends in Taxation in Developing Countries." *IMF Staff Papers* 18 (July): 264–321.
Chelliah, R. J. et al. 1975. "Tax Ratios and Tax Effort in Developing Countries, 1969–1971." *IMF Staff Papers* 18 (March): 187–240.
Contini, B. 1979. *Lo Sviluppo di Un'Economia Parallela*. Milan: Edizioni di Comunita.
———. 1981. "Labor Market Segmentation and the Development of the Parallel Economy—The Italian Experience." *Oxford Economic Papers* 33: 401–12.
———. 1987. "The Second Economy of Italy." *Taxing and Spending* 3: 18–24.
Fua, G. 1976. *Occupazione e capacita productive: la realta Italiana*. Bologna: Il Mulino.
Gaetani-D'Aragona, G. 1981. "The Hidden Economy: Concealed Labor Markets in Italy." *Rivista Internazionale di Scienze Economiche e Commerciali* 3 (March).
Galtung, J. 1973. *The European Community: A Superpower in the Making*. Oslo: Univeersitetsfolaget.
Garrett, G. 1992. "International Cooperation and Institutional Choice." *International Organization* 46 (2): 533–60.
Gilpin, R. 1981. *War and Change in World Politics*. Cambridge: Cambridge University Press.
Haas, E. 1964. *Beyond the Nation State: Functionalism and International Organization*. Stanford: Stanford University Press.
Hoffman, S. 1982. "Reflections of the Nation-State in Western Europe Today." *Journal of Common Market Studies* 21 (1,2): 21–38.
Kennedy, P. 1987. *The Rise and Fall of the Great Powers*. New York: Random House.
Keohane, R. 1980. "The Theory of Hegemonic Stability and Change in International Regimes, 1967–1977." In *Change in the International System*, edited by O. Holsti et al. Boulder: Westview Press.
———. 1984. *After Hegemony: Cooperation and Discord in the World Political Economy*. Princeton: Princeton University Press.

Kugler, J., and M. Arbetman. 1989. "Choosing Among Measures of Power: A Review of the Empirical Record." In *Power in World Politics*, edited by M. Ward and R. Stoll, 49–78. Colorado: Lynn Reinner.

Kugler, J., and W. Domke. 1986. "Comparing the Strengths of Nations." *Comparative Political Studies* 19 (April): 39–69.

Kugler, J., and A.F.K. Organski. 1988. "The End of Hegemony?" *International Interactions* 15 (2): 113–28.

———. 1989. "The Power Transition Theory: A Retrospective and Prospective Evaluation." In *Handbook of War Studies*, edited by M. Midlarsky. Boston: Unwin Hyman.

Kuznets, S. 1971. *The Economic Growth of Nations*. Boston: Harvard University Press.

Lotz, J. R., and E. Morse. 1967. "Measuring Tax Effort in Developing Countries." *IMF Staff Papers* 14.

Maddison, A. 1989. *The World Economy in the Twentieth Century*. Paris: Organization for Economic Cooperation and Development.

Marer, P. 1985. *Dollar GNPs of the U.S.S.R. and Eastern Europe*. Baltimore: Johns Hopkins University Press.

Midlarsky, M. 1989. *Handbook of War Studies*. Boston: Unwin Hyman.

Mitrany, D. 1966. *A Working Peace System*. Chicago: Quadrangle Books.

Morgenthau, H. J. 1948. *Politics among Nations*. New York: Alfred A. Knopf.

Morrow, J., and W. Kim. In preparation. "When do Shifts in Power Lead to War?"

Organski, A.F.K. 1958. *World Politics*. New York: Alfred A. Knopf.

———. 1965. *The Stages of Political Development*. New York: Alfred A. Knopf.

———. 1993. "Europe and the Rest of the World." In *The History of Europe*, Vol. 1, edited by Perry Anderson, Maurice Aymard, Paul Bairoch, Walter Barberis, and Carlo Ginsburg. Turin, Italy: Einaudi Editore.

———. In preparation. *The Second American Century: The New International Order*.

Organski, A.F.K., and J. Kugler. 1977. "The Costs of Major Wars: The Phoenix Factor." *American Political Science Review* 71 (December): 1347–66.

———. 1980. *The War Ledger*. Chicago: University of Chicago Press.

Organski, A.F.K., J. Kugler, J.T. Johnson, Y. Cohen. 1985. *Births, Deaths, and Taxes: The Political and Demographic Transition*. Chicago: University of Chicago Press.

Ornstein, N.J., and M. Perlman, eds. 1991. *Political Power and Social Change*. Washington, DC: AEI Press.

Petenatti, P. "Illegal and Unrecorded Employment in Italy." *Economic Notes* 8 (1): 14–30.

Pinder, J. 1991. *European Community, The Building of a Union*. Oxford: Oxford University Press.

Rouyer, A. 1987. "Political Capacity and the Decline of Fertility in India." *American Political Science Review* 81, (2): 453–70.

Sbragia, A., ed. 1992. *Euro-Politics*. Washington, DC: Brookings Institution.

Singer, J. D., S. Bremer, and J. Stuckey. 1972. "Capability Distribution Uncertainty, and Major Power War, 1820–1965." In *Peace, War, and Numbers*, edited by B. M. Russett. Beverly Hills, CA: Sage.

Snider, L. W. 1988. "Political Strength, Economic Structure, and the Debt Servicing Potential of Developing Countries." *Comparative Political Studies* 20 (4) January: 455–87.

Tilly, C. 1975. *The Formation of National States in Western Europe*. Princeton: Princeton University Press.

Tokman, V. 1985. *Beyond the Crisis*. Geneva: PREALC International Labor Organization.

Wallace, H., ed. 1991. *The Wider Western Europe: Reshaping the EC/EFTA Relationship*. London: Pinter.

Conflict and Cooperation in International Economic Relations

Robert M. Stern

This chapter explores a number of conceptual and modeling issues that are germane to the analysis of conflict in international economic relations. The initial discussion is devoted to a number of issues involving conflict that have been treated in the theory of international trade. The section focuses on departures from the free-trade optimum that is the centerpiece of the theory of comparative advantage and the gains from trade. Also considered are conflict situations, stemming from departures from full employment and external balance, that figure importantly in international macroeconomic theory. In the following section, I draw on one of my research specialties, which is the use of computational models to analyze international economic relations and policies. In particular, I discuss the design and implementation of the Michigan Model of World Production and Trade, which is a multicountry and multisector general equilibrium model of the international trading system that my Michigan colleague, Alan V. Deardorff, and I have been working with since the mid-1970s. Four applications of the Michigan Model are discussed to illustrate how the model has been used to provide quantitative analysis of potentially conflictual and cooperative international economic actions and policies. The final section offers some concluding remarks.

Conceptual and Modeling Issues in the Analysis of Conflict in International Economic Relations

The Theory of Comparative Advantage and the Gains from Trade

In the simplest version of the theory of comparative advantage and the gains from trade—the central focus of international trade theory—it is assumed that there are two industries located in each of two countries that exist in isolation (autarky), and there is perfect competition in all markets for goods and factors of production. The productivity of factors (e.g., labor and capital) employed in the industries in each country is assumed to be different for unspecified technological reasons, which means that the relative prices of the two goods will be different under conditions of autarky. It is this difference in autarky prices that gives rise to the possibility of international specialization and mutually beneficial trade. Thus, if trade is permitted to occur, each country will specialize in the production and export of the good in which it has the greatest comparative advantage or least comparative disadvantage compared to the other country. This means that factors of production in each country will be shifted toward the country's export industry and away from what will become its import-competing industry. Factors of production are assumed to be perfectly mobile between industries within each country, but not to move between countries.

The assumption of perfect competition guarantees that there will be optimal use of factors of production since firms are not able to control the price at which they sell their output and will maximize their profits by simply equating their costs at the margin with the given market price. Individual consumers are assumed to have given preferences and to act rationally in making consumption decisions with respect to the market prices that are given to them and subject to a budget constraint imposed by the size of their incomes. As mentioned, factors of production will move frictionlessly between industries as firms expand or contract output. Given the assumption of no barriers to the entry and exit of firms and the domestic movement of factors, this means that the role of government is designed primarily to foster competition and to maintain the social order. It will be evident that this "ideal" state of affairs will emerge as firms and consumers pursue their self-interest. It is as if there were an "invisible hand" guiding the process.

The concept and ideal of free trade have remained at the core of international trade theory for more than two centuries. What is interesting for our purpose here is that unfettered international specialization and exchange will be welfare-maximizing and that economic conflict does not appear, therefore, to be an issue. This should not be taken to mean, however, that international trade theory ends at this point, for this is certainly not the case. Rather, a great deal of attention has been devoted in the past half-century or more to the theoretical analysis of departures from the free-trade optimum. International economic conflict figures importantly in several of these cases that involve efforts by nations to engage in exploitative behavior that will improve their welfare at the expense of other nations. Let us turn then to consider the issues involved in analyzing various departures from the free trade optimum. (The discussion that follows is drawn in part from Deardorff and Stern 1987a.)

Departures from the Free-Trade Optimum

National Monopoly Power and the Optimal Tariff

The idealized assumptions of the classic argument for free trade imply the optimality of free trade only for the world as a whole. For individual countries, the optimality of free trade requires the additional assumption that the country is too small to have any influence, through its policies, over the prices at which it trades. Without this assumption, free trade is not optimal from a national perspective, and instead there exists an optimal degree of government intervention in trade, known as the optimal tariff, that works by turning the country's terms of trade in its favor.

This argument is sometimes thought to require that the country in question be large and therefore to apply only to such large, industrialized countries as the United States. However, the size that is important is not the size of the country as a whole but rather its share of world trade in markets in which it exports and imports. Since many countries tend to specialize their exports in a fairly small range of goods—as the theory of comparative advantage predicts they should—even quite small countries may have enough market power over the prices of their exports for the optimal-tariff argument to apply.

The optimal-tariff argument has the important feature that it involves a benefit for the intervening country only at the expense of the country's trading partners. Indeed, since free trade is optimal for the world as a whole, it must be true that the rest of the world loses more than the tariff-levying country gains. It should be evident that a country that attempts to take advantage of its monopoly power in trade will create a situation of conflict with its major trading partners. The possibility of retaliation thus looms large in this setting, and it is likely that all countries will lose if they simultaneously pursue this kind of policy. This suggests that there may be complicated and perhaps unsolvable strategic issues that will arise when one or more countries attempt to exercise national monopoly power in foreign trade. But the more that governments realize the potentially damaging effects of optimal-tariff intervention and retaliation, the more likely they might be to avoid taking such measures in the first place. Of course, this does not mean that national governments will always recognize the potential losses from their actions, in which case the world will be made worse off.

"Second-Best" Arguments for Government Intervention

A crucial assumption underlying the classic gains-from-trade proposition is that everything within the domestic economy is working properly: all domestic markets are perfectly competitive, prices and wages adjust freely so that markets clear, and private and social costs and benefits coincide so that there are no positive or negative externalities or spillovers that arise in production or consumption. If any of the foregoing conditions fails to hold, there exists a "domestic distortion," and the first-best optimal results of free trade are no longer assured. There may be grounds, therefore, for government intervention to correct domestic distortions and thereby restore the first-best optimum.

What is interesting and important here is that government intervention in trade may not be the best policy to use when there are domestic distortions. Suppose, for example, that firms are producing an insufficient amount of a good that confers a positive external benefit on society. An import tariff could be used to encourage domestic production, but this would distort consumer choice and reduce welfare because of the higher domestic price involved. In this circumstance, a production subsidy would be the best policy to use since it would lead firms to increase their output of the good that confers positive social benefit while leaving consumers free to consume at undistorted market prices. The optimal or first-best policy is the one that addresses the original distortion most directly. A tariff is thus second best compared to a subsidy. By introducing two distortions rather than one, trade intervention may succeed in solving one problem but only at the same time that it causes another.[1]

Similar examples are rife in the theory of protection. The classic example is the "infant-industry" argument, where a tariff is said to protect a young industry while it learns to be efficient. The assumption here is that some market failure—such as an imperfection in the loan market or the impossibility of keeping new technical knowledge from being copied—makes it impossible for competitive firms to take advantage of what would otherwise be a profitable opportunity. A tariff or other import restriction can therefore be used temporarily to make the operation profitable even in the short run while the learning process is under way. Naturally, though, the success of such a policy depends crucially on a correct diagnosis of which industries offer the potential for such improvement over time. Also, it may be difficult politically to remove protection once it has been put in place.

As in the case of the production externality discussed above, the infant-industry argument may be valid in the sense that a tariff may be beneficial. But it is also true that some other policy would be superior. Once again a production subsidy, equal in size to the tariff, would yield the same benefits to producers as the tariff, without causing the additional costly distortion of consumer choice. Even better might be a policy that subsidizes or guarantees loans to the industry, if the capital market was the real source of the distortion, or a policy that permits firms to appropriate technology if that was the problem.

---

1. A. Deardorff (Deardorff and Stern 1987a, 39) has likened trade policy to "doing acupuncture with a fork: no matter how carefully you insert one prong, the other is likely to do damage."

Many other arguments for intervention can similarly be traced to the presumption of a distortion somewhere in the domestic economy. But what should be stressed in all of these cases is the need for a correct diagnosis of the distortions at issue and the point that they could be better dealt with by means other than trade policies. While this kind of reasoning is generally accepted by most international trade economists, it is not by any means accepted by practical policymakers who are in the business of trying to make only marginal improvements in the economic environment. If they can find some feasible policy that will work, they are unlikely to worry that some other policy might have worked better.

Thus, it may be argued that first-best policies are politically unacceptable and, therefore, that trade interference, though only second best in economic theory, may be first best in political reality. This may be true, but it is a dangerous argument for several reasons. First, if trade intervention is politically more acceptable than domestic taxes and subsidies, it is probably because the electorate has less understanding of its true effects. If the public would not approve a direct subsidy to an industry, for whatever reason, then that fact should perhaps be taken as evidence that protection of that industry through trade intervention is also socially undesirable because of the consumption distortions involved. Second, it is always a very difficult empirical question whether the benefits of offsetting a domestic distortion exceed the costs that arise from the second distortion caused by trade intervention. While it is very difficult to make precise calculations of the costs and benefits of different policies, there is nonetheless substantial empirical evidence that suggests that the net effects of trade intervention are detrimental to welfare. A strong case can thus be made for using first-best policies. A final and important consideration here is that reliance on first-best policies to correct domestic distortions avoids the potential for conflict between nations that trade intervention entails.

Trade Intervention in Imperfectly Competitive Markets

Recognizing that many markets, domestic and international, are imperfectly competitive, growing attention has been directed in recent years to analysis of trade and trade policy in an imperfectly competitive world. It is clear that the classical case for the gains from trade does not apply directly in such a world. However, we do not yet have a clear understanding of the alternatives. Instead we have several suggestive ideas about the role of trade policy in particular situations that have not yet been established with any generality.

The first such idea is probably also the most important and is also simple. If a domestic market is not competitive, competition can be fostered by removing barriers to trade. Often a major reason that domestic markets are dominated by a small number of producers is that these producers are protected from foreign competition by tariffs or other trade restrictions. If given a choice, producers for the domestic market will opt for quantitative import restrictions, since these increase the profit that can be made by monopoly pricing in the domestic market. The trade policy that will best improve this situation does not require any subtle effort to offset the effects of monopoly power. Instead a simple opening of markets to free international trade will remove the market power itself and restore the benefits of competition. A domestic market with only a few domestic firms may, therefore, approximate free competition if those few firms must compete with a larger number of foreign producers. The removal of trade barriers in these circumstances will accordingly remove a source of international conflict and promote national and world welfare.

Unfortunately, there is sometimes no assurance that even worldwide free trade will confer the benefits of perfect competition in all markets. Some products are not tradable or are not readily available as substitutes from abroad. In addition, the world market itself may be imperfectly competitive, due perhaps to the historical dominance of a few firms or the nature of the product. Many products in today's international trade seem more and more to lend themselves to product differentiation and the use of large-scale and aggressive marketing techniques. In such cases, while free trade still increases competition, the nature of that competition is sufficiently imperfect that the benefits from it are no longer assured.

Two issues need to be addressed here. First, to what extent are our earlier arguments undermined by the persistence of imperfect competition even under free trade? In particular, is it still true that trade intervention constitutes only a second-best means of dealing with domestic distortions? Second, do imperfect market structures give rise to any new arguments for trade intervention other than the traditional ones?

The first question cannot be answered definitively since there is no single model of imperfect competition that can provide the basis for a conclusive proof. But, as shown in Deardorff and Stern (1987a, 43–44), it seems likely that the general principle favoring a domestic policy rather than trade intervention to remove a distortion would continue to hold in cases of imperfect competition.

As for the second question, free trade may fail to ensure perfect competition even in traded goods if world markets are not perfectly competitive. If world markets are monopolistic or controlled by a small number of oligopolistic firms and excess profits are being made at the expense of either foreign or domestic consumers, this suggests that trade intervention may benefit a country if it is able to capture a larger share of these profits. This idea has considerable appeal. Certainly, if you must be exploited, it is better politically to be exploited by domestic residents than by foreigners. Even economically, there may be a valid case for trade intervention.

Consider two possible cases (Deardorff and Stern 1987a, 46–50). The first involves an effort to capture a portion of foreign monopoly profits by means of an import tariff. In this case, the importing country gains from the tariff only if the price paid to the foreign monopolist falls. The tariff works here much like the optimal tariff mentioned above insofar as it improves the importing country's terms of trade. But, as before, a situation of conflict is created and there is no guarantee that this profit-seeking policy will succeed if the foreign government retaliates by taking measures on its own to prevent or offset the shifting of profits abroad.

A second case involves the use of trade intervention to alter the outcomes of "strategic games" played by imperfectly competitive firms so as to increase the profits they can share with their sponsoring governments. In effect, the government uses its policy to precommit firms to behavior that would otherwise appear to be—and be known by their competitors to be—suboptimal. It turns out that the theoretical models used in generating such results are rather fragile conceptually so that changes in key assumptions can be shown to negate or even reverse the conclusion that profit shifting is possible. Furthermore, this case for intervention is once again exploitative and, therefore, may give rise to retaliation. Thus, if both governments were to try to play this particular game, both countries would be worse off. Again, to the extent that governments recognize this and desist from exploitative measures, the scope for international conflict is reduced.

Countervailing and Strategic Intervention
However one may feel about the case in economic theory for free trade, the fact remains that countries do make extensive use of policies that interfere with trade, perhaps for the reasons that have been discussed. This raises the question of whether the cases for and against intervention are altered at all for countries whose trading partners use such policies.

There seem to be two distinct rationales for responding to the trade policies of other countries. One is to try to neutralize, offset, or countervail the presumed adverse effects of a foreign country's trade policies. The other is to try strategically to discourage the use of such policies by foreign countries by threatening, or actually implementing, policies that will affect them adversely. The difference between these two approaches is the following. In the former case the policy is to be chosen with a view to benefiting the domestic economy directly. In the latter case, since the purpose of the policy is to alter behavior abroad, a policy might be chosen in spite of having adverse effects domestically.

Countervailing intervention makes sense only if it benefits the domestic economy on its own account. It is not enough that it partially undoes the effect of the foreign-country trade policy to which it responds. The familiar example of this use of trade policy is the national use, sanctioned by GATT, the

General Agreement on Tariffs and Trade, of countervailing duties to offset the effect of foreign export subsidies. This countervailing policy normally does benefit the country using it, but only to the extent that the importing country is large enough to improve its terms of trade by imposing the duty. Where this is the case, the country could have benefited from a duty even had there been no foreign subsidy, assuming that it could have avoided retaliation. The question then is whether the fact of the subsidy, together perhaps with the official sanctioning of a countervailing duty, reduces the likelihood of retaliation. Only in this case does it appear that the use of a countervailing duty is a responsible policy in a competitive environment.

If instead we have an imperfectly competitive world, subsidies may be used to give a country's producers a competitive edge in a foreign market. In this case, a countervailing duty of some sort may be an optimal response on the part of the importing country's government as it tries to balance the gain from cheaper subsidized imports against the loss of monopoly profit earned by its domestic firms. While this is a possibility, it suggests the more general question of whether countervailing measures may be justified as a means of discouraging the use of export subsidies in the first place. This takes us into the topic of strategic intervention.

We have seen that there are a number of arguments suggesting that trade intervention may benefit one country at the expense of others. Many of these arguments, relating especially to national monopoly power and use of the optimal tariff, have long been familiar to international trade economists. But interest in the analysis of trade under conditions of imperfect competition has seemed to expand the scope for strategic intervention and in turn has led to new interest in the strategic issues of how countries may use intervention to exploit others and to keep from being exploited themselves. For the purposes of this chapter, it is most appropriate to focus attention on the question of how policymakers should act in a world of exploitative trade intervention.

In simple terms, what we have is the classic Prisoners' Dilemma game, in which each player has an incentive to act at the other's expense, and both lose if both act. Although it is clearly optimal for them collectively to refrain from acting (from intervening in trade), each has an incentive to depart from that optimum if it is ever reached. What is interesting, according to analyses by trade theorists such as Thursby and Jensen (1983) and political scientists such as Axelrod (1984), is that *the greater the perceived likelihood that a government expects its trade intervention to be retaliated against, the closer the solution will lie to free trade*. This suggests that, although trade intervention itself is harmful for reasons already discussed, it may nonetheless be desirable that countries expect intervention by other countries in response to intervention they themselves may undertake.

Alternatively, one could attempt to pursue negotiated solutions to games such as the foregoing. Such negotiations, however, pose the well-known problem of enforcing whatever agreement is reached. On the other hand, the incentives to enter into such negotiations are strong, even if one has no intention of abiding by their outcome. It is, therefore, not surprising that the trade policy community has managed to keep such negotiations going during a large part of post–World War II history.

Trade Intervention for Foreign Policy Reasons

The strategic uses of trade intervention just discussed were focused specifically on influencing analogous policies abroad. But trade intervention is sometimes also used as a means of influencing foreign policies that have nothing to do with trade. Because countries depend on and gain from trade, policies that interfere with trade can serve as weapons and can be used for a variety of aims. Still, one must ask whether trade intervention can succeed in changing foreign country policies and, if so, whether it is worth the cost.

To take the second issue first, trade as a political weapon makes sense only if it is capable of inflicting relatively great harm abroad compared to any disruption it causes at home. For a small country this would clearly not be the case, but for a large country like the United States, it does seem likely that we could do rather severe damage to at least some of our smaller trading partners at relatively little obvious cost to ourselves. But one must be very careful here, especially because markets often work far better than anyone expects. Even the United States might find that long-run effects of its policies will go against it in ways that would be hard to predict. When foreign markets and foreign suppliers are lost, either because the United States accidentally hurts them more than intended or because they look elsewhere for a more certain trading environment, the U.S. claim that it was only manipulating trade to promote the general welfare will fall on deaf ears.

There is also reason to doubt that even draconian trade policies such as embargoes can ever be very effective in changing the behavior of foreign governments and their constituencies. Trade can have powerful effects. But when used as a weapon, it seems more likely to generate resistance, rather than fear, in the hearts of its victims. The world's considerable experience with the use of embargoes does not suggest that they have been particularly successful in drawing concessions from those they were intended to influence. On the other hand, it is conceivable that trade policy might be more successful in influencing policies abroad if it were oriented toward providing positive rather than negative incentives in the political sphere. This is certainly worth exploring further.

International Factor Movements

The theory of comparative advantage and the gains from trade assumes that factors of production move costlessly between industries within countries but do not move internationally. While this assumption helps to clarify the role of trade and its effect on the returns to factors of production, it is, of course, unrealistic in view of the often substantial movements of labor and capital from one country to another that in fact occur.

For our purpose here, it is movements of real capital rather than financial capital that are important. Such movements of real capital constitute foreign direct investment (FDI) by international firms. There is a large body of theory of the determinants of FDI, but its main motivation derives from the apparent profitability involved in the internal control by the parent company of the operations of foreign affiliates. There are significant gains in economic efficiency and consumer welfare in both investing and host countries that result from FDI. But in some circumstances there may be costs as well, and conflicts may emerge as governments seek to regulate the investment activities of international firms. In host countries, for example, disputes may arise if it is believed that foreign firms can charge monopoly prices and thus earn excessive profits that they then transfer abroad in large measure. There may be complaints that indigenous workers are not given adequate opportunity to acquire skills and training, and that the host country is held back because it cannot acquire and develop foreign technologies on its own. It may be believed, furthermore, that foreign firms undermine the efficacy of host-country economic policies and maybe even threaten host-country political sovereignty. As for investing countries, they may have their own concerns about the loss of jobs and technological benefits, including spillover effects, as operations are transferred abroad. Strategic and national defense considerations may also be important.

Population movements between countries have been taking place for centuries for both economic and political reasons. These movements have been subject to varying degrees of control and restriction, depending upon the historical circumstances and countries involved. It is generally accepted that host countries maintain the right to limit immigration, whereas countries that attempt to constrain emigration especially for political reasons may be subject to international criticism. Just as in the case of FDI, the international movement of labor may be beneficial to both the sending and receiving countries insofar as it increases economic efficiency and welfare. But there may be costs here as well. The sending country may lose as its stock of human capital is diminished, particularly since those who leave may be among the most skilled and productive workers. Offsetting effects here would include somewhat higher wages for those that remain and the receipt of remittances from those who move abroad. In the receiving country, immigration may displace domestic workers and result in lower wages, and there may be added social costs depending upon the use that immigrants make of the available social infrastructure.

It is evident then that FDI and the international movement of labor may provide the basis for conflict between nations, apart from the conflicts that may arise as countries attempt to deal with the various departures from the free-trade optimum that have been discussed. The international community has not developed mechanisms and institutions for dealing with problems posed by FDI and the international movement of workers. Policies here remain the province of individual nations.

Departures from Full Employment and External Balance

The standard model of comparative advantage and the gains from trade assumes that all factors of production are continuously employed, given that markets for goods, services, and factors are perfectly competitive and function smoothly. Any unemployment of factors that occurs is treated as if it were a domestic distortion arising from difficulties in adjustment, especially in the short or medium run or because of the existence of market imperfections that act as a barrier to entry or exit of factors in particular sectors. As discussed, the first-best policy to deal with distortions is a domestic tax or subsidy that is directed at the source of the distortion. Trade policy will generally be second best or even worse than second best because of the production and consumption costs involved.

This same conclusion applies at the macroeconomic level. Departures from full employment may occur for a variety of reasons. For example, there may be exogenous real shocks due to an unexpected increase in oil prices or some other type of supply disruption. It is also possible that there may be unemployment or inflationary pressures because of cyclical fluctuations in economic activity. Such fluctuations may originate domestically or be transmitted from other countries via induced changes in imports and exports and international capital movements. Finally, changes in monetary or fiscal policies may in themselves constitute a disturbance that will affect aggregate employment and involve international transmission effects working through changes in foreign trade and capital flows.

These types of disturbances can have profound effects on aggregate employment, prices, the balance of payments, and exchange rates, and, accordingly, give rise to conflictual situations internationally as countries seek to offset the domestic consequences of the disturbances or to shield themselves from the adverse transmission of foreign influences. Trade intervention seems obviously a suboptimal way of dealing with these macroeconomic disturbances when the underlying problems stem from difficulties of adjustment in the markets for goods and services, labor, and foreign exchange.

International macroeconomic issues and problems have been analyzed at length over the years. To relate these issues and problems to the subject of this chapter, it may be helpful to distinguish between the defensive and offensive uses of policies in trying to cope with various types of macroeconomic disturbances and interactions. For example, if a country were to impose import restrictions to raise the level of employment and improve its current account balance, this could be considered an offensive policy since it would represent an effort by one country to improve its position at the expense of another. A currency devaluation designed for the same purpose would work similarly, since it would improve conditions in the home country while at the same time worsen conditions abroad. Policies designed to improve a country's macroeconomic performance through changes in exports and imports thus appear to be exploitative, and, to the extent that other countries may respond in kind, output and employment will be reduced at home and abroad. By the same line of reasoning, the defensive use of macroeconomic policies may appear to be justified if a country wishes to shield itself from the effects of foreign-induced changes in international trade and capital movements.

There is a very interesting and important lesson of macroeconomic policy that has emerged from the foregoing theoretical reasoning that is similar to our earlier point concerning first-best policies. The difference here arises from the international-transmission effects noted. Thus, suppose two countries are both experiencing a recession or inflation. In either case, the optimal policy for each country would be to undertake domestic expansionary or contractionary macroeconomic policies designed to deal with the unemployment or inflationary pressures. If one country were to use trade or exchange-rate policies, this would be exploitative since it would exaggerate the other country's problems.

One can also imagine situations in which one country may be experiencing a recession and another country experiencing inflationary pressure. Depending on the type of exchange-rate system in effect, this may or may not result in a conflict situation. It will if exchange rates are fixed, since expansionary domestic policies in the country with the recession will worsen the country's current-account balance and have opposite effects abroad, and conversely if the country with inflation were to implement contractionary domestic policies. This problem does not arise, at least in theory, if the exchange rate is flexible, since the exchange-rate movement should help to stabilize each economy.

In any event, the point is that there might be conditions when international harmony will be obtained by nations introducing macroeconomic policies that are targeted on domestic objectives. But international disharmony may ensue if countries use trade or exchange-rate measures for dealing with domestic problems or if countries introduce incorrect domestic macroeconomic policies that work in a destabilizing manner internationally. In these instances, it may be desirable accordingly for countries to attempt to cooperate by coordinating their policy actions rather than going it alone.

A Computational Modeling Approach to Analyzing
Multilateral Trading Arrangements and Policies

The preceding discussion was intended to clarify the issues that arise in the analysis of conflict between nations when there are departures from the free-trade optimum or departures from full employment and external balance. We now turn to one line of applied economic research—computational modeling—that has been used extensively to investigate a variety of important issues of potential policy conflicts and cooperation in the global trading system. The focus here will be on the Michigan Model of World Production and Trade.

The Michigan Model was developed initially in the mid-1970s to analyze the economic effects of the Tokyo Round of Multilateral Trade Negotiations in the GATT. It is a computer-based general-equilibrium model of the world trading system, providing sectoral detail for the eighteen major industrialized countries, sixteen major developing countries, and the rest-of-world. Complete details on the theoretical structure and equations of the model, data, and solution procedure are given in Deardorff and Stern (1986, 1990a).

Of the many applications of the Michigan Model that have been carried out over the years, four have been chosen for discussion here. These include: (1) analysis of unilateral U.S. introduction of tariffs coupled with defensive responses of other major trading countries; (2) safeguards policies to deal with import disruptions; (3) evaluation of alternative negotiating options in the Uruguay Round of Multilateral Trade Negotiations; and (4) comparison of the employment effects of a unilateral U.S. embargo and a multilateral embargo by all major Western trading countries on the export and import of armaments.

Tariffs and Defensive Responses

One important source of conflict in the international economic system in the 1980s stems from the disruptive effects of the Reagan Administration's monetary and fiscal policy mix on the U.S. foreign sector. At the political level in the United States, it is probably understood, though not always acknowledged readily in public statements, that the U.S. foreign-trade imbalance is a macroeconomic phenomenon related to the U.S. budget imbalance. Yet, because a political stalemate has developed over whether to raise taxes, reduce expenditures, or both, to reduce the budget deficit, emphasis has shifted instead to trying to correct the U.S. trade deficit. Thus, in 1985 and 1986 especially, a spate of legislative proposals designed to assist trade-impacted sectors of the economy were introduced in Congress. Several of these proposals involved the imposition of a general tariff surcharge on U.S. imports from all sources as well as a surcharge on imports from countries with large bilateral trade surpluses vis-à-vis the United States.

U.S. legislation actually condones the use of import restrictions under certain specified conditions, although, if the United States were to act unilaterally to impose an import surcharge, it would technically be in violation of its obligations under the GATT not to increase its statutory tariff rates. It would also be subject to foreign retaliation under GATT provisions.

Circumstances might arise, of course, in which the United States did decide to act unilaterally. To investigate this issue, the Michigan Model was used to determine how our major trading partners might respond to the imposition of a unilateral U.S. import surcharge. The alternative responses of our trading partners include: (1) passive acceptance of the U.S. import surcharge; (2) defensive response designed to neutralize the adverse effects of the surcharge; and (3) retaliation in kind, either on a multilateral basis or with reference to all or selected categories of U.S. exports to the country.

As described in Deardorff and Stern (1987b, 1990a), the modeling procedure followed was first to assume that the United States imposed a general import surcharge of 10 percent on imports from all sources, and that initially there were no changes of any kind implemented abroad. This would indicate what might be expected if there were passive acceptance of the U.S. action. It would also be indicative of the initial effects of the import surcharge prior to any reaction abroad. Assuming that our major trading partners had certain objectives that they wished to attain with respect to avoiding worsening of their terms of trade, balance of trade, and aggregate employment, the model was used to calculate how each country might be affected by the surcharge. Further calculations were then carried out to determine how large a surcharge would be required in each country in order to undo the adverse effects that the U.S. surcharge might have.

The results are interesting insofar as six industrialized countries—Australia, Austria, Canada, Finland, Norway, and Switzerland—showed a zero response. This is because a U.S. surcharge might affect them positively or because their own responses to a U.S. surcharge might prove detrimental to them. But what is also interesting is that the results suggest that these countries might not be spared damage since they could be affected adversely by actions that other countries might take in response to the U.S. action. The results further suggested that Japan, Germany, Italy, and the United Kingdom would be adversely affected by the U.S. action and might feel compelled to introduce countermeasures to defend themselves. But the results showed the defensive responses of these countries to be rather complex because a given country might not know or be able to anticipate the effects of the responses of all other countries.

Of course, it would be most desirable for the international economic system if the United States were to avoid introducing an import surcharge in the first place. But what this modeling exercise revealed was that some of our trading partners would be spared damage from a U.S. import surcharge because the main effects would be felt by other countries. And, further, for those countries that might be adversely affected, it would be difficult for them to frame an appropriate response unless they could determine the outcome of the complex interactions affecting all of the major countries in the world trading system. In any event, since a retaliatory process would make things worse for all those nations directly involved, this could reinforce the incentive for international cooperation.

Safeguards Policies

Nations may at times be subjected to a sudden surge of imports that can be disruptive to firms and workers in an import-competing industry. It is in recognition of the possible adjustment problems that can occur in these circumstances that safeguards or escape-clause arrangements have become part of national trade laws and have been incorporated into the Articles of the GATT. While these formal arrangements have unfortunately been bypassed by the use of other means of "administered protection" in many importing countries, it remains the case that an import surge routinely gives rise to some sort of protective response in the affected country or countries. What is interesting for our purpose here is that policy responses to import surges are often implemented without much consideration of their effects on other trading countries. Since safeguards issues were to be addressed in the Uruguay Round of Multilateral Trade Negotiations, which was launched in 1986, it appeared worthwhile to examine the implications, both for the world economy and for the protected industries, of the systematic use of safeguards policies of various types.

The Michigan Model was used to analyze the effects of alternative safeguards policies that might be undertaken by the United States and other industrialized countries in response to an unexpected surge in the imports of clothing from developing countries. This particular experiment was chosen in light of the crucial importance especially to the newly industrializing countries (NICs) of continuing access to the import markets of the advanced countries. The objective was to explore the general equilibrium effects of alternative safeguards policies across both industries and countries, taking into account the possibility that an import surge is likely to affect not just one country but many and, consequently, that safeguards actions will be pursued by many importing countries simultaneously.

The procedure followed was to assume that there was a 10 percent increase in clothing imports in all of the major industrialized countries at the same time. The model was then solved for the effects of this import surge on trade and employment in all sectors for the thirty-four countries covered in the model. The results of this solution were then used to construct a variety of safeguards policies responding to the import surge, based on the effects that the surge was calculated to have in the absence of any policy response. The policy responses were then introduced into the model together with the import surge itself in order to calculate the effects of the two together. Eight alternative policy responses to the import surge were explored, including: (1) maintenance of existing quotas on clothing imports in all industrialized countries; (2) a unilateral U.S. tariff on clothing imports; (3) a unilateral U.S. quota on clothing imports; (4) a multilateral tariff by all industrialized importing countries; (5) a multilateral import quota; (6) a unilateral U.S. production subsidy to domestic clothing producers; (7) a multilateral production subsidy to domestic clothing producers; and (8) a multilateral subsidy to keep employment unchanged in all industries.

What is interesting about the results is that the use of import protection—tariffs and quotas—turned out to be questionable even when practiced by only one country, since it shifted the burden of adjustment onto other countries. Furthermore, when protective safeguards actions were assumed to be taken by countries multilaterally, then even the beneficial effects in the protecting countries were undermined to some extent. This was especially the case since the protective policies served to raise the prices of production inputs in the protecting countries, thus having adverse effects on employment and output in export industries and perhaps also in the clothing industry itself. It was not clear, therefore, that the industrialized countries as a group would gain collectively from using trade policy measures for safeguards purposes. In contrast, when domestic policies were assumed to be used in dealing with the assumed import surge, they were noticeably more effective in limiting the decline in employment. This was particularly the case for the multilateral production subsidy—policy 7 above—which seemed capable of achieving what trade policies could not: a marked improvement in the employment situation in all industrialized countries.

The results of the Michigan Model experiments thus suggest that unilateral safeguards measures may shift adjustment burdens onto other countries and that trade policy measures may be particularly detrimental to the importing countries' own interests. Unilateral policy responses to an import surge appear to be undesirable therefore from the standpoint of the international economic system. The safeguards policy that appears to work best in terms of mitigating employment declines due to a broad import surge is when all the industrializing countries act together to subsidize domestic output. In designing a safeguards code in the GATT negotiations, the message of this research is that it might be desirable to rule out tariff and quota measures and instead to specify that domestic subsidies be used. This conclusion, it should be noted, is consistent with the central theoretical message of our earlier discussion that the use of trade policy measures is generally suboptimal. While it is not clear at the time of writing (February 1993) how the Uruguay Round negotiations on safeguards will turn out, it may well be that a safeguards code will permit the use of trade policies as well as domestic measures. If countries were then to use trade polices for safeguards purposes, this could have undesirable international consequences for the reasons that the aforementioned research has suggested.

Negotiating Options in the Uruguay Round of Multilateral Trade Negotiations

The Uruguay Round is the eighth round of multilateral negotiations that has been held under GATT auspices since the end of World War II. Because there are many different trade-liberalization options available to individual countries and groups of countries, it is important to consider the potential economic effects of these options in order to help define national interests and to suggest ways in which tradeoffs may be chosen among the different items on the negotiating agenda. The Michigan Model is well suited for this type of computational analysis. As mentioned above, it was originally developed to analyze negotiating options in the Tokyo Round negotiations. In this connection, the Senate Finance Committee of the U.S. Congress commissioned Deardorff and Stern (1979) to use the Michigan Model to evaluate the actual offers that were negotiated in the Tokyo Round by the United States and other major countries. This was done as part of the Committee's mandate to seek independent and impartial studies of the possible economic effects of the negotiations as an input into the Congressional deliberations on whether to ratify the changes in tariffs and other policies that the U.S. had agreed to implement.

Deardorff and Stern (1989b, 1990a, 1990b) have since addressed the issue of multilateral trade liberalization again by analyzing several different scenarios pertinent to the Uruguay Round. The scenarios were chosen to illustrate what might be expected to occur if it were possible to eliminate completely existing tariffs and nontariff barriers (NTBs) in the world's major trading countries. Of course, the scenarios chosen for analysis do not in actuality correspond to what was being proposed in the Uruguay Round or what might in fact actually be implemented. Nonetheless, we believed that the modeling results would be useful in helping the United States and other countries choose among the available options that would best serve their own national interests and in developing a consensus about which options might be mutually beneficial for the various countries participating in the negotiations.

The scenarios analyzed were as follows:

1. Elimination of all post–Tokyo Round (1987) tariffs in the eighteen major industrialized countries.
2. Elimination of NTBs in the major industrialized countries (excluding agriculture and textiles and clothing).
3. Elimination of domestic agricultural-production subsidies in the major industrialized countries.
4. Elimination of NTBs on textiles and clothing imports in the major industrialized countries.
5. Elimination of all tariffs and NTBs in the major industrialized countries (scenarios 1 + 2 + 3 + 4).

The results of each of these scenarios are too detailed to be reported here, but some of the overall conclusions can be mentioned. For scenario 5, which involves elimination of all existing barriers by the major industrialized countries, it was estimated that world exports would rise by around $70 billion, which was an increase of 5.1 percent above the 1980 level. U.S. exports would rise by an estimated $9 billion. The number of U.S. workers who would have to change jobs was an estimated 285,000, which was only 0.29 percent of the U.S. labor force. On a sectoral level, U.S. agriculture showed the largest estimated increase in employment, of about 2 percent of the 1980 agricultural labor force. Employment in most other major sectors varied by much smaller percentages, depending upon the particular negotiating option chosen for eliminating tariffs and NTBs. Given the structure of the Michigan Model and the different scenarios noted, it was possible to calculate employment effects by sector for each country in the model. These results disclosed several instances in a number of countries in which there could be considerable dislocations in labor markets if the trade liberalization were to take place all at once. This suggested the desirability of phasing in any liberalization over an extended period in an effort to mitigate any adjustment costs that might occur.

While there were instances of sizable net employment changes at the industry level in individual countries, the results also suggested that there were many industries in which the estimated employment changes were relatively small for the different scenarios analyzed. The reason for the small results is that the reductions in tariffs were small, reflecting the fact the tariff rates had already been reduced appreciably as the result of the seven previous rounds of GATT negotiations. Also, the tariff equivalents of the NTBs were on the whole fairly small. In addition to the scenarios noted above, experiments were run involving the assumed removal of tariffs in the major developing countries. In all previous GATT rounds, these countries were exempted from having to reduce their tariffs. However, in the past decade especially, the East Asian NICs have come under increasing pressure to reduce their import restrictions. We thus calculated what might happen if trade barriers were to be removed in all of the major industrialized and developing countries. The results suggested an even larger increase in world exports than the 5.1 percent increase noted above for scenario 5 and, further, employment reductions in some sectors might be smaller because of the broader liberalization involved.

Of course, how the United States and other participants actually behave in the Uruguay Round will depend on how they view their interests as related to both the reduction of tariffs and NTBs and the negotiation of rules governing other items on the negotiating agenda, especially safeguards policies, international transactions in services, and protection of rights to intellectual property (e.g., patents, copyrights, and trademarks). In any event, the types of calculations that have been made using the Michigan Model should be helpful in identifying the sectors in the United States and other countries that are potential beneficiaries from greater liberalization as well as sectors that could be vulnerable to the increased competitive pressures that liberalization may engender. Such information may, therefore, reinforce international cooperation and the accomplishments of the GATT on important matters of trade policy in the international economic system.

Unilateral and Multilateral Arms Trade Embargo

A question that has often been discussed is how important international trade in armaments is to employment and output in individual industries in the United States and other major countries and how these industries might be affected if this trade were to be stopped. This question is obviously pertinent should it ever be possible to effect unilateral or multilateral reductions of trade in armaments directly or via reductions in military spending.

Grobar, Stern, and Deardorff (1989) have used the Michigan Model to investigate the importance of international trade in armaments in the major Western industrialized and developing countries. For this purpose, a data set of the exports and imports of armaments for 1980 was constructed for the thirty-four Western countries included in the model. The trade was disaggregated into military ships, aircraft, communications equipment, and a variety of other military goods. Total exports of armaments by the major Western countries were $18.3 billion in 1980, with the United States accounting for about one-third of the total. The other major arms exporters included France, Italy, the United Kingdom, and Germany. Israel was the largest arms exporter among the major developing countries. The arms trade was allocated to seven industries included in the Michigan Model that produce military goods: wood products; rubber products; iron and steel; metal products; nonelectrical machinery; electrical machinery; and transport equipment.

It was then possible to calculate the ratios of military exports and imports to total exports and imports for each of the industries for each country in the model. Using these ratios, the importance of trade in military goods with respect to industry output and employment in each country could be determined. The procedure was to assume, first, that the United States imposed a unilateral embargo on its exports and imports of armaments. To implement this, it was assumed that the industry ratios of military to total exports and imports were reduced to zero, and these values were entered as exogenous changes in the model. The model was then solved to yield a variety of percentage changes in the important economic variables by sector as well as economywide weighted averages. Absolute changes were then calculated using the 1980 reference-year data. The second experiment involving a multilateral embargo was carried out on the assumption that all of the countries in the model reduced their military trade ratios to zero.

The estimated aggregate results of the unilateral U.S. arms trade embargo were to reduce U.S. total exports and imports by about $2 billion, which was about 1 percent of their 1980 levels. Some 140,000 U.S. workers were estimated to have to change jobs as the result of the U.S. embargo. This was a comparatively small 0.14 percent of total 1980 U.S. employment. There were similarly small changes in the U.S. terms of trade, the exchange rate, and domestic prices. The aggregate effects on the other countries were also small. At the industry level, the largest estimated net reductions in U.S. employment were in transport equipment (1.9 percent of 1980 employment) and electric machinery (1.7 percent). These same sectors showed an expansion of employment in the other industrialized countries.

The aggregate results for the multilateral embargo indicated a slightly larger decline in U.S. total exports and imports as compared to the U.S. unilateral embargo. For all countries, total exports and imports were reduced by more than $9.9 billion, which was less than 1 percent of total 1980 trade. An estimated 118,000 U.S. workers—0.12 percent of 1980 employment— were estimated to have to change jobs. At the sectoral level, the results for the United States were similar to the U.S. unilateral embargo. But for other countries, the results depended on whether they were net exporters or net importers of military goods. France and Italy showed employment declines in the transport equipment and electric machinery industries, while Japan showed an increase in employment in these industries as did most of the smaller countries. In percentage terms, the detailed industry results suggested that there might be significant adjustment pressures in a number of industries in several industrialized and developing countries, although the orders of magnitude were not of major proportions in most instances.

The general conclusion of this analysis is that the importance of trade in armaments for aggregate and sectoral employment in the United States and other major Western trading countries should not be exaggerated. Of course, there is the larger question of what the effects would be if a sizable reduction in domestic military spending in the major countries were possible. In order to investigate this question, information is needed on the sectoral composition of military spending to correspond to the trade in military goods already included in the model. It would then be possible to use the model to assess the aggregate and sectoral effects of unilateral and multilateral reductions in military spending together with embargoes on trade in military goods. (In this connection, see Haveman, Deardorff, and Stern 1992 and 1993, and their references to other studies of the international effects of changes in military expenditures.)

Of course, it remains to be seen whether unilateral or multilateral arms trade embargoes or reduced military spending can be attained. This will depend upon whether the international political environment is conducive to making the necessary changes. To the extent that economic analysis may be helpful in evaluating different alternatives and informing actual decisions, the Michigan Model could be used to establish whether particular policy options of reducing arms trade or domestic military expenditures would be disruptive to aggregate and sectoral output and employment in the United States and other major countries. The answer here would obviously depend on the size and timing of the changes involved. Thus, in the analysis of negotiating options in the Uruguay Round, we saw that the possibly disruptive effects of trade liberalization could be mitigated by phasing in the reduction or removal of the tariffs and NTBs involved. Presumably, reductions in military expenditures and trade could be phased in as well over a period of years.

Lessons from Computational Modeling

Having used the Michigan Model for several years to analyze a variety of trade policy issues, we have learned a great deal about the advantages and drawbacks of computational modeling.

The first and by far most significant lesson has been how important it is to have a multicountry and multisector model in order to analyze the effects of changes in trade policies. Time and again, it has been found that foreign tariffs and NTBs have a major impact on an individual country in addition to the impact that the country's own policies may have. A second lesson is that policymakers and their constituents are greatly concerned about the employment and output effects of changes in trade policies in the short-to-medium run. This concern underscores the need for a modeling capability that allows for disequilibrium in labor markets in response to changes in trade policies. In using the Michigan Model, we maintained close contact with staff economists in U.S. government agencies, in Congress, and in the major international organizations concerned with trade matters. The various papers describing the model experiments and results have been widely circulated in government circles, and, on occasion, government agencies have commissioned studies of important trade policy issues using the Michigan Model. While it is difficult to know whether the computational results of the model have been taken explicitly into account in making policy decisions, many government officials and their staff are certainly cognizant of the capability and uses of the model.

Over the years, certain drawbacks of the Michigan Model have become evident. These include the inability of the model to handle bilateral (as opposed to multilateral) policy changes, problems of separating real from purely financial effects of policy changes, and the need to take imperfect competition and economies of scale into account especially in certain manufacturing industries. In continuing work on computational modeling, an effort is being made to construct modeling options that address certain of these limitations. (See, for example, Brown, Deardorff, and Stern 1992.) It is planned, accordingly, to continue providing computational estimates of the economic effects of actual and hypothetical changes in trade policies. Of course, political considerations will ultimately govern the choice and implementation of policies. But government officials will, we hope, continue to find the computational results of the Michigan Model useful in evaluating existing policies and deliberating among different options for making changes in policies.

Conclusion

An effort has been made in this chapter to demonstrate how issues of conflict in international economic relations are handled conceptually in the theory of international trade and international macroeconomics.

To illustrate how certain issues could be analyzed in a pragmatic manner, we described briefly four applications of the Michigan Model of World Production and Trade. In the cases of tariffs and safeguards policies, the focus was on how unilateral U.S. actions would affect other countries. As far as tariffs are concerned, because of the possibility of retaliation, the conclusion was that it would be best if the policy action were not taken in the first place. With respect to safeguards policies, it appeared that the preferred policy was a multilateral domestic production subsidy rather than a unilateral or multilateral import tariff or quota. The third case, the analysis of negotiating options in the Uruguay Round was intended to show how countries might choose to formulate their negotiating positions and identify tradeoffs on particular options in the light of their national interests. The emphasis here was on the employment effects of different options, and the setting was one of cooperation for mutual gain by means of trade liberalization under the authority and influence of the GATT.

The focus of the fourth case, the experiments on unilateral and multilateral embargoes of international trade in armaments was again on employment effects in the major Western countries. It was shown in particular that the United States would experience only comparatively minor employment shifts if trade in armaments were eliminated. Other countries might experience more disruption of employment, but the effects could be mitigated by phasing in the changes in policies. In this last case, it would require agreement at the highest political levels to effect the reductions in trade armaments. In reaching such a decision, it would be important to know how disruptive such changes would be. The Michigan Model results suggest that the effects involved would be manageable. If this conclusion were accepted by those countries concerned, then cooperative steps could be taken to defuse the potential for conflict to arise as the result of international trade in armaments.

The Michigan Model is only one example of the contribution that international economists can make to the analysis of conflict and cooperation in the international economic system. One can point to other economic modeling efforts that deal with different aspects of the global trading and payments system. The insights from empirical economic modeling thus have much to offer to analysts and government officials who are involved in the international policy process.

REFERENCES

Axelrod, R. 1984. *The Evolution of Cooperation*. New York: Basic Books.
Brown, D. K., A. V. Deardorff, and R. M. Stern. 1992. "A North American Free Trade Agreement: Analytical Issues and a Computational Assessment." *The World Economy* 15: 15–29.
Deardorff, A. V., and R. M. Stern. 1979. *An Economic Analysis of the Tokyo Round of Multilateral Trade Negotiations on the United States and the Other Major Industrialized Countries*. MTN Studies 5. Washington, DC: U.S. Government Printing Office.
———. 1986. *The Michigan Model of World Production and Trade: Theory and Applications*. Cambridge: MIT Press.
———. 1987a. "Current Issues in Trade Policy: An Overview." In *U.S. Trade Policies in a Changing World Economy*, edited by R. M. Stern, 15–68. Cambridge: MIT Press.
———. 1987b. "Tariffs and Defensive Responses: A Computational Analysis." *International Economic Journal* (Summer) 1: 1–23.
———. 1989a. "A Computational Analysis of Alternative Safeguards Policy Scenarios in International Trade." In *The Political Economy of International Trade*, edited by R. W. Jones and A. O. Krueger, 261–87. New York: Basil Blackwell.
———. 1989b. "A Computational Analysis of Alternative Scenarios for Multilateral

Trade Liberalization." Discussion Paper No. 363, August. Ottawa: Economic Council of Canada.

———. 1990a. *Computational Analysis of Global Trading Arrangements*. Ann Arbor: University of Michigan Press.

———. 1990b. "Options for Trade Liberalization in the Uruguay Round Negotiations." *Proceedings of the Academy of Political Science* 37: 17–27.

Grobar, L. M., R. M. Stern, and A. V. Deardorff. 1989. "The Economic Effects of International Trade in Armaments in the Major Western Industrialized and Developing Countries." *Defence Economics* 1: 97–120.

Haveman, J. D., A. V. Deardorff, and R. M. Stern. 1992. "Some Economic Effects of Unilateral and Multilateral Reductions in Military Expenditures in the Major Industrialized and Developing Countries." *Conflict Management and Peace Studies* 12: 47–78.

———. 1993. "Sectoral Effects of Reductions in NATO Military Expenditures in the Major Industrialized and Developing Countries." *Open Economies Review* 4: 247–68.

Thursby, M. and R. Jensen. 1983. "A Conjectural Variation Approach to Strategic Tariff Equilibria." *Journal of International Economics* 14: 145–61.

An Organizational Approach to International Negotiation

Robert L. Kahn

The title of this chapter, "An Organizational Approach to International Negotiation," implies a link between problems of international relations, on the one hand, and the potential contributions of organizational theory, on the other. Allison (1971) proposed such a link more than twenty years ago, in his analysis of the Cuban missile crisis, and demonstrated some of the differences between explanations that depended on the rational-actor model and those that emphasized organizational process and bureaucratic politics. He concluded that, although organizational models offered the potentiality of improved explanation and prediction in the international domain, "studies of organizations have had little influence upon the existing literature of international affairs" (pp. 68–69). In the years since Allison's observation, scientific study of the negotiation process has expanded significantly, and the comparison of competing paradigms has begun (Zartman 1978). Economic models developed to explain wage determination have been applied to international negotiation (Cross 1978), and the "social psychology of negotiations" (Rubin and Brown 1975, Druckman 1977) has emerged as an ambitious integrative effort.

The potential contributions of organizational theory and research to the understanding of international negotiations, on the other hand, have received little attention. The title of a recent book by Lax and Sebenius (1986), *The Manager as Negotiator*, implies the relatedness of the organizational level to negotiation and bargaining, but the light is shining in the opposite direction from what Allison envisioned: general principles from negotiation theory and experimentation are used to illuminate the nature of organizational management. Winham's (1977) article on negotiation as a management process is

This chapter draws in part on a chapter entitled "Organizational Theory," in *International Negotiation* (1991), edited by Victor A. Kremenyuk and published by Jossey-Bass; and on a lecture presented in August 1988, on receiving the Kurt Lewin Memorial Award from the Society for the Psychological Study of Social Issues, American Psychological Association. A more complete exposition of this theoretical approach is provided in *Organizations and Nation-States* (1990), edited by Robert L. Kahn and Mayer Zald, and published by Jossey-Bass, San Francisco.

almost unique in urging the use of organizational phenomena to approximate the complexity of negotiations between nations.

As a student of large-scale organizations, I am glad to acknowledge the contributions of negotiations research to understanding organizational decision making, but I am eager to encourage the reciprocal process. In this chapter, we first describe three substantive areas of organizational research that are relevant to problems of negotiation at the international level. We then discuss each of them, in a sequence that suggests the extent to which their potential contributions can be immediately realized. The first, the behavior of people in organizational boundary roles, draws on a substantial research literature. The second, the recognition of organizations as a means for sustaining negotiated agreements, derives from the resource-dependence approach to interorganizational relationships. And the third, the problem of negotiating an acceptable procedure for decision making among units of unequal size and power, has only been touched on by organizational scholars but is likely to become an increasingly important problem in international relations.

Three Uses of Organizational Theory

The Concept of Organizational Boundary Roles

One way in which theory and research at the organizational level can contribute to understanding international relations is by taking account of the *organizational embeddedness* of negotiators, that is, of certain determinants of individual behavior that are common both to organizations and to nation-states. Acts of war, the making of peace, and the conduct of diplomacy, which von Clausewitz (1943) regarded as an activity intermediate between the two, cannot be fully understood as the formal acts of nations qua nations. Still less can they be understood entirely as behaviors of individuals acting as free agents. They are more fully understandable at the individual level, I believe, as behaviors of people acting in organizational roles.

The stability of organizations and of governments requires that the demands and expectations associated with each role in large part determine the behavior of the individual occupying that particular position. Admittedly, as one ascends the organizational hierarchy, the enactment of the role increasingly reflects attributes of the individual as well as the formalized requirements of the position. Generals have more discretion in their role behavior than do foot soldiers. But even at the highest levels, the demands of the role tend to overwhelm individual values and preferences.

Dramatic reminders of the dominance of role demands at high levels are provided when we compare the statements of national leaders while in office and after leaving it. For example, Eisenhower's (1961) remarkable warning to the American people about the dangerous power of the military-industrial complex came only in his farewell address. And Robert McNamara's (1983) proposal that the United States make a public declaration that it will not use nuclear weapons first, even at the "battlefield level" and even in response to an attack by conventional arms, was not made during his tenure as secretary of defense but in a 1983 article on the military role of nuclear weapons.

Negotiators, although often physically separated from their home organization or country, are not exempt from the requirements of role. When they negotiate, they are in part expressing their own values and personalities, but they are motivated in large part by organizationally mediated rewards and penalties, the hope of organizational preferment, organizationally generated feelings of solidarity with others, and identification with organizationally defined missions and with organizationally determined standards and values. Admittedly, the negotiator's role is unusual in that much of the required interaction is with people outside his or her organization (or nation). But this is not unique; people in sales, service, and liaison positions of various kinds also interact primarily with others who are outside their own organization.

Such people occupy positions that organizational theorists call *boundary roles*, and the conceptual language of role theory as developed in organizational settings gives us a way of dealing simultaneously with behavioral determinants that are self-generated, those that are generated by the immediate interaction of the negotiation itself, and those that are mediated by the constituencies that the negotiator willingly or unwillingly represents. This conceptual approach is one way in which organizational theory and research are relevant to international negotiations.

The Problem of Interdependence

A second way in which organizational theory and research can contribute to the domain of international negotiation involves the conceptualization of interdependence, which is a core problem in both fields. If nations were not interdependent in some respects, actually or potentially, there would be nothing to negotiate. It is the fact of a nation's interdependence with others in its environment that generates the content of negotiations.

How such interdependence of a social system with its environment can best be conceptualized and managed has been a central concern in organizational theory and research for more than twenty years. Early research in organizations concentrated almost entirely on internal issues, especially the relationships of supervisors and subordinates, but in the 1960s the emphasis began to shift toward the conceptualization of organizations as open systems whose existence required continuing, interdependent exchange with their environments (Emery and Trist 1973; Miller 1965a, 1965b; Katz and Kahn 1966; Thompson 1967; Lawrence and Lorsch 1967).

Scholars who adopted the open-systems view of organizations, and who thus agreed on the importance of organization-environment interdependence, did not therefore agree on how the environment of an organization should be conceptualized and measured. Scott (1987), in an excellent summary of the ways in which different investigators have approached the problem of organization-environment interdependence, distinguishes three levels of environments. The first, that of the *ecological field* (Hawley 1950) or the *interorganizational field* (Warren 1963), focuses on a specific geographic area and concentrates on the pattern of relations among organizations in that area. A second approach, usually designated *population* or *population-ecology* (Hannan and Freeman 1977), is based on categories of organizations that resemble each other in crucial respects, much as members of the same biological species resemble each other.

The third level at which organization-environment interdependence has been studied is based on the concept of the *organization set* (Blau and Scott 1962, Evan 1966). This approach, which can be regarded as an extension of role theory, is most readily extrapolated from the organizational to the national level and is most relevant to the process of international negotiation. It assumes that the relevant environment for any given organization consists of the other organizations with which it interacts directly. Thus, a company manufacturing automobile wheels might have in its set the steel corporation from which it buys material, the utilities that supply its power, the labor union that represents its employees, the auto manufacturer that buys its product, and the other wheel manufacturers with which it must compete.

The concept of the organization set assumes our interest focuses on a particular organization, one whose success or failure we want to understand and predict. It is from the viewpoint of this focal organization that the members of the set are defined, and it is the relationships between the focal organization and the separate members of its organization set that must be negotiated. As we shall see, the extrapolation of this approach to the concept of focal nations and their respective nation sets allows us to characterize interdependent relations between nations in ways that draw on organizational research and can be tested at the national level.

Negotiation of Formal Decision Making

A third domain in which organizational research might contribute to identifying and clarifying issues in international negotiation has to do with formal decision making. Human organizations, large and small, function by making decisions, choosing among alternative actions. Indeed, some organizational theorists regard organizations primarily as formal structures for making decisions linked to such goals as making a profit, attaining growth, and insuring survival.

Any organizational decision can become the subject of negotiation, but limitations of time and resources require that most decisions be made without formal or extended negotiation. The organizational hierarchy deals with this problem by subdividing and allocating the prerogatives for making decisions. Such subdivision and allocation may themselves become the subject of occasional intraorganizational negotiation, but most of the numerous operating decisions by which organizations function are not negotiated.

The decision-making process becomes more complicated when organizations are large and consist of numerous semiautonomous subunits, and when the decisions to be made involve significant questions of resource allocation, market share, distribution of profit, major product change, and the like. The decision-making situation then involves a number of executives, each responsible for some part of the organization, each representing therefore a constituency, but each also bearing some share of collective responsibility for the viability and success of the enterprise as a whole. To these must be added a further complicating factor: these organizational subunits are certain to differ in size, in resources, and in power.

The question that arises under such circumstances is how decisions can be reached that are accepted as legitimate and binding on all of the organizational units represented. This question, which must be dealt with by every organization large enough to contain components of significant size and autonomy, is relevant to international negotiation in two ways. First, international confederations, from the United Nations and the European Community to regional groupings of lesser size and more restricted function, must deal with the same problem: inventing a formal method for making collective decisions that will be treated as legitimate and binding by all of the participating units. Second, as Raiffa (1982) has pointed out, the task of inventing and adopting such a decision-making procedure is itself a negotiation problem of a peculiarly difficult kind.

These three conceptual areas—the explanation of behavior in boundary roles, the management of interdependence between organizations, and the making of major decisions in organizational systems consisting of unequal components—are domains in which the potential contributions of organizational research to international negotiations can be readily demonstrated. In the remainder of this chapter we will consider each of them in greater detail.

Negotiation as Behavior in Boundary Roles

As Cross (1978, 30) points out, models of negotiation have in common a fragmented approach to the problem; they differ mainly in the fragment on which they concentrate. I agree with this observation and with his judgment that the fragmented models are "a natural consequence of our limited understanding of an extremely complicated phenomenon." Approaching negotiation in terms of role theory, as it has been developed in social and organizational psychology, has the advantage of breadth. It allows us to deal simultaneously and in commensurate terms with attributes of the negotiator, the behaviors of his or her antagonist or counterpart, and the demands and expectations of constituents or coworkers. The main disadvantage of current role models of this holistic kind is that their quantification and measurement are not well developed.

The Role Model

The concept of *organizational role* is basically behavioral. It refers to a set of activities that are associated with a given position in an organization or other social system and that are therefore expected of anyone who occupies that position. For convenience, that occupant of a position on which our interest is focused at any particular time is referred to as a *focal person*. The people whose own work is interdependent with that of the focal person (supervisor, subordinates, peers occupying adjacent positions in the work flow, and the like) hold specific expectations about what activities the focal person shall perform and how they shall be performed. These people are referred to collectively as the *role set* or *role senders* for that position.

The members of a person's role set not only hold expectations for his or her behavior. They communicate them as attempts to influence and shape that behavior. The orders of hierarchical superiors, the suggestions of peers, and the requests of subordinates are all attempts by members of a role set to influence the behavior of a focal person; in combination they constitute the *sent role*. The focal person who is the target of these attempts perceives them more or less accurately; his or her interpretations constitute the *received role*. The focal person continues to perform his or her role, responsive in part to the expectations and communications of the role set, and in part to his or her own beliefs and preferences. That *role behavior* is observed by members of the role set, who may either modify or intensify their expectations, and thus the cyclical process of role sending and role enactment continues. Moreover, this core process for any given person takes place in a context that includes formal properties of the organization as a whole (e.g., size, climate), enduring properties of the focal person (e.g., personality, demographic characteristics), and interpersonal relations that have developed over time (e.g., degree of trust, liking, power).

The main elements in this approach to explaining the behavior of people in organized settings are presented diagrammatically as figure 1. It is, of course, a simplification. One of the complexities not illustrated is the likelihood of disagreement among members of the role set about the requirements

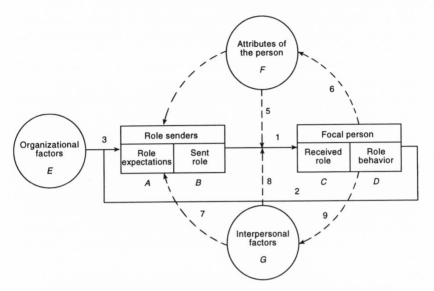

Fig. 1. A theoretical model of factors involved in the taking of organizational roles. (Katz and Kahn 1978, 196.)

of the focal role or the performance of the focal person. For example, a factory supervisor might be told by workers that the production demands are excessive and by the superintendent that productivity is below standard. This is one form of *role conflict*, and it has been studied extensively as a form of stress in work settings (Winnubst 1984, Cooper and Payne 1978).

Boundary Roles

The nature of role conflict, the ways in which people cope with it, and its consequences for their performance are issues of importance for understanding negotiation because negotiators' positions are particularly prone to role conflict. The reasons have to do with the nature of their role sets. For most organizational positions, the members of the role set are also members of the organization. For negotiators, however, members of the role set are partly within their own organization and partly outside it. The company representative who negotiates a new labor contract must deal simultaneously with the role expectations of management, workers, and union representatives. Negotiators, like salespeople and liaison specialists, are thus working across the boundaries of their own organizations and are said to occupy *boundary roles* (Kahn et al. 1964).

Boundary positions, as Adams (1976) pointed out, have a number of unique characteristics. People in such roles are more distant from members of their own organization—often more distant physically as well as psychologically—and they are necessarily closer to people in the external environment. Second, people in boundary roles must represent their organization to those outside it. Third, and more difficult, they must attempt somehow to influence outside people in ways that serve the organizational interest. Finally, they bring information about the external environment into their own organization, and not infrequently they attempt to bring their own organization to a more realistic understanding of that environment and its demands.

There is a substantial research literature on boundary roles, much of it based on organizational studies of salespeople and labor negotiators, or on experimental simulations of organizational transactions involving people in such roles. We summarize here those findings that seem particularly relevant to international negotiation, using the concepts and causal sequence described above and illustrated in figure 1. Major sources for these findings are Rubin and Brown (1975), Adams (1976), Druckman (1977), Zartman (1978), Katz, Kahn, and Adams (1980), and Putnam (1988).

Perhaps the most consistent cluster of findings involves the visibility and accountability of boundary persons to members of the role set in their own organization. High visibility and accountability, either during or after negotiation, have negative effects. Negotiators under these conditions tend to make smaller initial concessions in bargaining and encounter more deadlocks. Rubin and Brown (1975) explain similar results in terms of the negotiator's need for positive evaluation from the role set.

The main bases on which negotiators are evaluated appear to be their success and their compliance with the role expectations of the internal role set. When negotiator performance is not directly observable, the criterion of apparent compliance assumes increased importance.

The responsiveness and obedience of boundary persons to their internal role sets seems to depend on three factors—their personal need for approval, the strength of their attraction to the organization and their role in it, and the extent to which the members of the role set control rewards and penalties important to the boundary person (Hermann and Kogan 1977).

It is plausible that the climate of interpersonal relations established over time between boundary person and role set would affect the extent to which accountability is demanded, but only one relevant variable appears to have been much investigated. It is trust, and high trust by the role set leads to increased freedom for the negotiator, which in turn is associated with optimizing outcomes. Trust is established, on the other hand, by demonstrating obedience to role set expectations and by having produced successful negotiation outcomes. One can earn discrepancy credits, but at the cost of previous conformity.

In contrast to the research literature on the negotiation and bargaining process as such, the role-based research concentrates less on the responses of the negotiator to his or her counterpart outside the organization. Two factors appear significant, however: the boundary person's perception of the other's bargaining behavior and the expectation of future interaction. The boundary person acts more flexibly when the other (bargaining partner or antagonist) is seen as cooperative and when future interaction is likely. The boundary person becomes more demanding when the other negotiator is seen as exploitative and when future transactions seem unlikely.

Finally, research with Australian managers (Crouch and Yetton 1987) indicated that the benefits of "working through" conflicts depend upon the manager's skills in this kind of problem-solving negotiation. An earlier experiment (Bazerman and Neale 1983), which utilized a population of undergraduates in a simulated labor-management dispute, had shown a main effect of training on frequency of successful resolution. The training apparently had the immediate effect of decreasing the experimental subjects' initial expectations of success and increasing their willingness to make concessions. These changes in turn led to the increase in successfully negotiated outcomes.

This review of role-oriented research suggests that it is in some respects complementary to the dominant pattern of work on negotiation and bargaining. At least as it has developed in organizational psychology, this research has concentrated on explaining the behavior of people in organizational roles, most of whom are acting within the boundaries of the organization. Even for boundary-role persons, the emphasis has been on intraorganizational determinants of behavior. Bargaining theory, on the other hand, has concentrated on explaining the behavior of bargainers primarily in terms of their reactions to the behavior of their opposite numbers in the bargaining game and secondarily in terms of their own personalities.

We still await the development of a model that incorporates fully the strengths of both approaches. The nearest approximation to such an integration is contained in a chapter by Druckman (1978) on negotiation as dual responsiveness. He proposes that the characteristic conflict and stress of boundary roles reflect the necessity of performing simultaneously two quite different functions: "monitoring the other side for movement and monitoring one's own side for evidence of preferences" (p. 87). I agree with the distinction, and I concede the limitations of the organizational role model, at least in its present form, for dealing with the first of these functions. Its contributions to explaining the second function, however, deserve increased attention by students of negotiation.

The Management of Interdependence

Most books on negotiation do not include a definition of the term, either assuming that colloquial understanding will suffice or that meaning will emerge in the course of exposition. Those authors who do offer definitions, however, show substantial agreement. Lax and Sebenius (1986, 11), for example, say that "negotiation is an attempt by two or more parties to find a form of joint action that seems better to each than the alternatives." And Rubin and Brown (1975, 2) state that bargaining or negotiation is a "process whereby two or more parties attempt to settle what each shall give or take, perform and receive, in a transaction between them."

The central element in these definitions and others that resemble them is the assumption of interdependence of interests, actual or potential, between the negotiating parties. The negotiation process is then an attempt to reach agreement on how that interdependence shall be managed. In the simplest cases, the alternative to reaching agreement is complete separation. If a potential buyer and seller are unable to agree on a price, they separate, and there is no continuing interdependence. On the other hand, if two competing organizations cannot agree on a division of the market, the competitive interdependence is not thereby dissolved; it is more likely to be intensified. And if two nations cannot successfully negotiate a boundary dispute, their geographically determined interdependence is not lessened; it is simply unmanaged. Negotiation, in my view, is essentially an attempt to manage the interdependence.

That task, the management of interdependence, is what organizations and organizational theory are about, at levels from the interpersonal to the international. The recognition of interdependence between individuals at the level of the work group was central to the early work of the human-relations school (Mayo 1933, Roethlisberger and Dickson 1939, Argyris 1957, McGregor 1960, Likert 1961), which treated the management of interdependence at that level as the central task of supervision and regarded participative decision making as the most effective way of accomplishing that task. Emery and Trist (1973) proposed an analogous proposition at the organizational level. In their exposition of the sociotechnical concept of organizations, after acknowledging the importance of interdependence within work groups, they added, "Similarly, the primary task in managing the enterprise as a whole is to relate the system to its environment and is not internal regulation per se" (p. 220).

Scholars who attempt to explain the behavior of organizations in terms of the resource-dependence model, as we have seen, emphasize the exchange of resources between a given organization and others that constitute its organization set. Such exchanges presuppose some kind of agreement about the terms of exchange. Agreements in turn imply that a process of negotiation has occurred. Negotiations, successful or failed, involve interdependence. Interdependence of some kind is thus an inevitable part of cooperation and a precondition for conflict, interorganizational and international. Without some degree of interdependence with respect to resource acquisition, territorial boundaries, and the like, there would be no incentive to assume the risks and costs of conflict or the efforts of cooperation.

The Continuum of Managed Interdependence

Two persisting questions for every organization and nation are how best to manage unavoidable interdependencies and how to realize the gains of potential interdependencies. Let us begin with the organizational case and assume that the avoidance or elimination of a given interdependence between two specific organizations is impossible and that its nature is dominantly conflict-generating or mixed-motive rather than wholly symbiotic (Scott 1981) or promotive (Deutsch 1973). We can then imagine a hypothetical continuum in which the identifiable scale points represent specific structural arrangements for the management of interdependence between these two organizations. Arranged in order of increasing proportions of managed (i.e., successfully negotiated) as compared to "unmanaged" interdependence, we then have an ordinal scale anchored at one end by total combination (merger or absorption) and at the other by no-holds-barred conflict. (See fig. 2.)

In total organizational combinations, whether voluntary mergers or hostile takeovers, all of what had been an interorganizational relationship is made intraorganizational. Problems of conflict and negotiation are not thereby eliminated, but they are moved inside the organizational boundary and thus made subject to the authority structure and problem-solving machinery of the organization. It is in that sense that they become managed and, as Lax and Sebenius (1986) point out, the negotiation of intraorganizational conflicts is a manager's chief task. The other end of the continuum, no-holds-barred conflict between organizations, is not encountered in civil society. The social norms and the laws of the land limit the ways in which interorganizational conflict can be expressed, so that the more common situation is that of the market, in which competition is demanded but the expression of conflict is constrained by sociolegal factors. For example, criminal law prohibits physical assault on one's competitors or demolition of their production facilities.

The continuum of managed versus unmanaged organizational interdependence as represented in figure 2 was developed from organizational research. Each of the designated structural arrangements for managing organizational interdependence, however, seems to have its counterpart at the international level. Organizational mergers and takeovers resemble international federation and conquest. Organizational joint ventures have many international counterparts, from bilateral, single-purpose arrangements like the U.S.-U.S.S.R. Antarctic expeditions to multinational, multipurpose structures like the European Community or the United Nations itself. Organizational contracts resemble treaties, in that both are formal agreements regard-

Total combinations (mergers, takeovers)

Joint ventures

Contracts/treaties (as hierarchical documents)

Spot contracts (one-off)

Normative agreements (oral, informal); regimes

Markets (sociolegal constraints)

No-holds-barred conflicts

Fig. 2. Hypothetical continuum of managed interdependence between organizations

ing the future performance of the parties and both are governed by law, although international laws lack the enforcement powers that can be applied within nation-states.

The distinction between spot or one-off contracts and contracts as hierarchical documents is based on the scope of the agreement, both in terms of time span and range of activity. A spot contract is drawn, for example, when a manufacturer arranges to purchase a single shipment of component parts from a supplier. Suppose, however, that the same manufacturer contracted to purchase components from that supplier on a continuing basis, and that the contract included agreed-upon procedures for coordinating shipments with manufacturing schedules, adjusting prices to take account of cost changes, and settling incidental disagreements. The contractual relationship would then have acquired some of the functions typically carried out by management hierarchies within organizations, and in that sense the contract would have become what Stinchcombe (1985) calls a hierarchical document.

Such contracts involve a two-way relationship with the process of negotiation. They are the product of negotiation, of course, as are all agreements to manage interdependence that go beyond no-holds-barred conflict and the behavior of competing organizations in a hypothetical free market. But contracts that include procedures for settling future conflicts of interest that arise in their fulfillment are also vehicles for negotiation.

Less formal, noncontractual agreements between organizations resemble the agreements between nations that political scientists refer to as regimes. As

Keohane (1984, 115–16) put it, "International regimes neither enforce hierarchical rules on governments nor substitute their own rules for autonomous calculation; instead, they provide rules of thumb in place of those that governments would otherwise adopt."

Interdependence and Negotiation

The differences among these several ways of dealing with unavoidable interdependence are important, but they should not lead us to neglect their commonalities. Chief among these is their dependence on negotiation. Normative agreements, contracts of all kinds, joint ventures, and voluntary mergers or federations come into existence only as the products of negotiation. Idealized free markets, while preventing negotiation between competing producers, assume continuing negotiation between buyers and sellers, suppliers and purchasers. The hostile takeover of one organization by another may be undertaken unilaterally—that is, without negotiation—but the effect of such a takeover is not the elimination of conflict or of negotiation. Rather, the conflicts of interest that existed between organizations before takeover are moved within the boundaries of the enlarged organization, where they become subjects of negotiation by the management of the combined enterprise. Even a no-holds-barred conflict typically arises out of a failed negotiation; it is, in Boulding's (1962) terms, a system break, and its resolution will require the resumption of negotiations on some basis.

To the extent that both parties to a negotiated joint action are objectively better off, the negotiation game has been of the non-zero-sum variety. This calculation is made more complicated, however, by the fact that the alternative to a successful negotiation may not be a simple reversion to complete independence. Total lack of interdependence may be impossible, and the alternative to a given agreement may involve penalties, brute force, or other negative costs imposed by either or both negotiating parties.

A further complication stems from the fact that real-life situations, unlike many experimental games, are typically mixed—that is, neither simple zero-sum or non-zero-sum. Negotiations therefore take place, as Raiffa (1982) puts it, between cooperative antagonists, who must often discover for themselves the *potentiality for "creating value"* and thus making joint gains. And even when such value enhancement has been achieved, the problem of sharing remains. The pie may have been enlarged, but it still must be divided.

The process of sharing is eased when negotiators are able to take advantage of differences between themselves (Lax and Sebenius 1986). To the extent that the parties to a negotiation do not have identical value preferences, it becomes possible for each to give up something valued less than the thing that he or she receives in exchange. Such trading on differences or "dovetailing," however, implies a lengthy process of building trust, disclosing preferences, "creating value," and negotiating exchanges. The process implied is thus one of continuity rather than one-shot or episodic negotiations.

Joint ventures offer such continuity. They are by definition the product of successful negotiation, and they can also provide the context for continued success. For the latter reason, I believe that they deserve particular attention from scholars and practitioners of international negotiation.

Joint Ventures

The sequence of organizational arrangements from no-holds-barred conflict to merger reflects an underlying continuum of managed versus unmanaged conflict. There are therefore presumptive advantages as we ascend the scale— less risk of unmanaged, unconstrained, and perhaps survival-threatening conflict. On the other hand, there are costs associated with each higher point on the scale, and those costs involve sovereignty. Additional aspects of autonomy or sovereignty are surrendered at each higher point, and at the point of merger the identity of the organization itself is lost.

The leaders of organizations, like the leaders of nation-states, value sovereignty so highly that acquisition is resisted unless the personal or protective advantages are overwhelming. Add to this the power of nationalistic identity, and the limited appeal of total combination across national boundaries is readily understandable.

Joint ventures, however, offer some of the advantages of outright merger with virtually none of the risks. They entail only a limited pooling of resources (Scott 1987, 189), and they can be designed for a variety of formally stated and explicitly limited purposes. They can be sufficiently insulated from their parent organizations to permit the development of a cooperative subculture even when the parent organizations continue to compete or conflict in other spheres. And, most reassuring to those who insist on uncompromised sovereignty, joint ventures are not irrevocable. Unlike mergers, organizational and national, from which the component parts cannot secede without civil war or its corporate equivalent, joint ventures continue only as long as their parent organizations permit them to do so.

These characteristics give organizational joint ventures a certain plausibility at the international level, and there are some successful examples. The failures are numerous, however, and during the years of the cold war few of the successes involved both the United States and the Soviet Union as participants. One success in which both nations were major participants is the multilateral arrangement for the exploration of Antarctica. It is additionally remarkable because of its scale (eighteen voting nations and seventeen "acceding"), because of its duration (1965 to date), because the cooperative joint venture superseded earlier stages of conflict and informal regime agreements, and because the agreements to which the United States and U.S.S.R. were signatories, include the definition of Antarctica as a nuclear free zone.

The success of this special case appears to be more celebrated than understood. It has evoked a scholarly literature predicting a range of outcomes from competing national claims and international conflict to complete internationalization of the Antarctic continent, the first move on a continental scale toward the long-envisioned one world (Shapley 1988). As researchers, we stand to learn much more from comparative research on a population of successful and unsuccessful joint ventures, and from longitudinal case studies of specific joint ventures as they go through periods of varying success. The Standing Consultative Commission is a case of the latter sort, and some such analyses have been published (Graybeal and Krepon 1985, Buchheim and Farley 1988).

The Standing Consultative Commission (SCC)

The Standing Consultative Commission is of particular interest because it involves two points on the continuum of managed interdependence (fig. 2), the treaty or contract and the joint venture. The Commission was an outgrowth of SALT I, the Strategic Arms Limitation Talks between the United States and the Soviet Union begun in 1969. It is a unique example of a joint venture created as part of a treaty negotiation (the Antiballistic Missile or ABM Treaty of 1972), dealing with a subject of great military importance and sensitivity, operative over a substantial time period, and characterized within that period by sharply different patterns of success and failure. The Commission's stated purpose was to contribute to the continued viability and effectiveness of the treaty by resolving questions of interpretation and compliance as they arose. The Commission was thus the creature of one set of negotiations (the ABM Treaty) and the intended vehicle for another (dealing with questions of interpretation and compliance).

A review of SCC successes and failures over fifteen years shows that the successes dominate during the years before 1980, and the failures in the years from 1980 through 1987. For example, the pre-1980 achievements of the SCC included the negotiation of procedures for dismantling weapons in excess of the treaty limits, enacting treaty provisions limiting strategic offensive arms, regulating the replacement of ABM systems and components, and providing immediate notification of suspected use of nuclear weapons by other countries or terrorist groups. In addition, the SCC dealt successfully with eight questions of compliance raised by the United States, each of which tended to evoke a similar question from the U.S.S.R.

Beginning in 1982, however, a series of public and official statements from the United States charged the Soviet Union with generalized and intentional noncompliance (Duffy 1988). The U.S.S.R. made similar accusations against the United States, and both governments turned away from using the SCC as a forum for negotiation and conflict resolution. Disuse, moreover, gave increasing validity to charges of SCC ineffectiveness, the most florid of which was the statement of Caspar Weinberger, then secretary of defense, that the SCC had become an "Orwellian memory hole into which U.S. concerns had been dumped like yesterday's trash" (Duffy 1988, 285).

Success and Failure in Joint Ventures

A comparison of SCC accomplishments before and after 1980 suggests that the potential utility of such treaty-nested joint ventures is very great, but that the realization of that potential depends in part on factors external to the joint venture itself. The most obvious functions of joint ventures of the SCC, treaty-nested type are the interpretation and fleshing out of an agreement that is appropriately general rather than specific in many respects, and the application of the agreement to new political and technological developments. Viewed in these terms, a treaty-nested joint venture would function as a vehicle for continuing international negotiation as long as the treaty signatories wished to maintain the kind of cooperation prescribed in the treaty itself.

The more-difficult question posed by the short and varied history of the SCC is whether such joint ventures can help to preserve a mode of problem-solving negotiation even at times when the cooperative mood of the principals to the agreement has weakened. This is a familiar issue to organizational researchers, and to managements that have attempted field experiments in which some new organizational subculture is created within an environment of older norms and values. The tendency in such cases is toward erosion and absorption of the new (Morse and Reimer 1956, Walton 1978), and the major antidote consists in guarantees of autonomy for the new enterprise, preferably accompanied by some insulation from the parent organizations. Autonomy as a general condition is made up of such tangibles as the explicit delegation of decision-making authority, the commitment of resources for extended periods, and the appointment of members (representatives) for substantial terms.

One can imagine building such autonomous characteristics into organizational joint ventures at the international level, with commitments made at times of cooperative, long-sighted high tide, and the joint venture serving to continue such cooperation during periods of wavering commitment. There may, of course, be disadvantages to such designs. Increasing the autonomy or "distancing" of a joint venture from its parent systems may increase its ability to function as a cooperative cultural island, but it may reduce the likelihood that it will fulfill its larger social function; that is, that the cooperative example of the joint venture will lead, through a process of organizational learning or contagion, to more widespread cooperation between the principals themselves.

No systematic comparisons have yet been made between joint ventures that are successful and those that are not, between those that endure and those whose life is short, or between those that have the effect of inducing cooperation between their principals and those that do not. Research of this kind can help to realize the potential contributions of organizational studies to international relations.

Negotiation of Formal Decision Making

Our discussion thus far has concentrated on bilateral joint ventures between equal partners. Let us now turn to the complicating factors of numbers and inequality. International joint ventures like the European Community and the United Nations consist of many nations that differ greatly in size and power, a fact that makes it extremely difficult to reach initial agreement about the basis for making decisions. The principle of national sovereignty implies that the decisions of such multinational bodies be made on the basis of one nation, one vote. This principle is predictably unsatisfactory to nations with large populations, which are more likely to argue for a formula of one person, one vote. And considerations of power, economic and military, raise further complications. In addition to these competing principles, there is the question of what voting proportions are required to enact a decision—a simple majority, some larger fraction, or unanimity.

None of these problems is new, but none has been fully resolved in theory or in practice (Arrow 1951, Raiffa 1982). The bicameral Congress of the United States is an attempt, successful on the whole, to deal with the problem of unequal size among states. The structure of the United Nations, with the differentiation of the Security Council from the larger Assembly, is another attempt to deal with the problem of unequal size and power.

Despite occasional unanimous or near-unanimous decisions, such as the sanctions against Iraq after its invasion of Kuwait, the U.N. organizational design can be considered only a limited success, and there have been proposals to modify it. The most original of these, developed and given some testing in simulations, is the "binding triad" (Hudson 1986). This would require that the votes in the United Nations Assembly be counted in three ways—first, on the basis of one nation–one vote, then weighted according to the population of the voting nations, and finally weighted according to their power (i.e., rated according to gross national product, which is already the agreed-upon basis for determining national assessments for support of the U.N.). If the vote carried on all three bases, it would become binding on all member nations—hence the proposed designation, binding triad.

The dilemma of attaining joint decisions by units of unequal size and power that maximize the long-term collective good is another problem for which the potential contributions of organizational research appear promising. Most large organizations encounter this problem in some form. Many universities, for example, have councils of deans that act as decision-making bodies on the basis of formal votes. The colleges represented by the various deans differ greatly, however, in size of the student body, the size of the faculty, and allocated space and resources. The situation is replicated at the next-lower hierarchical level, when deans convene the heads of departments that also differ greatly in size, resources, and institutional importance. And in most large corporations, the various vice-presidential domains differ substantially in these respects. Nevertheless, the vice-presidents as a group are charged with acting in the interests of the organization as a whole when they participate in decision making at the organizational level.

It is certain that organizations have evolved many different ways of dealing with the core problem of collective decision making, and it is almost certain that their various solutions, formal and informal, hierarchical and participative, are not equally successful. This, however, is conjecture rather than the result of empirical research or theoretical derivation. Research to document the ways in which organizations deal with the problem of joint decisions by collectivities made up of unequal components remains to be done, and the contributions of such research to solving the same problem at the international level remain to be realized.

Conclusion

It is easy to pose questions to be answered by future research. The more difficult question, of course, is whether we can offer any advice to negotiators on the basis of organizational research already done. I believe that we can. For example, research on boundary roles tells us that negotiation skills can be taught, that the selection of people suited by personality for such roles is also important, and that negotiators are likely to be more successful if they are given substantial autonomy than if they are held to continuing and detailed accountability.

Research on the management of organizational interdependence, while at an early stage, suggests the advantages of treaty-nested joint ventures as a way of monitoring the fulfillment of treaty obligations and keeping treaty agreements viable under changing conditions. Finally, research on formal mechanisms of representative decision making by unequal components is so little advanced that we can only call attention to the importance of the topic as one that international organizations should address.

These advisory fragments are only illustrative of current possibilities. I offer them with a keen sense of the need to strengthen the research base and with awareness that, on the long continuum from art to science, negotiation is very much an art and likely to remain so. Like medicine, however, it is an art already informed to some extent by scientific theory and research, and we can hope to see increases in the science-based component. It is in that hope that this chapter has been written.

REFERENCES

Adams, J. S. 1976. "Organizational Boundary Behavior." Paper presented at the 84th Convention of the American Psychological Association, Washington, DC, September.

Allison, G. T. 1971. *Essence of Decision: Explaining the Cuban Missile Crisis.* Boston: Little Brown.

Argyris, C. 1957. *Personality and Organization.* New York: Harper.

Arrow, K. 1951. *Social Choice and Individual Values.* New York: John Wiley & Sons.

Bazerman, M. H., and M. A. Neale. 1983. "Heuristics in Negotiation: Limitations to Dispute Resolution Effectiveness." In *Negotiating in Organizations*, edited by M. H. Bazerman and R. J. Lewiski, 51–67. Newbury Park, CA: Sage.

Blau, P. M., and W. R. Scott. 1962. *Formal Organizations.* San Francisco, CA: Chandler.

Boulding, K. E. 1962. *Conflict and Defense.* New York: Harper.

Buchheim, R. W., and P. J. Farley. 1988. "The U.S.-Soviet Standing Consultative Commission." In *U.S.-Soviet Security Cooperation*, edited by A. L. George, P. J. Farley, and A. Dallin, 254–69. New York: Oxford University Press.

Cooper, C. L., and R. Payne 1978. *Stress at Work.* New York: John Wiley & Sons.

Cross, J. G. 1978. "Negotiation as a Learning Process." In *The Negotiation Process: Theories and Applications*, edited by I. W. Zartman, 29–54. Beverly Hills, CA: Sage.

Crouch, A. G., and P. Yetton. 1987. "Manager Behavior, Leadership Style, and Subordinate Performance: An Empirical Extension of the Vroom-Yetton Conflict Rule." *Organizational Behavior & Human Decision Processes* 39 (3): 384–96.

Deutsch, M. 1973. *The Resolution of Conflict.* New Haven: Yale University Press.

Druckman, D., ed. 1977. *Negotiations: Social-Psychological Perspectives.* Beverly Hills, CA: Sage.

———. 1978. "Boundary Role Conflict: Negotiation as Dual Responsiveness." In *The Negotiation Process: Theories and Applications*, edited by I. W. Zartman, 87–110. Beverly Hills, CA: Sage.

Duffy, G. 1988. "Conditions That Affect Arms Control Compliance." In *U.S.-Soviet Security Cooperation*, edited by A. L. George, P. J. Farley, and A. Dallin, 270–92. New York: Oxford University Press.

Eisenhower, D. D. 1961. Farewell address. *New York Times*, January 18.

Emery, F. E., and E. L. Trist. 1973. *Toward a Social Ecology*. New York: Plenum.

Evan, W. M. 1966. "The Organization Set: Toward a Theory of Interorganizational Relations." In *Approaches to Organizational Design*, edited by J. D. Thompson, 173–88. Pittsburgh: University of Pittsburgh Press.

Graybeal, S. N., and M. Krepon. 1985. "Making Better Use of the Standing Consultative Commission." *International Security* 10: 183–99.

Hannan, M. T., and J. Freeman. 1977. "The Population Ecology of Organizations." *American Journal of Sociology* 82: 929–64.

Hawley, A. 1950. *Human Ecology*. New York: Ronald.

Hermann, M. G., and N. Kogan. 1977. "Effects of Negotiators' Personalities on Negotiating Behavior." In *Negotiations: Social-Psychological Perspectives*, edited by D. Druckman. Beverly Hills, CA: Sage.

Hudson, R., ed. 1986. *Global Report, 20*. New York: Center for War/Peace Studies.

Kahn, R. L., D. M. Wolfe, R. P. Quinn, and J. D. Snoek. 1964. *Organizational Stress*. New York: John Wiley & Sons.

Katz, D., and R. L. Kahn. 1966. *The Social Psychology of Organizations*. New York: John Wiley & Sons.

———. 1978. *The Social Psychology of Organizations* (2d ed.). New York: John Wiley & Sons.

Katz, D., R. L. Kahn, and J. S. Adams, eds. 1980. *The Study of Organizations*. San Francisco: Jossey-Bass.

Keohane, R. O. 1984. *After Hegemony: Cooperation and Discord in the World Political Economy*. Princeton: Princeton University Press.

Lawrence, P. R., J. W. Lorsch. 1967. *Organization and Environment*. Boston: Graduate School of Business Administration, Harvard University.

Lax, D. A., and J. K. Sebenius. 1986. *The Manager as Negotiator*. New York: Free Press.

Likert, R. 1961. *New Patterns of Management*. New York: McGraw-Hill.

Mayo, E. 1933. *The Human Problems of an Industrial Civilization*. New York: Macmillan.

McGregor, D. 1960. *The Human Side of Enterprise*. New York: McGraw-Hill.

McNamara, R. 1983. "The Military Role of Nuclear Weapons." *Foreign Affairs* 62 (Fall): 59–80.

Miller, J. G. 1965a. "Living Systems: Basic Concepts." *Behavioral Science* 10: 193–237.

———. 1965b. "Living Systems: Structure and Process." *Behavioral Science* 10: 337–79.

Morse, N. C., and E. Reimer. 1956. "The Experimental Change of a Major Organizational Variable." *Journal of Abnormal and Social Psychology* 52: 120–29.

Oskamp, S., ed. 1988. "Psychology and the Promotion of Peace." *Journal of Social Issues* (special issue) 44 (2).

Putnam, R. D. 1988. "Diplomacy and Domestic Politics." *International Organization* 42: 427–60.

Raiffa, H. 1982. *The Art and Science of Negotiation*. Cambridge: Belknap Press of the Harvard University Press.

Roethlisberger, F. J., and W. J. Dickson. 1939. *Management and the Worker*. Cambridge: Harvard University Press.

Rubin, J. Z., and B. R. Brown. 1975. *The Social Psychology of Bargaining and Negotiation*. New York: Academic Press.

Scott, W. R. 1981. *Organizations: Rational, Natural, and Open Systems*. Englewood Cliffs, NJ: Prentice-Hall.

———. 1987. *Organizations: Rational, Natural, and Open Systems, 2d. ed.* Englewood Cliffs, NJ: Prentice-Hall.

Shapley, D. 1988. "Antarctica: Why Success?" In *U.S.-Soviet Security Cooperation*, edited by A. L. George, P. J. Farley, and A. Dallin, 307–35. New York: Oxford University Press.

Stinchcombe, A. L. 1985. "Contracts as Hierarchical Documents." In *Organizational Theory and Project Management: Administering Uncertainty in Norwegian Offshore Oil*, edited by A. L. Stinchcombe and C. A. Heiner. Oslo: Norwegian University Press.

Thompson, J. D. 1967. *Organizations in Action*. New York: McGraw-Hill.

von Clausewitz, K. 1943. *On War*. (Translated from the German.) New York: Modern Library.

Walton, R. E. 1978. "The Topeka Story. Part II." *Wharton* 3: 36–41.

Warren, R. L. 1963. *The Community in America*. Chicago: Rand McNally.

Winham, G. R. 1977. "Negotiation as a Management Process." *World Politics* 30: 84–114.

Winnubst, J. A. M. 1984. "Stress in Organizations." In *Handbook of Work and Organizational Psychology*, vol. 1, edited by P. J. D. Drenth, H. Thierry, P. J. Willems, and C. J. de Wolff, 553–71. Chichester, England: John Wiley & Sons.

Zartman, I. W., ed. 1978. *The Negotiation Process: Theories and Applications*. Beverly Hills, CA: Sage.

International Conflict and the Individual; or, What Drives That Person with Whom I Have to Negotiate, and Can Understanding His Motivation Really Help?

Helen R. Weingarten

For change agents, the test of any theoretical model of human behavior rests in its ability to clarify effective ways of making decisions and taking action in specific circumstances, not in its power to illuminate general causal laws. For social scientists concerned with developing "knowledge for practice," the consequent challenge is to develop models that provide knowledge useful either for carrying out appropriate interventions or for selecting among a range of possible action alternatives. Models may accomplish this end through their ordering and organization of experience.

The interpersonal conflict model described here is such an effort. First developed and applied in an organizational context (Leas 1985), then extended and refined for family disputes (Weingarten and Leas 1987). The Levels of Interpersonal Conflict Model (LICM), it is hoped, can contribute to the actual process of choosing and generating effective and nonviolent strategies for conflict management in international disputes.

The LICM was developed out of dissatisfaction with academic theories of interpersonal conflict that did not help practitioners to diagnose differentially and manage the diversity of conflicts they faced. To date the model has been useful in helping disputants and third-party intervenors in organizational and family contexts both to recognize the types of conflict they face and to plan their subsequent actions. It identifies critical dimensions of conflict interaction and helps to organize what is often a confusing array of facts into coherent conceptual categories. Those who aid in the resolution of conflict need models that will help them design interventions to fit a world considerably more complex than an iterated Prisoners' Dilemma game. In the family

This chapter was made possible in part by funding from the Program for International Peace and Security Research through a Carnegie Corporation Grant.

field, practitioners long ago abandoned the assumption that people render decisions rationally, in favor of the proposition that people select means and goals primarily on the basis of their values, emotions, and social bonds. So, too, the assumption that people choose to maximize one utility (usually identified as personal pleasure or interest) has been replaced by the proposition that people have multiple objectives that include, but are not limited to, needs to solve problems, to maintain self-esteem, to win, to control others, to stabilize power, and to enact revenge. It is not that rationality is denied. Indeed, a working definition of "rationality" as an efficient choice of means to advance one's goals is presupposed. Rather, the LICM is designed to clarify the factors that influence the exercise of rationality in conflict interaction and to identify the motives, goals, emotions, and cognitions that thereby play a critical role in shaping conflict behavior.

The Model

The LICM delineates individual differences in motivation and world view that systematically influence approaches to contested issues. It is not a theory of behavior. It does not posit a dominant motivational construct as the determinant of behavior in diverse interpersonal conflict situations. Rather, the model identifies five different levels of interpersonal conflict: (1) problems, (2) disagreements, (3) contests, (4) fights, and (5) war. As table 1 summarizes, each level has characteristic (a) motives, goals, or intentions, (b) assumptions about the situational context, (c) views of a third party, (d) emotional climates, and (e) behavioral styles.

Questions the model can be used to clarify include: What dynamic does a given instance of interpersonal conflict reflect? What personality and structural factors determine leverage points for change? What approach to a given conflict is likely to result in its satisfactory resolution? Is a particular strategy of conflict resolution that worked in one case likely to work in another? If not, why not, and what alternative should be tried? Within the model, the presence of conflict per se is not viewed as a sign that a relationship or organization or nation is in trouble. Rather, conflict may signal a social system's level of vitality. It is the way that people handle the conflicts that inevitably arise that strengthens or weakens their relationships, and the social systems of which they are a part.

For conflict-management strategies to be effective, the LICM assumes that principals and third parties must take into account situationally specific dynamics. Furthermore, techniques and strategies that are effective in helping group *A* resolve a dispute over money do not work with group *B*—even though the presenting problem is the same. Behaviors that may signal to an American businessman that a final settlement has been reached may be interpreted by his Chinese counterpart as evidence that the building of trust and a

TABLE 1. Levels of Interpersonal Conflict Model

Level	Major Objective, Motive, or Aim	Key Assumption	Principal's View of Third Party	Emotional Climate	Negotiation Style
I. Problem to solve	Solving the problem	We can work it out.	Advisor/facilitator	Hope	Open, direct, clear, and non-distorted communication; common interests recognized.
II. Disagreement	Self-protection	Compromise is necessary.	Enabler/mediator	Uncertainty	Cautious sharing; vague and general language; calculation beginning.
III. Contest	Winning	There are not enough resources to go around.	Arbiter/judge	Frustration and resentment	Strategic manipulation; distorted communication; personal attacks begin; no one wants to be the first to change.
IV. Fight	Hurting the other	Winning is impossible.	Partisan ally	Antagonism and alienation	Verbal/nonverbal incongruity; blame; perceptual distortions evident; refusal to take responsibility.
V. War	Eliminating the other	Other people are less human than oneself.	Rescuer or intruder	Hopelessness and revenge	Emotional volatility: no clear understanding of issues; self-righteousness; compulsion; inability to disengage.

working relationship has just begun. While some of the intervention strategies that work with marital partners in conflict (see Weingarten and Leas 1987) have been found to be equally effective with business associates or neighbors, it is anticipated that additional strategies will be needed in international conflict situations in which language, culture, and political ideology and structures radically differ.

Theoretically, the LICM postulates that, across contexts, any given individual may interact with others at escalated levels of conflict (i.e., contests, fights or war). In practice, however, some individuals never appear to engage in the more-escalated levels of conflict interaction, even when they fail to resolve their disputes peacefully and the situational pressures to escalate are intense. In contrast, other individuals continue to function at escalated levels even when some differences have been successfully resolved. In addition, the LICM recognizes that an individual's expressed level of conflict may reflect organizational or situational role constraints rather than more stable character traits or preferences. Thus, while the level of conflict in a system usually reflects the motivational dynamic of the most powerful individuals or coalitions, shifting a conflict to a different level is made considerably easier if even one key actor is inclined to move. Viewed from within the LICM, it is how individuals approach given issues that defines the conflict dynamics needing redress, rather than the substance or magnitude of those issues.

Level I: Problems

Individuals or groups engaging in level-I conflict interaction are motivated by a desire to solve identifiable problems. Department heads in a Fortune 500 company, at odds because one wants resources allocated to research and development and the other wants to increase the budget for sales and promotion, are as likely to be in level-I conflict as are co-op members trying to decide whether to use plywood or pine boards for the shelves in their newly purchased produce market. A husband and wife arguing over where to spend their summer vacation may approach one another from the same conflict level as U.S. and Russian negotiators arguing over where to make strategic cuts in arms.

At level I, real differences exist, and relational tensions stem from the fact that people perceive their goals, needs, action plans, or values to be in conflict. Communication problems may exist, but they are not to be confused with the differences in interest that generate level-I conflict. Occasionally, it is believed that problems will disappear if clear communication can be fostered—indeed many track-III diplomatic efforts seem grounded on such a hope. (Track III negotiation refers to a diplomatic meeting that takes place among actors not necessarily in formal diplomatic positions but with influence on policy.) Yet, while improvements in communication can make it easier to discover joint interests, solve problems, and negotiate differences, individuals who learn to communicate more clearly are also in a better position to discover interpersonal differences that communication barriers previously masked.

Although individuals in level-I conflict may feel somewhat uncomfortable with one another, the overall emotional climate of level I is hopeful. Principals in level-I conflict not only are willing to work together to overcome their differences; they want to do so and are seeking to discover how. While problem-solving strategy preferences vary, in general, individuals at level I tend to express a sense of individual responsibility for solving the problems they face and would rather "do it themselves" if circumstances permit than defer to representatives or mediators to do it for them. Consequently, when third parties are called in at this level, it becomes important that they not overstep a consultative role.

Unlike individuals embroiled in higher-level conflicts, individuals at level I are able to focus on substantive issues and differentiate between the problem and the people involved in it. Level I individuals do not get involved in the personalities of those with whom they differ. Rather, with minimal encouragement and support, level-I disputants are likely to share information openly, in language that is relatively specific, oriented to the here and now, clear of blame, and free of innuendo.

An assumption of interdependence and a respect for difference undergirds the interpersonal approach of principals at level-I conflict. While there may be some resistance to self-disclosure among disputants, because of their dominant belief that "we are in this together," they will not withhold critical information to save face or to "protect" selfish interests. Consequently, the sticky problems that do emerge at level I tend not to derive from personality or ideology but rather from skill deficits in problem solving or cross-cultural communication.

The expectation that one negotiating strategy or method of rational problem solving is appropriate for all disputes (cf. Fisher and Ury 1983), regardless of the substantive issues or cultural context, may undermine understanding or agreement even when there is evident goodwill and willingness to cooperate. Following a program to develop a mutual definition of the problem, gather data, search for alternative solutions, and choose a solution by consensus, while facilitative of successful negotiation in some circumstances, may be obstructive in others, if, for example, the differences between disputants lie in fundamental motives, values, or needs.

A track-III diplomatic meeting of prominent Israeli and Palestinian political activists that I attended was almost derailed by the program developer's prior experience with Middle East delegations who approached one another and the issues competitively. On the assumption that this group of delegates would also interact with one another as a level-III "contest," the dialogue design stressed the importance of third parties who would present themselves as "neutral" when feelings got hot and interrupt the dialogue between the principals to reduce tension.

Although these strategies had worked in previous dialogue situations, the individuals coming to this meeting were strongly motivated to cooperate. They wanted to understand one another and felt little pressure to reach agreement. Furthermore, as most of the delegates believed that the United States was a partisan player in Middle Eastern affairs, they were both suspicious and critical of the "neutral stance" adopted by the U.S. mediators and devoted considerable time and energy trying to engage them in substantive discussion. In this instance the meeting organizers were not only willing to consider participant criticisms, they were able to make on-site, program-design adaptations that allowed the meeting to progress. Frequently, however, individuals who approach conflicts as "problems to be solved" lack the conceptual, behavioral, or dispositional skills required for success in their endeavors. Even if individuals are motivated to solve problems, they may be unable to decide upon appropriate strategies. The psycholinguist George Miller has said, "Compared with television or telephone systems, human beings are more like bottlenecks than channels for the efficient flow of information" (Earl 1988). Further, even if we can assume skill in decision making, the information needed to determine or reach satisfactory outcomes may be unavailable.

It is important that the knowledge of skilled conflict managers not be lost and that the work of academic social scientists be informed by their experience. Research on practice has demonstrated that if fundamental value or sovereignty issues are at stake, setting up negotiations prior to working to promote greater understanding between the parties is more likely to escalate the level of interpersonal conflict than resolve it (Weingarten 1986). Similarly, in the absence of personal trust, the goal of cooperation is more likely to be achieved if the initial problem-solving strategy is to listen to the other's point of view rather than to try to persuade him or her of one's own.

Level II: Disagreements

Individuals in level-II conflict, "disagreements," believe that somebody is likely to get hurt, and they do what they can to avoid taking that role upon themselves. Here, the principals' motivation is significantly changed from a level-I focus on substantive problem solving to a level-II concern with establishing a safe and trustworthy relationship. Although substantive differences are as likely to exist at level II as at level I, at level II the relationship between disputants is perceived as ambiguous and risky. Consequently, concerns with self-protection and saving face must be addressed in their own right if any progress is to be made in resolving specific matters of contention.

Because trust is a critical dynamic of level-II conflict, principals at this level are likely to avoid confronting one another directly about their concerns and disagreements, although they may express occasional barbed comments when tensions mount. The earliest warning sign of systemic dysfunction is not conflict but lack of skill in dealing with it. This often brings on a lessening hope that it can be resolved satisfactorily.

Level II is a stage at which coalition building and utilization become important. People start looking for help, and their most common strategy is to enlist friends to discuss problems, listen to frustrations, and provide advice. Those drawn into the role of advice giver must realize that people at level II don't feel safe sharing everything. Consequently, they tend to mention only those things that are favorable to their particular position. Disputants' efforts to manipulate others without revealing much about themselves also distort the quality of information shared at this level. Systems in which there is considerable level-II conflict frequently suffer from information deficits and confusions.

The inclination to withhold information that might be seen as unfavorable to one side and favorable to the other is often justified by the belief that, in any open confrontation, someone will have to settle for less than at present. The assumption that compromise is likely to be a lose-lose proposition reduces each principal's willingness to collaborate in problem solving. Unlike principals in level-I conflict, who would rather solve their problems themselves, level-II disputants actively seek out third-party assistance. A cautionary note should be sounded in this regard, however. Experience in family and organizational disputes has shown that professionals brought into level-II conflict can easily escalate interpersonal mistrust if their presence limits the opportunities principals have to establish or demonstrate their trustworthiness to one another in face-to-face encounters.

Although principals at level II feel tense and vulnerable, they are more uncertain with one another than antagonistic. At this level, decisions to call in third parties to negotiate agreements need to be considered carefully. Future cooperation may be seriously undermined if disputants miss an opportunity to work together at a critical juncture early in the process. Often at level II, a crisis event triggers the realization that unless something is done soon, the conflict may escalate and the relationship among disputants deteriorate further. Although the disputants may feel ambivalent about the compromises they perceive would be required to resolve their differences, in level-II conflict they recognize their interdependence and want to maintain a working relationship. Nonetheless, as the climate of uncertainty characterizing level-II conflict promotes defensiveness, it inhibits the establishment of the open communication required for optimal problem solving—at least in traditional bargaining situations.

An example of a conflict-resolution strategy that takes into account level-

II face-saving concerns and barriers to open communication is provided by Leonard Woodcock's account of his experiences negotiating with the Chinese during 1977 and 1978 as President Carter's representative, and later as Ambassador, to Beijing (personal communication by letter 1990). When Woodcock took office, the U.S. position was that, in return for U.S. normalization of relations with the Beijing government, China needed to guarantee it would not use force against Taiwan. According to Woodcock, it was politically unfeasible in the United States to normalize relations with Beijing without either that guarantee or an agreement that the United States could continue to sell defensive arms to Taiwan. However, the United States had effectively accepted the proposition that there was only one China (with Taiwan being a part of China) in the Shanghai Communiqué of February 28, 1972, and demanding that China not use force against a part of itself was seen by Woodcock to be both an infringement of China's sovereignty and an initial bargaining position that the Chinese could not accept.

Woodcock felt himself to be in a dilemma. He must communicate to the Chinese that the United States needed to reserve the right to sell defensive arms to the Taiwanese authorities, and he must do so in a way that would not undermine the forthcoming formal meetings about normalization of relations between the two countries. Needing to establish himself as trustworthy in the eyes of his Chinese counterparts, and sensitive to their concerns with "face," this, in his own words, is how he proceeded:

In late ·1977 and early 1978, a few, but not many, American tourist groups were coming to Beijing. Many wanted briefings from the Liaison Office and these were given in our Public Dining Room (which was then our only Conference Room). Inevitably the Taiwan question came up and that was always left for me to reply. My answer was given, not as an Ambassador, but as an American citizen deeply concerned about the need to normalize relations between China and the United States. I said that in my opinion, the President should recognize Beijing as the one government obviously representing China. I then went on that no American President could do this without being in a position to assure the American people that the well-being of the people on Taiwan was reasonably protected. This required reserving the right to sell to the authorities on Taiwan, if need be, defensive arms.

Adjacent to this dining room, separated only by a swinging door, was a big kitchen in which the Chinese house staff was usually located, one or two of whom readily understood English. I had always assumed the staff reported to their own government and, of course, I wanted them to convey my position.

In order to make sure my position got back to the Chinese leadership, I sought meetings with three foreign Ambassadors in Beijing who I knew were very close to the Chinese. To them I conveyed that President Carter had decided to normalize relations in his first term and my position as to how it could be done while finessing the use of force question. When, out of these efforts, I got no answering echo from the Chinese, I felt confident in assuring my President that this could be done, if other matters could be handled satisfactorily. . . . The arms sales question was made a confrontational issue on September 19, 1978, but, by that time, both sides knew that a way to a solution was open given a resolution of other items for which there were precedents.

Level III: Contest

As hope diminishes that problems can be solved and face saved, power motives are aroused and "winning" becomes the focal dynamic of interpersonal conflict. In response to perceived differences of goals, needs, or preferences, disputants at level-III "contests" lose sight of their potential common interests, and this loss impairs their ability to recognize or appreciate their interdependence. The rhetoric of level-III conflict frequently stresses the right of persons (or nations) to act independently. Level III is the domain of the "self-determining" actor who seeks personal gain in an intrinsically competitive (i.e., resource-deficient) universe. This is the level of conflict in which disputants identify "freedom" and "independence" as their most cherished values and then wonder why the victories they achieve at each other's expense seem hollow.

At level-III conflict, issues have piled up and are hard to disentangle. The emotional climate is one of frustration and resentment. Anger erupts easily— often over issues the disputants themselves view as trivial—and dissipates slowly. Principals in a contest no longer find it easy to talk to one another informally. They point out inaccuracies in the other's position more to score points than to advance understanding, facilitate agreement, or solve problems. Perceptual distortions abound and are reflected in communication styles; emotional appeals are common; each party assumes it knows the other's "real" intentions. At level III there is reluctance to take the first step toward change, because the individual fears that such a move will be perceived by the other as a prelude to capitulation.

While level-III contestants are profoundly concerned with control and power, they recognize that it will be impossible to achieve these ends if their relationship to one another is entirely severed. At levels IV and V, antagonists are often satisfied by getting rid of the other. But at level III, contestants recognize the game can't continue without the other, and thus the relationship cannot be broken. Principals in level-III conflict may describe themselves as trapped. Their way of approaching their differences feels unsatisfactory. Yet the solutions they repeatedly try to implement–changing or controlling the other—do not seem to work.

Fisher and Ury (1983) point out the dangers of rigidly adhering to intervention strategies that emphasize contest and ignore the common interests of people in conflict. They argue that victories achieved by one party's defeat will turn out to be self-defeating in the long run. Yet, rather than suggesting a fundamental transformation of the motive to win that adequately deals with the issues of power and resource scarcity, they propose a better mousetrap.

According to their immensely popular work, *Getting to Yes*, Fisher and Ury (1983) contend that if disputants follow their negotiation methods, it is possible to achieve long-term resolutions to conflict in which everyone wins and no one loses. Psychologists, however, have long recognized that many people (surely as well represented in politics as in the family or the market) seem to have very little interest in the long-run gains to be had from cooperation and considerable interest in maintaining or increasing their personal power in the here and now. Given some disputants' reluctance to abandon their quest for power, it seems that Fisher and Ury's model of conflict resolution may be less applicable to level-III contests as understood within the LICM and more applicable to what I would identify as "pseudo-contests." A "pseudo-contest" is a level-I strategy of problem solving that mimics the level-III contest but is not motivated by entrenched desires to win or resource scarcity. Instead, a pseudo-contest occurs when acting competitively is the way principals have been socialized to behave when confronted by perceived obstacles to need satisfaction or goal achievement.

Competition is likely to be unavoidable when activities are structured so that one person's success requires others' failure. In contrast, pseudo-contests do not require competition. Rather, the competition that occurs in such situations is not inherent in the structure of the activity but stems from participants' false perception that one's win necessitates another's loss. Fisher and Ury clarify that many conflicts can be resolved without requiring that anyone lose. But in claiming that everyone can be a conflict "winner," they fail to discriminate the diversity of intentions or objective conditions that underlie conflict behavior—a failure that appears to derive from their acceptance and promotion of a competitive game metaphor as a cross-situationally applicable conflict analogue.

Political science and anthropology provide ample evidence that the degree to which different cultures depend on competition to organize and structure their political, economic, educational, or recreational systems varies broadly. As one commentator puts it:

> At one end of the spectrum are societies that function without any competition at all. At the other end is the United States. . . . Not only do we

get carried away with competitive activities . . . but we turn almost everything else into a contest. Our collective creativity seems to be tied up in devising new ways to produce winners and losers. (Kohn 1986)

If we accept that cultures differ in their reliance on competition as an organizing principle, it becomes critical to consider whether a scholarly literature rife with game analogies to describe the dynamics of interpersonal conflict plays a role beyond mere prediction in promoting or maintaining competition. Social psychologists have carried out innumerable studies that demonstrate that if you treat a person prepared to cooperate as a competitor, he is likely to reciprocate in kind. Given this, scholars must consider the political role "science" plays when it encourages readers to take seriously an iterated Prisoners' Dilemma game as a conflict analogue and to use theory based on this reductionist metaphor to plan their actions.

In *The Evolution of Cooperation*, Axelrod writes that, to change a situation in which cooperation is not stable to one in which it is, "[it] is only necessary to make the long-term incentive for mutual cooperation greater than the short-term incentive for defection" (1984, 134). Yet, when we consider such real-life situations as the Palestinian-Israeli conflict, for example, this proposal clearly seems easier said than done. Although more refined and comprehensive models of reality than that assumed by Fisher and Ury (1983) are available (e.g., Axelrod 1984, Etzioni 1988), it is frequently the case that such models do not easily translate into situationally specific strategies of action. Thus, while it would be hard to quarrel with Axelrod's conclusion that, to promote cooperation, we should: "enlarge the shadow of the future; change the payoffs; teach people to care about each other; teach reciprocity; and improve recognition abilities" (1984, 126–39), we are given few guidelines or even examples of how this actually can be accomplished in the real world.

Getting individuals in pseudo-contest (i.e., with level-I motives—the desire to solve substantive problems—and a competitive style of interacting) to adopt cooperative methods of negotiating is a relatively straightforward educational task. Similarly, if people are motivated to compete because they believe not doing so will threaten their survival in a resource-scarce world, demonstrating that their assumption of scarcity is false often results in collaborative problem solving. Difficulties resolving level-III conflicts in collaborative ways will persist, however, when the goal of winning is personally or culturally entrenched or the scarcity of resources is real.

Disputants in contest generally seek out third parties when they want to bolster their own positions or when impasse occurs. In the latter circumstance, a common strategy is to call in outsiders to serve as arbitrators, judges, or peacekeepers. Third-party intervention can effectively reduce manifest expressions of level-III conflict. But when substituting external pressures to comply for personal commitments to change, further outbreaks of conflict may merely be postponed. As long as disputants understand their own interests to be independent and exclusive of those with whom they compete, they are likely to abandon competition only for as long as they are compelled to do so (Kelman 1958).

Level IV: Fights

Principals in level-IV conflicts, "fights," are noteworthy for their persistence in conflict behavior when chances of goal attainment are slim or nonexistent. Believing it impossible to change their circumstances or to get important needs met with circumstances as they are, combatants at level IV act as if making their opponents hurt is more critical than either solving their problems or winning.

Level-IV conflict is often a critical turning point for individuals. As hope for winning within the context of the circumstances dies, the emotional climate becomes one of alienation and antagonism. Outsiders are enlisted, not to help "save" the relationship between principals as at levels I or II or to legitimize heirarchy as at level III, but as allies to challenge the status quo. In such a system, images of the other become fixed and stereotyped. Even when there is evidence to the contrary, each side believes the other cannot or will not change. Indeed, when the other side attempts to modify its position, its motives are questioned and charges of hypocrisy or manipulation are leveled.

Within organizations characterized by level-IV conflict, factions emerge because individuals believe independent actions will expose them to too much risk. Consequently, the approval and support of a known group of allies become critical. In level-IV conflict, individuals know who is part of their group and who is not. If a person wants to become part of a faction, he or she may well have to do something to prove loyalty. Indeed, individuals may not feel like good members unless they can do something that demonstrates their willingness to "stand up and be counted."

The behavior of guerilla fighters often appears to reflect level-IV conflict dynamics. Thomas Friedman, in describing the response of the Palestinians in 1982 after the Israeli army cut through their lines in less than a week and reached Beirut, writes of his interview with George Habash, the leader of the Popular Front for the Liberation of Palestine (1989, 150–51):

> This pediatrician-turned-guerilla had been fighting the Israelis since 1948, when he was twenty-one. . . . To him the fact that the battle in south Lebanon had been lost seemed totally insignificant. The most important thing was that there had been a battle at all. . . . "I thank God," he shouted, oblivious to the irony of the great Arab Marxist invoking the Almighty. "I thank God," he continued, bringing his fist

down onto the table, "that I lived to see the day that a Palestinian army fought an Israeli army. Now I can die. I don't need to see any more." Waving his arm around at his young acolytes, he added, "I feel sorry if anything happens to these young men, but now I can die, for we really fought them."

Implicit in this anecdote is another feature of level-IV conflict. As part of the faction dynamic of level IV, strong, often charismatic leaders will emerge who are comfortable with the leadership role and the exercise of power. Leaders in level-IV conflict are generally available to their followers and willing to expend considerable personal energy and initiative working on group goals. They inspire loyalty not only because they oversee followers effectively but also because they appear willing to make personal sacrifices themselves.

Given the strong within-group interdependence of level-IV actors (e.g., "It's us against them"), it becomes difficult for individual members of a faction to argue with the leadership, and the quality of information available suffers. Furthermore, when individuals find themselves at odds with a leadership decision that necessitates comment, they will not do so where they can be observed by the members of the opposition. At level IV, the "public" expression of in-group differences is likely to occur only when individuals are challenging the leadership hierarchy itself—as appears to have been the case when Zhao Ziyang broke party ranks to speak with student demonstrators prior to the Tiananmen Square massacre in June 1989.

As part of the dynamic of level IV, within-group cohesiveness and solidarity become more important than reconciling diverse constituencies or interest groups. At level IV, antagonists are tied to a strong commitment to their "position" and resist suggestion that the priorities of their faction might be less important than the priorities of the larger organization or the reduction of tension within the system as a whole. In level-IV conflict, individuals measure their success primarily by whether they have subordinated opposing groups; only secondarily are they concerned with whether they have achieved their ends or those of the larger system as a whole. As a result, if a subgroup's actions harm other factions, group members may express some sorrow or remorse that people had to be hurt, but will readily rationalize their behavior in terms of "the truth" being more important than any pain and suffering resulting from their actions. At level IV, priorities and values have changed profoundly from those of levels I, II, or III. Individuals have become more fixed on ideology and their own personal (or subgroup) agenda. Commonly, they lose sight of the importance of community, diversity, and relationship.

The key to level-IV behavior rests in the fact that the conflict is structured so that antagonists come to envision themselves as guardians of fundamentally exclusive principles. To outsiders it may seem as if the disputants are merely incompatible. To the person experiencing level-IV intent, it appears that the course of action he or she is taking is necessary "to preserve identity," "to insure democracy," "to combat anarchy," and so forth. In other words, this is not a problem to be solved or even a contest to be won. Level-IV actors see themselves as fighting oppression, perversion, or some other serious moral and ideological threat.

It may further clarify level-IV conflict dynamics if, keeping in mind that a characteristic feature of escalating conflict is that the strategies of response become increasingly entrenched, we consider the evolution of the events culminating at Tiananmen Square in June 1989. According to the report of a Stanford historian living in Beijing for the year prior to and shortly beyond the "Massacre" (Benedict 1989), the initial demonstrations following Hu Yaobang's death on April 15 could be seen as a level-I strategy focused on criticism and reform of Deng Xiaopeng's regime, not its overthrow, and confined to a relatively small group of activist students:

> . . . during the early weeks of the movement, most non-students continued to insist that they were simply not interested in politics. They seemed more amused than anything else by the earnest young students. On Tuesday, April 25, I was on a bus which passed some students from Beijing Normal University, carrying their school banner and talking to people on the street. A young worker on the bus cracked: "The Red Guards have arrived!", a remark that was met with laughter by others on the bus. (16)

For the first week of the protests, Benedict's observations support newspaper reports that the Chinese authorities did not respond to student demonstrations with any show of force. On the morning of Hu Yaobang's funeral, April 22, however:

> . . . those of us who came late to the square were blocked from seeing much of anything by the thousands of police who stood shoulder to shoulder all around the perimeter of the square. (15)

According to Benedict, a further turning point in the evolution of the protest movement can be dated from April 26 when the *People's Daily* carried an editorial that charged that the student movement was a "planned conspiracy" calling for "grave political struggle" against the students. As a result of the editorial making clear that the government might well use force against the students, the "laogaixing" (common people) joined the April 27th march, swelling the ranks of demonstrators to over 150,000.

With the expansion of the ranks of demonstrators to include the common people, the character of the protest shifted. By May 15, Benedict writes,

> Common people, the janitor in our building, the cafeteria workers, people I talked to on the street, all supported the students. Many did so because they believed that the students were the best hope of solving the twin problems of inflation and corruption: they were not particularly concerned with the broader issues of democracy and press freedom. . . . This outpouring of support had a darker side. . . . The student movement had become, almost overnight, one governed by emotion and passion. Now the demonstrators were out for blood, and they would not settle simply for a real "dialogue," they wanted nothing less than the collective resignation of the leadership. Where in the world, let alone the Communist world, would a government voluntarily leave power under such circumstances? (29–30)

According to the LICM, it is a hallmark of level-IV conflict that antagonists seek the assistance of third parties only as allies. To people fighting for survival or principles, you are either with them or against them—there is no other option. Neutrality is perceived as added power for the other side. Only if an outsider is on one's own side can he or she be tolerated. Given this dynamic, third parties can easily raise rather than reduce the stress experienced by level-IV principals. In general, as stress within a social system rises, the individual's ability to approach problems creatively and flexibly within that system declines (Janis and Mann 1977). As "saving face" is a particularly important aspect of Chinese culture, a public loss of face is likely to be a particularly potent stressor within the Chinese cultural context, and the role of the media as a shaper of conflict becomes critical.

Although we don't generally think of the media as a third party, in many instances it performs such a function—and in Tiananmen Square the media appears to have played a central role in escalating a level-I protest into a level-IV fight. Perhaps if the foreign press had not been so insistent in promoting the student cause; perhaps if the protesters' disruption of Gorbachev's visit had not been so public a loss of face; perhaps if the students could have "improved their recognition abilities" and shifted their strategy when confronted with mounting opposition, cooperation between the antagonists could have been promoted and the violence avoided.

To the extent that outsiders such as the world press became involved in the outcome of events in China, the LICM predicts that face-saving and competitive motives would be aroused to a degree that could lead principals to become both too stressed to solve problems and too invested to quit. Just as the involvement of third parties at level II can escalate the conflict by diverting the trust-building process between principals, the involvement of non-allied third parties at level IV is likely to do the same unless their dealings with the principals occur out of the public eye. In working with level-IV combatants, change agents must learn that it is easier to block destructive exchanges by highlighting the costs of current competition rather than the benefits of future cooperation. This is often best done in private session. Similarly, helping level-IV disputants recognize how their current methods interfere with achieving important personal values often motivates a willingness to change whereas a focus on the harm they are doing to the other does not. Such strategies take into account that the incentives for action at level IV are vested in individual interests rather than in relationship.

Principals in level-IV conflict have lost sight of interdependence. Deng justified the Tiananmen Square massacre as a rational response to an irresponsible factional effort to bring down the system of government he was committed to support. Considering this, on what basis then can either Deng's view of "the facts" or his choice of response be challenged? These questions are raised not because there are readily apparent answers but rather to highlight that understanding the contribution of values as an inextricable part of conflict and its resolution becomes increasingly critical as the stakes of conflict mismanagement become increasingly profound.

Level V: War

At level V, "war," conflict has become intractable. Differences of interest are not only viewed as mutually exclusive, the claims of one party are perceived by the other as a threat to ontological security. Enemies at level V experience high levels of anxiety, which they believe can only be assuaged by the other's defeat. At war, combatants have no compunctions against the use of compulsion and force—they are relentless in trying to accomplish their aims, and vengeful and vindictive when frustrated.

Objectivity has been lost to subjectivity. Information is skewed, and irrationality is rampant. There is no longer any clear understanding of the issues—personality has become the issue. Level-V behavior is part of a simple and heroic drama that the combatant has fixed in his head and that may or may not be related to what is actually going on in the world. Disputants see themselves as utterly responsible for the survival of their cause. They view themselves as the sole protectors of important principles, facing detractors, invaders, and destroyers who must be stopped at all costs.

The emotional climate of enemies at war is characterized by volatility, rage, and hopelessness. Combatants feel hopeless about their ability to achieve security or satisfaction while the enemy still exists. Because of this loss of confidence in their individual ability to achieve important ends, they seek out and are susceptible to external directives and guidance. In addition, because they believe there is no place untainted by the other, principals see the costs of withdrawal as greater than the costs of engaging in a battle to the death. Consequently, at level V, there is often focus on tales of martyrdom— Masada for the Israelis, and the promise of Paradise for Islamic fundamentalists who die fighting in Allah's jihad (Wright 1985).

At both levels IV and V, group members may perceive themselves to be part of an eternal cause, fighting outsiders for unambiguous principles. However, unlike leaders at level IV, who consider themselves and their followers to be "comrades in arms," level-V leaders generally are career-oriented professionals who have undergone training that encourages them to consider their followers to be resources or chess pieces rather than unique and irreplaceable individuals. Level V leaders are drawn from specialized elites; they are generals from academies rather than enlisted men or draftees who rise from the ranks.

If we consider modern and global warfare, a critical distinguishing feature is the diversity of intentionality that characterizes its principal participants. *Modern warfare and "war" as defined by the LICM are not synonymous.* If soldiers are invested in level-V intentionality as defined by the LICM, they cannot choose to stop fighting because to do so would be immoral and irresponsible. Mercenaries or generals, in contrast, may view their participation in warfare more as a level-I problem-solving exercise than as a result of uncompromisable principles. Consequently, interventions for dealing with the realities of war must necessarily be inclusive of all the levels of conflict so far considered, rather than being attentive solely to the fifth category within the model, designated as "war."

Within the LICM, the distinction made between level-IV and level-V conflict inheres in fundamental issues of intentionality and value rather than of behavior or attitude. At both levels, there are principals who believe that to quit is to be more than disloyal; to rein in one's zeal is to be a traitor to the cause. At both levels, those who are really committed will sacrifice all. Only at level V, however, will participants treat not only their antagonists as less than human but their compatriots as well.

Ends are all important at level V, and any means are seen to justify them. A characteristic of level-V conflict is that one doesn't have to do much thinking about the ethics of means. Though the losses may be great (and though important principles, like freedom or the dignity of individuals, may have to be compromised), the ends are so important that one need only worry about "temporary" breaches (e.g., such as sending troops on missions known to be suicidal) after the principles one is fighting for have been restored.

A key assumption of individuals at level V is that other people are less human than oneself. This is the realm of "I/it" relationships dominating and eliminating "I/Thou" (Buber 1970). Theoretically, war as defined by the LICM can exist without the use of physical force or armaments. In practice, however, it appears that, once human beings are reified and seen as manipulable objects, rationalizing violent use of them and violence against them to achieve one's ends becomes inevitable.

When enemies objectify and do violence not only against each other but also against their allied subordinates, the prognosis for human survival is bleak. Even when powerful third parties levy pressures or incentives compelling the principals to restore a semblance of "peace," periods of nonviolence under such conditions are rarely stable. To manage battering couples, separating the partners and maintaining the partition between them long enough so that agreements of nonaggression can be put into operation and enforced has been shown to be a more-effective first step than are programs that initially attempt to work with the principals conjointly.

However, experience with intimate enemies suggests that agreements of nonaggression will only be sustained over the long run if the individual's sense of identity becomes invested in nonviolence and cooperation rather than if these behaviors are compelled by pressure from outside. An implication for action that derives from this insight is that persons concerned with creating the conditions for peace must attend as much to the building of character as to the dismantling of bombs.

Summary and Conclusion

The Levels of Interpersonal Conflict Model was designed to clarify the multiple and divergent conflict dynamics that are usually lumped together when questions such as "Why do people fight?" are put on the table. The title of this chapter asks how important it is to know the intentionality of a negotiator. Throughout, situations are described that demonstrate not only how different motivational dynamics lead to different behaviors under similar stimulus conditions of conflict but also how seemingly similar conflict behaviors that derive from different intentional bases will be responsive to different incentives and pressures for change.

From such a model, it is hoped that practical knowledge can be derived so that conflict need not escalate to "contests," "fights," or "war." There is a great deal of biological, historical, and psychological evidence documenting and justifying the propensity of human beings to engage in violent conflict with one another. Far less attention is given to understanding the circumstances that lead human beings to sustain situations of cooperation and peace in the face of scarce resources and pressures to compete.

Comparisons of human beings to hypothetical prisoners or to other species are useful when they allow us to recognize that doing violence against one's own is an easily evoked human potential. The shortcomings of such comparisons are evident, however, in their failure to explain the behavior of an Oscar Arias or a Mother Teresa. In their failure to take into account these prototypically human actors, these comparisons promote the illusion that biology in the absence of culture is the determining influence in human affairs.

Understanding that human behavior is influenced not solely by "objective conditions" but also by what situations "mean" requires models of interpersonal conflict that account for the fact that human beings interpret reality as they respond to it. Knowing that a person pursues sexual gratification or happiness tells us very little about him or her that is individually predictive; for that, we need to know the principle under which these goals are operative. There are people who are happy only in meeting the needs of others and people who feel pleasure or arousal only in the face of another's total subjugation and humiliation.

Models of human behavior that fail to take these divergences into account are, at best, merely reductionistic and of interest to a limited audience. When interpersonal differences are misconceived, mishandled, and escalated because the models available to interpret and influence them conceive of conflict only as a process at level III and above, such models can be downright dangerous. The LICM recognizes that it is not the seriousness of the issue that determines the level of interpersonal conflict, but the motivation and behavior of the principals. In surfacing difference, conflict presents each of us with the opportunity to advance human development through the discovery of integrative and nonviolent solutions to problems. Only if we model ourselves after the best of humanity, the creators and caretakers among us rather than the exploiters and killers, may we yet avoid what Hobbes predicted for humanity—a future that is "mean, nasty, brutish and short."

REFERENCES

Axelrod, R. 1984. *The Evolution of Cooperation*. New York: Basic Books.
Benedict, C. 1989. *Beijing Journal*. Unpublished manuscript, Stanford University.
Buber, M. 1970 (1937). *I and Thou*. New York: Scribner.
Earl, P. E., ed. 1988. *Psychological Economics*. Boston: Kluwer Academic Publishers.
Etzioni, A. 1988. *The Moral Dimension*. New York: Free Press.
Fisher, R. and W. Ury. 1983. *Getting to Yes*. New York: Penguin Books.
Friedman, T. 1989. *From Beirut to Jerusalem*. New York: Farrar, Straus, Giroux.
Janis, I. L., and L. Mann. 1977. *Decision Making: A Psychological Analysis of Conflict, Choice, and Commitment*. New York: Free Press.
Kelman, H.C. 1958. "Compliance, Identification and Internalization." *Journal of Conflict Resolution* 2: 51–60.

Kohn, A. 1986. *No Contest*. Boston: Houghton Mifflin.

Leas, S. 1985. *Moving Your Church Through Conflict*. Washington, DC: Alban Institute.

Weingarten, H. 1986. "Strategic Planning for Divorce Mediation." *Social Work* 31(3): 194–200.

Weingarten, H., and S. Leas. 1987. "Levels of Marital Conflict Model." *American Journal of Orthopsychiatry* 57(3): 407–17.

Woodcock, L. 1989. Personal communication with the author by letter April, 1990.

Wright, R. 1985. *Sacred Rage*. New York: Linden Press/Simon and Shuster.

How the Mind Preserves the Image of the Enemy: The Mnemonics of Soviet-American Relations

Eugene Burnstein, Mark Abboushi, and Shinobu Kitayama

This chapter begins with a brief review of the various approaches social scientists have taken over the past forty years in their analysis of intergroup conflict. It then discusses several recent social psychological experiments demonstrating that ill will toward an out-group is initiated with little or no external pressure. Finally, there is a series of studies on how knowledge about the out-group is organized in memory and why this organization serves to sustain or even augment such ill will once it is initiated.

Explanations of Intergroup Conflict

Instrumentalism

Social science is of two minds about how to explain antagonisms between groups (see reviews in Horowitz 1985, Smith 1986). The most popular account, often called *instrumentalism*, emphasizes the rationality of decisions to engage in conflict. The basic assumption is that people act as a group to the extent that they believe that they have common goals and perceive that these goals can be most readily achieved collectively. Groups, therefore, are merely vessels of individual interest, like a trade union or manufacturers association. The more extreme versions of instrumentalism even hold that the group is ideology, an agreed-upon abstraction or a social representation constructed for partisan ends (Breuilly 1982, 1–41, Hobsbawm and Ranger 1983, Moscovici 1988).

In any case, conflict is said to occur whenever the goals of one group are incompatible with those pursued by another group and each is determined to resolve matters to its advantage. From the instrumental perspective, therefore, intergroup conflict is the result of objective forces and not of some obscure, visceral urge to dominate. Groups decide to compete because their members calculate that more is to be gained (or less is to be lost) from this course of

197

action than from cooperation; their decision does not depend on atavistic emotions such as fear or envy of the out-group. In short, according to the instrumental model, groups fight each other when their members think fighting is the most efficient means of protecting their interests in the circumstances.

Finally, instrumentalism assumes that members' interests stem from the material conditions of life, which leads instrumentalists to believe that, in the last analysis, groups contend over goals that are concrete and objective (e.g., territory, wealth, and power) rather than abstract or subjective (e.g., god, liberty, and the pursuit of happiness). This argument can also be made on psychological grounds, that interests giving rise to group formation and intergroup conflict must be tangible, otherwise individuals would have difficulty comparing their position with those of others and deciding whether the positions are compatible.

The finest social psychological expression of instrumentalism is found in the work of Sherif. His pioneering field experiments left no doubt that competition over material resources can cause strong antagonisms between collectivities (Sherif 1966). He observed under well-controlled conditions that if two arbitrarily formed groups have incompatible goals, the members of one group dislike those belonging to the other and, given the opportunity, physically attack them with energy and craft. Moreover, when their interests are made compatible—the researchers establish a *superordinate goal* whose achievement requires intergroup cooperation—antagonisms vanish and are replaced by alliance and friendship. Hence, having their outcomes organized in a zero-sum fashion is *sufficient* condition for conflict between the groups; and having their outcomes organized in the form of a coordination game (or, in Sherif's terms, when the groups are linked by a superordinate goal) is *sufficient* condition for intergroup cooperation. Whether they are *necessary* conditions is another story.

To get at the necessary conditions for intergroup conflict, it might be instructive to start with *ethnies*—clans, bands, tribes, and nationalities who on objective grounds seem compelled to quarrel but do not do so. For example, if there is an ethnic division of labor so that groups specialize in complementary occupations, differences in economic function may inhibit conflict even though one group gains from the arrangement more than the other does. Needless to say, the notion that a disadvantaged group appreciates the economic activities of the advantaged group does little for instrumental theories.

This issue has been highlighted in analyses of the *middleman minorities* hypothesis, a derivation from the instrumental model (e.g., Bonacich 1973, van den Berghe 1981). According to this hypothesis, foreigners from the metropole who descend on rural areas to buy the crops and sell manufactured goods exploit the local citizenry and as a result build up a reservoir of resentment toward themselves. However, the evidence that peasants frequently welcome rather than resent the alien merchant is considerable (Horowitz 1985, 185–228).

The same theme in a somewhat different guise is found in theories about the resurgence of ethnic awareness that is thought to be associated with *modernization* (Barth 1969, Hannan 1979, Olzak and Nagel 1986). These formulations see group mobilization and intergroup conflict stemming from competition for jobs between members of different *ethnies*; and intensification of job competition, particularly in the secondary and tertiary sectors of the economy, is a normal by-product of modernization. However, there is considerable research indicating that the relationship between ethnic conflict and modernization is not so straightforward. In Wales, Belgium, and Quebec, three of the most studied cases, ethnic mobilization, say, as evidenced by the amount of support for nationalist parties, was often strongest in the least "modern" (i.e., the most rural) areas (Ragin 1979, Nielsen 1980, Olzak 1982). To accommodate findings of this kind some researchers have given up the notion of competition as an objective economic process and argue that intergroup conflict is caused by economic competition only when the competition is *perceived* by members to be *unfair* (Belanger and Pinard 1991, Pinard and Hamilton 1986).

Social psychological research has also found that, contrary to the instrumental hypothesis, tangible threats from an out-group do not necessarily lead to intergroup conflict. To take a well-known study in the area, during two successive mayoral elections involving a white candidate and a black candidate, Kinder and Sears (1981) interviewed a large sample of white suburbanites around Los Angeles to assess their beliefs about the dangers posed by minority groups in four domains of considerable importance to the respondents' personal lives: neighborhood desegregation, racial busing, black violence, and preferential treatment in hiring and promotion. They found no relationship between perceived threat in respect to any of these issues and the tendency to favor the white candidate for mayor. If anything, a white voter who believed blacks posed a real threat in a domain where he or she was actually vulnerable (e.g., the respondent had a child who was likely to be bused or who lived in a neighborhood that was likely to be affected by black violence) was just about as inclined to cast a ballot for the black candidate as for the white candidate, whereas a white person who was not vulnerable and on objective grounds had little to worry about from black people was much more likely to vote for the white than the black candidate.

More surprising from the perspective of instrumental theories was the finding that perceptions of black threat in these cases was unrelated to whites' schema or stereotype of blacks, what Kinder and Sears called *symbolic racism*. The latter refers to highly abstract, general, and unqualified evaluations of the out-group as indicated by agreement with sweeping propositions such as "blacks get more than they deserve." While the level of symbolic racism was not trivial—64 percent of the sample assented to that statement— whether respondents agreed or disagreed with it did not depend on how menaced they felt by neighborhood desegregation, racial busing, black violence, or hiring and promotion preferences. Nor did vulnerability even to that most emotion-laden threat, busing, predict opposition to its implementation. In fact, the single statistically significant effect regarding attitudes toward busing was that the average white who had children in high school and who thought they were likely to be bused to a black school was *less* opposed to busing than a white with children in high school who thought busing unlikely, which is an anomalous finding to those who believe that opposition to a menacing out-group increases in intensity as the menace becomes more palpable.

Finally, most problematic for instrumentalism, are some pervasive facts of group life. Intense conflicts frequently occur between groups whose members have only the foggiest idea of the tangible interests underlying the dispute (and those who believe they do know them often disagree). However, the members *are* aware of the cost, and believe that it is disproportionate to whatever it is they are fighting over. If, for example, someone surveyed the Sinhalese and Tamils in Sri Lanka or the Bosnians, Croats, and Serbs in what was Yugoslavia and asked them to list their reasons for fighting, we propose that the responses would not support the instrumental model: when members of these *ethnies* computed their gains and losses, the sum would be negative. But, of course, it is irrelevant to our argument whether they actually do the arithmetic since most of the people of Sri Lanka and the former Yugoslavia know intuitively that for them the material benefits of conflict at best— assume they give no thought to defeat—will hardly compensate for the destruction and bloodshed, not to mention the opportunity costs. Nonetheless, in the case of conflicts between collectivities, some scholars would argue that the rational model can be more appropriately applied by postulating that the group, rather than the individual, decides. If the group is viewed as a unitary actor, theoretically, a policy that is profitable for its purposes could be perceived as dear by the average member. However, this presumes that we can determine the utility of intergroup conflict for a collectivity at least as well as we can determine this utitility for an individual and that the former value is relatively independent of the latter, neither of which is true. Be this as it may, what is striking to us is the frequency with which groups engage in conflicts that ordinary members find unprofitable and prefer to avoid. In addition, we do not think it rare for the elites responsible for initiating and directing such conflicts to do so while disparaging its value. The *New York Times* recently (June 2, 1992) carried an interview with the senior commander of the Serbian forces laying siege to Sarajevo in which he despaired that "Serbs and Bosnians . . . have done such terrible things to each other that they will never again be able to live side by side. . . . After living so well in Yugoslavia, and creating this disaster, we should get a Nobel Prize for stupidity."

Primordialism

If no tangible profit is to be had, why then fight? Because, according to our second theory of intergroup conflict, called *primordialism*, there is a more fundamental source of antagonism than that assumed by the instrumental model. In contrast to the notion that groups are vessels of special interest with no status or integrity—to use Campbell's (1958) pithy term, no *entitativity*—independent of these interests, primordialists take it as self-evident that there *is* a visceral urge to distinguish invidiously one's own group from other groups. It is undeniable, they say, that since time immemorial people everywhere have been differentiated into certain categories (see Rosch 1977), usually defined in terms of culture, religion, language, phenotype (i.e., race), and proximity (i.e., territory). Peculiar to these social categories is the belief that membership signals a common origin and a common fate; individuals who belong to the same group are perceived as biologically and historically interdependent, as having the same ancestry and the same destiny. Among other things, this means that virtually all members of a disadvantaged *ethnie*, especially those who have prospered and have high status in the larger society, feel concern about their community in what they perceive as a struggle against subordination ("we Malays have to emulate the Chinese or we will remain behind them forever") or even extinction ("for us Ossetians a Georgian-dominated state means that in time our community will disappear"). In any case, their concern often is strong enough that it leads them to make extraordinary sacrifices for the good of the group, sacrifices of a kind that typically occur, if at all, among close kin.

Interestingly enough, like instrumentalism, the primordial model also implies that intergroup conflict stems in part from the social representations that societies adopt to explain social differentiation. For the primordialist, these myths constitute schematic rules for deciding who belongs in what social category, particularly whether the other belongs in same category as oneself or in a different category. The rules constitute a member's implicit theory of the social unit or a mental model specifying the boundary between in-group and out-group. Most important, unless the person makes a conscious effort to control their application, the rules operate automatically—it is psychologically impossible to conceive of other individuals without immediately categorizing them in terms of gender, age, speech, or a variety of other features having to do with physique and dress that connote group membership—in parallel with more deliberate processes (e.g., the conscious calculation of common interest) in order to estimate the quality of a potential social relationship. Is it likely to be cooperative or competitive, beneficial or costly, enduring or temporary, intense or superficial? Will I be dominant or subordinate? In sum, the conjecture is that, upon encountering others, we immediately identify them as in-group or out-group, often without any awareness on our part, and respond to them appropriately in terms of their membership.

Whatever the merits of these speculations, the primordialist does have a point: it is clear that intergroup conflict can have an egregiously costly, nonrational, self-sacrificial aspect that is difficult to explain within an instrumental model. At the same time, however, there remains the nontrivial problem of coming up with a psychological theory that spells out how notions of common descent and common destiny can lead collectivities to quarrel and fight. We will not review the various attempts (e.g., Alexander 1987, Daly and Wilson 1988, Trivers 1985) but simply note that the primordial model's insight is that, as a species, we have been so persistently and intensely social that whatever the biological roots of *ethnie*, the category itself has become symbolically encoded, its distinctive features being language, culture, territory, and phenotype, each of which has been a distal but not totally unreliable cue to biological kinship for most of human history.

Even if during the past few centuries the concept of a nation, people, or tribe has been deracinated and transformed, there are reasons for it remaining a pervasive and powerful social representation. To begin with, the transformation probably has not been enormous; and, whatever the extent, it stems not from an abrupt qualitative change in group life but rather from a gradual decline in the ecological validity of language, culture, territory, and phenotype as kinship cues. Moreover, this gradual decline may have been vastly compensated for by an increase in the human capacity for self-deception, or however else one wishes to describe our ability to attribute beliefs and emotions originally associated with kin relations to those involving nonkin ("he's not heavy *Father*, he's my *brother*"). Nonetheless, while proximity and familiarity, common culture, phenotypic similarity, and even designation by group consensus or experts (e.g., one's parents) may no longer predict kinship as well as they did in the past, the feeling that one knows who is likely to be trustworthy and cooperative remains useful even in the most ordinary social exchanges, if only as a *self-fulfilling prophecy*. Hence, categories denoting nationality, peoplehood, and ethnicity may still benefit the person to the extent that they actually detect "cheaters" or that they reduce anxiety about others in the situation and thereby encourage cooperation. To this extent, these categories remain adaptive concepts, and our capacity to deploy them in encoding will likely persist.

Current Social Psychological Analyses of Intergroup Conflict

Although Sherif's research was extremely influential, there were at about the same time other theoretical developments occurring in social psychology that pointed to noninstrumental sources of intergroup conflict. Interestingly enough, in these theories the urge toward establishing invidious distinctions between groups is more cerebral than visceral. They assumed that we store information in memory in as stable a form as possible. To this end, if the information in question is social, we "chunk" it so that positive relationships appear to occur between members of the same set, and negative relationships between members of different sets (Heider 1958; Harary, Norman, and Cartwright 1965; Davis 1967).

When knowledge is encoded in this fashion it is said to satisfy the principle of *structural balance* (Heider 1958). The evidence that this principle is an important source of bias in the cognitive representation of social relations is considerable: balanced social structures are not only easy to remember, they are also perceived as consistent, logical, and typical, whereas imbalanced social structures are difficult to remember and are perceived as inconsistent, illogical, and atypical. Hence, individuals expect social relations to be balanced and recall them as such. Should their expectations be violated, they reconstruct social relations in memory to approximate a balanced structure (Burnstein 1967, Cottrell 1975, Crockett 1982, Sentis and Burnstein 1979).

As an illustration, suppose that you read in dispatches from the trans-Caucasus that the relationship between group A and group B is extremely hostile, as is the relationship between group C and group D, whereas A and C have an extremely friendly and cooperative relationship. You know little about these groups but think this is interesting and file the information away in memory. Later, a colleague asks you about the potential for intergroup conflict in this region of the ex–Soviet Union, especially between A and D, D and B, and B and C, relationships that were not touched upon in the dispatches. What do you say?

The balance-theory prediction is that over time you will be incapable of distinguishing relationships described in the dispatches from those that were not and that you will have "filled in" and recoded the information in memory as representing two antagonistic *alliances*, namely, A and C versus B and D, with friendly, cooperative relations between groups in the same alliance and hostile, competitive relations between groups in different alliances. Hence, you are inclined to recall that there is great potential for conflict between *A* and *D* and between *B* and *C* but little potential for conflict between *B* and *D*, even though the original information was silent in these respects (also see Davis 1967, whose formulation permits more than two alliances or "clusters" under these conditions). In short, balance theory, or any of the other models of cognitive consistency, assumes that the mind organizes intergroup relations as much as possible according to an in-group versus out-group schema whose principles can be summarized in the following homey statements (Campbell and LeVine 1968, 555):

1. An ally of an ally will be an ally.
2. An enemy of an ally will be an enemy.
3. An ally of an enemy will be an enemy.
4. An enemy of an enemy will be an ally.

Inexplicably, current analyses of intergroup conflict are not much influenced by Heider's (1958) work. Instead, they attempt something different but equally interesting, namely, to describe the *minimal* conditions under which in-group members will act in a hostile fashion toward out-group members (Brewer 1979; Horwitz and Rabbie 1982; Insko and Schopler 1987; Insko et al. 1990; Rabbie and Horwitz 1969; Tajfel 1970, 1981; Turner 1987). The signal and very important contribution of all this newer work has been to demonstrate that even if neither the nature of the groups nor the relationship between them is specified—individuals merely know that they belong to one social category whose meaning eludes them and that others belong to a different and equally elusive social category—members, who as individuals have nothing tangible to gain or lose, still opt to help the in-group and harm the out-group. Put differently, members act as if the default value for intergroup relations is competition, which is similar to the point Heider made years earlier.

The experimental procedure Rabbie and Tajfel followed is probably the most widely used. Subjects, often high school students, are arbitrarily divided on trivial and incomprehensible grounds (e.g., a flip of a coin, their preference in unfamiliar artists). They are then presented with series of matrices consisting of pairs of payoffs, one of which will be given to the members of the subject's category (but not to the subject) and the second, to members of the other category. The pairs exemplify different strategies ranging from maximizing joint gains ("$20 to my group and $25 to the other group") to maximizing differences ("$10 dollars to my group and $1 to the other group"). When asked to choose, the preference is for payoffs that advantage the in-group relative to the out-group, that is, something approximating a difference-maximizing strategy. Note two things about this finding. First, it means that rather than both groups benefiting similarly, individuals prefer to have their own group experience a cost as long as the cost inflicted on the other group is appreciably greater. Second, the *mere presence* of an unfathomable and ephemeral in-group and out-group boundary is sufficient to evoke the preference.

The procedures used by Insko and his colleagues are somewhat more complex. For instance, they had in-group and out-group members actually engage in an exchange; and, equally important, their payoff matrices unconfounded strategies so that inferring members' intentions toward the out-group from their choice of payoffs is not problematic. Moreover, they were concerned not just with what happens if individuals belong to different social categories but with what happens when they actually recognize this difference and act accordingly. The goal, as we suggested earlier, is to identify how little it takes for individuals to perceive that they are interacting with each other as members of distinct social entities (in-group versus out-group) instead of individuals interacting qua individuals.

Insko and colleagues discovered that thinking in terms of in-group versus out-group required more than arbitrary categorization (cf. Tajfel, whose categories had no clear meaning to people, e.g., *we* in the cubicles on the left side of the laboratory versus *them* in the cubicles on the right). In addition, individuals belonging to one category had to discuss and arrive at some consensus regarding their exchange with those belonging to the other category. As to the exchange itself, the decision as to who gets what reflected ill will but mixed with realism. In-group members seemed to take into account that the out-group was not going to disappear after one exchange: compared to when there was no categorization or discussion, individuals were inclined to choose payoffs that benefited the in-group more than the out-group, but their choices did not reflect a true difference-maximizing strategy; rather, there was a compromise between conflicting impulses, a desire to maximize joint gain as opposed to a desire to maximize differences. In short, individuals preferred those payoff pairs that produced the greatest benefits for both groups *and* at the same time benefited the in-group more than the out-group. Let the tide raise both our boats, but let it raise mine higher than yours. Hence, one could say that Tajfel's subjects behaved as if it were a "war of each group against all," and Insko's subjects acted in the spirit of "enlightened capitalism."

Neither researcher argues that competition is inevitable, only that it is inherent to intergroup settings. Here Insko's findings make a key contribution by demonstrating, first, that noncompetitive predispositions are also inherent; and, second, that due to these countervailing tendencies, the default value for intergroup relations is a compromise between pure cooperation (i.e., maximizing joint gain) and pure competition (i.e., maximizing the difference between in-group and out-group gain). Rather than competition at any cost, it may be more accurate to say the preferred strategy is the largest joint gain *but* with the in-group gaining more than the out-group. Keep in mind, moreover, that this preference is manifested when the social context is extraordinarily uninformative and members operate under ignorance; there are no clues to goals or intentions. Hence, the implication is that, at bottom, humans are "enlightened capitalists" in the sense that, under conditions of minimal knowledge, in-group members do not try to overwhelm the out-group and appropriate its resources. Instead they pursue a more nuanced strategy, distrusting the out-group but at the same time taking into account the *shadow of the future*, sensing the possibility of a useful alliance and intuiting the permanence of in-group interests as against the impermanence of enemies (Axelrod 1984).

Be that as it may, despite the differences, both Tajfel and Insko agree about in-group members' initial attitude toward an out-group: in the absence of countervailing knowledge, humans view members of an out-group more negatively than they do members of the in-group. Not much is known about *why* they feel this way. Insko does suggest, however, that negativism toward the out-group stems primarily from a fear on the part of in-group members about the intentions of those in the out-group (Insko et al. 1990), which seems to beg the question. Tajfel (1981) and Turner (1987) took a more elaborate stab at it via their theory of social identity. This formulation assumes that self-worth depends on social identity, that is, the group(s) to which individuals perceive they belong. Belonging to a high-ranking group confers a positive social identity and belonging to a low ranking group, a negative social identity. In the former case, self-worth is high; in the latter, it is low. Intergroup conflict, therefore, reflects attempts by members to enhance self-worth by improving the standing of the in-group, a change that, if successful, is inevitably at the expense of the out-group. As a consequence, in a ranked system, in-groups automatically sense general ill will or malevolence on the part of out-groups. When the out-group ranks higher than the in-group, the ill will is perceived to be overlaid with scorn or contempt, and when the out-group ranks lower, with envy or resentment.

While the Tajfel-Turner model is most widely used in social psychological analyses of intergroup relations, many of its more-important implications remain to be tested. For example, an obvious hypothesis is that intergroup conflict increases as the likelihood of social mobility, the ability to change group membership and, thus, one's social identity, decreases. However, no study has varied mobility opportunities; indeed, virtually all of the experimental work has used groups or social categories that individuals can readily leave (or enter) and that, therefore, should engender little conflict. Nonetheless, the findings from this research, together with those of Insko and his colleagues, are the main social psychological evidence for primordialism, and it is reasonably good evidence. As a result, instrumentalists have difficulty arguing that members of one group will not act antagonistically toward those of another group when there is no tangible profit to be derived from doing so. They clearly will. And although we may not as yet have a good theory to explain why, demonstrating that sociality at its most meager is from the very outset stamped by conflict is a useful and important corrective to Sherif's (1966) formulation that antagonism toward the out-group is simply an attempt by in-group members to gain some tangible end and does not occur otherwise.

In this chapter, we assume that Tajfel and Insko are essentially correct. Given that relations between groups are inherently but not inevitably antagonistic and that in-group members are predisposed to attribute ill will to out-group members, we go on to ask why the antagonism persists in the absence of support, and often in the face of evidence to the contrary. What mechanisms of mind sustain the belief that the out-group is the enemy? We will argue that this is due in part to the structure of human memory and the process of recall, which constrain thinking so that information about an out-group's malevolence is easier to access than information about its benevolence.

Recalling What We Know About the Out-group: Two Search Strategies

Memory stores information and makes it available to consciousness, which uses it to make decisions and communicate ideas. To minimize the cost of deciding and communicating, memory strives to be Gricean; that is, the concepts brought into consciousness should be: (1) as informative as is necessary but not more so; (2) as consistent as possible with each other and with the underlying evidence; (3) relevant; and (4) as unambiguous and coherent as circumstances warrant (Grice, 1975). To satisfy these principles, memory has evolved a particular structure which, as it turns out, also lends itself to maintaining one's habitual view of others. A good way of understanding the nature of this structure is to examine how one recalls information about an out-group.

Over several years in the 1980s we asked individuals two questions: Is the Soviet Union a threat to world peace? The simplest way of deciding is to search memory for an appropriate past opinion, terminate the search at this point, and use the opinion as a ready-made answer. As an example of such a self-terminating procedure, a person who did not want to consider the issue at length might remember having decided at some time in the past that "the Russians want to dominate their neighbors" and that "they will risk war to do so," and answer the question affirmatively. If the person was even more pressed by other matters, she might merely recall that, the last time an issue like this arose, she concluded that "the Soviet Union will cause a war," which seems to fall in the same category as "the Soviet Union is a threat to world peace" and without further to-do use the past opinion as her present judgment. We call this mnemonic strategy of activating old opinions about an out-group and immediately terminating the process upon finding one that is good enough to serve as a response, *limited-search*.

Because limited-search permits the person to sidestep the hodgepodge of details underlying an opinion, it is relatively effortless and can be carried out even while one is really deliberating about something else. In this sense, it is a mindless strategy. Nonetheless, on occasion a "control process" of this kind may be preferable, considering the alternative strategy, namely, *exhaustive-search*. Suppose individuals do not stop once they have recalled an old, seemingly pertinent opinion; instead they go on to analyze the opinion just to be sure it really can be used as a response. Once the search extends beyond the representation of the opinion, it brings to mind *case information*. Whereas opinions are abstract and unqualified, case information is concrete and specific. It is the representation in memory of the distinct events that were used to form (as well as to update) one's opinion of the out-group. When the out-group is as complex as was the Soviet Union, case information is bound to be mixed. Thus, some events that a person remembers about the Soviet Union imply that it had a policy of cooperating with the United States, while other events that come to mind imply a policy of competition.

The upshot is that, compared to limited-search, exhaustive-search is bound to sow confusion. Individuals who might otherwise have believed an old opinion they happened to recall, that "the Soviet Union is expansionist," which means the same as "the Soviet Union is a threat to world peace," grow increasingly unsure of themselves as they probe more deeply and become conscious of qualifications (e.g., ". . . hey, they don't always pursue an expansionist policy—remember the case of . . .") and context (e.g., ". . . did I read that in the *National Enquirer* or was it in Kennan? . . ."), the caveats and nuances that are the essence of case information. Hence, a strategy of limited-search enables the uninterested or the preoccupied to avoid being temporarily perplexed by pros and cons, the disparate details underlying the old opinion. Obviously, however, steering clear of facts has the long-term cost of a poorly grounded decision.

In summary, in order to make a judgment about an out-group individuals must retrieve relevant information from memory. There are at least two ways of going about this. Limited-search is a strategy whereby individuals cease thinking about the out-group as soon as an old opinion comes to mind that is good enough to use as a ready-made response. Additional knowledge about the out-group is deemed unnecessary and is not accessed. The alternative strategy, exhaustive-search, leads individuals to continue thinking about the matter in question even after summoning up a suitable past judgment. As a result, there comes to mind a variety of details about the out-group (i.e., case information) that may qualify and even contradict the opinion.

The reason these different search strategies call up different kinds of information has to do with the way memory is organized. Assume individuals had not yet formed an opinion of the out-group. They were knowledgeable but had not taken a position one way or another as to, say, whether the Soviet Union was a threat to world peace. To form an opinion, they retrieve various pieces of case information (e.g., ". . . they were bloody ruthless in Afghanistan . . ."), connecting them with other pieces (". . . which is what they did earlier in . . ."), and making a series of inferences terminating in a judgment (". . . yes, the Soviet Union is a threat to world peace . . ."). The opinion itself, therefore, is the gist or summary of case information and is represented separately from the latter. Finally, an opinion such as the Soviet Union being a threat to world peace is linked to other opinions to constitute a larger structure, called a *schema* or *stereotype*, representing the person's most general conception of the out-group.

In essence, forming an opinion about the out-group involves connecting and summarizing heretofore disjoined knowledge. These operations produce a hierarchical structure in which abstract concepts, those contained in one's schema of the Soviet Union, are stored near the top and concrete knowledge, the specific events of Soviet history that make up case information, is stored near the bottom. How this organization is achieved has been a fundamental issue in theories of social cognition (Abelson et al. 1968, Fiske and Taylor 1991). In general, the process is assumed to be one of continuous culling and refining in the service of coherence. As a consequence, certain ideas represented at one level of the structure are *discounted* and lack representation at levels above it. The discounting principle is well known: in order for a proposition to be represented at a higher level it must be *consistent* with the other propositions at this level. Hence, case information that is inconsistent with an old opinion will not be reflected at the level of the opinion, nor will opinions that are inconsistent with the schema be reflected at the level of the schema.

Inconsistent information, however, is not erased from memory. A person with an extremely negative stereotype of the Soviet Union can, when pressed, recall considerable case information that is positive. Discounted events remain part of the knowledge structure underlying the opinion and will be accessed when memory search is exhaustive (Schul and Burnstein 1985, Kitayama and Burnstein 1989). Nevertheless, as a result of discounting, the information represented at higher levels is coherent, unqualified, and categorical—sweeping generalizations—whereas the information represented at lower levels consists of a jumble of concrete images, anecdotes, and narratives whose implications tend to be disparate and tempered. It follows then that, when individuals pondered whether the Soviet Union was a threat to world peace, the answer they came up with depended on how they search memory.

In thinking about collectivities like the Soviet Union, top-down processing is probably most common. The level at which search begins generally corresponds to level of the concepts instigating the search, and the concepts that get us thinking about out-groups of this kind are typically abstract. Indeed, because the entity to which it refers is so complex and heterogeneous, the very concept of "Soviet Union" must be quite broad as must many of the concepts associated with it, like "world peace." Hence, when individuals concern themselves with a question containing these concepts, they start their analysis near the schema level. If they terminate the search at this point, the information available will be unqualified and unidirectional. As a result, their judgment is likely to be extreme. However, if the search is exhaustive, individuals eventually access case information which is qualified and mixed, and they take a moderate position. This implies that a limited search leads to a more anti-Soviet opinion than does an exhaustive search. The critical question is under what conditions individuals use one or the other strategy.

To try to answer this question, let us again suppose that individuals were faced with the relatively abstract issue of whether the Soviet Union was a threat to world peace. They would resolve the matter effortlessly with schematic knowledge, that is, by outputting some cut-and-dried past opinion *or* effortfully with case information, that is, by integrating the mix of events represented at that level of memory. Hence, issues that focus on abstract features of the out-group allow the person to *decide* between terminating memory search early or searching exhaustively. In these circumstances, strategy is a matter of preference or predisposition. However, issues that deal with concrete matters—Did the Soviet Union, in building the radar installation at Krasnoyarsk, violate the SALT treaty?—compel memory search to begin at the level of case information ("well, it's a phased-array system, that means . . . ," and "the treaty permits other radar systems like . . . but not systems like . . ."). Under these conditions, therefore, individuals have little choice. Unless they are experts, they do not possess a preintegrated, ready-made response for issues of this degree of specificity; instead, regardless of personal inclination, they are obliged to access case information.

The preference for a particular search strategy, we assume, depends on the capacity of working memory. In arriving at a judgment how many separate and unrelated chunks of knowledge can it take into account? As memory search moves from schema to case information ideas and images not only increase in number and concreteness but they also become relatively more disjoined and less coherent. Individuals differ in their tolerance for knowledge of this kind. Some who have a difficult time holding in mind many disparate pieces of information are inclined to search in a limited fashion and to make up their mind quickly based on past opinions. Others whose tolerance is large are inclined to search exhaustively and to make up their mind slowly based on case information.

Study 1: Judgments That Rely on Schemas of the Out-group Cluster While Those That Rely on Case Information Do Not

One of the more straightforward consequences of our analysis is that since the ideas represented in the schema are more cohesive than case information, decisions that reflect schematic knowledge will covary or cluster more than decisions that reflect knowledge of cases. In the former there is a single (abstract) representation or mnemonic structure that informs the judgments a person makes about the out-group; in the latter, there are many (concrete) representations or structures, each referring to a distinct event and each giving rise to a judgment peculiar to that event.

A useful statistical technique for testing notions of this kind is factor analysis. The existence of a factor means that there is a set of judgments (or issues) that are highly correlated with each other and poorly correlated with those in a different set. The implication is that a common structure or factor underlies the correlated set, whose judgments are said to define or load on the factor. In this context our analysis suggests, first, that abstract and concrete judgments of the Soviet Union load on different factors; and second, that the abstract judgments all load on the same factor whereas the concrete judgments load on as many factors as there are cases to which these judgments refer.

Finally, we argue that abstract concepts permit individuals to choose between searching memory in a limited or an exhaustive fashion but concrete concepts do not. In a limited search, a judgment can use either knowledge represented in the schema or case information; in an exhaustive search, only case information. If this is true, then abstract judgments should vary with individual differences in strategy preferences, and concrete judgments should not. In our first study, strategy preferences are assumed to depend on a person's general aversion to thinking and remembering as well as his or her tolerance for disjoined knowledge. A flawed but not unreasonable clue to such capacities is the person's level of authoritarianism (Altemeyer 1981, Dillehay 1978, Forbes 1985): individuals high in authoritarianism characteristically avoid extensive exploration of memory more and have less tolerance for unintegrated information, or a stronger desire for coherence and consistency, than those low in authoritarianism (Brown 1965, Frenkel-Brunswik 1949, Rokeach 1960).

Our first study, therefore, attempts to predict information-processing strategies and the resulting judgments on abstract or concrete issues involving the former Soviet Union, using a standard measure of authoritarianism, the F-scale. If authoritarianism as measured by the F-scale is negatively related to the capacity for encoding disjoined knowledge in working-memory, then it follows that individuals high in authoritarianism prefer limited search and those low in authoritarianism, exhaustive search. Inasmuch as abstract judgments of the Soviet Union are hypothesized to be affected by differences in memory-search strategy more than concrete judgments are, authoritarianism should predict the abstract judgments better than the concrete judgments. Specifically, individuals high in authoritarianism will be more anti-Soviet than those low in authoritarianism when responding to questions that can be answered at the schema level (i.e., abstract issues), but they will not differ in anti-Soviet sentiment when responding to questions that must be answered at the level of case information (i.e., concrete issues).

The data we used to test these ideas were from a brief survey in 1986 of over 200 undergraduates at the University of Michigan. They responded to four items about the Soviet Union, two abstract and two concrete (see table 1), as well as seven F-scale items devised by Fillmore Sanford (1950, Janowitz and Marvick 1953), plus two from the original scale (Adorno et al. 1950). The respondents' judgments were subject to two different analyses. First, we examined the factor structure underlying the judgments, and next, the relationship between each kind of judgment and individual differences on the F-scale.

TABLE 1.   Abstract and Concrete Issues Used in Studies 1 and 2

Abstract Issues
1. The Soviet Union has gotten away with more than it deserves to. (Study 1)
2. The Soviet Union really is an "evil empire." (Studies 1 and 2)
3. The Soviet Union keeps its word. (Study 2)

Concrete Issues
1. Recent proposals by the new Soviet leadership indicate an increased willingness to come to an agreement on arms control. (Study 1)
2. It is a good idea to prohibit the sale of our advanced computer systems to the Soviet Union. (Studies 1 and 2)
3. I admire what Gorbachev is trying to do. (Study 2)
4. The Soviet Union is prepared to negotiate a withdrawal of its forces from Afghanistan in the near future. (Study 2)
5. It is mainly because of Soviet support that the Vietnamese have been able to continue their occupation of Cambodia. (Study 2)
6. In its relations with Finland, the Soviet Union demonstrates that it will allow small neighboring countries to be independent and prosperous. (Study 2)
7. The number of meetings going on between top U.S. and Soviet officials indicate that a period of friendly relations could be about to begin. (Study 2)

An exploratory factor analysis with varimax rotation produced a three-factor solution quite consistent with our predictions. The normalized loadings shown in table 2 demonstrate that the two abstract issues define a single factor, suggesting that judgments of this type reflect a common mnemonic structure, whereas the two concrete issues form separate and orthogonal factors, suggesting that each judgment has its own distinct structure in memory.

Multiple regression analysis was carried out to determine the differential effect of memory-search strategies on abstract and concrete judgments of the ex–Soviet Union. The relationship between authoritarianism, our memory-search measure, and abstract judgments was substantial ($\beta = .46, p < .001$). The relationship between authoritarianism and each of the concrete judgments was just moderate ($\beta = .12, p < .01$, for the arms control item; and $\beta = .28$, $p < .01$, for the computer item). In short, abstract judgments become markedly more anti-Soviet but concrete judgments only slightly more anti-Soviet as the tendency to engage in limited-search increases. The difference in the strength of the two relationships is quite reliable ($t[211] = 4.58, p < .001$).

These findings demonstrate that judgments of the Soviet Union varied depending, first, on whether an issue is abstract or concrete and, second, on whether the person calls up the schema or case information. When the issue is abstract, either kind of knowledge can be used to arrive at a judgment. Individuals who are high in authoritarianism terminate memory search at the schema level to avoid the incoherence associated with case information. Consequently, the ideas available to them are categorical, and their judgment of the out-group is extreme. On the other hand, those low in authoritarianism have greater tolerance for disparate knowledge. As a result, they are more inclined to search exhaustively and access case information, which gives a qualified, less black-and-white picture of the out-group and leads these individuals to be relatively moderate in their judgments. In sum, our initial study suggests that, unless the issue in question is sufficiently concrete so as to force

TABLE 2. Normalized Factor Loading for the Judgments about the Soviet Union (Study 1)

Judgments	Factor		
	1	2	3
Abstract			
Evil	.625	(.312)	(.203)
Deserve	.814	(.011)	(.195)
Concrete			
Computer	(.282)	(.118)	.951
Arms control	(.137)	.942	(.099)
% Variance explained	28.8	53.7	78.5

individuals to access case information, or unless they themselves are already disposed to search exhaustively, human memory is prone to extreme opinions. In this sense, we can say it is built to sustain ill will between groups.

Study 2: Memory-Search Strategies and Opinion Polarization

We have argued that limited search activates the schema but not the underlying case information. Since schematic knowledge is categorical, a limited-search strategy would lead a person to take a relatively extreme anti-Soviet position. Exhaustive search, however, calls up case information which, being qualified, gave rise to a relatively moderate opinion of the Soviet Union. Moreover, it was predicted that these effects will be observed for abstract but not for concrete issues. In our second study, we not only measure search-strategy preferences using a new scale in addition to the F-scale (see below) but also perform an experiment in which individuals are *instructed* to engage in mental operations that correspond to one or the other search strategy. The expectation is that, when the issue is abstract, those instructed to use limited search will take a more anti-Soviet position than those instructed to use exhaustive search. Again, when the issue is concrete, there should be no difference in judgment regardless of what strategy the person is instructed to use.

The data for this study stem from a survey of nearly 500 students at the University of Michigan conducted in early 1987. They were asked to give their opinions with respect to two abstract and six concrete issues involving the Soviet Union (see table 1). In addition, they responded to the same F-scale items used in the previous study as well as a new scale called the *Need-for-Cognition* scale. A major objection to the F-scale as a measure of cognition is that the items are so heavy-handed and moralistic (e.g., "There are only two kinds of people in this world, the weak and the strong.") that it is difficult to know what individuals are responding to. Are they reacting more to the content of the item or to its style? In light of this, critics say, we cannot clearly tell the extent to which the response reflects a person's characteristic way of thinking (e.g., his or her tolerance of ambiguity) or ideology (e.g., his or her liberalism). The Need-for-Cognition scale avoids such problems by eschewing ideology and asking the respondent to make straightforward estimates of the frequency with which they engage in or their liking for Proustian bouts of recall. A typical item is, "I avoid situations where there is a likely chance I will have to think in depth about something." We assume that the scale reflects a tendency opposite to that of the F-scale, so that the greater the Need-for-Cognition score, the more exhaustive the memory search. There is reasonable support for this assumption. For instance, in studies to validate the scale, individuals who scored high remembered more facts to support their position on an issue than did individuals who scored low (Cacioppo and Petty 1982).

Immediately before answering the items about the Soviet Union, roughly a third of the respondents, those in the limited-search condition, received written instructions to the effect that they were not to think at any length about the upcoming questions but instead to give the first answer that sprang to mind. Another third, who were in the exhaustive-search condition, were instructed to think awhile before answering and not to give the first response that came to mind. The remaining respondents received no instructions.

An exploratory factor analysis with varimax rotation replicated the findings of the preceding study. That is to say, the two abstract judgments loaded on a single factor, and the six concrete judgments loaded on six separate and orthogonal factors, again demonstrating that opinion expressed on abstract issues are based on the person's schema of the out-group while opinions expressed on concrete issues are based on case information (see table 3). Moreover, as in the first study, the F-scale predicted the abstract judgments ($\beta = .18$) appreciably better than it did the concrete judgments overall ($\beta = .08$; $t[488] = 2.92, p < .01$). Similarly, there is fairly good evidence that respondents high in Need for Cognition searched more exhaustively than did those low in Need for Cognition. In deciding about abstract issues, high Need-for-Cognition individuals took a relatively moderate position toward the Soviet Union, whereas those low in Need for Cognition took a relatively extreme position ($\beta = -.21$). The difference in opinion extremity was considerably smaller, however, when these same individuals responded to concrete issues

TABLE 3. Normalized Factor Loadings for Judgments about the Soviet Union (Study 2)

Judgments	Factor						
	1	2	3	4	5	6	7
Abstract							
Word	.83	(−.02)	(.02)	(.04)	(.10)	(.09)	(.21)
Evil	.67	(.03)	(.09)	(.10)	(.08)	(.00)	(.11)
Concrete							
Gorbachev	(.17)	(.06)	.95	(−.06)	(.08)	(.04)	(−.01)
Afghanistan	(.16)	(.03)	(.09)	(−.01)	.98	(.06)	(.04)
Meeting	(.00)	.98	(.06)	(−.04)	(.03)	(.13)	(−.07)
Vietnam	(.12)	(−.04)	(−.06)	.99	(−.01)	(−.03)	(.03)
Computer	(.29)	(−.07)	(−.02)	(.03)	(.05)	(.08)	.93
Finland	(.08)	(.13)	(.04)	(−.03)	(.06)	.97	(.07)
% Variance explained	14.7	27.0	39.1	51.5	63.8	76.0	87.7

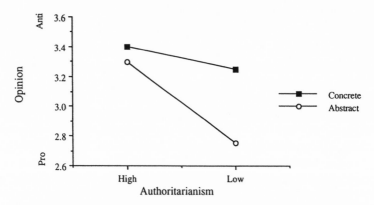

Fig. 1. Opinion toward the Soviet Union as a function of authoritarianism and type of issue

($\beta = -.08$; $t[488] = 2.92$, $p = .01$). In short, authoritarianism and Need for Cognition had similar but opposite effects on opinion polarization.

To assess the effect of instructing respondents to use particular search strategies, an analysis of variance was performed. Respondents were split at the median on the F-scale as well as on the Need for Cognition scale, and a comparison was made between their answers to abstract and to concrete questions under the three conditions of instruction. All the theoretically important effects were statistically significant. First, highly authoritarian respondents were more anti-Soviet than those low in authoritarianism on abstract issues but not on concrete issues ($F[1, 475] = 15.22$, $p < .0002$). Second, there was a comparable effect in respect to Need for Cognition, in that respondents scoring low on this scale were more anti-Soviet than those scoring high—but only on the abstract issues, not the concrete issues ($F[1, 475] = 17.73$, $p < .0001$). These results are shown in figures 1 and 2.

Finally, there was a reliable interaction between instructions and opinion polarization ($F[2, 475] = 3.57$, $p < .03$). On abstract issues, limited-search instructions gave rise to the most-extreme anti-Soviet opinions; no instructions, to opinions that were moderately anti-Soviet; and exhaustive-search instructions, to opinions that were the least anti-Soviet. Again consistent with the model, judgments on concrete issues did not differ as a function of memory search instructions (see fig. 3).

Study 3: How Case Information Affects the Perception of Events

Our schema of the out-group provides a general interpretive structure prompting us to view its actions vis-à-vis the in-group as a coherent sequence of

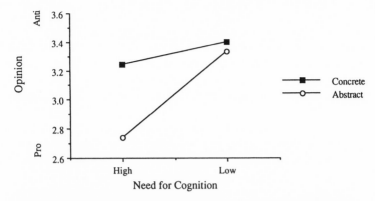

Fig. 2. Opinion toward the Soviet Union as a function of Need for Cognition and type of issue

events, often as cause-and-effect. Hence, the mere knowledge that an incident involved the Soviet Union and the United States permitted us to locate it within a particular historical framework that integrates and makes comprehensible what might otherwise be disjoined and difficult to understand. If, for example, someone said, "In 1961, Tolo attempted to invade Pongo, which is allied to Apat," we would not have an inkling. At best our understanding of what this meant would be dim, depending on our conception of "invade" plus idiosyncratic ideas such as the recollection of movies in which collectivities with names like these inhabited islands in the South Pacific. However, we would have a clear and distinct understanding of the meaning if the person said, "In 1961, the United States attempted to invade Cuba, which is allied to the Soviet Union." In the latter instance, we automatically activated our schema of the Soviet Union and its relations with the United States and interpret the event in terms of general notions about "clashing Soviet aspirations and American intentions . . . it's simply another instance of the parry and thrust . . . goes on between us all the time since the cold war began . . . the Soviets try to expand their influence and we repulse them, then we try to expand our influence and they repulse us."

Case information, on the other hand, implies familiarity with particular events that have occurred between the Soviet Union and the United States. Not only is this knowledge concrete, but it is also peculiar to an event, distinguishing it from other events. When individuals possess a great amount of case information within some domain, we consider them *experts*, and when they possess little case information, *novices*. Experts as well as novices have stereotypes about the former Soviet Union. Both, therefore, are prone to integrate events involving the Soviet Union and to perceive them in some sense as fundamentally similar, reflecting *grand strategies, national goals*,

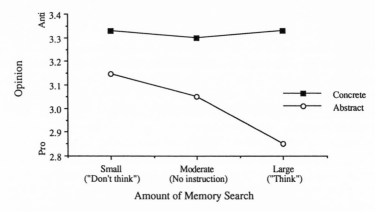

Fig. 3. Opinion toward the Soviet Union as a function of memory-search instructions and type of issue

operational codes, and the like. The critical difference, of course, is that experts have considerably more case information. Compared to novices, they are more capable of identifying features that are unique to an event and to categorize the event differently than other events. Put starkly, novices, having few categories available to encode events, miss recognizing the differences between events and as a result, perceive them as similar. Experts, however, having many categories (and subcategories) available, can readily detect the dissimilarities between events (Solomon 1990). An important implication is that changes in behavior signaling a decrease in ill will on the part of the out-group are likely to be noticed by experts but not by novices.

These hypotheses about the effect of expertise on encoding the out-group's actions follow from Tversky's (1977) theory of psychological sim-ilarity, which assumes that the perceived similarity between any two events is a function of the number of features a person recognizes that they have in common compared to the number the person recognizes that are unique to each. That experts possess more case information means they know more than novices know about the unique circumstances surrounding incidents like the United States lifting the embargo on grain shipments to the Soviet Union or the Soviets shooting down one of our spy planes, two incidents typical of those used in the present study. Consequently, when experts think about one of these two events, the set of features that come to mind overlap little with the features that come to mind in thinking about the other; however, for novices, with only schematic knowledge of the Soviet Union, the two sets of features may overlap a great deal. The upshot is that experts should per-ceive events of this kind as different, and novices should perceive them as similar.

In light of our earlier studies, comparisons between the way experts and novices think about the Soviet Union ought to take into account the effort these individuals make to recall what they know. That is to say, because experts know more, they can analyze an event in greater detail than a novice, *if* they bring this knowledge into play. Whether they do, needless to say, depends on how they search memory. An expert who uses exhaustive-search will access a vast amount of case information and, thereby, have a different perception of events, one containing more unique elements, than an expert who uses a strategy of limited search. On the other hand, having relatively little case information to begin with, novices should not differ as a function of memory-search strategy to the same extent as do experts. Hence, when deciding whether two Soviet actions are similar or different, experts who search memory exhaustively are more likely to base their judgment on case information and take into account features peculiar to an event than are experts who engage in limited search. However, since novices possess little case information, whether they adopt a strategy of exhaustive search or limited search should make relatively little difference. This implies, first, that novices will perceive events as fundamentally similar or as belonging to the same category, whereas experts will perceive them as fundamentally dissimilar or as belonging to different categories. Second, novices who search memory exhaustively should be only slightly less likely to perceive events as similar than novices who search memory in a limited fashion, while experts who search memory exhaustively should be much less likely to perceive the two events as similar than experts who use limited search.

Our final study tests these ideas using the technique of cognitive mapping to describe an individual's mental representation of incidents involving the ex–Soviet Union and the United States (e.g., Axelrod 1976). Cognitive maps consist of a set of points and lines. In our research, a point represents a specific event, such as lifting the grain embargo or shooting down a spy plane, and a line connecting two points, a perception that the events are similar in nature. According to our analysis, cognitive maps become increasingly differentiated with expertise and effort in searching memory. Hence, an expert's representation should be less connected, that is, contain fewer lines, than a novice's representation. In addition, the representation of experts who follow a strategy of exhaustive search should be less connected than that of experts who follow a strategy of limited search, while the difference in connectedness between the representation of novices using exhaustive search and those novices using limited search, although perhaps similar in direction, should be much smaller in magnitude.

The expert respondents were twenty-two doctoral candidates in political science at the University of Michigan, specializing either in international relations or in Soviet politics. The novices consisted of ninety-eight first- or second-year undergraduates. All respondents were given thirteen events (see table 4) involving the Soviet Union and the United States and rated the similarity between all nonredundant pairs on a nine-point scale (1 = very dissimilar; 9 = very similar). After completing the similarity ratings, they filled out the Need-for-Cognition scale.

Since the neutral point of the scale is 5.0, we assume a connection (line) exists between two events if the average rating of similarity is 5.5 or greater. The resultant cognitive maps are shown in figure 4. As predicted, the experts' network is more sparsely connected than that of the novices (chi-square [1] = 4.57, $p < .05$). In fact, the novices have more than twice as many connections as the experts. To test the hypothesis that differentiation depends not only on the amount of case information individuals possess but also on their effort in retrieving such knowledge, we divided both experts and novices into those who are inclined to search exhaustively (high Need for Cognition) and those who are inclined to limit their search (low Need for Cognition). The cognitive maps for the two sets of experts are presented in figure 5. Consistent with our hypothesis, those who search exhaustively tend to have a more differentiated representation, that is, events are perceived as less similar, than those who terminate memory search quickly (chi-square [1] = 3.33, $p < .07$) . The corresponding networks for novices are shown in figure 6. Unlike the cog-

TABLE 4. List of Events Used in Similarity Rating

1. 1958: Soviet leader Krushchev vows that his country will "bury" the U.S.
2. 1960: The U.S.S.R. shoots down an American spy plane over Soviet territory.
3. 1961: The U.S. attempts to invade Cuba, which is allied with the U.S.S.R.
4. 1973: The U.S. and the U.S.S.R. provide weapons to the opposing sides during a Middle East war. That is, the U.S. provides weapons to one side, while the U.S.S.R. provides weapons to the other side.
5. 1973: The U.S.S.R. sends an exhibit of masterpieces from its National Gallery to tour the United States.
6. 1973: The U.S. and U.S.S.R. (among others) sign a treaty forever halting tests of nuclear weapons in the atmosphere.
7. 1979: The U.S.S.R. invades Afghanistan.
8. 1981: Soviet Premier Brezhnev sends get-well wishes to Ronald Reagan during the President's recovery from an assassination attempt.
9. 1981: The U.S. lifts its grain embargo against the U.S.S.R. (i.e., resumes selling grain).
10. 1981: U.S. President Reagan expresses hope that upcoming talks with the U.S.S.R. will provide for respect and a better relationship between the two countries.
11. 1982: The U.S.S.R. promises never to be the first to use nuclear weapons in a war with the U.S.
12. 1983: Ronald Reagan publicly declares the U.S.S.R. "evil."
13. 1987: American pop star Billy Joel plays several concerts in the Soviet Union.

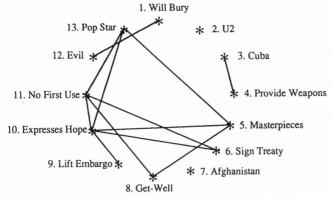

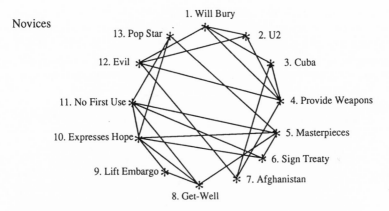

Fig. 4. Cognitive maps of experts and novices. Events connected by a line are perceived as similar; events not connected by a line are perceived as dissimilar.

nitive maps of experts, they contain a relatively large number of connections and this number does not vary much with recall effort (chi-square [1] = .07, *ns*).

Given these findings, it is reasonable to conclude, first, that case information allows individuals to recognize significant differences between actions; and, second, that as the effort made to recall this information increases, so does the recognition of differences. As a result, those who lack case information and are obliged to rely on the highly abstract ideas contained in

High Need for Cognition

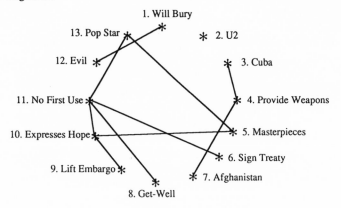

Low Need for Cognition

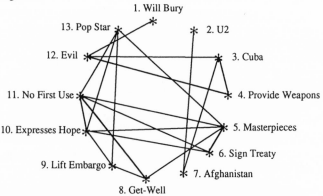

Fig. 5. Cognitive maps of experts who differ in Need for Cognition. Events connected by a line are perceived as similar; events not connected by a line are perceived as dissimilar.

their schema of the Soviet Union are naturally prone to categorize various Soviet actions as similar, while those with an abundance of case information are just as prone to see these actions as belonging in different categories.

From the point of view of cognitive theory, none of this is surprising. After all, the out-group even as a general concept, is complex and multi-dimensional. The complexity increases by an order of magnitude if the concept refers to a large, heterogeneous collectivity with a long and turbulent

High Need for Cognition

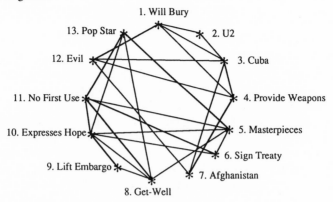

Low Need for Cognition

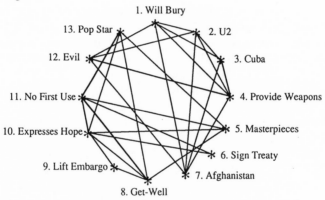

Fig. 6. Cognitive maps of novices who differ in Need for Cognition. Events connected by a line are perceived as similar; events not connected by a line are perceived as dissimilar.

history. Hence, when people characterize the former Soviet Union and its relations with the United States, not only is the number of features that could come to mind enormous, but there are no clear rules of categorization to tell which features are criterial. In short, most of us do not have a distinct prototype of the Soviet Union; we cannot imagine *the* Soviet Union (or any large nation for that matter) as a unitary concept, not in the sense that we can imagine the prototypical apple or the prototypical horse. At best, most of us would come up with a small number of "is a . . ." propositions like "is a huge country," "is a country with many different ethnic groups," "is a communist nation," and "is a dictatorship of the proletariat."

Merely to think of an event involving the ex–Soviet Union, say, the lifting of the grain embargo, and attempt to list its causes requires considerable analysis even for experts. The task becomes even more difficult when one must compare these features with those leading to the shooting down of a spy plane, the sending of an exhibit of masterpieces, and the like. Perhaps most daunting of all is the feeling that the events have important features that one cannot remember or about which one is ignorant. In these circumstances, individuals welcome any guidelines, even those that are highly abstract and general. If the novice's schema describes the Soviet Union and the United States as having been in a continuous conflict that waxed and waned ("the cold war . . . détente . . .") for most of the century, then grain embargoes and spy planes and sending masterpieces may be categorized as aspects of a seamless historical flow. The novice, remembering nothing particularly unique about any event other than signaling a certain intensity of conflict, may perceive them as not too dissimilar. In the language of Tversky's model, encoding at the schema level increases the ratio of common to distinctive features. The experts, on the other hand, can, if they try, remember many things unique to each of these events. The ratio of common to distinctive features *ergo* decreases, and they become aware of changes or differences in Soviet-U.S. relations that escape the novice.

General Discussion

To the chagrin of instrumentalists, the historical evidence has long suggested that intergroup conflicts occur even though the parties know ahead of time that whatever tangible benefits they might derive from the conflict will not cover costs. More recently, social psychologists have carried out experiments demonstrating that in-group members will express ill will toward the out-group with no observable justification for doing so. To the (theoretical) satisfaction of the primordialist, this implies that antagonism—probably reflecting a mixture of fear and distrust tempered by the shadow of future alliances—is the default relation between groups. Hence, although there is no good understanding of *why* these feelings occur so readily, we know that unless there are mitigating circumstances (e.g., a common foe), the members of one group believe that the members of another group are likely to be enemies. In this chapter we attempt to extend this line of reasoning by demonstrating how the natural operations of memory sustain and even augment such beliefs.

Our analysis focuses on a large collectivity, the former Soviet Union, and argues that because judgments about an out-group depend for the most part on what one happens to remember, some individuals will take a more polarized position than others even though they have the same knowledge of the out-group. In this connection, we examine differences in opinions that are due to the effort individuals make in recalling what they know about the out-group. Two strategies are contrasted: under limited search the person terminates recall as soon as an appropriate past opinion about the out-group comes to mind; under exhaustive search, the person continues recall until all relevant knowledge about the out-group has been accessed. Hence, depending on their search strategy, individuals have different amounts and kinds of information available with which to make their judgment.

In addition, our model assumes that a person has in the past made many judgments about the Soviet Union, which over time have been integrated to constitute a schema or stereotype that is represented separately from the concrete events underlying the judgments. It also assumes that knowledge of the Soviet Union is organized hierarchically so that abstract information, namely, the system of opinions making up the schema, is located near the top and knowledge of concrete events, namely, case information, near the bottom. Since schematic knowledge has undergone considerable culling and refining to maximize consistency, it is unqualified and categorical, whereas case information is mixed and moderate.

Finally, where individuals enter memory depends on the issue. Abstract issues activate abstract knowledge, and concrete issues, concrete knowledge. With abstract issues, therefore, search begins at the top, and with concrete issues, near the bottom. Suppose that, in deciding where they stand on an issue, individuals follow a limited-search strategy: they access their schema of the "Soviet Union," find a past opinion contained in the schema that links concepts similar enough to those specified in the issue (e.g., a person may decide a belief she just recalled, "Russia is expansionist," is the equivalent of "the Soviet Union is a threat to world peace") and use this past opinion as a ready-made response (e.g., "Yes, the Soviet Union is a threat to world peace."). Since the schema summarizes a large number of specific events, it changes very little upon receipt of a new case, especially when the new case is inconsistent with the schema. Such incidents are stored in memory as case information; limited search simply does not give one access to knowledge of this kind. Therefore, despite "knowing" better—the case information is there to be recalled—the person who engages in limited search continues to distrust and fear the out-group in the abstract and, through the lens of these emotions, persists in viewing its various actions as an unmitigated expression of ill will. In the mind of these individuals, the enemy remains the enemy.

Those following an exhaustive-search strategy, of course, also possess concrete knowledge that would serve to temper sweeping generalizations about out-group ill will. However, unlike individuals who use limited search, they make an effort to access this knowledge and use it to interpret out-group behavior instead of relying on old opinions. Hence, they are less antagonistic toward the out-group and view its actions as more differentiated, less driven by a single animus, than do individuals inclined toward limited search. The implication is that individuals who are more capable of analyzing an out-group's actions and recognizing the differences between them are also more likely to access this knowledge as case information when judging the out-group's intentions. If correct, then, when there is an actual change in out-group behavior, individuals who search memory exhaustively are likely to take this change into account and to alter "the image of the enemy," whereas those who limit their search are not.

Summary

The results of the three studies provide reasonable support for our main hypotheses. When the issues involving the former Soviet Union were abstract, opinion polarization was predicted by both indices of memory search, that is, the F-scale was found to be positively related, and the Need-for-Cognition scale negatively related, to anti-Soviet opinions; when the issue was concrete, the relationship between the two scales and opinion polarization was greatly attenuated. Comparable results were obtained by experimentally manipulating the search strategy. When the issues were abstract, respondents who were instructed to limit their search subsequently expressed more anti-Soviet opinions than those who were instructed to search memory exhaustively. However, when the issues were concrete, memory search instructions had relatively little effect on opinions.

Furthermore, factor analysis demonstrated a factor structure that was consistent with the assumption that knowledge about the Soviet Union was organized hierarchically. According to our model, abstract and concrete issues are processed at different locations in memory. Issues involving abstract concepts activate information at the schema level, and issues involving concrete concepts activate case information. Schematic information is coherent and unidirectional, whereas case information is disjoined and mixed. That judgments regarding abstract issues all loaded on a single factor while judgments regarding concrete issues loaded on as many factors as there were cases supports this argument.

Finally, individuals with a large amount of case information (experts) readily differentiated between a variety of events involving the Soviet Union and the United States. The extent of differentiation depended on the effort made to retrieve this information; that is, experts who searched exhaustively differentiated more than experts who limited their search. On the other hand, individuals with little case information (novices) are unable to differentiate; instead, they "chunk" events and see them as similar. The implication is that novices have difficulty in detecting changes in out-group behavior. As a result, when such changes actually occur, novices are more prone than experts to miss them and continued to judge Soviet-American relations in terms of stereotypes.

REFERENCES

Abelson, R. P., E. Aronson, W. J. McGuire, T. M. Newcomb, M. J. Rosenberg, and P. H. Tannenbaum, eds. 1968. *Theories of Cognitive Consistency: A Sourcebook*. Chicago: Rand McNally.

Adorno, T. W., E. Frenkel-Brunswik, D. Levinson, and R. N. Sanford. 1950. *The Authoritarian Personality*. New York: Harper & Row.

Alexander, R. D. 1987. *The Biology of Moral Systems*. New York: Aldine De Gruyter.

Altemeyer, B. 1981. *Right-Wing Authoritarianism*. Winnipeg: University of Manitoba Press.

Axelrod, R. 1976. *Structure of Decision: The Cognitive Map of Political Elites*. Princeton: Princeton University Press.

———. 1984. *The Evolution of Cooperation*. New York: Basic Books.

Barth, F. 1969. "Introduction." In *Ethnic Groups and Boundaries: The Social Organization of Culture Difference*, edited by F. Barth, 9–38. Boston: Little, Brown.

Belanger, S., and M. Pinard. 1991. "Ethnic Movements and the Competition Model: Some Missing Links." *American Sociological Review* 56: 446–57.

Bonacich, E. 1973. "A Theory of Middleman Minorities." *American Sociological Review* 39: 583–94.

Breuilly, J. 1982. *Nationalism and the State*. Manchester: Manchester University Press.

Brewer, M. B. 1979. "In-Group Bias in the Minimal Intergroup Situation: A Cognitive-Motivational Analysis." *Psychological Bulletin* 86: 307–24.

Brown, R. W. 1965. *Social Psychology*. New York: Free Press.

Burnstein, E. 1967. "Sources of Cognitive Bias in the Representation of Simple Social Structures: Balance, Minimal Change, Positivity, Reciprocity, and the Respondent's Own Attitude." *Journal of Personality and Social Psychology* 7: 36–48.

Cacioppo, J. T., and R. E. Petty. 1982. "The Need for Cognition." *Journal of Personality and Social Psychology* 42: 116–31.

Campbell, D. T. 1958. "Common Fate, Similarity, and Other Indices of the Status of Aggregates of Persons as Social Entities." *Behavioral Science* 3: 14–25.

Campbell, D. T., and R. A. LeVine. 1968. "Ethnocentrism and Intergroup Relations." In *Theories of Cognitive Consistency*, edited by R. P. Abelson, E. Aronson, W. J. McGuire, T. M. Newcomb, M. J. Rosenberg, and P. H. Tannenbaum, 551–64. Chicago: Rand McNally.

Cottrell, N. B. 1975. "Heider's Structural Balance Principle as a Conceptual Rule." *Journal of Personality and Social Psychology* 31: 713–20.

Crockett, W. H. 1982. "Balance, Agreement, and Positivity in the Cognition of Small Social Structures." In *Advances in Experimental Social Psychology*, Vol. 15, edited by L. Berkowitz, 1–57. New York: Academic Press.

Daly, M., and M. Wilson. 1988. *Homicide*. New York: Aldine De Gruyter.

Davis, J. A. 1967. "Clustering and Structured Balance in Graphs." *Human Relations* 20: 181.

Dillehay, R. C. 1978. "Authoritarianism." In *Dimensions of Personality*, edited by H. London and J. E. Exner, Jr., 85–127. New York: Wiley.

Fiske, S. T., and S. E. Taylor. 1991. *Social Cognition*. New York: McGraw-Hill.

Forbes, H. D. 1985. *Nationalism, Ethnocentrism, and Personality: Social Science and Critical Theory*. Chicago: University of Chicago Press.

Frenkel-Brunswik, E. 1949. "Intolerance of Ambiguity as an Emotional and Personality Variable." In *Perception and Personality: A Symposium*, edited by J. S. Bruner and D. Krech, 108–43. Durham, NC: Duke University Press.

Grice, H. P. 1975. "Logic and Conversation." In *Syntax and Semantics*, edited by P. Cole and J. Morgan, 41–58. New York: Academic Press.

Hannan, M. T. 1979. "The Dynamics of Ethnic Boundaries in Modern States." In *National Development and the World System: Educational, Economic, and Political Change, 1950–1970*, edited by J. W. Meyer and M. T. Hannan, 253–75. Chicago: University of Chicago Press.

Harary, F., R. Z. Norman, and D. O. Cartwright. 1965. *Structural Models: An Introduction to the Theory of Directed Graphs*. New York: Wiley.

Heider, F. 1958. *The Psychology of Interpersonal Relations*. New York: Wiley.

Hobsbawm, E., and T. Ranger, eds. 1983. *The Invention of Tradition*. Cambridge: Cambridge University Press.

Horowitz, D. L. 1985. *Ethnic Groups in Conflict*. Berkeley: University of California Press.

Horwitz, M., and J. M. Rabbie. 1982. "Individuality and Membership in the Intergroup System." In *Social Identity and Intergroup Relations*, edited by H. Tajfel, 241–74. Cambridge: Cambridge University Press.

Insko, C. A., and J. Schopler. 1987. "Categorization, Competition and Collectivity." In *Group Processes*, edited by C. Hendrick, Vol. 8, 213–51. New York: Sage.

Insko, C. A., J. Schopler, R. H. Hoyle, G. J. Dardis, and K. A. Graetz. 1990. "Individual-Group Discontinuity as a Function of Fear and Greed." *Journal of Personality and Social Psychology* 58: 68–79.

Janowitz, M., and D. Marvick. 1953. "Authoritarianism and Political Behavior." *Public Opinion Quarterly* 17: 185–202.

Kinder, D. R., and D. O. Sears. 1981. "Prejudice and Politics: Symbolic Racism versus Racial Threats to the Good Life." *Journal of Personality and Social Psychology* 40: 414–31.

Kitayama, S., and E. Burnstein. 1989. "The Relation between Opinion and Memory: Distinguishing between Associative Density and Structural Centrality." In *On-line Cognition in Person Perception*, edited by N. Bassili, 91–122. Hillsdale, NJ: Erlbaum.

Moscovici, S. 1988. "Notes towards a Description of Social Representations." *European Journal of Social Psychology* 18: 211–50.

Nielsen, F. 1980. "The Flemish Movement in Belgium after World War II: A Dynamic Analysis." *American Sociological Review* 45: 76–94.

Olzak, S. 1982. "Ethnic Mobilization in Quebec." *Ethnic and Racial Studies* 5: 253–75.

Olzak, S., and J. Nagel. 1986. "Competitive Ethnic Relations: An Overview." In *Competitive Ethnic Relations*, edited by S. Olzak and J. Nagel, 1–14. Orlando: Academic Press.

Pinard, M., and R. Hamilton. 1986. "Motivational Dimensions in the Quebec Independence Movement: A Test of a New Model." In *Research in Social Movements, Conflicts and Change*, edited by L. Kriesberg, Vol. 9, 225–80. Greenwich, CT: JAI Press.

Rabbie, J. M., and M. Horwitz. 1969. "Arousal of Ingroup-Outgroup Bias by a Chance Win or Loss." *Journal of Personality and Social Psychology* 13: 269–77.

Ragin, C. 1979. "Ethnic Political Mobilization: The Welsh Case." *American Sociological Review* 44: 619–35.

Rokeach, M. 1960. *The Open and Closed Mind.* New York: Basic Books.

Rosch, E. 1977. "Human Categorization." In *Advances in Cross-Cultural Psychology*, Vol. 1, edited by N. Warren, 3–49. London: Academic Press.

Sanford, F. 1950. *Authoritarianism and Leadership.* Philadelphia: Institute for Research in Human Relations.

Schul Y., and E. Burnstein. 1985. "When Discounting Fails: Conditions under Which Individuals Use Discredited Information in Making a Judgment." *Journal of Personality and Social Psychology* 49: 894–903.

Sentis, K. P., and E. Burnstein. 1979. "Remembering Schema-Consistent Information: Effects of a Balance Schema on Recognition Memory." *Journal of Personality and Social Psychology* 37: 2200–2211.

Sherif, M. 1966. *In Common Predicament: Social Psychology of Intergroup Conflict and Cooperation.* Boston: Houghton Mifflin.

Smith, A. D. 1986. *The Ethnic Origins of Nations.* Oxford: Blackwell.

Solomon, G. E. A. 1990. "Psychology of Novice and Expert Wine Talk." *American Journal of Psychology* 103: 495–517.

Tajfel, H. 1970. "Experiments in Intergroup Discrimination." *Scientific American* (November): 96–102.

———. 1981. *Human Groups and Social Categories: Studies in Social Psychology.* London: Cambridge University Press.

Trivers, R. 1985. *Social Evolution.* Menlo Park, CA: Benjamin/Cummings.

Turner, J. C. 1987. *Rediscovering the Social Group: A Self-Categorization Theory.* New York: Basil Blackwell.

Tversky, A. 1977. "Features of Similarity." *Psychological Review* 84: 327–52.

van dan Berghe, P. L. 1981. *The Ethnic Phenomenon.* New York: Elsevier.

Interest, Principle, and Beyond: American Understandings of Conflict

Don Herzog

To understand U.S. foreign policy, we need to understand the concepts and categories that Americans bring to bear. After all, we see the world through our concepts and categories. They identify what's possible, what's desirable, indeed what's visible in the first place. There is simply no possibility of junking all our concepts, stepping outside them, and gaining an unmediated grasp of the world. Here, I offer a sketch of American understandings of conflict. Understandings, not understanding: even in the realm of foreign policy, Americans have long brought intriguingly different categories to bear, categories whose richness isn't captured by some standard academic models.

I want to begin by suggesting that it's mistaken to assume that each culture must have some unified account of "conflict." U.S. culture clearly doesn't. It's not just that we have a number of competing accounts of conflict, though we do. Nor is it just a matter of cultural pluralism, of WASPs and Cuban-Americans and so on seeing the world differently, though they do. "Conflict" itself is an abstract category, that is supposed to bring together and illuminate different activities in very different social settings. I conjecture that the term itself comes more easily to social scientists (and those who have been through certain kinds of psychotherapy) than it does to the ordinary speaker. Those tempted to think that "conflict" is the name of some deep essence that all kinds of conflict have in common, that we use the category to strip away merely contingent and accidental details and illuminate what's central, are tempted in precisely the wrong direction, one inviting a Wittgensteinian rejoinder: concepts need have no deep core or essence at all, no property or properties found in each and every instantiation of the concept; they tie things together by loose relations of family resemblance, no more.

Think about the following familiar scripts, which I present in a deliber-

Hearty thanks to Charles Stein, who tolerated endlessly disjoint conversations and contributed some of the ideas and formulations of this chapter.

ately stylized way. It's an open question whether they actually capture what goes on in the world. Nonetheless, they provide some of our most familiar accounts of various sorts of conflict.

The playground fistfight. The schoolyard bully swaggers up to a bespectacled nerd and demands his lunch money. To the bully's astonishment, the nerd doesn't deliver. Anxious but defiant, he says, "no way." The bully pushes him around a bit; the nerd pushes back. Fists are swinging blindly, and the nerd's glasses get crunched, an untimely demise. Suddenly the nerd's friends appear and tell the bully to get lost. After some uncertain blustering, he does.

The marital spat. Jim gets home late from work, and to his disgust the meat loaf is burnt. He glares at Kathy. In a moment he'll regret later, he impulsively lobs a characteristically barbed sarcasm: "You've made this 3000 times before, so you really should have it down by now." Fed up with what she's recently learned to think of as sexist crap, Kathy responds with some contempt, "Why don't you go out and grab some beer?" Jim decides to do just that. Before he's out the door, though, the two have exchanged increasingly cutting remarks on in-laws, the household budget, and their sex life.

Market competition. Wizzabee's Widgets, long thought to have a lock on northeastern sales outlets, have been slipping in quality, and some of the dealers are disgruntled. The chairman of the board of Spacely Sprockets pores over a report by an ambitious junior executive suggesting that Spacely enter this new market. "Risky," he murmurs, shaking his head, "risky." Then he looks at the depressingly flat graph of company growth in the last three quarters and decides to enter the widget business. Wizzabee's is caught asleep at the switch, and within a year most dealers are happily buying Spacely Widgets, still priced a bit under cost to secure the new market.

Scholarly dispute. At the national meetings of the Society of Medieval French Historians, two professors continue their long-standing debate on criminal behavior in rural communities. One, a *marxisante* historian, wants to cast such behavior as a desperate response to the ongoing exploitation of the peasants by their bastard feudal lords. Another, more influenced by Durkheim than Marx, wants to think of the criminals as deviants testing and demonstrating the boundaries of communal identity. The evidence is tantalizingly sketchy, the argument on each side increasingly intricate, the audience alternately amused and stupefied.

Racial tension. "The old neighborhood just isn't what it used to be," sighs Glen, trying to explain to his daughter why they're selling their home. Away at college, she explodes with indignation. "You just mean that finally blacks are buying some homes. Dad, I never thought I'd hear *you* talking this way." Glen dodges. "Well, not quite that. But property values are falling. And there's something different about the tone of the neighborhood that your mother and I just don't like." The local newspaper runs a story on white flight; rumors of a cross-burning abound. The neighborhood may be integrated, but people's social networks are completely segregated.

Sibling rivalry. Timmy, four years old, greets the new baby with a measured equanimity that leaves his parents surprised but deeply pleased. Once he'd found out what Mom's big tummy meant, he'd been increasingly sullen, and sometimes had lashed out with fearsome anger, even threatening to flush his new brother down the toilet. Still, they're home from the hospital, with the baby, and, after a lot of anguished thought and consultation, no gift for Timmy, lest he think they're bribing him. And Timmy seems quite happy. He even gives the baby a perfunctory peck on the cheek. Now it's time for him to go to daycare, and he wheels around. "Mom?" "Yes, dear?" "Just one more thing. When I come back today, I don't expect to see this baby here any more."

I could, of course, go on. Since the United States is a highly differentiated society, with crisply demarcated roles and institutions built on different internal logics, I could, in fact, go on for some time. Don't these familiar facts militate against thinking that "conflict" names some deep common essence worth capturing? If there is something in common, isn't it going to be completely banal and uninteresting? (Compare this all-too-familiar riddle from social science: "What do courts have in common?" "Courts are instruments of dispute resolution." This would be worth telling a six-year-old, or a visiting Martian anthropologist, but it doesn't tell us anything we didn't already know.) There may in fact be *nothing* that all these sorts of conflict have in common. Again, what unites various sorts of conflict may be nothing more than a loose family resemblance.

There's an important point here about the logic of comparative studies in political science. Often people respond to case studies or stories about some other country by demanding, "What generalization emerges from this? What does this have in common with other cases, other times, other places?" Typically, though, what's interesting about comparative studies is what's different, not what's the same. Anthropologists don't go to Bali or study potlatch to show that lo! they're just like us. The differences they discover aren't just inherently interesting, a way of providing the pleasures of tourism in an armchair. Rather they throw what's distinctive about our own way of doing things, what we had taken for granted, into high relief. We learn not just about them, but also about us. Similarly here: I take it we're interested in sorting out the American and Japanese and Russian and Chinese views of conflict not because we think that they must ultimately be the same, but because we want to know more about the differences, and how the differences make a difference. But then one can repeat the same point within each country. Again, there may be some distinctively national style informing or even governing conflict in what seemed like different social settings: whether there is such a style is just another empirical question. Given what I know, my best bet is that we won't gain anything interesting by trying to isolate The American View of conflict. Instead I want to focus specifically on American views of war.

One other prefatory point (the penalty for inviting a political theorist to contribute to such a project), on what we tend too grandly to call methodology. Investigating Americans' view of conflict is not best viewed as a question about their behavior, even their "verbal behavior." It's more an interpretive enterprise, trying to reconstruct the concepts and criteria they use to sort out the world, to understand what does and should go on. If, to invoke Wittgenstein yet again, we are pursuing a language-game or a set of language-games, then we want to try to figure out the rules and principles of the game.

Political scientists are wont to think of concepts and especially ideology as constraints. But that is, by and large, a mistake. (It's not a mistake unique to political scientists. Durkheim makes a similar mistake about social facts in *The Rules of Sociological Method*; Bentham casts law simply as a matter of prohibiting certain courses of action; and so on.) True, concepts rule out some courses of action. Any vocabulary will downplay certain possibilities, will make them elusive or invisible or presumptively unacceptable. More important, though, concepts, even ideological concepts, open up new possibilities we wouldn't notice without them. Think of a social actor with no concepts at all. Such a curious fellow wouldn't be the most flexible actor of us all, the one uniquely well positioned to grasp far-flung possibilities in nuanced detail. Like someone trying to study the natural world without any concepts, he'd be mute, blind, paralyzed.

Concepts of war can, I suppose, serve as causes of war. Some views of war make it inevitable in any actual or even imaginable circumstances; others serve as self-fulfilling prophecies. (Consider: war is the rightful response to not always getting our way. Or, war is our destiny, our divine assignment, the only road to historical progress. Or, war is an ordinary and uninteresting social practice, in need of no special justification or excuse. Or, in a different way, war is what you must do whenever circumstances *xyz* arise, and, undeniably, we now find ourselves in such circumstances.) Ordinarily, though, the concepts we use to understand and appraise war neither preclude nor necessitate any war. A road map doesn't tell you what your destination must be. The rules of grammar don't tell you what you ought to say. Engineering doesn't tell you whether or where to build a bridge. Similarly, views of war don't make you fight particular wars. They set up a complicated and partly indeterminate game, allowing the players to make different interpretive moves in coming to terms with political events. Launching or continuing or withdrawing from war turns out, sometimes surprisingly, to be at the end of some path in the game we launched on. So it doesn't all hang on the concepts. Much of it hangs on the way lots of little contingencies happen to come together in the world.

It's not just a question of what war in fact is (not that that's an easy question itself). We want also to know how war arises. Most important, we want to know what counts as a justification of war, or what Americans take to count as a justification. (Those who believe that social science depends on a fact/value distinction have no reason to avoid this agenda, for it's just a matter of fact that some consideration is taken in some community to count as a justification, and scholars can report the fact without endorsing or condemning it.) Studying the criteria that can be brought to bear in justifying war ought to be a central concern of the most bombs-and-rockets-oriented scholars among us. For those bombs don't go off, those rockets don't get fired, unless someone can tell a convincing story about why they ought to be. "Because I felt like it" isn't a good reason; indeed it isn't any kind of reason at all. Not, anyway, in America.

There's an obvious political reason for treating the justification of war as central in the United States. Since this is a democracy, framing a justification that (most of) the public will accept is a precondition of pursuing any military expedition effectively. (One way to write the story of Vietnam is to cast it as a war in search of a justification—not a fanciful suggestion in light of those internal memos later published in the *Pentagon Papers*.) The point remains central even if one is generally of the bent we weirdly call realist, even, that is, if one is inclined to think of state policymakers as unswervingly devoted to the pursuit of the national interest. Even if that's the only story they care about, it's not, in fact, a story that can always be told in public. (Nor, in fact, are our policymakers such unswerving realists. To give just one example, Richard Nixon frequently invoked the concept of honor in discussing Vietnam. It's implausible that he had no regard for honor, but was opportunistically trying to manipulate public opinion. The best bet is that Nixon himself was captivated by the concept.) So one could profitably reconstruct the tacit rules governing the permissibility of invoking interest.

Sometimes invoking national interest does work amazingly well. Consider for instance the U.S. decision to send ships into the Persian Gulf, ostensibly to protect Kuwait's oil tankers. Presenting that decision to the American public, President Reagan invoked the national interest—but he never explained quite what interest was at stake, or how the presence of U.S. ships would protect it. Still, despite the carping of some critics, the appeal seemed largely successful. There's an ironic twist here: Americans sound and behave most like realists when they're asleep at the switch, when they're paying no attention whatever to any actual calculation of costs and benefits.

Sometimes an appeal to the national interest appears, but isn't the central point. In 1893, President Harrison urged that a decision to annex Hawaii "will be highly promotive of the best interests of the Hawaiian people, and is the only one that will adequately secure the interests of the United States. These interests are not wholly selfish."[1] More recently, we could say that we liberated the people of Grenada from an oppressive regime; we could lamely add that we protected American medical students. But we had to appeal to the interests of the people of Grenada, not our own. Similarly we couldn't publicly say what many believed must be true, that U.S. policy in Nicaragua was motivated by our own interests. We had to say that the Sandinistas had broken the revolutionary promises that they had made to their own people (just as Adlai Stevenson told the U.N. after the Bay of Pigs that "The Castro regime has betrayed the Cuban revolution"[2]); though again we could lamely add that they were only hundreds of miles from Texas, one of the more whimsical uses of worries about dominos. More recently yet, President Bush found himself fumbling for other and putatively better reasons after suggesting that we saved Kuwait because the price of oil and American jobs were on the line. Here, perhaps, we centrally appeal to the interests of others, and tack on some story about national interest to explain why we're bothering to get involved.

Sometimes, though, an appeal to the national interest is a nonstarter. Think about all the policy options that never get seriously considered. At the height of OPEC's power, William F. Buckley, Jr., suggested that we conquer Libya, thus gaining some oil and getting rid of Qaddafi. That might have been in our interests. So might grabbing Quebec and the Yucatan as vacation spots, or for that matter turning sharply against Israel and South Africa, so escaping international opprobrium and saving lots of money besides. One can always generate a story about why doing any of those things wouldn't *really* be in our interests, by emphasizing indirect consequences and the like. But those stories don't show that indeed U.S. policy is diligently devoted to the national interest. Instead they remind us how marvelously pliable talk of interest is, how soft this allegedly hardheaded guide to the world is.

Realists have sometimes acknowledged, but sometimes forgotten, that it's often very hard to figure out what our interests are and how to attain them, that lurking behind the apparently hardheaded category of "interest" are knotty disagreements about empirical and moral matters. The permanent availability of disputes about our interests means that realism could never furnish the brisk sort of foreign policy its patrons want it to. Walter Lippmann, for instance, criticized Woodrow Wilson for giving "legalistic and

---

1. James D. Richardson, comp., *A Compilation of the Messages and Papers of the Presidents* (New York: Bureau of National Literatures, 1917), 9: 348ff.

2. Henry Steele Commager, ed., *Documents of American History*, 8th ed. (New York: Appleton-Century-Crofts, 1968), 2: 681.

moralistic and idealistic reasons" instead of appealing to "durable and compelling reasons," namely "the substantial and vital reason that the security of
the United States demanded that no aggressively expanding imperial power,
like Germany, should be allowed to gain the mastery of the Atlantic Ocean."[3]
And Henry Kissinger has suggested that American foreign policy lacks "staying power" because of our "denial that our interests are involved."[4] But even
if the United States became a far more thoroughgoing realist actor than it is
and has been, its foreign policy could still swerve and stagger, thanks again to
unending disputes about what our interests are and how to attain them.

Again, though, even if American policymakers were hard-boiled realists,
even if they were to wake up and go to sleep citing chapter and verse from
Morgenthau, the rest of us aren't like that. So even realist policymakers hell-
bent on pursuing the national interest would have to figure out how to justify
their military adventures to ordinary citizens, to the rest of us. In fact, I
suspect, our policymakers are no more single-minded realists than the rest of
us are. I don't doubt that their subculture is different, that people buried in the
bowels of the State Department employ some peculiar concepts and categories. And it may be that their subculture is closer to realism than American
culture at large is. Still, no matter what their own beliefs, they have to find
some way of talking not just to Congress but ultimately to the rest of us. It will
be useful, then, to spend some time considering formal political documents:
Presidential addresses, Congressional debates, declarations of war, and the
like. Not that such documents provide transparent access into the deepest
mental states of their authors: far from it. For these purposes, what matters
isn't what the policymakers really think, but what they think the rest of us
think.

To underline how systematically American views of war depart from
realism, I want briefly to recall Robert W. Tucker's somewhat hysterical
contribution to the debate on North-South relations, *The Inequality of Nations*. Tucker's disdain for the thought that poor countries in the global economy have any claims of justice to press against rich countries hangs partly on
a crude variant of moral skepticism common among social scientists. But
that's not what makes his book interesting. Tucker senses that the kinds of
arguments often advanced on these subjects aren't readily captured by the
structures brought to bear by realists, game theorists, and the like. I mean,
broadly speaking, what we call rational-choice analysis. If we understand

3. Walter Lippmann, *U.S. Foreign Policy: Shield of the Republic* (Boston: Little, Brown,
1950), 37.

4. Henry Kissinger, *American Foreign Policy*, 3d ed. (New York: Norton, 1977),
91–92.

what's distinctive about that approach, we'll be able to grasp what's different about American views on war. Perhaps I should emphasize that it would beg the question, it would lean too heavily on mere words, to suppose that American departures from "rational-choice analysis" show that Americans are irrational or unreasonable.

In a rational-choice view, war is indeed the continuation of politics by other means, where politics in turn is the pursuit of advantage by actors with well-defined goals. They may find themselves in coordination dilemmas, in prisoners' dilemmas, in zero-sum games, in games with no determinate solution: regardless, they are in the business of weighing costs and benefits. Ordinarily one assumes those costs and benefits are commensurable and (idealizing for the sake of the mathematics) infinitely divisible, that one can think of giving up or putting in a bit more or less. That view, familiar in the academy, doesn't resonate in American culture. In fact, a casual survey suggests that Americans pride themselves on reviling any such account of war.

A first point: many of the famous battle cries of Americans stake out all-or-nothing positions that don't permit calculations of marginal payoffs or trade-offs or anything of the sort. 54' 40" or fight, unconditional surrender, give me liberty or give me death: such categories aren't shrewd second-order bargaining strategies, an attempt to precommit to an unbudgeable position to force the opponent to back down. They might end up working that way (though given a conventional story about the failures of the Versailles Treaty and the rise of Hitler, that wouldn't make them a triumph of rationality). But the actors don't understand them that way. They take themselves simply to be insisting on the right outcome.

A second point: appeals to morality have long played an important role in American foreign policy. President Carter wasn't eccentric in making human rights a central justificatory resource in foreign policy. The Four Freedoms, making the world safe for democracy, trying to compel the Soviet Union to let Jews emigrate: Americans have embraced such familiar causes not because they have a roundabout story about why they're in our interests, but because they're morally attractive or even required. Tucker's worry about moralism in foreign policy isn't just a skeptical worry that there's nothing really there, that it's all arrant nonsense. It's a worry that moral principles don't lend themselves to quasi-economic calculation. One doesn't compromise, we often think, when an issue of principle is at stake. Compromise would be evidence not of rationality, not of realism, but of reprehensible lack of integrity. Only scoundrels pursue interests when principles are at stake. That is why John Kennedy sounded such deliberately anti-economic tones in his frequently quoted dictum that the United States would "pay any price, bear any burden, meet any hardship, support any friend, oppose any foe to assure the survival and the success of liberty."

It's too quick, though, to think that self-interest and principle are simple opposites, that those not committed to some version of realism about foreign policy are Wilsonian idealists. The juxtaposition between self-interest and principle, realism and moralism, isn't only stale; more important, it doesn't come close to exhausting the alternatives. Notice here Secretary of State Stimson's 1931 address to the Council on Foreign Relations. Wilson, urged Stimson, had departed from long-standing U.S. policy in deciding not to recognize Mexico because it wasn't a "just government based upon law," wasn't based on "the consent of the governed." Americans had never previously paid—and, if Stimson had his way, would never again, pay—attention to "the *de jure* element of legitimacy"; instead, they would regard only a new government's "*de facto* . . . control of the administrative machinery of the state" and the like. Stimson sympathetically echoed Jefferson's view "that every nation has a right to govern itself internally under what form it pleases."[5] But that too, of course, is a principle. Stimson no more than Wilson wanted to decide whether to recognize a new government by asking if doing so would serve U.S. interests. He was pursuing neither the national interest nor Wilsonian moralism. And he was restating long-standing U.S. policy. That policy at least sometimes really did have clout. President Cleveland reversed Harrison's stand on Hawaii, urging in part that the toppling of Hawaii's government had been accomplished "by a process every step of which . . . is directly traceable to and dependent for its success upon the agency of the United States acting through its diplomatic and naval representatives."[6] That meant there was no autonomous support of the Hawaiian people, and so Cleveland decided not to annex Hawaii.

It's not just that there are different kinds of principle. The juxtaposition between interest and principle isn't only stale; more important, it doesn't come close to exhausting the alternatives. My third point concerns a curious mixture of views surrounding the categories of purity, cleanliness, filth, and redemption, views that have nothing to do with interest *or* principle. Consider a category familiar to U.S. historians, that of American exceptionalism. From the founding, there was supposed to be something different about America, something making this nation pure and shining and even divinely favored as against those corrupt Europeans. Tom Paine deliberately manipulated Americans' religiosity by arguing in *Common Sense* that America, the new world, was also America the promised land, a fresh beginning. Like Israel after Egypt, like life after the flood, America was God's starting from scratch. American society would be purged or cleansed of the characteristic sins of the ancien régime, among them the style of diplomacy that realists would en-

---

5. Commager, *Documents*, 2: 225–26.
6. Richardson, *Compilation*, 9: 461ff.

shrine as the very model of judicious behavior. The same sentiments animate Washington's famous Proclamation of Neutrality, holding out to Americans the promise of using the once vast Atlantic Ocean to distance themselves from the filthy maneuvering for interest that ensnared Europeans in endless war: "Our detached and distant situation invites and enables us to pursue a different course." Celebrating the accomplishments of the Pan-American group in 1939, FDR would contrast the Americas' "serenity and calm" with "the tragic involvements which are today making the Old World a new cockpit of old struggles."[7]

Here peace is what makes America pure. (There are other dimensions to purity, like the racial purity that has tantalized many Americans since the founding, when Jefferson mused about sending the slaves back to Africa, and Benjamin Rush found scientific evidence that blacks were just whites suffering a curious kind of leprosy. This sort of purity itself has implications for foreign policy—recall, for instance, disputes about Asian immigration during this century, or how the thought of admitting eight million Mexicans to the Union led John Calhoun to temper his imperialism by noting, "Ours, sir, is the government of a white race"—but I can't pursue it here.) Isolationists and Christian pacifists follow this tradition. Critics of U.S. policy have sometimes found it useful to invoke the same tradition as part of their critique. So, I take it, arises the subversively critical force of Walter LaFeber's referring to the history of American policy in terms of empire and second empire, political and economic domination: those categories were supposed to apply only to those bellicose European dynasties, not America, so it should come as an alarming revelation that American policy can be cast just the same way.

If peace is purity, war is filth. Like everyone else, I suppose, Americans have always romanticized war: our boys abroad make us proud; they are involved in the great adventure hailed by Teddy Roosevelt, fighting one splendid little war or another. But some Americans have always tried to puncture the romantic illusions, to hammer home the familiar lesson that war is hell. So the dubious hero of *The Red Badge of Courage* learns the lesson that Thomas Hobbes long ago stated drily: "When Armies fight, there is on one side, or both, a running away."[8] William James, appalled by Roosevelt's rhetoric, tried to make room for what he called the moral equivalent of war, other settings in which men could strive heroically. Literature is one thing, though; television is another. There is nothing for stripping war of its romanticism like beaming it live into millions of American households on the evening news, as happened during the Vietnam War. (The day after announcing he wouldn't run for re-election, Lyndon Johnson mused, "As I sat in my office last evening,

---

7. Richardson, *Compilation*, 1: 214; Commager, *Documents*, 2: 414.
8. *Leviathan*, chap. 21.

waiting to speak, I thought of the many times each week when television brings the war into the American home. No one can say exactly what effect those vivid scenes have on American opinion." No one could say exactly, but Johnson had some inklings. He went on to wonder what would have happened after the Battle of the Bulge or during defeats in Korea had Americans been able to watch television coverage.[9]) After years of that exercise, Frank Capra films could never be viewed quite the same way. One source of the appeal of the lightning surgical strike, what we might call the Grenada effect, must lie here: we're victors before we have to witness the carnage as we eat dinner.

That peace is pure, war filthy, isn't distinctively American: it's a banal truism, a syrupy slogan one might hear in Sunday school. But there's also an intriguing inversion. War itself can be purifying, cleansing, restorative: an ocean of blood can wash away the sins of a failed America. The best-known case is the reaction of many Northern intellectuals to the civil war. Charles Eliot Norton, for one, had no patience with any "feeble sentimentalities" about overestimating the value of human life: "I can hardly help wishing that the war might go on and on till it has brought suffering and sorrow enough to quicken our consciences and cleanse our hearts." Emerson, for another, had the characteristically questionable taste to console the bereaved parents of a colonel "that one whole generation might well consent to perish, if by their fall, political liberty & clean & just life could be made sure to the generations that follow."[10]

Nearby is another twist on the ideas of cleanliness and purity: war is the struggle between light and darkness, good and evil. One doesn't have a conflict of interest with Nazi Germany: that's the sort of thought that leads to Chamberlain's appeasement, which here looms not just as bad calculation but as a deal with the devil. Instead the Third Reich is evil incarnate, what we must be justified in sweeping off the face of the earth. (The deep appeal of this moral view, instructively, is almost completely absent from Bruce Russett's account of why America shouldn't have entered World War II.) Or think of Kennan's famous Mr. X article: it argues that the Soviet regime has an inherently expansionist dynamic, so that if it is successfully contained it will inevitably collapse; but the article can be taken, and has been taken, as urging something very like a quarantine. Or recall the celebration as well as the brouhaha surrounding Reagan's reference to the Soviet Union as the evil empire, before he warmed up so dramatically to Gorbachev. Many Americans were happy to have a leader finally willing to say what was simply true,

---

9. James MacGregor Burns, ed., *To Heal and to Build: the Programs of Lyndon B. Johnson* (New York: McGraw-Hill, 1968), 468.

10. George M. Fredrickson, *The Inner Civil War: Northern Intellectuals and the Crisis of the Union* (New York: Harper & Row, 1965), 74, 80, 81.

instead of uttering mealymouthed pieties in the name of diplomacy. The bleakly comic possibilities in thinking of war as sanitation didn't escape the erratic geniuses of Monty Python, who offered a history of the Vietnam War as a cartoon commercial for a laundry detergent named Uncle Sam's—I think these are the details—which promises to get the red out, as the viewer watches a red, white, and blue gauntlet pouring detergent over a teeming map of Southeast Asia.

A fourth point: there's an entirely different American approach, a chillingly confident one, to thinking about conflict. It qualifies, I suppose, as a political version of bad faith. War isn't anything like a conflict of interest because it isn't in any interesting way elective or voluntary and because *they*, whoever they are at the moment, just have no standing. War here is necessary, inevitable, divinely appointed. Manifest destiny wasn't in any strong sense a justification of conflict. It's better viewed as a denial that there was any conflict that needed justifying, any land grabbing or Indian killing that might be morally objectionable in the first place. (Indian killing—I use the contemporary name—is another occasion for celebrating the cleansing power of murder. Robert Bird's best-selling novel of the 1830s, *Nick of the Woods*, can be read as a celebration or a critique. It features a Quaker, Nathan Slaughter, who, it turns out, secretly and gruesomely kills Indians because they once killed the members of his own family. His public protestations of pacifism ring hollow once we learn that he is Nick of the Woods; and—this may be literary clumsiness more than practiced ambiguity—it's not clear whether the reader is supposed to identify with Quaker Nathan or genocidal Nick.) Champions of manifest destiny not only appealed to Scripture, what even one so sagacious as John Quincy Adams once had read into the *Congressional Record* to explain what right Americans had to push the Indians ever westward. They also likened the expansion of America to the laws of gravity, arguing that America must surge west (and north and south, for that matter; a minor instance I've always found amusing is Walt Whitman's Brooklyn editorials urging that the United States seize the Yucatan) just as an apple must fall from a tree. Or again, while inviting Congress to declare war against Britain in 1812, Madison said the United States "shall commit a just cause into the hands of the Almighty Disposer of Events, avoiding all connections which might entangle it in the contest or views of other powers." War here is nothing but a judicial appeal.

I want to quote one example of the rhetoric of manifest destiny at length. This is from William Gilpin's 1873 book, *The Mission of the North American People*:

> The calm, wise man sets himself to study aright and understand clearly the deep designs of Providence—to scan the great volume of nature—to

fathom, if possible, the will of the Creator, and to receive with respect what may be revealed to him.

Two centuries have rolled over our race upon this continent. From nothing we have become 20,000,000. From nothing we are grown to be in agriculture, in commerce, in civilization, and in natural strength, the first among nations existing or in history. So much is our *destiny*—so far, up to this time—*transacted*, accomplished, certain, and not to be disputed. From this threshold we read the future.

The *untransacted* destiny of the American people is to subdue the continent—to rush over this vast field to the Pacific Ocean—to animate the many hundred millions of its people, and to cheer them upward—to set the principle of self-government at work—to agitate these herculean masses—to establish a new order in human affairs—to set free the enslaved—to regenerate superannuated nations—to change darkness into light—to stir up the sleep of a hundred centuries—to teach old nations a new civilization—to confirm the destiny of the human race—to carry the career of mankind to its culminating point—to cause stagnant people to be re-born—to perfect science—to emblazon history with the conquest of peace—to shed a new and resplendent glory upon mankind—to unite the world in one social family—to dissolve the spell of tyranny and exalt charity—to absolve the curse that weighs down humanity, and to shed blessings round the world!

Divine task! immortal mission! Let us tread fast and joyfully the open trail before us! Let every American heart open wide for patriotism to glow undimmed, and confide with religious faith in the sublime and prodigious destiny of his well-loved country.

Gilpin's rhetoric is incoherent in much the same way vulgar Marxism often is. He invites us to cooperate with our destiny, to choose to do what we must inevitably do. Its incoherence, though, doesn't mean it's politically unattractive. Nor, I think, should we be cavalier in dismissing such rhetoric as mere fluff, or for that matter as something we've outgrown.

Similarly, the Monroe Doctrine has sometimes been treated not as a contingent policy we've staked out, a choice we've made, but as a natural fact, not subject to our control or revaluation. Their missiles in Cuba aren't the least bit like our missiles in Turkey, because theirs just don't belong here. Communist influence in South America flouts long-standing U.S. policy, which drifts readily into U.S. tradition, which drifts readily into, flatly, the way things are. It's unnatural; when we move against it, we are simply restoring things to their pre-appointed harmony, the normal or natural state. I doubt American policymakers are taken in by this enough to be as virtuously astonished as they often sound in condemning foreign interference in Latin

America, in refusing to see any parallels with American policy; I don't doubt that they find it politically useful to pretend they're astonished. That particular message is for domestic consumption.

A closely connected point: if conflict is hard to justify, just deny there's any conflict at all. James Polk was a master of this move. In a single message to Congress, he described the impending annexation of Texas as a "union . . . consummated by . . . voluntary consent," adding,

> This accession to our territory has been a bloodless achievement. No arm of force has been raised to produce the result. The sword has had no part in the victory. We have not sought to extend our territorial possessions by conquest, or our republican institutions over a reluctant people. It was the deliberate homage of each people to the great principle of our federative union.

Talk of victory, though, was a revealing slip. Though war had not yet broken out, Mexico's ambassador to the United States had already demanded his passport and returned home, after informing Polk that Mexico viewed these moves as a wholly aggressive violation of its sovereignty. That's why Polk moved blithely on, as though it was a separate subject, to say, "I regret to inform you that our relations with Mexico since your last session have not been of the amicable character which it is our desire to cultivate with all foreign nations."

At the same time, what looked very like conflict was brewing with Britain over the Oregon territory. Calm as ever, in the very same message, Polk reported that Britain had made "extraordinary and wholly inadmissible demands," that "our title to the whole Oregon Territory [is] asserted, and, as is believed, maintained by irrefragable facts and arguments." Note here the salutary political advantages of the passive voice, which enables Polk to avoid posing the embarrassing question, *who* believes it? (At the very least, one suspects, not the British.) Polk again disguised a contestable political judgment as an unquestionable fact when he added, "The civilized world will see in these proceedings a spirit of liberal concession on the part of the United States, and this Government will be relieved from all responsibility which may follow the failure to settle the controversy." To disagree with the U.S. position here is presumptively to declare that one isn't civilized: and then, of course, one's judgment doesn't count anyway.

Something finally might be said about Americans' views of soldiers. Again, they are our young men, even our boys, bravely shouldering their rifles and heading off to do us proud. They are also warriors out to win honor and glory, categories that may smack of Homer or the royal court but survive full-blown in the military. They're also grunts, cannon fodder, surly interchangeable parts as wont to frag their commanders or smoke marijuana as to fight the enemy.

In part, there are real chronological changes here brought about by social change. The rise of increasingly awesome technology, for instance, makes it harder to tell a story about a certain kind of bravery in battle: for every talented fighter pilot, we think, there must be thousands of soldiers nowhere near the front lines, soldiers who wait for someone else to push some button or other. And the turn to a volunteer army enables us to think of soldiering as just another job.

But, in fact, all these views are always available, and they're invoked for different purposes. Soldiers are our boys when we want to rally 'round the flag and brand domestic dissent as a profound act of betrayal, not just something lending aid and comfort to the enemy or sapping the unified national will we need to grind out victory, but a moral failure to resonate to the heroic sacrifice our loved ones are making for us. (Recall how hard it was to rebut the plea, "Support our troops in the Gulf!" by urging that the best support would be bringing them home at once.) Soldiers are grunts when we want to despise war or mock the mindless robots who would go along with such inexcusable policies. (Savaging U.S. war in Mexico and support of slavery, Henry David Thoreau derisively referred to "the soldier, of whom the best you can say in this connection is, that he is a fool made conspicuous by a painted coat."[11]) Then again, soldiers are our boys when we want to puncture abstract stories about glory and justification by underlining the savage human toll of war. Instructively, though, there's not complete symmetry here. I know of no case where someone has described American soldiers in demeaning or derisive ways in order to assure us that it's okay to be fighting because the price is so low. Though some have come close: take John W. De Forest, who knew full well the hardship of war. He insisted that "We waste unnecessary sympathy on poor people. A man is not necessarily wretched because he is cold & hungry & unsheltered; provided those circumstances usually attend him, he gets along very well with them; they are annoyances, but not torments. . . ."[12]

And, of course, soldiers are heroes when one wants to underline what a grand and glorious cause this war (or war generally) is. Take Arthur Bird's *Looking Forward* of 1899, a late but all-too-typical specimen of manifest destiny prose. In looking forward to the happy days of 1999, those of the United States of the Americas that cover both continents, Bird celebrates the soldier who gets God's work done:

---

11. Henry David Thoreau, "Slavery in Massachusetts," in his *Reform Papers*, ed. Wendell Glick (Princeton: Princeton University Press, 1973), 95.

12. Fredrickson, *Inner Civil War*, 87.

"The man behind the gun," anxious to lay down his life by the side of the powerful breech-loading destroyer he loved so well to train and groom; "the man behind the gun" who loved and cared for his mighty weapon as a father would his child; watching it by night and day, praying for the hour when he might belch from its throat missiles of destruction into the enemy's ranks,—"the man behind the gun," God bless him, is America's own true born.

A closing caution: if Americans have so many views of war, so many views of soldiers, then it might seem that ruthless opportunism reigns, that one can always tell a story designed to come out the way one antecedently wants it to. (This is the opposite of the worry that our concepts compel us willy-nilly to certain wars.) That's false. Rich as they are in some domains, these concepts fail us in others. It's a commonplace among some academics that familiar views about bipolar conflict and state sovereignty fail us in coming to terms with the emerging international order. We can generalize the point: Americans find some (actual and potential) wars wholly baffling. We can't always describe the situation the way we already want to. Sometimes we can't figure out any way to describe it at all that makes sense to us. The poverty of our vocabulary in such cases must be one of the reasons, along with changing administrations and the rest, that American policy so often vacillates indecisively. So a richer vocabulary, a more intelligent conversation between rulers and ruled, would help us sort out what we're up to and why.

One-Minded Hierarchy versus Interest-Group Pluralism: Two Chinese Approaches to Conflict

Donald J. Munro

China's hard-line leaders explain all conflict in society as being the result of an undesirable absence of uniformity of thought. They especially stress as an explanation its absence among officials. Thus in the eyes of Deng Xiaoping, one of the most direct causes of continued student unrest in the spring of 1989 was an absence of uniformity among top leaders, on whom China's university students could model. Party Secretary Zhao Ziyang had publicly differed on certain policy issues with Deng.[1] But all along, even concerning less dramatic conflicts, the explanation of conflict was the same. Thus in January, 1989, a member of the Standing Committee of the Chinese People's Political Consultative Congress explained differences between the central government and local regions on economic issues in these terms:

> This state of affairs has been caused by numerous factors, such as structural problems, policy problems, and the practical conditions in various localities, but the fundamental and internal cause is the lack of a political idea to unify all people.[2]

---

1. I know of no better statement of the hard-line theoretical position prior to the Tiananmen massacre than an article by Bo Yibo in *Xinhua ribao* (New China Daily), June 1, 1987, 1–2. The article decries the trend to attack leftism and not rightism, and it condemns the trend to allow economic considerations to supplant party rectification work. Thereby the trend obstructs the goal of "unity of thought." Bo reminds party members that what they have to offer the country is leadership in thought and politics. Virtue and technical ability must go hand in hand, with the stress on the former. Theoretical dimensions of the alternative approach to that reflected by Bo Yibo are developed in the present chapter, but they culminate in the public split between Zhao Ziyang and Deng Xiaoping in the spring of 1989. An alleged copy of a speech attributed to President Yang Shangkun details how Mr. Zhao opposed Deng Xiaoping and the Political Bureau, and also kept students informed of the split. See Hong Kong AFP of May 29, 1989, from Beijing, in Foreign Broadcast Information Service (henceforth FBIS) Chinese, May 30, 1989, 16–22. Michel Oksenberg brought this document to my attention.

2. Beijing, *Xinhua*, January 30, 1989, in FBIS, January 31, 1989, 39–40. The same report contains reference to a colleague's comments to the effect that bribery and other forms of corruption are also political problems, to be corrected by ideological unity.

Until the Tiananmen massacre in early June, 1989 there was an embry-onic countertrend on how to explain conflict. Its most-visible form was the emergence of the Independent Student Union and various regional student associations (such as the East China Teacher's College Autonomous Student Union) and the Independent Labor Union, all subsequently declared illegal, and the intellectuals' union, founded in mid-May, 1989, and the journalists association.[3] This alternative approach explains conflict in terms of inevitable differences in the interests of people belonging to different groups, some unorganized and some organized. Former General Secretary Zhao may have previously supported this position.

Organized voluntary associations (clubs, professional associations) con-stitute a subdivision of "interest groups." As identified by persons outside of their cohorts, such as political leaders and social scientists, many interest groups are large amorphous groups without any formal structure or member-ship. The existence of the subdivision, organized voluntary associations, has the most interesting possible implications for political developments in China. This is because they provide a means whereby an individual can transcend the unit (*danwei*) to which that person is assigned by the state. Such units consti-tute the bottom line of the official structure whereby society is organized for social control and other purposes. Transcending their units, individuals can associate with persons of similar interests in the voluntary associations, in some cases with the potential for political lobbying.

This chapter concerns the contrast between the two explanations of con-flict, culminating in the suppression, for the moment, by the hard-liners of aspects of the countertrend. It ends with the projection that if the uniformity policies of the hard-liners are in time modified, the trajectory will be for China to resume a course that I here describe as interest-group pluralism.

---

3. The following facts constitute typical background to the emerging demand for indepen-dent unions and associations. A report at the end of 1988, on the eve of the 11th Congress of the All-China Federation of Trade Unions, identifies 378,000 basic-level trade unions in China. However, the report complains that they are emasculated by not having their duties clearly defined, by being unable to represent or safeguard the interests of workers and speak on their behalf because the government has not attached importance to their legal status, and by having their chairmen appointed rather than elected. See *Gongren ribao*, December 28, 1988, 3, in FBIS, January 23, 1989, 26–27. In spite of this, a union official reported over 100 strikes in 1988. Hong Kong AFP from Beijing, in FBIS, February 1, 1989, 47. The efforts of journalists to begin to protect their professional interests through legal means is reflected in the establishment of the China Press Law Research Center, which made recommendations to be forwarded to the State Council and to the National People's Congress concerning freedom of the press. Beijing, *Xinhua*, February 2, 1989, in FBIS, February 3, 1989, 25. In February, 1989, a group of journalists independently organized a campaign against the Three Gorges plan for damming the Yangtse River.

One-Minded Hierarchy

For nearly six hundred years, until 1905, there was a philosophical orthodoxy in China. All males who sought power and privilege through the civil service examinations had to study the commentaries on the classics by Cheng Yi (1033–1108) and Zhu Xi (1130–1200). And many other male elites, over the centuries, absorbed Cheng and Zhu's ideas in schools, where their works saturated a somewhat standardized curriculum. There is an answer in these works to the question of how to avoid conflict. The practice of enforcing an orthodoxy meant that large numbers of influential people had been taught much the same thing about that answer. None of this is to deny that individual Confucians may have been more or less opposed to the government's attempt to enforce an orthodoxy. And there is a long history of the imperial government dealing with a number of intellectually diverse Confucian private academies.

The teaching was to avoid conflict through uniform acceptance of the same ethical principles and of the practical rules of social conduct by which they are observed. The literati called attaining this uniformity "one-mindedness", and it referred to everyone in a group or in the country thinking the same on these issues. The ethical position was a social-role ethic, meaning that duties and expectations are functions of reciprocal social roles (husband-wife; father-son; older brother–younger brother). Specific duties and expectations (rights) were not generally discussed as possessed by humans as humans. Rather, they were described as varying depending on the relationship of one role to another, for all roles come in sets of two and are relationally defined. The core principles concern special obligations owed to family members and elders, and loyalty to the throne. The practical rules were called rules of ritual conduct, codified in early texts, and aimed to ritualize all interpersonal contact in a manner akin to practices in temple sacrifices, weddings, and funeral ceremonies.

In its original formulation by Mencius (372?–289? B.C.), this Confucian ethics had a place for duties common in content for all humans. An example would be the duty to react with sympathy to all humans in distress. But as Confucianism evolved under the influence of state sponsorship, sets of five and of three social roles with different duties took front stage in ethics as against the common duties of all humans. The result was that even sympathy was said to be expressed in role terms: as compassion in the case of superior to inferior and as filiality in the case of inferior to superior. Those superiors sufficiently advanced on the path to sagehood implement compassion by facilitating natural processes of change, especially by nurturing life cycles in humans and then in other living things.

The plausibility of uniformity as a goal rested in the belief that all persons are born with a mind having the same innate moral sense. It contains the social-role duties and also the rules that account for all objective regularities, such as seasonal plant growth. The principles contained in it and open to intuitive insight are universally present. Only some minds presently are clear enough to grasp them. But the assumption was that the more that education enlightened the cloudier minds, the more everyone would naturally think the same.

The social roles were hierarchically ranked. Their occupants together formed such commonplace Confucian social units as the family, lineage, community (one or several villages), county, and empire. These units also had moral significance because they were held together by individuals exercising role duties that originate in human nature. Their participants were interrelated because of their exercise of innate emotions that originate in the family setting and that can be extended beyond it to other people. And the rules indicating their duties were also believed to be innate in the mind. The groups did not exist primarily to serve some utilitarian end (though they might have done so); rather, they existed because individuals fulfilled their natures by participating in them and contributed thereby to realizing some holistic goal ("the whole world as one body"). The constitution of other legitimate organizations (a military unit, for example) was often based on the family model. Thus, individuals in them would role play in a manner akin to family roles, treating a senior male as a patriarchal figure. When the members of any of these groups realized their natures by participating in them, the organizations fulfilled their functions (a descriptive matter), and they were morally good groups (a value matter). So fact and value combined in discussing them. Historians would rank dynasties and lineages in terms of virtue, as well as individual fathers, husbands, wives, patriarchal figures and emperors in them.

Sharing the ideal of one-mind uniformity, Confucians and Maoists both promoted that ideal by rank ordering social roles. That is, they carved up society into the occupants of semifixed, hierarchically ranked social units. In the Confucian social role ethic, the expectation was that husbands, fathers, older brothers, and princes are superior and to be emulated. Others may match that superiority by emulating their virtues or obeying their orders. The key to avoiding conflict was for the subordinates (wives, children, lesser people) to each of these superior roles to adopt the standards and judgments of the superiors (so long as they themselves remained in line with orthodox rules of conduct). In Maoism, the proletariat (the Party), the peasantry and sometimes the set workers/peasants/soldiers had the same elevated status, in name, as did Mao and the Party in reality. The population was to model on the teachings of the supreme leader (Mao) who manifested the values and wisdom of the morally superior social class. Or they could model on a national model adept at copying Mao or the best class traits (Lei Feng), or copy more local figures skilled at governing their lives in accordance with official values. The Confucian ranks derive from Heaven and are imprinted by Heaven in all human minds, thereby being accessible to intuition. Maoist ranks derive from History, which casts different groups into progressive and reactionary roles in different stages of history.

Why would anyone expect the one-mind solution to apply to avoiding conflict about all problems? The answer within this school of philosophical orthodoxy and within Maoism was that all matters are moral matters. That is, all significant matters concern obligations possessed by humans or natural objects (in the Confucian case), for which general rules exist, and in the observance of which, praise or blame are justified. In Confucian orthodoxy, the psychological basis was that with the proper cultivation, an innate moral sense is able to (and should) dominate all psychological activity involving desires or motives or feelings ("the moral mind should rule the human mind"). Example: the desire to eat is controlled by an awareness of the rules applicable to the manner of eating and type of food to be eaten, so when a person acts accordingly, his eating is "proper." So, few thoughts about any nontrivial matter are immune from the control of this moral sense, and any event involving humans thereby becomes a moral event.

Objectively, moral principles are built into natural processes. Development through a process is good; divergence from it is bad. Example: Knowledge of a plant involves acquaintance with the changes it regularly undergoes from buds to blossoms to withering to dormancy, (a descriptive matter) and also knowledge of how it should behave (a normative matter). All minds potentially have the ability to identify the principles or rules at work in those natural processes and thereby to agree on a resolution to any problem that facilitates rather than obstructs the natural process. I will return to this issue below.

The moral mind has the authority to dominate whenever an issue of role-based obligation is present. When no obligation is in question, there may be license to act as one pleases. But the ubiquity of natural processes (especially concerning matters such as climate, that affect plant and animal life) ensures that someone could usually find occasion to shout that a sage person has an obligation to intervene to assist Nature and its creatures.

One sign that any individual participates in the one-mindedness is his choice of words. To participate, he must use words that simultaneously describe actions and pass judgment on them in accordance with accepted standards in the official orthodoxy. A person accepts the standards by repeating officially accepted words in an officially accepted word order. Word order often is significant because priority of placement reveals acceptance of priority of importance. For example, to cite a passage from the early Confucian classic, *The Great Learning*, in which one places the section on the investigation of things before the section on sincerity of the will, is to signal one's affiliation with the orthodox Cheng-Zhu school. To reverse the order of priority shows one's allegiance to the alternative Wang Yangming school. In 1910, to have described what goes on in reformed private schools as the teaching of "self-cultivation, national language, the Confucian classics, and mathematics" was to demonstrate one's acceptance of the policy that even with modernizing reforms, moral self-cultivation would come first in the curriculum. Similarly, during the Maoist period, to use the phrase "virtue, education, and physical fitness" (*de*, *yu*, *ti*) to describe the curriculum was also to affirm acceptance of treating moral education as the most important part of teaching.

Reliance on this practice is a legacy of the "rectification of names" doctrine dating from the Warring States period (403–221 B.C.). The basis of the doctrine is the recognition that the speaker's words reflect his values, and thus words can persuade others, changing their acts. Controlling word choice is a way of controlling how people influence each other on matters of principle. In its earliest form, the standard for guiding word choice was the Confucian compilations of ritual rules of conduct, especially the *Book of Rites (Li ji)*.

Modern partisans of the one-mind solution to conflict have continued to place great stock in the analysis of word choice as a clue to thought conformance. And they have acted as though the persuasive power of words makes correct language capable of altering reality. Falling lockstep into this pattern in the post-Mao era, even many opponents of one-mindism and proponents of all sorts of reforms talk of changing the old definitions as a way of generating support for the new wave. They note how their adversaries form expressions simultaneously to describe and criticize. For example, one writer cites the expression "commerce through science (*ke shang*)" to describe those who use science to make things that can be commercially profitable.[4] The "science" character is positive, the "commerce" one pejorative. So the expression describes the activity and condemns it at the same time (fact-value fusion). The writer advocates changing the meaning of the commerce character so that it has a positive connotation. This is a very popular accompaniment to political and economic reform, derided by one critic as "rectifying the name" of whatever was criticized in the past.[5]

Another sign of being "one in mind and will" is obedience. In the past, this meant obedience to the emperor as central authority, today, to the Party. This way, "the interest of the part obeys the interest of the whole."

The social scientist or the cynic may deride the test of word choice as evidence of thought conformance. He will say that word choice may itself

4. *Renmin ribao* (People's Daily) overseas edition, June 6, 1988.

5. Yuan Bozhao, "'Zheng ming' yu guannian 'gengxin'" (The "rectification of names" and the "renewal" of concepts), *Zhexue yanjiu* (Philosophical investigations), November, 1985, 19–22.

become faked or ritualized, adopted to fit occasions and revealing nothing about inner thoughts, which may be of a sort contrary to the words. This is certainly the way real people did and do, in fact, sometimes choose their words. However, the Confucian teachings were not ignorant of the matter. They treated the disparity between what we think and what we say as a problem in self-cultivation to be overcome. There is an introspective and a behavioral side to cultivation. Confucians were fond of quoting *The Great Learning*, that "the superior man must be watchful over himself when he is alone," ensuring that his words and acts are proper even when no one is around. Then the right habits will develop and the individual's acts will not be faked on other occasions. This all involves introspective self-examination.

The behavioral part of the personal-cultivation process involved practicing rituals, including speech. A consequence was supposed to be the transformation of the mind, bringing beliefs into consistency with the spirit of performed rituals. Such a person, nurtured within and without, will have the virtue of sincerity (*cheng*), meaning that there is no inconsistency between his inner thoughts and his outer actions. The Confucian also did not recognize a bifurcation between the private, subjective world of beliefs and the public, objective world of overt behavior, including speech. Inner beliefs will inevitably emerge as words and as other acts. The skilled scholar can identify those that are sincere and not fear trickery. In contemporary China, the problem of the disparity between what people say and what they believe is well known. In controlled settings, such as prisons, officials prove the disparity through the study of words in confessions. Elsewhere in society, the disparity often lingers unattended.

There were Confucians not affiliated with the doctrines that became orthodoxy who granted the existence of private interests that were none of the state's business to evaluate or to edify morally through education. Those other Confucians even lived at the same time as the founders of orthodoxy, Cheng Yi and Zhu Xi. But the school of Cheng and Zhu believed that it is the state's business to intrude into the realm of people's minds. It helps ensure that the principles innate to the moral mind do rule.

In the Maoist period, the one-mind approach continued, as did the ethics of hierarchical social role-fulfillment. However, the officially sanctioned roles were no longer the Confucian sets mentioned earlier (though unofficially they endured) but rather ones based on rank-ordered social classes. Each class had its roles to play in realizing the target of revolutionary victory or socialism. Their moral station now derived not from Nature or from principles innate to human nature, but from History.

The one-mindedness goal continued in a mixture with a theory about the creative consequences of fostering conflict. I will set aside and not discuss the purposive, violent, physical abuse justified for enemies of the people (and for random souls during the Cultural Revolution and in the Tiananmen massacre).

For the rest of the population, the explanation of conflict was ideological deviancy. The method of resolution was officially instigated public criticism (thereby creating new conflict and shifting its focus onto one or more of the participants). The end result was to be the restoration of one-mind uniformity. One-mindedness was the goal, fostered conflict the means.

The values that gave content to the one mind were those of the proletariat as interpreted by the Party. Members of other classes demonstrated their progressiveness to the degree that they assimilated these values. The operational principle in all of this was "unity-criticism-unity," and its echoes have been heard on into the 1980s:

> Under the guidance of this principle, when contradictions occur among the people, it is necessary to proceed from the desire for unity and resolve contradictions through the method of criticism and self-criticism.[6]

All nontrivial conflicts fell within this approach because of the continued official proclamation that all problems are moral problems.

Gradually in the post-Mao era, however, some unorthodox Chinese writers dared specifically to identify and criticize this traditional concern with uniformity as an obsession to be corrected. One recent writer recorded a shift, now, in the national spirit "from seeking uniformity and getting rid of diversity to having both." He traced the deep roots of the goal of uniformity back to Dong Zhongshu (179?–104? B.C.), who helped formulate orthodoxy in the Former Han.[7] The writer describes even the details of mundane clothing choice covered by Dong's sweeping proposals. Other writers identified the Confucian "monolithic unity of everything" with the patriarchal clan system that enforced uniform duties for occupants of standardized social positions:

> The Confucians' "Grand Unity of Everything" [*da yitong*] is then the chief aspect of the Chinese cultural tradition. The "Unity of Everything" that is treated as "Grand" (venerated) by this tradition is the "orthodoxy" of a patriarchal clan system with strict ranks. It was based on a self-sufficient natural economy. This kind of a tradition required that each person occupy for his entire life an unchanging position in the societal network. It caused each individual to be dependent on his own superior and patriarch (the "respected" and "parents"). With no independent personalities, how could they allow the concept of free competition?[8]

---

6. *Guangming ribao*, September 13, 1984, 2, in FBIS, September 20, 1984, K10.

7. *Renmin ribao*, May 2, 1988, 5.

8. *Renmin ribao*, overseas, May 17, 1988, 5. Article by Li Honglin, "Lun jingzheng" (On competition) is one of the most substantive of the theoretical articles on the alternative approach to conflict.

The author went on to say that the centralized socialist state after 1949 only reinforced this attempt to create a grand unity of everything. Thus, he and others advocated a dramatic departure from this one-mind approach to conflict avoidance. It was not a departure that all accepted, as the Tianamen tragedy underscores, but it had sufficient momentum to have made an impact.

Some events of the post-Mao era, such as economic decentralization, the availability of Western economic models, and access to the lectures of Western experts on everything, serve as background to this shift away from the one-mind approach to conflict avoidance. I want to table these matters. Instead, I want to understand the shift from the point of view of participants. If I had been a Chinese affected by the deflection away from uniformity toward some toleration of pluralism, how would I have explained it to myself? How would I have justified it? In investigating this, I realized that two different kinds of question lead to different aspects of the explanation. The first, with which I deal in the next section, searches for concrete historical events with which the embryonic toleration of diversity and conflict of beliefs was linked. The second question, to be faced in the final section, asks if, concurrently, there were emerging theoretical justifications for toleration. I turn now to the alternative approach.

Interest-Group Pluralism

The attempt by Chinese leaders to impose uniformity of belief and judgment has been a barrier to modernization. Chinese ethical writings of the 1980s reveal the beginnings of a deflection away from the traditional road, on which philosophers and political leaders prized uniformity as a way of eliminating conflict. Instead, the countertrend was to celebrate pluralism and be permissive of conflict. I now identify the conditions under which the alternative, that is, the move to pluralism, arose and could be justified. One of my conclusions is that pluralism of interest groups and organizations (with their often-conflicting viewpoints) is entirely compatible with the existence of a highly authoritarian central leadership of the state. The state's function can evolve from being enforcer of uniformity of thought to being arbiter of conflicts between different interest groups and organizations. This may mean deciding whose viewpoint is correct. More important, it means deciding, among the competitors, who gets the pork out of the state's barrel.

My thesis is that, in China, the emerging intellectual toleration of pluralism had required a shift away from classifying people by using social categories differentiated in terms of moral worth. This move in turn could be justified by drawing on the admissions by some recent Chinese thinkers that not all matters are moral matters. This departure from the Zhu Xi orthodoxy of the late empire had its advocates under Republican China. However, with the Communist assumption of leadership in 1949, the principle that all matters are moral matters was promulgated as part of officially supported Maoist thought.

Let me sum up what was new and not new about these alternative developments before I begin the analysis of them. The "New" column of the ledger starts with the position that pluralism of beliefs or judgments is not necessarily a sign of a social defect needing correction. Although it may not be desirable, it is inevitable and not to be feared. The diversity in question concerns judgments about the allocation of resources and policies affecting social, intellectual, and artistic life. The next new entry was that groups and organizations are not rank ordered in terms of moral worth, and, therefore, their viewpoints permissibly conflict in the open until some arbiter decides among them. In other words, no one group can be assumed consistently to have an enduring access to the truth. Finally, the acceptance of pluralism of beliefs means that individuals are under no obligation publicly to affirm daily their acceptance of the single truth. Some privacy of belief follows.

On the other side, in the "Not New" column, single-party authoritarianism remained, even in this alternative approach. Pluralism did not refer to multiparty political pluralism. Second, there was no challenge to the holistic understanding of the relation of groups to the state. Otherwise stated, there was no theory of the rights of groups to adhere permanently to their positions. This provides central authorities with considerable legitimacy in mediating conflicts among groups in the name of the interest of society as a whole.

A Plurality of Minds and Morally Neutral Social Groups

The concrete historical event that keeps popping forth from small mountains of recent articles, books, and memories of conversations, is that writers were redefining the kind of people who will participate in conflict situations, substituting morally neutral groups for hierarchically ranked ones. With this redefinition, they ensured that conflict can no longer be resolved by identifying the group that has the right moral or political principles and then requiring that others model on its members until societal one-mindedness is achieved. Second, these voices denied the possibility of one-mindedness (except on vague and unproblematic goals). Third, simultaneously, they accepted the inevitability of conflict. The three points with which I introduce this section marking the historic shift appear clearly in the following statement:

> The traditional way to differentiate social classes is no longer useful under the present conditions. The new social relations, group relations, and interpersonal relations can no longer be classified in light of the owning of the means of production. Vocational, technical, and other sociological standards are becoming more and more useful. No single

person or social organization or group can absolutely and completely represent and realize the interests of all people in society. The false impression of "no conflict" no longer exists. People's interests are no longer monolithic, but are plural.[9]

There was a continuing change in the nature of the social categories and in their membership:

Part of the members of the original social groups, such as the peasants, have disintegrated into agricultural producers, worker-peasant households, and individual industrial and commercial households. A population of one million of the demobilized servicemen have been converted into other social groups of every category. New social groups such as entrepreneur groups, individual household groups, and employer groups have already taken certain social places in the group structure. We may say that the social group structure in China is undergoing a turbulent new period of continuous reorganization and gradual optimization.[10]

By the 1980s, there were those who repudiated dividing society in accordance with social units or social stations ranked in terms of moral worth. In their place, they spoke of a variety of morally neutral social groups. There was also the shift from focusing on social roles related functionally to some large entity or goal (lineage, community, state, society) to focusing on independent groups. One of these was "interest groups" (*liyi jituan*), a term borrowed from Western political science that, significantly, had its first imprimatur from Zhao Ziyang. Another was morally neutral voluntary social organizations. A third was voluntary organizations that had structure (unlike broad interest groups) and yet that seemed primed to serve as politically active interest groups advocating the members' goals to other groups, including government agencies. These new, morally neutral social groups differed from their Confucian and Maoist predecessors (lineages, classes) in that they would not routinely be subject to moral evaluation; nor were they composed of occupants of intrinsically superior or inferior social stations. Furthermore, they derived their relative worth from utility, not from human nature (as with Confucian-sanctioned social groups or social roles) or from History (as with Maoist classes).

Sometimes the term "interest groups" referred to those with shared attitudes deriving from common occupations but not having any formal organization. They are like the social strata (*jiezeng*) in more traditional Marxist

---

9. *Shanghai shijie jingji daobao*, August 10, 1987, 12, in FBIS, August 19, 1987, K12.
10. *Guangming ribao*, February 29, 1988, 3, in FBIS, March 22, 1988, 20.

sociology. Examples would include aged cadres, enterprise managers, private entrepreneurs, government employees, intellectuals, residents of coastal areas, residents of hinterlands, and central and local authorities. Specifically, within rural areas, the groups would include enterprise owner-managers, specialized personnel (teachers, medical workers, and agricultural technicians), and leading cadres at the township and village levels.[11] One reason for identifying such groups was to caution policymakers of a variety of different opinions they would be wise to solicit before formulating a policy and of the potential sources of conflict it might elicit. The interests of an enterprise and of its workers are, in important ways, different; their responses to the same policy will be different. There were attempts to formalize consultation with these groups through a method called the "social dialogue system," using newspapers, radio and television:

> Establishing the social consultation and dialogue system will be conducive to forming closer ties between leading organs and the people and to building a bridge of mutual understanding between people of different social strata. This system will become an effective form to correctly handle the relationship between different social interests and to alleviate contradictions between them.[12]

There are other new social units devoid of hierarchical or evaluative connotations that differ from mere interest groups in having formal organizations for a stated purpose. The act of forming such an association (*jie she*) was often discouraged in imperial China. Today they are variously called social cohorts (*shehui qunti*) or social groups (*shehui tuanti*).[13]

Until the 1980s the authorities blocked most such initiatives in the People's Republic as well. One writer states that "in the past we had a doctrine that strongly sought unity," and it obstructed lateral associations.[14] Lateral associations or economic lateral associations (*jingji lienho ti*) refers to one type of nonpolitical social organization, namely one between enterprises engaged in similar activity, something like a trade association. Such organizations are not entirely grass roots in origin, as they may be initiated by enterprise leaders eager to share technical information. However, they accomplish the same end as the other voluntary organizations in affording members the chance to transcend their *danwei*.

11. *Beijing Review* 48 (November 20–December 6, 1987): 18; 12 (March 21–27, 1988): 31; and 17 (April 25–May 1, 1988): 28.

12. "Overcoming Bureaucratism, Building Democratic Politics—Commentary on Political Structural Reform," Hong Kong, *Liaowang Overseas Edition* 44, (November 2, 1987): 8–10, in FBIS, November 9, 1987, 37.

13. *Renmin ribao*, April 29, 1988, 5.

14. *Renmin ribao*, July 12, 1986, 5.

Examples of associations in a city might include a *weiqi* (go) players club, a physics society, and a federation of literary and art circles.[15] Shanghai registered 2,627 of them in 1984.[16] A government report in 1989 referred to over 1,000 national-level organizations and over 100,000 local ones.[17]

Within the field of Chinese philosophy and related cultural subjects, an interesting example of a voluntary social organization is "The International Academy of Chinese Culture." Established in Beijing in 1984, it takes as its own model an earlier institution of considerable symbolic significance. This is the private academy, which began to flourish in Southern Song times (1127–1279) in opposition to the Imperial College. One member described its aims in these words:

> We discussed the question [of Chinese failures in the past century] and concluded that all of the failures resulted from the lack of the social class called literati, which is a symbol of social rationality. Without rationality, a society is bound to progress like a blind person groping for direction.[18]

Apparently members of the Academy regard themselves as representing the goals of a subgroup of intellectuals able to articulate societal goals.

These associations were legal bodies (*fa ren*), the membership of which was voluntary (*zi ying*).[19] This legal status brought them under party and government leadership when the rulers so chose, making the organizations acceptable.

A recent study of Chinese nongovernmental organizations (NGOs) found that they must be affiliated with governmental counterparts (*gua kao danwei*). They rely on these counterparts for wages, transportation, and administrative support. This reduces their autonomy.[20] November 1, 1989 marked the national implementation of a law on the registration and supervision of social organizations.[21] The aim was to tighten governmental supervision. The implementation of the law suggests that previously some organizations were only loosely tied into governmental organs or, in the minds of some leaders, operated too autonomously.

The emergence of the new social organizations after the Cultural Revolution was not without conflict itself. Much of it centered on opposing govern-

---

15. Article by Yan Jiaqi, "The Scientific Meaning of 'Separation of Party and Government'" in *Renmin ribao*, November 7, 1987, 5, in FBIS, December 7, 1987, 17.

16. *Renmin ribao*, April 29, 1988, 5.

17. *Renmin ribao*, overseas, November 1, 1989, 1.

18. Quoted in *China Daily*, May 2, 1988.

19. *Renmin ribao*, April 29, 1988, 5.

20. Susan Whiting, "The Non-Govenmental Sector in China: A Preliminary Report," prepared for the Ford Foundation, July, 1989, 5.

21. *Renmin ribao*, overseas, November 1, 1989, 1.

ment intrusion into the affairs of the economic lateral associations. And conservative political voices criticized the populace as "rushing headlong into mass action" by establishing associations, academic societies, research societies, foundations, centers, and trans-trade and trans-area national organizations without the approval of central authorities.[22]

When the self-employed formed an organization, public reports stressed that it had a constitution, meaning that it had rules for the members to follow, and that on that basis it would handle disputes.[23] I treat an organization such as that of the self-employed as a third type. Unlike most broad-interest groups, it is organized. Yet it seemed able to defend and promote its members' economic and political interests, unlike some benign voluntary organizations (such as hobby clubs). The student and journalist associations of the spring of 1989 belong to this third type.

A recent study of NGOs found nongovernmental research institutes to be the most autonomous and most involved in political advocacy of the NGOs. Of these, the single most highly publicized politically was the Stone Institute of Social Development, founded with a grant from the Beijing Stone Computer Corporation. The Stone Institute and several other research institutes were attacked following the repression of the June, 1989 demonstration.[24]

In any case, the voluntary social organizations were tolerated after the Cultural Revolution and, under strict supervision, after November 1, 1989. Among the important reasons given as to why the voluntary associations were to be tolerated was that in China's present historical era, class conflict has disappeared, but less-violent differences endure. These social organizations provided a forum for resolving these more-benign conflicts:

> Although the economic basis for heated opposition and conflict of interest between members of society has disappeared with the establishment of the socialist system based on public ownership, and the unity of fundamental interests of all the people has been realized, the existence of various different social cohorts is objective and necessary. This is because, in the initial stage of socialism there continue to exist differences between urban and rural areas, industry and agriculture, mental and manual labor, and there continue to be differences among people in occupation, income, preferences, habits, race, and even psychology and culture.[25]

---

22. Beijing, *Xinhua*, December 11, 1984, in FBIS, December 12, 1984, K1.

23. "Premier Zhao and the Self-employed," in Beijing, *Xinhua*, December 4, 1986, in FBIS, December 8, 1986, K13. Discusses a visit made by Zhao Ziyang to the Self-Employed Association.

24. Whiting, "The Non-Governmental Sector in China," 39–40.

25. *Renmin ribao*, April 29, 1988, 5.

The social organizations that cater to different groups can solve social problems. Their semi-independent status means that they can react more quickly than government departments.

The citation immediately above reveals a picture of historical change in China that serves as background to the legitimation of a variety of different social cohorts. It speaks of "the initial stage of socialism." The reference to stages suggests a *process* of change. At one point, class struggle was appropriate, as were certain coercive ways of resolving it. But the "initial stage" of socialism (beginning in 1956) is a later point in the long process leading to socialism. So different social organizations are appropriate now, as are other means of resolving conflicts between them. A plurality of interests is inevitable at this stage. One function of government is to discover conflicts of interest and resolve them.[26] There is a suggestion in the citation that sometime in the future, differences among people and conflict may evaporate. All of this is reminiscent of Mao's pre–Cultural Revolution idealization of China's ability peacefully to resolve "contradictions among the people."

In the emergence of these new social cohorts there was one point of continuity with earlier forms of social analysis. Writers talked about groups rather than individuals. It seemed legitimate to speak of pluralism among the interests of groups, less so of the plurality of individuals' interests. This suggests the endurance of a perspective on groups that differs from that in Western liberal ethics. The Western liberal sometimes regards the group as a mere instrument or tool to help him achieve an interest that he has apart from it. In the evolving Chinese group pluralism, the group may have had an interest or goal of its own apart from those of its members. Participation by the members may bring such group interests into existence. An example of group interest would be attaining a reputation of effectiveness as an arbitrator of conflicts among members, or in preserving harmonious feelings among members, or in synthesizing the differing wise insights of the individual members.

What was new in these social cohorts was a conscious shift in the range of activities that count as significant for purposes of classifying into named groups the persons who perform the activity. The range was broader than the focus on production activity by people having similar relations to property, favored by Marxists.[27] Also, the key activities no longer centered on fulfilling or avoiding reciprocal social-role duties within Confucian or Marxist class

---

26. Andrew Nathan informs me that this theory can be traced back to a 1979 speech of Su Shaozhi, former director of the Institute of Marxism, Leninism, Mao Zedong Thought. Arguing that China is not yet socialist nor even building socialism, he said that instead it is in a transition period between capitalism and building socialism. Hu Qiaomu and others attacked the theory, but others picked it up.

27. *Lilun yu shijian* (Theory and Practice) 15 (August 6, 1987): 46.

categories. Rather, they involved the pursuit of varied interests, the performance of professional skills, taking part in hobbies, sharing trade information, or promoting philosophical or religious teachings. One writer romantically portrays the spectrum of pluralistic views that may be anticipated as the goal of one-mindedness fades: "Socialist society should be a garden with a rainbow of colors; it should be a sparkling period in which human talents massively burst forth."[28]

Pluralism was in the picture because of the recognition of the epistemological principle that those affiliated with these different groups look at the same facts differently:

An indisputable fact in China today is that there exist different interest groups whose understanding of the objective situation is different, and that the interest structure and distribution pattern are gradually being replaced by new rational ones.[29]

Chinese analysts acknowledged the resultant conflict of ideas. Within the same field, benign conflict between varying interpretations of the same facts can be a good thing. It can generate confidence and thereby enthusiasm for production. One writer said that the Chinese should reevaluate their traditional opposition to "individualism" so long as it does not mean seeking private gain at the expense of others:

[O]nly this society [one promoting independence of personality] can completely arouse people's positive outlook, and greatly develop the productive forces. Therefore, I think, Marxists will welcome the changes in Chinese society to which competition gives rise and welcome people's acknowledgement of self-worth, mastery of their own destiny, and the respect for their own personality.[30]

The most common forms of tolerated competition include competition through examinations for limited positions in universities and free market competition among commercial enterprises. Obviously, many of the disagreements and conflicts among groups concern money:

The period of reform is one in which contradictions in human relations can easily grow intense. Because of the imbalance in the distribution

28. *Renmin ribao*, overseas, May 17, 1988, 2.
29. *Beijing Review* 48, (November 30–December 6, 1987): 18.
30. *Renmin ribao*, overseas, May 17, 1988, 2.

relations between groups, it will inevitably lead to contradictions and conflicts between groups.[31]

Thus, economic competition of all kinds is the most obvious form of conflict to catch the public eye.

My thesis, then, is that moving away from the use of morally laden social categories (within the family or within production relations) was a prerequisite for toleration of conflict of beliefs, values, and interests. Inevitably, it brings in its wake a downgrading of one-mindedness as a goal and a toleration of a certain amount of pluralism. This is because no one social group is *by definition* the authoritative model for all the others. Each group has its permissible interpretation of the same objective event.

However, we witnessed a reduction, not a total elimination, of morally laden social categories. "Relational network" (*guanxi wang*) continues to be a pejorative term, referring to groups of people having some kinship, regional, school, or occupational ties on the basis of which individuals do favors for each other, circumventing normal bureaucratic channels. It is a fact of life, however, even among highest leaders. Often people cluster around a central figure whose social status and activities give him special access to privileges that he can dispense and protection he can secure. Because it is dependent on patronage, the network's endurance is unstable. Here is one description:

> Generally speaking [a relational network] refers to people inside and outside the party whose thoughts are not pure, whose style is not upright, who make use of their rank and power and make deals among themselves, and whose goal is to help each other gain selfish political and economic interests for individuals or small groups.[32]

One of the things that makes them intrinsically bad from an official perspective is that they act independently of higher authority.[33] They have been an effective and simultaneously disparaged way of getting things done for centuries, as this old aphorism attests: "The relation between fellow townsmen is more useful than an official seal" (*yi ge gongzhang ding bu liao yi ge lao xiang*).

Relational networks overlap in some ways with another enduring bad group, the feudal clan (*zongfa*). Clan mentality (*zongfa guannian*) lasts even if the clan does not:

---

31. *Guangming ribao*, February 29, 1988, 3, in FBIS, March 22, 1988, 21.
32. *Renmin ribao*, December 10, 1986, 10.
33. *Renmin ribao*, August 1, 1986, 5.

A "relational network" is a feudalistic clan concept . . . "when a husband has a high position his wife is honored," "when a father is in a high
position, it honors his sons." . . . This is one characteristic. Using the
relations of superior and inferior, of schoolmates, same native place,
same occupation, and same enterprise in order to help and protect each
other. This is the second characteristic.[34]

There is a difference between clan ties and relational networks in that not all
members of the latter have blood ties. The leader of a relational network may
not be a patriarchal figure whose status is partially due to age and clan position
but rather a person whose activities give him access to privileges to dispense.

Mayfair Yang distinguishes relational networks from a third negative
group, factions:

Factions are logical extensions of guanxi relational networks. Factions
are also made up of personal relationships of mutual obligations and
exchange. However, unlike guanxi networks which are made up of sets
of dyadic relations, each of which is usually not cognizant of the whole
extent of the larger network, factions are composed of members who
have a consciousness of belonging to a group and are ready to live up to
its obligations to any other member. . . . The links in a guanxi network
may differ in their familiarity base; one link may be based on a kinship
tie, another on a classmate tie, and yet another may be established
through the personal introduction of a mutual friend. Membership in
factions, on the other hand, is based on more uniform common ground-
ing, where all or most of the members might share a common place of
origin and regional dialect, or political and economical interest, or ideological stance.[35]

Factions dominated premodern Chinese politics, where they were known by
the term *pengdang*. Although factions had some apologists, most writers
treated them as intrinsically evil.[36] The reason is that they fragment the body
politic. Their members place their own selfish interests of themselves and

---

34. *Renmin ribao*, December 10, 1986, 1.
35. Mayfair Yang, "The Art of Social Relationships and Exchange in China" (Ph.D.
dissertation, University of California, Berkeley, 1986), 159–60.
36. During the Northern Sung, Ou-Yang Hsiu (1007–1072) defended some factions as
cohorts of virtuous, like-minded men. During the Qing dynasty, in the eighteenth century, the
rulers tolerated not gentry-based public factions but kinship-based private forms of political
solidarity, providing the lineage group was not too large. See Benjamin Elman, *Classicism,
Politics, and Kinship: The Ch'ang-chou New Text School of Confucianism in Late Imperial China*
(Berkeley: University of California Press, 1990), chap. 1.

those of the faction ahead of the interest of the state. This type of criticism carries over into the present, when several terms identify them (e.g., clique [*xiao jituan*] and gang [*bang*]). Writers treat factionalism as an expression of the individualistic or anarchistic guild mentality of the old society. One commentator said:

> Therefore, to put it briefly, factionalism is a manifestation of the exploiting class' ultraindividualism aimed at scrambling for power and profit, and seeking personal gains, by taking advantage of their position and power.[37]

"Individualism" here is an emotive term meaning selfish concern with the interest of a part rather than of the whole. The criticism was typical of criticism made of factions by those who placed one-mindedness in first place as a means of preventing conflict. Factions demand one-mindedness of their members. But the perception is that they shatter the one-mindedness of larger social units including the state.

One reason why factions and relational networks were open to attack in the premodern period is that they were not intrinsically of varying moral worth. People departed from orthodox, morally rank-ordered social units when they participated in them. Also, though factions might claim lofty purposes, outsiders attributed to them the utilitarian goal of maximizing the benefits of their members. This was at odds with the Confucian, human-nature or Nature-based moral standard. As for criticism of today's factions, a common critical approach is that too few people reap the benefits factions seek for them to be morally acceptable even to contemporary utilitarians, who are beginning to emerge in Chinese ethical circles. However, factions still remain another fact of life in Chinese politics, not much destabilized by the criticism. At the same time, like relational networks, the existence of a single actual faction may be vulnerable because of dependence on the patronage of officials who can lose power struggles.

One of the paradoxes of contemporary China is that the idea of a faction as a selfish and divisive group colors the understanding of what a political party is. This was true back in the 1920s and helps explain the avoidance by the New Culture leader Hu Shi of participation in the party process. A consequence is that members of voluntary groups that could make a political difference in furthering their beliefs often avoid political action, in part because it might suggest party behavior. They cherish unorthodox belief, but they avoid the activity that would make pluralism of the political process a reality.

---

37. "Guard against Factionalist Interferences in Comparison and Examination Work," in Nanjing, *Xinhua ribao*, April 27, 1984, 1, in FBIS, May 10, 1984, K11.

The concrete sins of cliques (*xiao jituan*) are often their economic crimes. They rob the government to line their own pockets, perhaps reselling at a profit production materials taken from government-owned industrial and agricultural enterprises. The cliques may simply be officers in one department of an enterprise.

Certain morally laden social groups endure from the past. They constitute the background against which to contrast the morally neutral social categories just discussed. At the same time, the relation of these unofficial groups to local or central governments in the past established patterns into which newer, legitimate voluntary organizations may flow if the alternative approach to conflict management reemerges. While not formally administering the relational networks or factions, officials often had to mediate between the interests of competing ones. Perhaps there is a clue here as to one of the functions of future governments in China: independent organizations compete for limited pork-barrel funds and favored treatment, and officials mediate between them on the basis of governmental goals. Of course, the informality of networks and factions means that there is not much regularized precedent or legal procedure for conducting such mediation.

Theoretical Basis for Morally Neutral Social Cohorts

There were doctrinal shifts in the 1980s that could be used to justify morally neutral social-groups, whose members are linked by interests or skills not describable in social-role terms. Such groups are not ranked in terms of moral worth. There were three distinct factors in this evolving theoretical position.

The first factor, in rough form a fairly old idea, was the division of the interests of all the people into two sets, fundamental interests, and all the rest. By declaration of the leaders, the fundamental interests of all the people are the same.[38] The more-recent twist was to assert that the people all accept modernization and socialism with Chinese characteristics as their fundamental interests and agree on them. The door was then opened for diversity of opinion on what constitutes the other interests. It was legitimate for people to join together in groups pursuing competing interests and for controlled conflict on such collisions of goals.

The second factor was backing off from the Confucian and Maoist assertion that all matters involving humans are primarily moral matters, where moral was defined in terms of social-role duties. As long as all matters are moral matters, an inevitable consequence will be to trivialize all concerns and

38. Zhao Baoyun and Li Shijun, "The Historical Evolutions of 'Separation of Three Powers' and Whether It Suits Our Country's National Conditions," in Beijing, *Lilun yuekan* 9, (September 25, 1987), FBIS, October 23, 1987, 25.

behaviors other than fulfillment of social-role duty, for social-duty is the content of morality. During the Maoist period it was common to identify work of different classes that contributes to socialism as alone worthy and to disvalue other activity. According to this criterion, only work relating to agricultural, industrial, or defense production (as interpreted then) had worth. Each class, including the intellectual "stratum," had its function in contributing to production or defense. Such functions were the role duties of members of the different classes or groups: workers, peasants, soldiers, intellectuals, and national bourgeoisie. This means that work or study in scientific management, much theoretical natural science, commerce, demography, environmental studies, law, philosophy, religious studies, social science, foreign cultures, and nonpropagandistic arts and letters work had no importance. But, according to an alternative theoretical position that also emerged, if people can highlight interests, skills, and activities that are not concerned with role duty and consider them important enough to be a basis for grouping people, then there is a basis for morally neutral groups.

Maoism carried on the spirit of the Zhu Xi–Confucian idea of the moral mind dominating all activity. This is symbolized by such slogans as "politics in command" (1950) and the "doctrine of the four firsts" (which includes the rule that political work should be first, above all other work). These slogans treated politics or morality (meaning the standards in the minds of participants) as the key to understanding and dealing successfully with any significant event of which they are a part. The morality in question takes as its standard the respective duties of an official set of social classes, led by the workers and peasants through their party.

As the contemporary Chinese philosopher Li Zehou put it, the "modern new Confucian" (Mao), like his Confucian predecessors, takes the individual rectifying his mind as the basis for building the country well and promoting peace in the world (to paraphrase *The Great Learning*).[39] Mao had said that "thought and politics are both leaders. If we relax thought work and political work, economic and technological work will both go down a bad road."[40] So morality and politics lead economics, technology, and everything else. As Li Zehou interpreted this position, Mao claimed that good and evil (proletarian and capitalist) traces can be found in everything touched by human thought in present-day China. Proletarian thought refers to the positive moral values of public/impartial/selfless (*gong*), previously associated with the heavenly principles (innately in the moral mind or Dao mind) of Cheng-Zhu thought.

---

39. Li Zehou, "Shitan makesi zai Chongguo" (Probing Marxism in China), in *Chongguo xiandai sisiangshi lun* (On the history of contemporary Chinese thought) (Peking: Dongfang chubanshe, 1987): 180, 181, 185, 186, 187, 194, 195.
40. Ibid., 186.

Capitalist thought refers to the negative values of private/partial/selfish (*si*) associated with the human desires (the human mind). So I conclude that Mao had bought into the legacy of the Cheng-Zhu belief that the Dao mind must always rule the human mind.

In the 1980s, there were fresh voices in China, and Li was among them, that openly condemned the traditional idea that "morality governs the world" (*daode lun li zhi tianxia*).[41] The new voices said that this viewpoint ignores economic conditions and managerial skill in analyzing actual problems. The traditional viewpoint focuses instead only on the content of the approximation to one-mindedness of the minds of participants, ignoring other variables. One critic says that it offers a simplistic account of motivation, ignoring material needs and interests.[42] People have biological needs as well as social ideals, and they are equally valid. In writing today about traditional Confucian ethics, other critics make a similar point. Fulfillment of family relational roles and other hierarchical roles in Confucian thought artificially shifted the concerns of all agents away from actual economic and interest relationships, keeping the concerns artificially focused on role duties.[43]

An example of a policy shift concretely reflects this theoretical move. This was the issuance of "The Law of the PRC Governing Enterprise Bankruptcy (for trial implementation)," originally scheduled to go into effect for state-owned industrial enterprises in November, 1988. To allow a company to go bankrupt means that the measure of what is important in the organization is no longer employee attitude toward role duties or "morality." Rather, it is management skill and economic prudence:

> It may seem inhuman and ruthless to let enterprises that are not properly managed, that cannot repay the departments even with their assets, and that show no improvement after remedy measures are taken to go bankrupt. But we should not show any sense of pity because this, after all, is not a question of morality.[44]

The third factor in the justification of morally neutral groups did not have the wide backing that the second factor has. But it was growing in prominence. This was a rejection of the social-role ethics in favor of another way of thinking about morality. The most-popular alternative was a form of utilitarianism that was coupled with the presumption (rebuttable in individual cases),

---

41. For an example of the explicit use of this phrase, see *Xinhua ribao*, January 25, 1988, 1. See also the critique of the idea by Wang Ruoshui in "On the Marxist Philosophy of Man," FBIS, July 24, 1986, K1.

42. *Chongguo qingnian* (China youth) 2 (February 1983): 18.

43. *Renmin ribao*, August 15, 1986, 5.

44. *Renmin ribao*, October 10, 1986, 5, in FBIS, October 21, 1986, K11.

that each human should be treated as equally worthy by virtue of universally shared traits. In moral decisions, each person's varying interest would count for something because of this equal worth. The shared characteristics are either Mencian in tone, centering on a sense of compassion, or they derive from the early Marx's discussions of basic human needs in the *Economic and Philosophical Manuscripts*. Those taking this position claimed that *official* authorization for it came from the third plenary session of the Eleventh CPC Central Committee, which defined the purpose of socialist production as the satisfaction of the people's needs. One prominent figure gave as examples of universal needs the need for self-realization and for material and spiritual enjoyment.[45]

This is precisely the alternative that Maoists vigorously rejected. The form that the Maoist repudiation took was authorizing only the division of humans into class categories while rejecting class-transcending characteristics:

> Is there such a thing as human nature? Of course there is. But there is only human nature in the concrete, no human nature in the abstract. In a class society there is only human nature that bears the stamp of a class; human nature that transcends classes does not exist.[46]

Even with the death of Mao, the standard official line on ethics has often been in spirit consistent with this Maoist statement. That is, there are no universal rights or duties. Rather, they vary as a function of time and the person's social group. One author says, "There is no abstract individual morality. It is always connected with a certain social phenomenon."[47] Politics and morality are equated. As talk of classes fades, the individual remains defined in terms of a social group. So, in the official line, the new talk has been of the legitimacy of individual interests. However, such interests have been explained in such a manner as to be the same as the interests of the collective. The bottom official line is still group morality; it is just that the size of the groups has expanded. The duties are still relational and reciprocal between the individual and the collective, just as they were between members of different classes.[48]

---

45. Wang Ruoshui in Shanghai, *Wen huibao*, July 18, 1986, 2, in FBIS, July 24, 1986, K1–3.

46. Mao Zedong, "Talks at the Yenan Forum on Art and Literature" (Peking: Foreign Languages Press, 1960), 31–32.

47. Ma Zuobin, "Jianchi you hong you zhuan de fangxiang" (Firmly adhere to the direction of both red and expert), *Hongqi* (Red flag) 8 (1981): 29, 31.

48. Sima Zhe, "Zemyang kandai ziyou" (How to regard freedom), *Hongqi* 23 (1985): 30–32.

In constrast, in the post-Mao period, the advocates of an alternative to a class-based social-role ethics stand outside of what remains of an older official position. These new voices located their theory of value within Marxism. They said that Marxism is a scientific theory that encompasses a value system. However, they said that the value system takes human needs and their history as its basis. One authoritative source cited says that "the general concept of 'value' is produced in those relations with external things in which people satisfy their needs." Another work states, "Simply put, when we say that something has value, it means that has a definite use for humans and that it can fulfill certain needs."[49] The needs always seem to be universal human needs, with no reference to role-differentiated needs. The change is to replace a social-role ethics with some kind of need-based utilitarianism.

If widely accepted, this utilitarian dimension to ethics in China would provide theoretical justification for a whole variety of new social groupings. And, of course, each group may have its particular perspective on any controversial issue, so the utilitarianism also fosters a plurality of points of view. The receptivity to and expectation of a diversity of groups would come about because this kind of utilitarianism involves no a priori assumption that any particular kind of activity has more utility than any other. Being receptive to a diversity of groups, it expects conflict in the form of the competition between groups for the supremacy of their perspectives. No group is assumed to be the bearer of truth or worth. This utilitarianism retains the option to evaluate groups after the fact, on the basis of their contribution to the satisfaction of human needs. In other words, unlike the case of certain Confucian roles and certain Maoist classes, no group is by definition morally superior (most useful). Some writers tried to argue that intellectuals are more useful than others and deserve higher wages. This was a plaintive plea that reveals long-standing official neglect or abuse of intellectuals.

Given the debatable nature of anyone's claim about which group is most useful, we could assume that the existence of a fairly full range of such new social groups will be assured along with conflict between them. This would be the case as long as the three-pronged theoretical underpinning grows in favor.

The bottom line was that in contemporary China, neither Nature nor History any longer provided a believable blueprint for the static rank ordering of groups in terms of moral worth. For those buying into the utilitarian alternative, such worth depends on how people construct society to gain certain goals. At one time it may be some groups, at another time others that make the strongest claims for worth. The social categories and their worth would always be changing.

---

49. Yuan Zhiming, "Makesizhuyi de kexue xing yu jiazhiguan" (Marxism's scientific nature and view of value), *Zhexue Yanjiu*, April, 1983, 37.

Changing the classification of social groups also has the positive result of broadening the range of facts that are relevant to explaining any human problem. No longer are the facts limited to the thoughts in the minds of participants concerning their social-role duties. Instead, any facts that bear on the utility of a solution are pertinent.

The Future

The one-mind approach ignores many aspects of societal change. Its approach to conflict is to purge officials who publicize their disagreement with the supreme leader(s) and to emphasize political indoctrination as a tool in achieving its goal.

If pluralism is permitted to reemerge, the pattern for its evolution will likely be through the legalization of a variety of voluntary organizations that may serve to lobby officials on behalf of the interests of their members. Yet there is much that remains unclear about the form of the relation that such organizations would have with the state.

The Confucian orthodoxy that saturated China until the twentieth century is sadly deficient in teachings about how individuals can simultaneously serve family or local organization and the state or society. Theorists during the Republican period did not do much to fill the void. The theory still needs to be written. But at this point in time, some aspects of what the content of an adequate theory will be are fairly clear.

Its basic principle would be the compatibility of both respect for a highly authoritarian state and toleration of a plurality of semi-independent social organizations. The social organizations would remain the focus of an individual's local loyalties. The state would change its function from being the administrator of everything and the indoctrinator of all minds. Instead, while retaining parts of these missions, its functions would shift to being the mediator of the conflicting interests of the semi-independent organizations. It formulates national goals. In accordance with these goals and its control over pork-barrel assets, it would decide who gets the pork.

Of course there would always be the danger that membership in relational networks rather than contribution to national goals would influence these decisions about distribution. Here is where laws controlling conflict of interest are required to foster impartiality.

In the months prior to June 4, 1989, a wide range of influential persons known to favor interest-group pluralism seemed heading in the direction of also regarding central-government authoritarianism as compatible with it. A debate focused on the term "New Authoritarianism" and the thesis of a young scholar named Wu Jiaxiang that history goes through three stages: old authoritarianism, new authority, and liberal democracy. Somewhat in the spirit of Sun Yat-sen's idea of a period of political tutelage prior to democracy, New

Authoritarianism insists on strongman politics for China in its current stage between traditional and modern society. It prizes political stability and social order. While Deng Xiaoping associated himself with the idea, though not the term "New Authoritarianism," so did some liberal economists. The Beijing Young Economists' Association and the China Economic Structural Reform Research Institute stated in their "Summary of the Symposium on the National Economic Situation": "China needs an authoritative supreme leading group which can rally the social elite and the nation in this complicated environment to firmly and rhythmically advance this historic reform."[50] And another economist proposed that the authority of the central administration must be enhanced and safeguarded in order to regulate the market and guide enterprises as a way of mitigating trade conflicts between localities.[51] Critics of the idea of New Authoritarianism point to its placing too much reliance on a single individual and on its inattention to any reform of the existing power structure.

Thus, liberalization would not necessarily take the form of Westernization, where that term includes a multiparty system. Playing with Western political symbols is playing with fire in China, because they suggest to many Chinese the claim that there is nothing valuable in Chinese social and political culture. They inflame the passion of humiliation. The bottom line of liberalization would be found in the plurality of semi-independent social organizations. Other principles would concern the means whereby the state can nurture respect for its new role. These would focus on the establishment of legal limitations on governmental intrusion into the activities of the voluntary social organizations. And they would deal with a key issue in state accountability, namely regularizing channels whereby state officials consult organizations and interest groups in the formulation of goals and policies. The sprouts of pluralism in China are fragile. To attend to these principles would be one way of nurturing them.

The former Soviet Union witnessed a similar growth of politically interested voluntary organizations during the 1980s, as documented by S. Frederick Starr. Emerging in Russia in the 1850s, they were nearly wiped out as a result of Lenin's New Economic Policy of the 1920s. Some benign clubs existed before the 1980s, but since then politically active groups have mushroomed. In the 1980s, they were publically given the right to exist, and they sent representatives to a 1987 meeting that called for a federation of such organizations that could maintain a dialogue with the Communist party. In 1988, one hundred of them met to form an independent "democratic union."

---

50. "Deng Xiaoping on Neo-Authoritarianism," Hong Kong, *Zhongguo tongxun she*, April 7, 1989, in FBIS, April 7, 1989, 15.

51. Lu Lu, "Eliminating Drawbacks in Policies and Structure Brooks No Delay," in Beijing, *Jianjixue zhoubao*, April 30, 1989, 1, in FBIS, May 10, 1989, 36–37.

The impact of Solidarity in Poland is well known. Given the rapid penetration of world news into some Chinese cities, a knowledge of the existence of such organizations in Russia, Eastern Europe, and elsewhere may continue to directly affect their future in China.[52]

There is an unavoidable but slippery and dangerous road ahead for foreign countries and for organizations in those foreign countries (including voluntary organizations) in dealing with China. This is because China is a country with strong advocates of both alternatives to viewing conflict. Many Westerners regard interest-group pluralism as essential to modernization because it is necessary for the organized competition out of which the best work methods emerge. So they will support its advocates. But the theory underlying interest-group pluralism is Western. To the extent that Westerners support such pluralism in China, they risk getting drawn into the struggle between the partisans of the two approaches to conflict and enflaming antiforeign sentiment. There is no avoiding this. But the consequences can be positive and the risks diminished by Westerners' helping to foster the evolution of individual Chinese voluntary organizations through formal association with their Western counterparts and by keeping them tied into relevant international organizations. On an individual basis, this can be accomplished without directly challenging the central authorities.

52. S. Frederick Starr, "Party Animals: Pluralism Comes to the U.S.S.R.," *New Republic*, June 26, 1989. Brought to my attention by Thomas Bernstein.

Conflict in Soviet Domestic and Foreign Policy: Universal Ideology and National Tradition

Roman Szporluk

At the turn of the century, a major social, economic, and political transformation was taking place in Russia, which at the time was a great multinational empire extending from Warsaw in the west to Vladivostok in the east. Many rival currents of thought and various political movements presented their solutions for Russia's political, social, and ethnic conflicts. For reasons that cannot be examined here, in 1917, the adherents of one Marxist current, the Bolsheviks, seized power in Russia and, after a prolonged and extremely bloody civil war, consolidated their regime in the early 1920s. Among the nations of the world, Russia alone adopted as its guide for the solution of its problems and conflicts the Marxist ideology, invented about seventy years earlier in Germany, an ideology that its founders thought offered a solution for all of the important problems of humanity at large. For, indeed, Marxism was a comprehensive system of thought, which claimed to explain the entire history of humanity and to offer a vision, a scientific blueprint, for humanity's future. In that blueprint, the phenomena of conflict, power, and politics were to make room for totally new principles of social organization—solidarity, cooperation, and a rational management of resources and people, i.e., planning.

Before the Communists seized power in Russia, the Russian empire was a multiethnic polity consisting of many peoples in Europe and Asia with diverse languages, religions, and historical traditions. After the revolution of 1917 and the civil war, a few of its peoples became independent nation-states, for example, Finland. The majority remained under Moscow as member states of the Union of Soviet Socialist Republics. By the early 1920s, it seemed that Communism had defeated nationalism as the principle of political organization.

Seventy years later, however, during the Gorbachev era, ethnicity in the Soviet Union had become one of the basic causes of demands for change. In the last phase of Gorbachev's rule, the leaders of the Soviet nationalities demanded that ethnic issues and conflicts be resolved through the establishment of autonomous or independent states. In the end, ethnic relations became transformed into international relations, and these conflicts, among others, led to the breakup of the Soviet state.

The collapse of the U.S.S.R. in 1991 and the reemergence of Russia as its principal successor state have brought back on the agenda all the fundamental problems that the Russian empire faced at the beginning of the century. The situation is now, however, much more critical than it was eighty years ago, because the country has been devastated in all possible ways and at the same time it is facing with a new intensity the consequences of the breakup of the old state itself. The Russia of today is a much smaller country than the Russia of 1914. Besides those areas that left Russia after World War I, it has also lost such essential regions of the old state as Ukraine, the Caucasus, and Central Asia. Areas that represented the sphere of interethnic relations in the context of Soviet domestic politics for over seventy years now belong to the sphere of Russia's international affairs. There is a Russian ambassador in Kiev today and a Ukrainian ambassador in Moscow.

In place of the bankrupt ideology of Marxism-Leninism, the Russians need to find a new system of values; in place of the collapsed socialist economy based on Plan, they are desperately trying to find their way toward a market economy. They are trying to establish a political system that will replace the Communist party-dominated Soviet regime. The Soviet experience in dealing with conflicts, the Soviet ideas about the nature of conflicts, in the opinion of many are totally irrelevant and practically useless in the emerging world of a post-Communist Russia. Which way will Russia go? What elements of its pre-Soviet cultural and political tradition will it revive now as it looks for guidance to its future? How will it reconcile its indigenous heritage—Soviet and pre-Soviet—with the influences and models now coming from abroad? These are dilemmas of the kind nineteenth-century Russia knew all too well, but the realities of present-day Russia are profoundly different from those of the previous century. If nineteenth-century Russia ultimately fell in 1917, and embraced a vision that collapsed in recent years, how can one be sure that the Russia of today will be more fortunate in its search for a new political and social order?

This chapter examines conflict in domestic and foreign policy throughout the Soviet period, in particular, the evolution of Soviet thought on the subject of conflict in state and ethnic politics, and in international relations. We are interested here in Soviet thought about the nature of issues rather than in how the policies were conducted during that period.

Two sources of Soviet thinking on these matters are evident. First, the new rulers of Russia were professed Marxists, and one has to refer to Marx to explain their position on matters that concern us here. Second, whether or not they acknowledged this, the Soviets were heirs of the Russian political tradition—even if they rejected it as a matter of principle and defined themselves in opposition to it—and were influenced by it.

Let us briefly summarize the basic propositions of these two points of view. The starting assumption of Soviet thinking was Marx's belief that humanity is divided into classes and that classes are in a relationship of constant conflict, which can be resolved by the violent overthrow of one class, the bourgeoisie, by the oppressed class of the proletariat. Marx believed that all power is class power and that once class rule was abolished the state would disappear along with the classes themselves, and, as a result, international relations and international conflict would disappear as well.[1]

Marx's approach to ethnic, cultural, religious, and national diversity and conflict arising out of it was therefore premised on those beliefs. Other conflicts therefore are either "sublimated" versions of class conflict, or examples of purely distorted, "false" consciousness. More fundamentally, one may say that Marx believed that relations between individuals and groups involving power are not a natural or proper condition of humanity: power, including power politics, would disappear together with classes. (He, too, believed that power corrupts, but his solution for the problem was to abolish the cause of power itself.) When true Communism became a reality, cooperation, not power, would be the principle of human interaction.

Any reader of *The Communist Manifesto* has noticed that no solutions are offered for interstate, international problems in the period following the proletarian revolution—obviously because there would be no problems. (It has been noted by many that this famous text does not mention Russia or the United States. Alexis de Tocqueville had been much more prescient in 1835.)

Marxism provided the theoretical basis for the Soviet approach both to domestic policy and to international relations. In the arena of international relations, Moscow argued that the world proletariat was represented by the Soviet state and that the international bourgeoisie opposed the proletariat in the form of foreign states hostile to the U.S.S.R. Accordingly, the Soviet leaders assumed that, fundamentally, the relations between their state and the rest of the world would remain antagonistic until the proletariat overthrew the capitalists and won power for itself in the major nations of the world. The world would achieve real peace when class conflict was resolved and the

---

1. See Walker Connor, *The National Question in Marxist-Leninist Theory and Strategy* (Princeton: Princeton University Press, 1984) and Roman Szporluk, *Communism and Nationalism: Karl Marx versus Friedrich List* (New York and Oxford: Oxford University Press, 1991), for Marx's view of nationality and nationalism, and for reference to other relevant works on the subject. Margot Light, *The Soviet Theory of International Relations* (New York: St. Martin's Press, 1988) considers the Marx and Engels legacy in the Soviet theory.

system of independent states was replaced by a new organization of mankind. Thus, in the Soviet view, ultimately derived from Marxism, social and political conflict would be abolished along with the abolition of capitalism.

The new Soviet concept of international relations was a translation of the classical Marxist-Leninist conception of class conflict into the interstate arena. Foreign policy for the first socialist state was an arena of class conflict in a peculiarly ideological form of interstate relations: what really mattered, according to this view, was that the proletariat continued to struggle with the bourgeoisie, which expressed itself in international relations as a conflict between the Soviet Union and the capitalist powers.

For reasons that, again, we cannot explain here, Russia under Communist rule chose to describe itself as the prototype of the future organization of all humanity. Even its name, Union of Soviet Socialist Republics, reflected the new rulers' conviction that they were opening a new era of human history. This commitment to world revolution was not simply an ideological slogan. It fundamentally influenced both the new state's domestic policies and its foreign-policy outlook. While people have often said that the Soviet state used foreign Communists to its own advantage, it needs to be stressed even more strongly that the domestic policies of the U.S.S.R. were fundamentally shaped by the global outlook of the Soviet state and by its ideological commitment to Communism as a worldwide program. There is no rational way of explaining the Stalinist industrialization and collectivization without reference to the Soviet Union's perception of itself in these Marxist ideological terms.[2]

With the Russian revolution of 1917, Lenin and his comrades had to face problems for which Marx had provided very little guidance other than proposing that a continentwide Communist revolution would take place very soon in Europe and international conflict would disappear thereafter. Trotsky himself has told us that upon being appointed foreign commissar of the Russian republic he expected to "close down the shop" after a few months at best.

Within Soviet Russia, the proletariat had yet to face the bourgeoisie, whatever was left of it, and the petty bourgeoisie, of whom there were plenty. Real politics were made in the party, and the party, of course, was not a federal organization. It was a strictly centralized organization as was proper

---

2. The very title of Elliot R. Goodman's book, *The Soviet Design for a World State* (New York: Columbia University Press, 1960), must sound strange if not quaint these days, but there *was* a time when the idea reflected in it was taken seriously. Goodman documents an important phase in the history of Communist thought on international relations. See Andrew C. Janos, "Social Science, Communism, and the Dynamics of Political Change," in *Liberalization and Democratization: Change in the Soviet Union and Eastern Europe*, ed. Nancy Bermeo, (Baltimore and London: Johns Hopkins University Press, 1992), 81–112, for the argument that both the rise and the fall of the Soviet regime need to be viewed in terms of a "world system paradigm." Janos asserts that "the domestic transformation of the Soviet Union was not an end in itself but rather was part of a larger international design" (96).

for a party of the working class which by its very nature was international. In order to accommodate—and control—the ethnic factor in its structure, the state was formally declared a federation. What mattered to the Communists was not only that the Soviet Union was a multiethnic country, but also that it was a country in which the overwhelming majority of the population consisted of the petty bourgeoisie, i.e., peasantry. They viewed the peasantry at home as a threat, just as they did the foreign bourgeoisie. Thus, in domestic matters, this ideological position prompted the Soviets to suppress the bourgeoisie and the kulaks, and then to collectivize agriculture altogether. Trotsky's view about the end of foreign policy had a counterpart in Lenin's early belief that it would be possible to abolish the market and money and regulate administratively the production and distribution of goods. Only in 1921 was N.E.P. (New Economic Policy) introduced, in a short-lived break with this design to bring about a Communist millennium.

The rulers of the Soviet state were not only disciples of Marx, they were also inheritors of the Russian political tradition. By the late 1930s, if not before, it became evident that Soviet political culture bore a striking resemblance to certain prerevolutionary political traditions. Even more surprising, Soviet political ways resembled the much-more-distant world of old Muscovy more than the world of late-imperial Russia. What was the Muscovite political tradition that found life in Stalin's Soviet Union? How did Stalin and his associates reconcile their professed adherence to Marxism with their evident closeness to the world of Muscovy?[3]

We need to examine the concept of politics, social organization, conflict, and conflict resolution that existed in imperial Russia before Bolshevik rule. What kinds of conflicts did the state recognize as legitimate? What procedures were recognized for dealing with those conflicts? Which body, individual or institution, was authorized to adjudicate conflicts?

In his "Muscovite Political Folkways" (1986), Edward L. Keenan argues that Soviet political culture as it was formed and consolidated in the 1930s, after what Keenan considers an "aberrant" phase in Russian political history, extending from the late nineteenth century to the early decades of the twentieth century, was a revived version of the old Muscovite culture. (In Keenan's view, late-nineteenth and early twentieth-century Russia was beginning to adopt modern, Western-style ideas and methods, but they never took hold and have to be seen as an aberration in view of what happened after 1917. Will the

---

3. The literature on the subject of "continuity and change" in Russian and Soviet history is so vast that to name any sampling of works would inevitably and rightly provoke questions regarding those left out. The reader will have to choose, but such authors of broader syntheses as Richard Pipes, Nicholas V. Riasanovsky, Hugh Seton-Watson, and Donald W. Treadgold would probably be on everybody's list. For a recent discussion of the problem see Robert C. Tucker, "Sovietology and Russian History," *Post-Soviet Affairs* 8, no. 3 (July–September 1992): 175–96.

post-1991 Russian politics be more successful in making the "aberrant" normal?) This term—Muscovite—designates the culture formed before 1700, and operating, as it were, in three social spheres: the peasant culture, the culture of the court, and the bureaucratic culture. These cultures, Keenan says, "while they occasionally have come into conflict, have always been essentially compatible and, in modern times, have merged."[4] It is not possible to summarize Keenan's involved and complex argument here. The following excerpts, however, will at least identify some of what he calls "common denominators of the Russian political culture":

1. All three were "informal" or traditional in the sense that political status and social function were determined not by the rules of a specifically political institutional structure (as distinct from social and kinship structures), but by a combination of birth, personal affiliation, and the *ad hoc* balance of the interests of other players . . . .

2. In these closed and informal systems, "membership," while it conferred significant rewards and an assured role in collective decision-making, was confidential, because it required acquiescence in the consensual governing mechanism of each unit. As a result, the status of an individual could not be assured independently of such mechanisms, and excessively aggressive attempts to increase individual power or status, since they were seen as potentially system-threatening, ran the risk of severe group sanctions.

3. The general tendency of policy in all three cultures was to strive for stability and risk-avoidance, rather than change, including "progress." In the village this tendency arose from the nature of subsistence agriculture; in the bureaucracy, from the political vulnerability (in fact, impotence) of the clerk class, from its hierarchical organization, and from the logistical magnitude of its tasks; among the political elite, from a tradition deeply rooted in the fear of uncontrollable factional strife . . . .

4. By comparison with other political systems of comparable complexity, antiquity, and comprehensiveness, the component sub-variants of Muscovite political culture were notably reluctant to promulgate, for the use or admiration of non-participants, "laws," i.e., generalized principles of their own operation, or "ideology." Although all members of any of these systems knew "how it worked," how to behave so as to maximize one's opportunities for power and wealth within the obligatory forms and taboos, none seems ever to have been moved to

---

4. Edward L. Keenan, "Muscovite Political Folkways," *The Russian Review* 45 (1986): 115–81.

codify this behavior, or to have indulged in justificatory or other generalized abstractions about it.[5]

Keenan further argues that, in the late 1930s, "the restabilization of Soviet society . . . produced a reassertion of traditional forms of political behavior." He lists three main reasons why this should have happened. First, he points out that

among the organizations and trends that had competed for hegemony in the revolutionary period, it was the Bolshevik party, whose creed of centralism, elitism, and conspiratorial rule was most compatible with traditional patterns, that became the principal agent and beneficiary of the reestablishment of political stability.

He adds that because of their activities before the revolution, the leaders of the Communist party "had shared relatively little in the cultural and practical experience of the first decades of the new century." Second, Keenan thinks that, in the course of the revolution and internal party struggles, those who had "become most profoundly committed to a non-traditional political culture" were eliminated. Finally, and most important, Keenan says, "the new political elite that emerged by the end of the thirties was dominated by individuals of proletarian or peasant background." They had been formed in "the village political culture" and their outlook was further "reinforced by the experience of the chaotic and risk-laden environment in which they had risen to power."[6]

From Keenan's perspective, the era of Khrushchev represented an attempt—a failed attempt—to break with these Muscovite-Soviet traditions; for example, Khrushchev's permission and encouragement of public discussion ran against the rule of "internal discussion" (p. 176) and so did his pro-decentralization measures (p. 177). The Soviet leadership tried to use the politics of détente to protect the old system from change, but Keenan makes the point that the whole issue of creating a new political culture more in tune with the modern age would not thereby be set aside:

But even had *détente* provided more rapid and significant gains, the leadership would only have had postponed confrontation with the problem that is, from the point of view of political culture, the crucial one: does the present political culture contain the capacity for change—the

---

5. Keenan, "Folkways," 157–58.
6. Keenan, "Folkways," 168–69.

"transcription speed" to permit rapid adaptation, with stability, to the vast and radical socio-economic changes that have occurred during forty years of stability and economic growth, or will it be "overloaded" by tasks of social and political change whose satisfactory accomplishment will require instrumentalities it has not developed, and attitudes it has not permitted to evolve?[7]

As our essay will argue, the answer to the Keenan question seems to be negative: in the sense that the old political culture did not adapt itself to change but, on the other hand, became "soft" enough to prevent a violent revolution.

It appears that the Leninist party and the Muscovite autocracy had a similar view of politics and resembled each other institutionally: for example, both the tsars and the Bolsheviks preferred to practice the real business of government in private, without revealing the issues or process to the general public. According to A. J. Polan, Lenin's view of politics amounted to the liquidation of politics—"the end of politics."[8] We might say that the aim of Muscovite rulers had been to prevent the birth of politics. Thus, by looking at Russian history in a larger historical perspective, we can see that Soviet Communism which abolished "politics" made recourse to a genuine indigenous tradition of Russia.

There was one fundamental difference between the tsars and the commissars, however, and that difference would prove to be a major reason for the ultimate collapse of Communism in the U.S.S.R. The ruling elites of Muscovy did not care in the least whether their government, their social and spiritual way of life, was adopted by other nations and peoples. It was enough that their ways served them, the Russians. The Russian Communists took universalism and internationalism from Marx. They believed that their system was universally applicable, and, of course, immediately after the revolution they did not imagine it would ever become like the old Muscovite system. They expected foreign Communists would seize power soon and proceed to build socialism in the Russian way. But this "internationalist" world view, by its very nature, placed the capitalist world in the role of an enemy of Communism, i.e., Russia. The Bolsheviks thus chose to define themselves so as to create an antagonistic relationship with the world around them.

Would they manage to have a better relationship with the outside world when it, or parts of it, adopted Communism in its Russian version? By the late 1930s, as we have noted, the Soviet system had acquired Muscovite features,

---

7. Keenan, "Folkways," 179.

8. A. J. Polan, *Lenin and the End of Politics* (Berkeley and Los Angeles: University of California Press, 1984).

and Marxism was blended with the Russian political tradition. Would that synthesis be acceptable outside Russia, or would it prove capable of self-transformation once Communism expanded beyond the borders of the U.S.S.R. as they existed before 1939, and thus made the Soviet state a part of a larger Communist system?

The first opportunity to face such questions came in 1939–40, when the Soviet Union occupied the eastern half of Poland, the Baltic states, Bessarabia, the northern part of Bukovina, and parts of eastern Finland. (The Soviet-Polish war of 1920 promised an earlier opportunity to do so—but it ended unsuccessfully for Moscow.) Later, in the aftermath of the Second World War, the U.S.S.R. made additional territorial gains, and also Soviet-inspired Communist regimes came to power in Eastern and Central Europe. If ever, this was the time for a rethinking, a redefinition of Communist ideas on government and conflict. Using the language of the dialectic, this was an occasion to explore in a new light the relation between the specific—the national—and the general or universal aspects of Communism by taking into account the Soviet experience and its reception in the newly socialist territories.

As we know, Moscow chose to reaffirm its model and to insist on its faithful implementation abroad. Stalin continued to see the Soviet experience as a universal model, not a national variant. But this was not enough. In justifying their domestic and internal politics and their system of government, the rulers of Moscow argued *at home* that the Soviet system was the right one for all the peoples of the U.S.S.R. because foreign nations were adopting it. They did not think about the possibility that this argument could work the other way, for opposite purposes: Should any foreign nations ever reject the Soviet regime, the fact of such a rejection could be used in *internal* Soviet political debate to justify opposition to Communism within the U.S.S.R.

The Chinese Communists never made a connection of this sort in *their* domestic ideological campaigns. Mao and his successors did not seek to convince the Chinese masses of the leaders' right to rule by pointing out that the Chinese kind of Communism was being adopted abroad, say in Vietnam or Laos, or by the Communist insurgents in Malaysia or the Philippines or Angola. Chinese Communism defined its legitimacy within the framework of Chinese history and politics, and by invoking the doctrine of Marxism as adapted to China.[9]

Even though the Soviet position, taken literally, implied a hostile relationship with the entire capitalist world, in practice Moscow accepted the

---

9. This becomes very clear from Donald J. Munro's chapter in this volume, "One-Minded Hierarchy versus Interest-Group Pluralism: Two Chinese Approaches to Conflict." One might further develop Mao's point, as quoted by Munro, that "human nature that transcends classes does not exist," to concede that "human nature that transcends states and nations does not exist."

possibility of relatively peaceful, indeed friendly, relations with this or that capitalist nation. The Soviets also understood that there were contradictions sometimes leading to wars among capitalist powers. Nonetheless the fundamental Soviet vision of the world assumed a conflictual relationship with the capitalist powers as long as they remained capitalist.

Soviet theory and practice maintained the assumptions of the early post-revolutionary years as late as 1939–40, when Stalin directly annexed the Baltic states into the U.S.S.R., for he continued to act on one of those assumptions: namely, that the U.S.S.R. was a universal state in the making and that when Communists came to power in any other country, that country would become associated with the U.S.S.R. in a common state structure. Looking back at those decisions from the perspective of our time, we may wonder whether that decision served the interests of the Russian center.

The new challenges of 1944 and after seemingly led to the abandonment of old Communist assumptions. The independent countries of Eastern Europe were independent in a formal, constitutional sense: they continued to remain sovereign members of the international community. At the same time, however, in Communist theory they were thought to be members of a larger entity, the socialist bloc or camp, and as such no longer sovereign in the conventional meaning of the term. They were expected, therefore, to become more and more like the Soviet Union, and in the not too distant future to become tied to it also legally and formally.

The post-Stalin era was marked by the recognition of the reality of Communist diversity, as exemplified by the Yugoslav-Soviet rapprochement in 1955, and of course by Soviet relations with the People's Republic of China. But even Khrushchev did not revise the ideology in a fundamental way. He could not control China or Yugoslavia, but when he spoke about those countries that remained in communion with the U.S.S.R., as he did in his celebrated speech in Leipzig in 1959, or in the party program of 1961, he insisted that the boundaries between not only the Soviet republics but also independent socialist states were "losing their [former] importance." The implication was that, sooner or later, some sort of a supranational community embracing the U.S.S.R. and Eastern Europe would emerge. On this ground, there arose the notorious Soviet-Romanian conflict in the early 1960s concerning the Danube River development.

Be that as it may, the Soviet theory of international relations involving socialist countries versus capitalist countries underwent rather important changes. The fundamental ideological assumptions remained the same, but they were no longer treated as immediately relevant for practical politics. The doctrine of peaceful coexistence contained a very-important policy-influencing component; namely, the possibility of removing the threat of war between the socialist camp and the capitalist countries. This amounted in practice to recognizing the nonsocialist countries as a permanent reality on the world map, and one that was independent of Moscow. Although Leninism and Stalinism did not regard the inevitability of military confrontation between the two camps as an ideological dogma, the real possibility and threat of such a war was always considered very seriously. "Imperialism means war" was a common slogan. However, this old slogan was quoted less often as the new realization that "the atomic bomb does not observe the class principle" gained currency among influential people in Moscow and, somewhat more slowly, in Beijing.[10]

The principle of peaceful coexistence, however, was explicitly applicable to relations between socialist and nonsocialist states, and expressly not applicable to relations between socialist countries. When Moscow proposed peaceful coexistence to Beijing, Moscow asked Beijing to admit that China was not a socialist state. The guiding principle in intersocialist relations was "proletarian internationalism," one of whose expressions came to be known in the West as "the Brezhnev doctrine." Khrushchev had considered peaceful coexistence to be the "general line" of Soviet foreign policy and this, some think, might imply its superior standing versus "proletarian internationalism." But one might also conclude that where the latter was in effect, one no longer dealt with foreign policy in the traditional understanding of the term because individual socialist states were treated as forever bound to a larger entity called Socialist Commonwealth or World Socialist System.[11]

For many years after 1968, the Soviet official line at home argued that in their relations with Moscow the socialist countries of Eastern Europe were basically following the same direction that the non-Russian Soviet republics followed before they joined Russia to form the Soviet Union in 1922.[12]

---

10. This startling intellectual discovery was made by *Pravda*, July 14, 1963, here quoted from William Zimmerman, *Soviet Perspectives on International Relations, 1956–1967* (Princeton: Princeton University Press, 1969), 5. Zimmerman covers an extremely important period in the evolution of Soviet thought and presents an analysis of the rise of a new academic discipline in the Soviet Union—that of international relations—and its connection to the policy-making process. For a more recent work in the same subject see Allen Lynch, *The Soviet Study of International Relations* (Cambridge: Cambridge University Press, 1987).

11. See William Zimmerman, "Soviet–East European Relations in the 1980s and the Changing International System," in *East-West Relations and the Future of Eastern Europe*, ed. Morris Bornstein, Zvi Gitelman, and William Zimmerman (London: George Allen and Unwin, 1981), 87–104.

12. Thus, for example, P. N. Fedoseyev, ed., *Leninizm i natsional'nyi vopros v sovremennykh usloviiakh* (Moscow: Progress, 1972), 285–99, saw similarities between the "military alliance" of Soviet republics prior to the formation of the U.S.S.R. and the organization of the Warsaw Pact. See also the collective volume published in Russian in Prague, *Sovetskii Soiuz i sovremennyi mir* (Prague: *Problemy Mira i Sotsializma*, 1972), with contributions by Soviet and East European ideologists. In Ukraine, official statements claimed that the Russian language was becoming a language of interstate communication of Eastern Europe, not only one used in

At the same time, scholars have argued persuasively that actual Soviet behavior in dealing with East European countries was premised on a quite different assumption: Moscow seemed to have accepted that in the long run the East European countries would remain tied to it through various international organizations but were not destined to join the U.S.S.R. itself. It is important to note these two facts because they reveal one of the weaknesses of the internal Soviet system. However realistic Soviet foreign policy may have become in abandoning the old dreams of the world going Soviet, Soviet ideology for domestic consumption remained committed to the argument that the spread of the Soviet model abroad needed to be cited as an argument to legitimize the Soviet system before its own citizens.

In a book published in 1989, Joseph Rothschild argued as follows:

> the hegemony over East Central Europe . . . has become a powerful justification of the Soviet system in the eyes of its own elite and public. That hegemony has been the most visible and palpable prize of the great Soviet victory and therefore continues to function as a powerful moral bond between the regime and its peoples . . . . Hence it probably can not be relinquished without jeopardizing that internal Soviet legitimacy for which it is both catalyst and keystone. And these considerations will override Soviet awareness that the East Central European objects of the hegemony are sullen and that its objective blessings even for the Soviet Union itself are mixed.[13]

Rothschild further pointed out that:

> any Soviet yielding of the area not only would undermine the ideological claims of Communism to be the unfolding of an inexorable historical process and degrade the Soviet Union's credentials as a confident global power, but would also gravely jeopardize a basic internal Soviet consensus and erode the domestic security of the system itself.[14]

communication between the U.S.S.R. and Eastern Europe, thus adding an argument in favor of using Russian in Ukraine. I cite these works in Roman Szporluk, "Nationalities and the Russian Problem in the U.S.S.R.: An Historical Outline," *Journal of International Affairs* 27, no. 1 (1973): 34–37, where I argue that after 1968 Moscow adopted a policy of intensive and accelerated Russification in the republics—a policy that went farther than anything that Stalin had done—because it reasoned that if the non-Russian republics retained their distinct cultural identity, they would become (or remain) receptive to the same disease that had affected Eastern Europe. As we now see, this was an unsuccessful race against time.

13. Joseph Rothschild, *Return to Diversity: A Political History of East Central Europe Since World War II* (New York and Oxford: Oxford University Press, 1989), 75.

14. Rothschild, *Return*, 222. See also 221: "there is no signal that Stalin's heirs are prepared to retreat from it [East Central Europe], nor any flagging of their political will to dominate

In the last phase of the Soviet system, the internal legitimacy of the regime was indeed subverted when it became evident that Communism was being overthrown in Eastern Europe. Thus, Moscow had to pay for its previous insistence that the success of Communism in Eastern Europe justified Communist rule within the U.S.S.R. (Admittedly, there were repercussions of East Europe in China, too, but the democracy movement there proved to be much easier to suppress.)

The most recent events in the U.S.S.R. have confirmed this analysis and have also added a new perspective. Now, we can not only see the changing Soviet ideas on the nature of conflict, but also observe how the leaders of the Soviet state handled what we now know was the state's terminal crisis. Whereas the spokesmen of the Baltic nationalities believed that their conflict with Moscow could be solved only through complete separation from the Soviet state, the leaders of the Soviet state misjudged the seriousness of the conflict and crisis, and their responses indicated that they did not understand what was really at stake. Moscow also failed to understand that other Soviet nationalities were adopting a program identical with that first put forward by the Balts.

While Moscow forcibly suppressed the reform movement in Czechoslovakia in 1968, it acted quite differently when it was faced with a much more serious challenge to its authority within the Soviet state, as was the case in Lithuania in 1990–91.

How is one to explain this change in dealing with conflict? There are several possible answers. The Soviets may have revised their views about the nature of conflict and the legitimate ways of dealing with it. The secession of the Baltic states came after the overthrow of Communist regimes in Eastern Europe. One might have thought that Moscow would respond with exceptionally severe measures to a domestic threat after it had peacefully accepted the breakup of the socialist commonwealth in Eastern Europe. Were the Soviets demoralized, unwilling to risk resistance that was to be expected? Was their willingness to tolerate Lithuanian independence a reflection of their weakness? I would like to suggest that, until it was too late, Gorbachev did not quite believe that the secession of the Balts was almost inevitable. His relatively moderate handling of the crisis reflected his underestimation of the power of nationalism. He believed that the Soviet Union was a single country held together not only by Communism but by a common experience dating back many centuries. He stated this view in his last message as president, addressed to the heads of independent republics as they met in Alma Ata on

---

the area. The domestic Soviet imperatives that were operative at the close of World War II still apply . . . that victory remains the most powerful legitimizing experience of the Soviet Communist system, the most authentic bond between the Soviet elite and its Slavic peoples as well as within that elite. Hegemony over East Central Europe compensates for their enormous sacrifices in the war and their enduring grievances since its end. It validates the Soviet system to itself."

December 18, 1991. In the meantime not only the Balts but also other non-Russians had made it clear that they did not regard the U.S.S.R. to be their country. For them, the U.S.S.R. was an empire not worth saving.

Just as the Soviet Union had won recognition as one of the world's two superpowers, forces emerged within the Soviet Union and demanded its breakup. What had traditionally been treated in the Soviet Union as "the nationality problem" and had been regarded by the Communists as a secondary question in relation to class conflict, became transformed into a movement for the establishment of international relations within the U.S.S.R., in other words, for the abolition of the U.S.S.R.

This paradoxical development can be explained by the failure of the Moscow leadership to adjust its political style to the changing domestic and international situation of the Soviet state. As we noted, by the 1930s, the Soviet leadership had adopted the traditional Russian, indeed Muscovite, view of politics, including the approach to the question of conflict and ways of resolving it. Moscow did not revise or transform its traditional "political folkways" even after the Soviet state annexed territories with different political traditions, such as the Baltic republics or western regions of Ukraine. It did not abandon those Muscovite folkways even after the Soviet Union established its control over East Central Europe—and yet, from the very beginning of the Soviet state, the ideology of Communism insisted on regarding Communism as an international force whose sphere of operation extended to the entire globe. Moscow kept on regarding the Soviet state as the prototype for a future organization of humanity. One might think that this was simply an ideological dogma, something not to be taken seriously when one dealt with real issues. But this would be too simplistic a view of ideology in Soviet conduct of foreign or domestic policies.

Since the Soviet state was organized as a federation or as an association of formally independent nation-states (the Union Republics), once the legitimacy of the system was questioned, the internal structure of the state, which was never intended to be taken seriously by the founders of the U.S.S.R., provided a ready framework for the articulation of nationalist secessionist demands *within* the U.S.S.R. Instead of creating an example for others to follow, the Soviets had organized their own state in such a way as to make it easier to be subverted from within.

We can suppose that had Gorbachev really understood the power of the nationalist challenge, he would have responded to it more decisively. Marxism's blindness on the question of nationality likely made it possible for the nationality conflict in the U.S.S.R. to unfold more peacefully than it would have if the Communists took it more seriously. Even Gorbachev could do no better than imagine that if more goods were sent to shops in Nagorno-

Karabakh, the Armenian-Azeri conflict might be brought to a peaceful resolution. He acted in the same spirit when he was faced with more direct challenges to his authority in Central Asia and in the Baltic region.

For many years Soviet Communists justified their rule by comparing the Soviet present with the pre-Soviet, tsarist past. It was a standard item in Soviet propaganda to compare any given Soviet achievement with conditions in Russia in 1913. The Soviet regime got into real trouble when Soviet citizens stopped comparing their lives with those of their grandparents and started making comparisons with life in other countries, first in Eastern Europe, then in the West. These comparisons in space rather than time became very damaging to the prestige of the Soviet system at home.

These unfavorable comparisons with foreign countries had an effect on the ethnic Russians, too. The sight of other nations, which for decades had been fellow members in the socialist commonwealth, adopting new views and practices proved infectious in Russia. This brings us to the next major reason why the Soviet regime failed in Russia. The Communist party, until the very end, remained organized in accordance with the Leninist principle that it was the only spokesman for the working class and the bearer of "scientific" Communist ideology, and not merely an organized expression of some specific social forces such as a class or nationality. On the contrary, the Communist party was said to be an international or supranational entity, and its grasp of social issues rose above the particular class perspectives of individual classes, even above the perspective of the proletariat. This conception of the party not only authorized it to manage ethnicity in accordance with the principles of "scientific Communism," but also denied the workers as workers, in Russia proper as well as elsewhere, the right to organize themselves independently of the party.

As we noted earlier, the Soviet system adopted the political patterns and rules of old Muscovy. That adaptation was functionally effective when, in the 1930s, the Soviet state was confined to the areas traditionally under Moscow's influence. After World War II, "Muscovite political folkways" became less and less adequate for coping with the diversity of the Communist world. Moscow refused to coopt the elites of the Baltic republics to its central leadership, and it failed to create any new structures that would accommodate the political aspirations of leaders like Tito or Mao by giving them a role in running the world Communist movement. Even after the breaks with Tito and with China, the Soviets did not reorganize their relations with the Communist nations of Eastern Europe in a manner that would allow the latter to share power equally with Moscow in running the socialist commonwealth. Finally, in the last instance of this failure to adjust the political "folkways," just as the republics were increasingly articulating their desire for expression and autonomy under Gorbachev, the central leadership in Moscow ethnically was becoming more and more Russian, that is, culturally "Muscovite." If the Moscow leadership had been less Muscovite and more "international," perhaps the conflict we have discussed would have been resolved differently.

But Russia proper was also increasingly rejecting the Muscovite-Soviet system. While this chapter has concentrated on Soviet ways of dealing with ethnic conflict, involving Moscow and the non-Russians, in Russia too there arose demands for depriving the Communist party of its constitutional right to hold the "leading role" in the state and society. The Communist party was forced to abdicate this right and to legalize other political parties. The new view of politics among the educated Russian public was summarized in the phrase "Democracy is conflict"—*Demokratiia est' konflikt.*[15] In other words, public life in a *normally* functioning society entails conflict, contest, competition of opposing views and forces.

This new concept of democracy, or more broadly, of politics, for this is what the statement means, was opposed not only to the Soviet ideas and practices, but also to the traditional Muscovite approach to conflict and conflict resolution.

By the summer of 1991, the defenders of the Soviet state felt that only a recourse to force could save the empire and thus prevent the internationalization of relations between the republics and, at the same time, save the traditional Russian and Soviet theory and practice of politics. Against them, there arose a Russia that defined itself by Western political ideals. That new Russia accepted the view that "democracy is conflict" as the basis of its internal organization and also agreed to treat its relations with the other nations of the former Russian and Soviet empires as belonging properly to the sphere of international relations. It remains to be seen whether this attempt to liberate Russia from both Communism and "Muscovy" will succeed.[16]

---

15. "Demokratiia est' konflikt. Poisk pravovogo resheniia natsional'nykh problem v SSSR," *Vek XX i mir* 12 (1988): 8–17.

16. For a discussion of prospects of democracy in post-soviet Russia and other new states, and of the new international scene after the demise of the U.S.S.R., see the essays of Timothy J. Colton and Robert Legvold in *After the Soviet Union: From Empire to Nations* (New York: W. W. Norton, 1992). Colton and Legvold are the editors of this volume. For a nation-by-nation overview, see Ian Bremmer and Ray Taras, eds., *Nations and Politics in the Soviet Successor States* (Cambridge: Cambridge University Press, 1993).

Managing Organizational Conflict in Japan: Implications for International Relations

John Creighton Campbell

"Today Japan is stepping out onto the world stage" is a commonly accepted proposition. The usual question is what effect this will have on Japan. My question is what effect this will have on the world stage. That Japan's own role will expand is obvious, but beyond that, how will the conduct, the playing of world politics be affected?

After all, the stage conventions and the acting style of international relations must come from somewhere. It is reasonable to suppose they will mainly be defined by the dominant powers of the day. An extreme example is historic East Asia, centuries ago, where countries that formally were vassals (though actually sometimes quite independent) would kowtow to the Son of Heaven. These ritualistic interactions among nations were essentially a projection of domestic Chinese politics. In fact, they cannot be understood without a grasp of fundamental Chinese thinking about conflict and other human relationships (see Donald J. Munro's chapter in this volume).

Similarly, in the postwar world it is the United States that has dominated. It looks natural enough to us, but to those from different cultures, the style as well as the substance of world politics has a distinctively American accent. It is easy for us to visualize the U.S.-Soviet security confrontation as a Western movie, but how would it look as *kabuki*? Or to switch metaphors, we often see economic battles with Japan or the Europeans as a poker game; they would seem quite different if perceived as mah jong.

One purpose of this chapter is to look at how conflict is perceived and handled in a different culture, as a way to shake our assumptions about what is normal or inevitable about conflict in world politics. A further purpose is to suggest specific directions in which international relations might evolve— even possible "lessons." As the world's agenda shifts toward economic problems, and as Japan gains in power, it seems likely that a more Japanese way of doing things will become more prevalent (as I will observe below, the U.S.-Japan trade relationship already has several such characteristics). What is that Japanese way?

Conflict and Japanese Culture

The argument here is avowedly cultural, on the side of the anthropologists (see Smith 1983) against the majority of political scientists who specialize on Japan. Political scientists tend to reject cultural explanations, as so often wrong or silly, as so convenient for those with a political axe to grind (pro- or anti-Japan), or as so contrary to hopes for elegant social science generalization. While recognizing all these dangers, I would point to the virtues of, for example, Michael Blaker's (1977) analysis of prewar Japanese negotiating style, or for that matter, on a different country, the classic characterization by Louis Hartz (1955, 285) of how America's "colossal liberal absolutism" came to be projected on the postwar world.

My interest is less in Japan's international behavior itself, however, than in following up the suggestion by Robert L. Kahn in this volume that how conflict is handled between organizations may be a productive analogy for international relations. More specifically, I think that a particular approach to promoting long-term cooperation within fundamentally conflictual relationships can be found in many Japanese organizational contexts, and that this approach has broader theoretical and practical implications. Between market and hierarchy, looser than contract but more binding than regime, we find "covenants" among organizations that endlessly negotiate about fair shares of costs and benefits in pursuit of survival and growth.

While each such covenant or other manifestation of Japanese-style conflict management has a variety of explanations, the appearance of similar patterns in many different settings suggests an underlying cultural trait. I would argue that the most-fundamental cultural traits are not characteristics ("Japanese are hardworking") or even values ("Japanese prefer group over individual interests"), but understandings of how the world works, of what constitutes the reality that requires attention. The central point here, as Takie Lebra (1976, 2) observes, is that "Japanese are extremely sensitive to and concerned about social interaction and relationships" rather than physical or symbolic objects.

This observation leads to some rather unconventional propositions. The common image of conflict and conflict resolution in Japan is that, in distinction with the West, decision making proceeds by "consensus," which is possible because of the value given to "harmony" or "trust." This statement is not incorrect. However, it is misleading if interpreted as meaning that Japanese are harmonious by nature, or that they see people as naturally harmonious, and therefore find it easy to cooperate. As a recent typical example, Fallows (1989, 28, 33) thinks that Japanese racial unity "expands the radius of trust to include everybody in the country," so that "the sense of bonding is intense and gives most Japanese an instinctive reason to cooperate with each other."

In fact, Japanese do not see themselves as particularly trustful and harmonious. A 1980 survey carried out in Japan and the United States by NHK, the Japanese broadcasting company, included two relevant questions. First, "would you say that most of the time people are helpful or that they are mostly just looking out for themselves?" "Helpful" was picked by 59 percent of Americans and 25 percent of Japanese; "look out for themselves" by 41 percent of Americans and 75 percent of Japanese. Second, similarly, 71 percent of Japanese compared with 33 percent of Americans agreed with the proposition that "most people would try to take advantage of you if they got the chance," rather than trying to be fair (Richardson and Flanagan 1984).

These responses reflect a fundamental pessimism about human nature, a view of people as intrinsically egotistical, selfish, and contentious. Here "harmony" and "consensus" are highly valued precisely because they are so hard to achieve. Disputes between individuals, groups, or institutions will destroy the best-laid plans unless extraordinary pains are taken to exclude or control them. Management of conflict in order to pursue other goals is seen as crucial, indeed a primary task for leaders at all levels of society.

The notion that conflict is just as important in Japan as elsewhere has recently become commonplace in Japanese studies, a reaction against over-celebration of the harmony or consensus model by pundits in Japan and abroad (see Najita and Koschmann 1982; Krauss, Rohlen, and Steinhoff 1984; Mouer and Sugimoto 1986; Pharr 1990; Eisenstadt and Ben-Ari 1990). I will not try to review the many interesting insights about the nature, causes, and implications of conflict in Japan even in this English literature, much less all the relevant analysis in Japanese. The focus here is quite narrow, a particular angle on how conflict has been managed in several organizational settings within Japan, in order to speculate about implications for dealing with international conflict.

Conflict Management within Organizations

The Japanese approach to dealing with conflict can be seen in how organizations are constructed and managed. Several practices are common to business firms, governmental ministries, and other organizations regarded as important in Japan. Recruitment is carefully controlled to screen out potential troublemakers, and long periods of apprenticeship or on-the-job training serve to socialize new members into the ways of the organization and to inculcate a sense of loyalty and solidarity. Personnel are rotated rapidly within the organization to inhibit sectionalism, and outside commitments (such as to professional associations with their own codes of ethics) are minimized. Members are encouraged to socialize after hours so that human bonds of trust will develop, with organizations often supplying recreation facilities, collective

housing, and expense accounts. Formal and informal ideological pronounce-
ments reiterate the uniqueness of the organization and the common fate shared
by all within its boundaries.

At a time of crisis or strain, the organization will step up all these
techniques for increasing internal solidarity. The image is everyone giving
their all and pulling together. Naturally, organizational leaders will often try to
stimulate a sense of peril or threats from outside in order to dampen internal
conflict or increase productivity. The "excessive competition" often seen in
many markets within Japan, as well as the zeal of export campaigns by firms
and the notorious fights among governmental ministries, are partly due to
these organizational techniques.

What if conflict is inherent in the structure or operations of the organization? When important goals require cooperation, as between the marketing
and product-design divisions of a manufacturer, quite elaborate structures for
negotiating differences will be developed. On the other hand, when cooperation is not so crucial, a much higher degree of inefficiency, functional overlap,
and fragmentation of purposes may be tolerated than in an equivalent Western
organization. Moreover, many important decisions that elsewhere would be
either analyzed rationally or fought out politically will be settled by mechanical rules. For example, resource allocation in Japan is often even more incremental or based on preserving "fair shares" than in the West (Campbell 1977).

Most important, enormous attention is paid to what Japanese see as the
most crucial relationship, that between high and low, bosses and employees,
at all levels. The value given to preserving status hierarchies while avoiding
the alienation of subordinates pervades Japanese organizational culture and
helps account for such practices as seniority-based pay and promotion, participatory management techniques, and the norm of passive leadership. In particular, *ringi*-style decision making, in which decisions are reached (at least
formally) on the basis of a document originated by a low-level unit and then
cleared up through the organization, is an elaborate mechanism for getting
everyone on board, especially at lower levels. It remains popular despite the
costs in time and diffusion of accountability.

All these characteristics reflect a view of organizations as essentially
political and conflictive. For example, while an important strain of American
theory on organizational behavior is based on a notion of inherent conflict
(e.g., Cyert and March 1963), in practice American managers often act as if
their firms should be harmonious and rational. When they encounter problems, they think about solving them with technology, money, revising the
organization chart, or some new technique for motivating workers or communicating management objectives more clearly—get things right and everything should run smoothly.

In contrast, as Clark (1979, 136) has observed, "the decision-making process in Japanese companies probably recognizes the existence of such a [Cyert-and-March type] coalition, and the need for a variable and politically determined set of aims, rather more clearly than in the American and British company." Japanese managers are more likely to recognize political problems when they occur, and when trying to solve even nonpolitical problems, to think about how a given solution will affect relationships among individuals and offices. A common response to a new proposal is that it will cause "trouble" (*toraburu*), meaning some difficulty in human relationships that must be dealt with from the start or else the idea should be dropped.

Because an organization brings its members together and provides them with a common purpose, it would seem that conflict within its boundaries would be relatively easy to manage. Nonetheless, Japanese managers think hard about how to deal with internal conflict, sometimes at the expense of values seen as more important elsewhere. Given the apparent effectiveness of many Japanese organizations, the principle of management by preventing "trouble" might have broader applicability, perhaps particularly in international organizations where institutionalized conflict is normal.

Conflict Management between Organizations

Conflict between organizations—as between nations—can often be easily handled simply by avoiding contact, but more elaborate contrivance is required in those cases in which interdependence makes avoidance impossible or too costly. Kahn's chapter outlines a continuum of "managed interdependence" or conflict management between organizations, each category corresponding to a type of relationship between nation-states.

Kahn's main focus is the "joint venture." In Japan, these are seen as extremely difficult to arrange because each parent organization has its own unique personality and its members will strongly identify with it. American executives who have negotiated with a Japanese firm about establishing some cooperative relationship are invariably impressed by how long the process takes, as the Japanese work hard at feeling out the other side to determine whether a match is possible, and then in constructing the social relationship necessary for effective communication and cooperation. Wining and dining, golf, requests for information and mere hemming and hawing may go on for months.

The length and intensity of this process are often even greater for negotiations between Japanese firms than in the cross-national case, because the costs of failure are seen as higher. In fact, mergers and acquisitions are relatively rare in Japan, and so are joint ventures for more than quite limited purposes. Similarly, in the bureaucracy, interagency committees rarely achieve more than a bland, lowest-common-denominator agreement that leaves the participating ministries quite free to proceed on their own. In the few exceptions, when matters are particularly significant and urgent, committee members must be put to work in the same room under high pressure for a long enough time that concern for their joint enterprise comes to outweigh loyalty to the parent organization (Fukui 1978).

Another approach to conflict between organizations, for shorter-term or less-encompassing problems, is to employ a mediator, a conciliator, or a go-between. Ideally, the mediator is higher in status than the two contenders and has an existing relationship with both (though not one of giving orders). After listening to both sides at length, he might suggest some guidelines for talks, or propose some solution that would not have been acceptable to either side unless backed with his prestige. Such "mediation from above" is an important function of the prime minister and other senior politicians in dealing with disputes within government, and of governmental ministries with regard to conflicts among private organizations (such as allocating shares in a cartel). Preservation of this important conflict-resolution role is an important reason why Japanese in positions of authority generally avoid both advocacy of substantive positions on issues and open demonstrations of power. Either would impair the ability to "persuade" both sides in a dispute (Campbell 1984).

A third approach to conflict management is more difficult to explicate. In describing some social interaction, a Japanese will often use the terms *tatemae* and *honne*, which can be glossed as "principles" and "true intentions," but which evoke (along with some related dichotomies—*omote-ura* or front-back, *soto-uchi* or outside-inside) a subtle interplay between public and private, formal and informal, dignified and mundane, onstage and behind-the-scenes, ritual and reality, symbol and substance (Ishida 1984).

Of course, such distinctions are not unknown in the West. In any parliamentary body, for example, a veneer of politeness among enemies is crucial to doing business ("my esteemed colleague the honorable gentleman from . . ."). Much of the art of international diplomacy lies in knowing how to maneuver between the formal level of open meetings and the behind-the-scenes chat. The point is that Japanese negotiators use such techniques particularly well: they see the flowery speeches and stilted interaction of the conference room on the one hand, and the boozy familiarity of the after-hours bar on the other, as equally crucial to making a deal.

And there is more to it. Robert Smith's (1978) dramatic account of a bitter fight about a chicken factory in a small village demonstrates many facets of conflict in Japan: the intensity of underlying resentments ready to explode in a putatively "harmonious" community, a taste for conspiracy and devious tactics, feelings of shame when conflict comes to the surface, the use of mediation from above (a political elder from the county seat was called in, though he failed), and especially, the role of rituals. By stiffly coming together at funerals and other formal occasions, and then starting to use formal polite phrases when meeting on the street, the two sides gradually restored relations. The assumption in Japan is that attitudes are likely to follow behavior, one reason why the surface or dignified *tatemae* level is often perceived as more fundamental than the *honne* level of "real" underlying motives and emotions.

The opposite pattern may also be important: symbolic conflict behavior on the surface, cooperation underneath. Annual labor-management disputes (especially in the public sector) bring out red flags, noisy parades, and radical rhetoric, allowing the expression of strong feelings that may be repressed the rest of the year, and helping labor and perhaps management as well to go along with the eventual deal (Cole 1979, Ben-Ari 1990). Fights about the budget between the Finance Ministry and spending ministries plus their political allies look similar: a lot of noise and conflict on the surface, cooperative negotiations to an easily predicted finish underneath (Campbell 1977). The conflict demonstrates the sincerity of participants to their constituents, and no doubt provides meaning and enjoyment to themselves.

While the wage- and budget-negotiation cases are extreme, many recurring conflicts between organizations will quickly take on ritualistic characteristics in the sense that both sides will act in rather predictable ways. Americans negotiating with Japanese are often annoyed to find themselves in some prescripted drama of conflict. "It's all *kabuki*," they say, which is true enough; the inexperienced or insensitive will go on to dismiss such techniques as trivial or hypocritical. Skillful negotiators learn how to get in on writing the script.

The end as well as these various means of interorganizational conflict resolution should also be noted. In brief, it is to restore, or to create, a social relationship, at the dignified or the mundane level—preferably both (Hanami 1984). If the parties can agree on a basis for talking together—perhaps a "philosophy" or perhaps just an implicit agreement on place, participants, and agenda—the details can be worked out later. An American contract between two firms (or between labor and management) will often include pages and pages of dispute-resolution procedures for various contingencies, while the equivalent in Japan might be a paragraph saying both parties agree to discuss any problems in "good faith." The central achievement in either case is just the principle that negotiations will continue.

As with managing conflict within organizations, the assumption here is that manipulation of social relationships is the way to solve problems. This point may offer some lessons: for example, a role in international dispute resolution for elderly world statesmen in formally high positions, even if they lack real authority or power. And the utility of rituals deserves more attention—as I will suggest below, the United States may already have learned something from Japan about how to ritualize a long-term fractious relationship, to mutual benefit.

Covenants with the State

In the discussion so far, we have found that Japanese "harmony" or "consensus" in many instances means not a lack of conflict but ways of dealing with conflict. What of the most celebrated instance of harmony, the cooperative relationship between government and business so often seen as the key to the Japanese economic miracle? Several recent studies by Western scholars point toward a new interpretation of that relationship.

The main debate over the role of government in Japanese economic growth has been fought between enthusiasts for "industrial policy" and mainstream economists. The former saw the engine of change as Ministry of International Trade and Industry (MITI) bureaucrats, cleverly using market forces to assure efficiency while they restructured industry, while the latter saw competition and entrepreneurship at the firm level as the key, with government playing a supporting role at best (Johnson 1982, 1990; Patrick and Rosovsky 1976). In short, the issue was seen as state versus market, one or the other.

Lately, however, an "in-between" interpretation has become prominent. Daniel Okimoto called his recent book *Between MITI and the Market* (1989) to emphasize the "networks" among firms that allow the state to stimulate and guide economic development. These come in various forms (some called "groups" or *keiretsu*—wordings vary): federations of companies in various industries centered on a bank (often former *zaibatsu* conglomerates), "family" arrangements of a large firm and its suppliers, formal trade and industry associations, informal cartels, research consortia, and so forth. Whether or not the government helped build such networks, they are a necessary condition for effective communication between bureaucrats and businessmen.

Writers like Okimoto, while not ignoring conflict, tend to emphasize cooperation between state and industry to achieve common goals. Other Japan specialists have taken a more political approach, finding a strong element of manipulation in how these groupings are formed, whether the initiative is top-down or bottom-up. Kent Calder (1988) writes of "circles of compensation" created by the LDP or by governmental ministries to attract support from various constituencies by drawing them into long-term exchange relationships. David Friedman (1988) describes how small and medium-sized companies (his main case is machine tools) band together to pressure politicians into providing subsidies, while resisting government attempts to reorganize the industry or guide its development.

A seminal conflict-oriented analysis of the government-business relationship is Richard Samuels's (1987) treatment of market transformations over many years in four segments of the energy industry. In reflecting on why the allegedly "strong" Japanese state has not played a large *direct* role in the market (e.g., through the public corporations so common in the energy field elsewhere), Samuels rejects the argument that MITI bureaucrats were clever enough to work through the market. He points out that MITI had, in fact, tried to take over again and again, but was rebuffed by active or passive resistance from private firms. The relationship was nonetheless quite intimate: Samuels calls it "reciprocal consent," a "permanent negotiation" between industry and government with the payoffs—profits or insurance against risk on the one hand, control or autonomy on the other—always on the table. The key is that the terms of the deal can always be renegotiated to reflect changes in the power balance, caused by changes in the economic environment or other factors. Samuels's picture of government-business relations is thus less one of cooperation than of institutionalized or regulated conflict. It is this pattern we call a "covenant."

Richard Boyd's account of alleged industrial restructuring in shipbuilding in the late 1970s is a detailed and sophisticated demonstration of how difficult maintaining or recreating a covenant can be in times of strain. It took long negotiations, with Transport Ministry officials as well as industry association leaders taking the lead, to develop intricate formulas for capacity reduction among builders on the one hand and for financing of exit costs among banks and other institutions on the other, as well as "to coax parties to those discussions to acknowledge even the most limited of commitments and to ensure that commitments are interlocking" (Boyd 1989, 12). In fact, the resulting policy was probably more significant as a symbolic affirmation of the covenant and its ability to deal with a "crisis" than as an effective solution to real problems.

Beyond economics, collaboration of a similar sort between state authority and outsiders can be found in a variety of unlikely areas. Battles between the ruling LDP and the opposition parties in the national Diet are mitigated or managed—often enough, ritualized—by a long-term exchange relationship that, like much else in Japan, includes money changing hands. The terms of the deal are affected mainly by election results (Krauss 1984). In many localities, police and gangsters, the *yakuza*, have developed a cozy relationship of live-and-let-live as long as lawbreaking is kept within boundaries. The boundaries shift from time to time with public opinion or other environmental change (Ames 1981). Even the student radicals of the late 1960s, violence-prone and dedicated to the overthrow of the system as they were, quickly worked up rules-of-the-game with university and municipal authorities covering the whats, wheres, and whens of their demonstrations and of reprisals. As the radicals waned in power, restrictions could be made tighter and tighter (Steinhoff 1984).

The student movement was a transitory phenomenon, but long-term protest movements, such as the decades of struggle by former outcastes (*bur-akumin*), may well be partially transformed into a clientele trading favors with local bosses, although radical goals and confrontational tactics are also maintained. Frank Upham (1987) dissects state-society legal relationships in this and three other policy areas to demonstrate how far the authorities will go to avoid talking about rights and general moral or legal principles, or about their own procedural obligations and the legal "standing" of others. Japanese legislation is notorious for procedural and substantial vagueness, leaving much discretionary authority to bureaucrats who then are free to be quite accommodating within a framework of "administrative informality."

All these cases have in common an approach to conflict well captured by Samuels's (1987) term for government-business relations, "reciprocal consent"; by Calder's (1988) phrase for ministry-interest group relations, "circles of compensation"; by Upham's (1988) characterization of how the legal system deals with outsider groups as "managed democracy"; or even by Friedman and Samuels's (1992) later word for technology communication among government and firms in the defense industry, "protocols." It is because no label exists to pull all these observations together that I use the term "covenant."

Covenants without the State

For that matter, I see a still-broader scope for this label. The writings mentioned above on "networks" and so forth mostly proceed from an assumption that the critical nexus is the relationship between state and society. It would therefore seem that such approaches to developing cooperation within conflictive relationships would not have much applicability to international relations, where there is no state. However, the Japan literature includes similar observations about relationships among organizations, particularly firms, that do not directly involve the government. Examples include purchasing arrangements between a large manufacturing firm and its suppliers, transactions among the several layers of the complicated distribution system, the *dango* system of rigged bidding among construction companies, space- or time-allocation deals between advertising agencies and mass media organizations, and the extraordinarily intricate work-sharing arrangements among small firms specialized in particular processing stages in the textile industry.

In fact, as many have observed, the Japanese economy seems to be full of cartels, groups, collaborative arrangements, and special deals. The analytic problem is that, according to textbook economics or to more-elaborate formulations like Mancur Olson's *The Rise and Decline of Nations* (1982), all this groupism amounts to rigidification and should be far less efficient and conducive to economic growth than free competition. Still, Japan grows very rapidly.

Ronald Dore addresses this problem in his aptly titled *Flexible Rigidities* (1986) by applying Oliver Williamson's transaction-cost approach to economic organization. Many situations of interdependence that in the West would be handled either through market or hierarchy—auctions or short-term contracts on the one hand, vertical integration on the other—are dealt with through "relational" or "obligational" contracting in Japan. Two or more firms buy and sell from each other for a long time, with prices and other conditions decided neither by unilateral command nor by immediate supply-and-demand conditions. Rather, they are negotiated, with the outcome depending partly on market prices, partly on shifts in the relative power of the participants and, not infrequently, partly on the willingness of one party to help out the other through a spot of trouble. In Dore's view, these and other Japanese "rigidities"—"permanent employment" at the firm level is the best-known example—actually provide more capacity for dynamic adjustment than the classical free-market prescriptions for economic efficiency.

Such deals can be interpreted as a set of techniques for conflict management. Consider the manufacturer-supplier case (the automotive and electrical industries are the most studied—e.g., Smitka 1991). "Just-in-time" inventory control is not only a way to avoid maintaining a large supply of expensive parts, it is a strategy to force repeated small interactions between the supplier and the manufacturer, with immediate attention and tit-for-tat response to a defective part or late delivery. Prices are renegotiated regularly, and the scope of bargaining is expanded by such devices as one-shot bonus payments that reward productivity gains by the supplier but still allow for cutting costs. Personnel exchanges and collaboration in designing parts keep additional channels of communication open.

The politics of such relationships get constant attention. There are frequent assertions of familylike ties, including formal and informal social events to encourage fellow feeling. On the other hand, each side also tries to increase its autonomy (and therefore power) vis-à-vis the other. For example, suppliers try to increase sales to outsiders (say, reducing dependence on the main customer from 70 percent to 60 percent), while manufacturers instigate competitions among their suppliers over who will get to make some new part. Because the implicit contract is seen as lasting forever, such marginal shifts of advantage promise enough payoff to make them worth pursuing, and both sides feel safe enough to fight vigorously.

The manufacturer-supplier relationship is hierarchical, but Dore (1986, 73) observes for horizontal relationships as well a

tendency for the balance between perceptions of competing interest and the perception of a common interest between rival producers of the same commodity to tilt more toward the latter than in most other countries, in spite of the business zeal which Japanese companies otherwise show.

Such perceptions of common interest provide support for cartels, *dango* bid rigging, effective trade associations, joint research projects among giant firms and, in a smaller context, cooperation in irrigation and other village projects among rice-farming households.

But in analyzing rice farmers, Robert Marshall (1984) departs from Dore's emphasis on the development of trust and cooperation. Writing from a game-theory perspective, he sees continued suspicion and fear of exploitation as accounting for Japanese-style collaboration. In a variety of collective decisions reached by farmers in a small village, the requirement of unanimity protects the individual against the group, but it is balanced by the threat of exclusion from future interactions if cooperation is withheld. An elaborate process of discovering each participant's true interests while maintaining a norm against "selfish" open advocacy is needed before the shape of a "fair" settlement can be discerned. This "mutual-investment" model can be effective as a defection-reduction device only when multiple transactions occur over time with no foreseeable end, within a stable and restricted group of participants. Marshall leaves an impression that all the talk of community and harmony is little more than ideology, a polite screen to obscure hardheaded and largely hostile bargaining.

In fact, a review of several studies indicates that the extent to which it is values or structures—feelings of community or trust versus economic or other sanctions—that best explain effective conflict management in horizontal covenants (and for that matter in hierarchical ones as well) will vary greatly depending on both objective circumstances and the predilections or theoretical perspective of the writer. Certainly trust by itself is insufficient to assure cooperation and prevent defection, particularly in the case of a cartel to fix prices and production levels, where cheating by price-cutting is often both easy and profitable. A political mechanism is needed.

The illegal cartel of television manufacturers, described by Yamamura and Vandenberg (1986), relied on secret monthly industry-wide reports of detailed information on prices, profits and rebates compiled by the electronics trade association. If the cartel had been legal, such information might have been enough for MITI to detect violations and assure compliance through "administrative guidance" or sanctions (e.g., the famous Sumitomo Metals case described by Upham 1987). Superordinate authority was lacking, however, so the "big seven" companies developed an extraordinarily intricate system of working groups, most of which met every month for at least ten years. The "TS group" and "Tenth-day group" included midlevel managers of all companies; the "Palace Preparatory Group" digested their materials to make an agenda of unresolved issues for the "Palace Group" (named for one hotel) of senior managing directors, whose decisions would be ratified by top executives in the "Okura Group" (another, better hotel). There was also an "MD Group" which actually voted on production levels and shipments.

The authors note in passing that "students of Japanese management will appreciate the evidence of *ringi*-style decision-making processes in the organization of this clandestine system" (Yamamura and Vandenberg 1986, n. 68). That and more: so carefully delineated a decision-making process, with such frequent meetings among so many people, becomes necessary because separate organizations with sharp conflicts of interest must cooperate. The trick, no doubt, was to accommodate changes in the environment and in the power balance among the companies, as well as the individual peculiarities of each, through incremental variations of the complicated provisions of the deal—many rules of thumb for doing so must have emerged over the decade.

American television manufacturers—or former manufacturers—can testify to the success of this cartel in maintaining high prices and profits in Japan, and helping to finance export drives, along with its companion export cartel that coordinated sales strategies (including very aggressive pricing) in the United States. In general, the Japanese proclivity for groupings of companies, with or without government participation, has often been attacked by Americans, such as the elaborate critique in the 1989–90 Structural Impediments Initiative. Since covenants are formed for the advantage of insiders, they obviously exclude outsiders, Japanese or foreign; moreover, they often raise prices or otherwise exploit consumers or the world at large. Whether all this is moral, fair, or legal, and whether the American or Japanese government can or should do anything about it, are interesting and important questions that need not concern us here.

Moreover, we need not be responsible for assessing the extent or significance of the covenant pattern compared with alternative forms of organization—markets, contracts, hierarchy, whatever—as an explanation of Japanese economic success or of how the political system works. That is too large a task. The point for us is simply that this approach to management of conflict is unusually prevalent in Japan and may offer some broader lessons. To see these more clearly, we need a more analytic view of covenant structure and function.

Covenants as Cooperation among Egoists

A covenant is an agreement to negotiate in perpetuity by two or more participants (usually organizations) who are interdependent but also have interests in conflict. Each participant is willing to give up some autonomy, profit, or other value in exchange for a permanent seat at the table, aid if its survival is threatened, predictability, and avoidance of open conflict. The membership is stable, and transactions with outsiders are discouraged. The ultimate price of defection is exclusion from future cooperation, but minor lapses will be met with less-drastic though immediate sanctions. Although the basis of the arrangement in self-interest is clear to all, it will often be buttressed with an ideology of friendship and "common fate," perhaps even with fictive kinship ties, and "off-the-job" relationships among participants will be encouraged.

The principle for allocation of benefits and burdens is understood to be a version of "fairness" or, as Boyd (1989) puts it, "consensus." That implies not only the decision-making rule of unanimous agreement (genuine or fictive), but the two substantive "operational principles of 'survival of all members' and an 'equal burden of adjustment.'" What "equal" means is subject to negotiation and renegotiation: the strong may have to assume more of the pain if that is necessary for the weak to stay in the game. For example, the deal in shipbuilding called for capacity reductions of 40, 30, 27, or 15 percent depending on the size of the firm. On the other hand, the heavyweights will take a bit of extra advantage when times are good.

While the principles of survival and equal adjustment are similar to "rights" in that they can be legitimately asserted by a participant, they have less content than either a set of explicit constitutional rights or the specific contract provisions of who will do what; moreover, they are not safeguarded by rules of procedure, and there is no real appeal beyond persuading the other members of the covenant. Instead of a legal process, one finds permanent, iterative, frequent negotiations.

As may be inferred from the examples above, the shape of these covenants may be vertical or horizontal; indeed, most are both, and the tension between the contradictory principles of hierarchy and community is an important internal dynamic. The more hierarchical covenants in particular are often more a set of dyadic relationships than a real group, resembling the "stem" form of organization that Nakane (1970) sees as typically Japanese. The government may be involved, but as a participant (albeit in a superior position) rather than a unilateral maker or enforcer of rules.

The covenant form as outlined here resembles the iterative games analyzed by Robert Axelrod in *The Evolution of Cooperation* (1984). Axelrod explores how Prisoners' Dilemma situations of interdependence plus conflict of interest can be managed to maximize the benefits to each participant in the absence of authority. Drawing on theoretical deduction and game simulations supplemented by observation of various cases, he envisions a long-term relationship of repeated negotiations among a stable, closed, relatively small group (the theory itself treats dyads), with good information about the interests of each member, a strong future orientation, tit-for-tat sanctions to inhibit defections for short-term benefit, and norms that discourage envy and encourage reciprocity.

This approach has yet to be extensively reflected in the Japan literature (except for Marshall 1984 and, in passing, Levy and Samuels 1989). However, the studies briefly reviewed above contain many correspondences to Axelrod's prescriptions. For example, Samuels (1987) stresses the stability of the small group of participants as a key condition for "permanent negotiations" and the norm of "reciprocal consent." Dore's (1986) account of regional textile firms' "obligational contracting" remarks on the constant evocation of the future (including grandiose "visions" without much objective reality), and on the regular surveys of economic conditions in the industry that provide accurate information to all. Indeed, many writers have seen *nemawashi* as the key to Japanese decision making: more than actual prenegotiation, this is a process of information exchange so that each participant knows the others' interests. Upham (1987) points to the importance of speedy sanctions, such as those brought to bear on Sumitomo Metals when it temporarily defected from a steel-industry cartel, and of keeping competing interests (consumer or environmental activists) out of the decision-making system.

This somewhat casual list could be extended, but perhaps is enough to indicate that scholars taking various approaches and examining various phenomena have come to emphasize—or have detected the Japanese emphasizing—many of the same ways of dealing with conflict that Axelrod derived theoretically. We might wonder, parallel to the remark by Clark cited above, whether the Japanese had read Axelrod's book about iterative Prisoners' Dilemmas along with Cyert and March on political processes inside companies.

Why So Many?

But of course, for the most part these are not consciously designed structures. As Axelrod's evolutionary approach might suggest, the prevalence of covenants in Japan is due less to anyone's intentions than to distinctive conditions that encourage their development or survival.

What distinctive features? One is homogeneity: the ability to understand the interests and predict the behavior of other participants is enhanced when all the participants are the "same sort of people," likelier in Japan than in a multiethnic country like the United States. Organizational homogeneity—the similarity of jobs, structures, and corporate cultures across companies—helps in the same way.

Another is stability: the long reign of the LDP and the important role of self-reproducing bureaucratic agencies means that key participants in national-level covenants do not change much. A third is rapid economic growth: material benefits are important to sustaining a covenant, and an expanding pie minimizes conflict. A fourth, particularly clear in the case of cartels or rigged bidding, is the legal framework: Japanese laws and their implementation allow much business collusion that would have been prosecuted in the United States (at least until the 1980s).

As well as such "objective" features of the environment, the development and maintenance of covenants has been supported by Japanese culture. A preference for stability and predictability is one factor: for example, "the Japanese uniformly claim that long-term stable relationships with credible suppliers [of uranium], even at higher than market prices, are preferable to the vagaries of the world market" (Samuels 1989, 640). The emphasis on exchange and reciprocity, such as carefully graduated formulas for gift giving, that run throughout Japanese society is another (Hamabata 1990). The legitimacy of household or village models of "community" as a template for many seemingly incompatible forms of organization is a third (Rohlen 1974). Fourth, Dore (1986) and others argue that Japanese ideas about social solidarity, whether Confucian or natively Japanese, are essential to support cooperation-within-conflict relationships in the long term.

Other supporting factors could be listed, but I will instead discuss two points at a bit more length, as they have often been cited as basic elements in Japanese culture, and are also closely related theoretically to the covenant pattern. The first is that Japanese tend not to believe in universal, transcendental principles. A given action is evaluated not as being right or wrong, but as being appropriate, proper, helpful, or not, within a particular context (Benedict 1946, Lebra 1976).

In general, covenants should be more difficult to form to the extent a society assumes that behavior should be constrained by universally applicable principles, whether those be the Ten Commandments, the Koran, the antitrust law, lists of human rights, detailed job descriptions, quarterly profit-and-loss statements, or free trade. That is, the possibility of making a deal is greater the more that is put on the table, or the less that is excluded a priori because it is subject to some transcendental set of norms. Moreover, for a covenant to be maintained indefinitely, the terms of the deal must be adjusted to changing conditions, and that flexibility is maximized when anything can be brought up for renegotiation.

Second, by the same logic, covenants are more likely to be found in the absence of strong central authority. Orders from above would also constrain the items available for making a deal, since participants would have to orient their behavior toward some authority outside of the covenant. As indicated above, although some have seen Japan as a "strong state," it is not one in the usual sense. With brief exceptions, Japanese history has not been characterized by clear-cut, decisive leadership. One manifestation of this pattern is that the prime ministership in postwar Japan is less of a power center than the office of the chief executive in almost any other country (Hayao 1990); many similar examples could be cited.

Did covenants grow up to fill a vacuum of authority, or conversely, as Samuels (1987) suggests, was it the power of private actors organized into covenants that rebuffed a state trying hard to assert authority? Such questions can be left open; the point here, as with the "situational ethic," is that Japanese ways and the covenant structure are well suited to one another.

Lessons for International Relations?

In fact, the two observations above are central to my rather heroic proposition that these Japanese approaches should be helpful in understanding, and perhaps in practicing, international politics. After all, the defining characteristics of the world system are precisely the weakness of universal norms and the lack of central authority. Our painfully developed system of international law—let alone the United Nations—is important but hardly adequate as a system for regulating interactions among sovereign states.

This gap has been filled to some extent by formal or informal "regimes," special-purpose groupings across nations, which are sometimes relatively egalitarian or "horizontal" and sometimes vertical, largely dominated by one or a few powerful nations. Like Japanese covenants, they are structures in between hierarchy and market, and their function is long-term management of conflicting interests so that each participant can gain the benefits of cooperation. Of course, they have rarely been as powerful or far-reaching as Japanese covenants, but we can speculate that they might become so.

The immediate objection to this identification of covenants and regimes is that the Japanese pattern rests on homogeneity and the international one on heterogeneity. On reflection, it appears that this difference should affect the style of the relationship more than its essence. True, Japanese believe they can communicate through nonverbal signals based on shared experience and assumptions. However, the extraordinary efforts devoted to gathering information about the interests of each participant demonstrate that shared assumptions do not go very far when working out the terms of a deal. The emphasis on internal solidarity and on competition in fact makes relationships between Japanese organizations look much like nation-states feeling each other out and reaching limited-purpose deals in their own self-interest. Japanese attempts to surround a covenant with an aura of family feelings can best be seen as a conscious attempt, along with sanctions against defection, to minimize the strong centrifugal forces that are inherent in such relationships.

The similarities in the two situations are more important. The relative weakness of central authority and of law as means for regulating conflict gives participants an incentive to work out deals on their own. Transcendental principles are not very constraining: in the Japanese case, perhaps by cultural predilection; in the international case, because each participant has his own set of moral convictions, which in effect have to be left at the door before a conversation can even begin. The logic of a covenant or a regime has to be its own, based on exchange with negotiable terms.

The postwar relationship that has evolved between Japan and the United States displays many characteristics of a dyadic, hierarchical covenant. Although Washington often tried to insist that the stakes were matters of principle or violations of norms, such as free trade, national treatment, reciprocity, regulations against "dumping," or a variety of purported ethics of international behavior, Tokyo has usually channeled disputes into a negotiation over specific concessions. Today, nearly anything can be talked about, including items that would be regarded as internal interference in most international contexts. The underlying assumption is that long-range mutual benefits make it worth going to considerable trouble to handle the inevitable "frictions" through repeated negotiations; indeed, despite public acrimony, real cooperation in the economic, military, diplomatic, and cultural spheres has expanded rapidly.

In general, the Japan-U.S. relationship looks more like internal Japanese approaches to managing conflict than it resembles either American domestic arrangements or other international deals. The care given to arranging schedules and levels of participation and the frequent, quite-sophisticated shifts back and forth between the formal and the "real" levels are indications. There is great stress on information gathering and on building personal ties—all those expensive Washington insiders are supposed to play both roles. The recent Structural Impediment Initiative talks, in which (formally at least) Japan as well as the United States made demands and the problems on both sides were discussed, indicate at least some capacity to alter the nature of the relationship to reflect shifts in power. All the special deals between the two countries resemble a Japanese-style bilateral covenant.

Conclusion

The argument here has been that Japanese think about and deal with conflict in distinctive ways, observable in how they construct organizations and in how organizations deal with one another—in particular, in the structures of long-term, negotiated conflict we have called "covenants." The fact that the U.S.-Japan relationship resembles such covenants in important ways indicates that these domestic Japanese patterns may be applicable in broader contexts.

Indeed, as our identification of Japanese covenants with Axelrod's theoretically derived prescriptions for cooperation among egoists indicates, there is no necessary connection with Japanese culture or social conditions. Various informal international regimes may be similar. In fact, the weakness of universal principles and of central authority suggests the suitability of the covenant form relative to alternative ways of handling conflict in both Japan and the international arena. Studying its characteristics and dynamics in Japan, where it is most fully developed, might thus yield some lessons.

Such lessons are all the more important to grasp, in that fragmented economic issues seem to be rising and polarized security issues declining on the world's agenda. The former lend themselves to long-term, pragmatic negotiations based on positive-sum game assumptions that allow payoffs to all participants from an expanding pie. For that matter, it is possible that Japan's "flexible rigidities" can provide models for preserving the benefits of market competition while accommodating pressures for more management of international trade and investment.

The idea that Japan might offer lessons to the United States in economic management is now commonplace, if controversial, but few have suggested that the theory or practice of international relations might benefit from Japanese examples. On the contrary, the usual prescription is that Japan must become more assertive, principled, and responsible—act more American—to respond to changes in world politics. But perhaps world politics will change more. In any case, observing how organizations manage to fight productively within Japan should widen our sense of the possible in dealing with international conflict.

REFERENCES

Ames, W. L. 1981. *Police and Community in Japan*. Berkeley: University of California Press.

Aoki, M., ed. 1984. *The Economic Analysis of the Japanese Firm*. Amsterdam: North Holland.

Axelrod, R. 1984. *The Evolution of Cooperation*. New York: Basic Books.

Ben-Ari, E. 1990. "Ritual, Strikes, Ceremonial Slowdowns: Some Thoughts on the Management of Conflict in Large Japanese Enterprises." In *Japanese Models of Conflict Resolution*, edited by S. N. Eisenstadt and E. Ben-Ari, 94–124. London: Kegan Paul.

Benedict, R. 1946. *The Chrysanthemum and the Sword*. Boston: Houghton Mifflin.

Blaker, M. 1977. *Japanese International Negotiating Style*. New York: Columbia University Press.

Boyd, R. 1989. "The Political Mechanics of Consensus in the Industrial Policy Process: The Shipbuilding Industry in the Face of Crisis, 1973–1978." *Japan Forum* 1 (1): 1–17.

Calder, K. E. 1988. *Crisis and Compensation*. Princeton: Princeton University Press.

Campbell, J. C. 1977. *Contemporary Japanese Budget Politics*. Berkeley: University of California Press.

———. 1984. "Policy Conflict and Its Resolution in the Governmental System." In *Conflict in Japan*, edited by E. S. Krauss, T. P. Rohlen, and P. G. Steinhoff, 294–334. Honolulu: University of Hawaii Press.

———. 1988. *Politics and Culture in Japan*. Ann Arbor: Center for Political Studies, University of Michigan.

Clark, R. 1979. *The Japanese Company*. New Haven: Yale University Press.

Cole, R. E. 1979. *Work, Mobility and Participation: A Comparative Study of American and Japanese Industry*. Berkeley: University of California Press.

Cyert, R., and J. G. March. 1963. *The Behavioral Theory of the Firm*. Englewood Cliffs, NJ: Prentice-Hall.

Dore, R. 1986. *Flexible Rigidities: Industrial Policy and Structural Adjustment in the Japanese Economy, 1970–80*. Stanford: Stanford University Press.

———. 1987. *Taking Japan Seriously*. Stanford: Stanford University Press.

Eisenstadt, S. N., and E. Ben-Ari, eds. 1990. *Japanese Models of Conflict Resolution*. London: Kegan Paul.

Fallows, J. 1989. *More Like Us: Making America Great Again*. Boston: Houghton Mifflin.

Friedman, D. 1988. *The Misunderstood Miracle: Industrial Development and Political Change in Japan*. Ithaca, NY: Cornell University Press.

Friedman, D. J. and R. J. Samuels. 1992. "How to Succeed without Really Flying: The Japanese Aircraft Industry and Japan's Technology Ideology." Paper prepared for the National Bureau of Economic Research conference on "Japan and the U.S. in Pacific Asia," San Diego, CA, April 1–3.

Fukui, H. 1978. "The GATT Tokyo Round: The Bureaucratic Politics of Multilateral Diplomacy." In *The Politics of Trade: U.S. and Japanese Policymaking for the GATT Negotiations*, edited by M. Blaker, 75–169. New York: Columbia University, East Asian Institute.

Hamabata, M. M. 1990. *Crested Kimono: Power and Love in the Japanese Business Family*. Ithaca, NY: Cornell University Press.

Hanami, T. 1984. "Conflict and Its Resolution in Industrial Relations and Labor Law." In *Conflict in Japan*, edited by S. Krauss, T. P. Rohlen, and P. G. Steinhoff, 107–35. Honolulu: University of Hawaii Press.

Hartz, L. 1955. *The Liberal Tradition in America: An Interpretation of American Political Thought since the Revolution*. New York: Harcourt, Brace and World.

Hayao, K. 1990. *The Japanese Prime Minister in the Policy Process*. Ph.D. Dissertation, Political Science, University of Michigan.

Ishida, T. 1984. "Conflict and its Accomodation: *Omote-Ura* and *Uchi-Soto* Relations." In *Conflict in Japan*, edited by S. Krauss, T. P. Rohlen, and P. G. Steinhoff, 16–38. Honolulu: University of Hawaii Press.

Johnson, C. 1982. *MITI and the Japanese Economic Miracle*. Stanford: Stanford University Press.

———. 1990. "The Japanese Economy: A Different Kind of Capitalism." In *Japanese Models of Conflict Resolution*, edited by S. N. Eisenstadt and E. Ben-Ari, 39–59. London: Kegan Paul.

Krauss, E. S. 1984. "Conflict in the Diet: Toward Conflict Management in Parliamentary Politics." In *Conflict in Japan*, edited by S. Krauss, T. P. Rohlen, and P. G. Steinhoff, 243–93. Honolulu: University of Hawaii Press.

Krauss, E. S., T. P. Rohlen, and P. G. Steinhoff, eds. 1984. *Conflict in Japan*. Honolulu: University of Hawaii Press.

Lebra, T. 1976. *Japanese Patterns of Behavior*. Honolulu: University of Hawaii Press.

Levy, J. D., and R. J. Samuels. 1989. "Institutions and Innovations: Research Collaboration as Technology Strategy in Japan." Paper prepared for the "Conference on

Oligopolies and Hierarchies: Strategic Partnerships and International Competition," Fondation de Royaumont, Asnieres-sur-Oise, France, April 20–23.

Marshall, R. C. 1984. *Collective Decision Making in Rural Japan*. Ann Arbor: University of Michigan, Center for Japanese Studies.

Mouer, R., and Y. Sugimoto. 1986. *Images of Japanese Society: A Study in the Structure of Social Reality*. London: Kegan Paul.

Najita, T., and J. V. Koschmann, eds. 1982. *Conflict in Modern Japanese History*. Princeton: Princton University Press.

Nakane, C. 1970. *Japanese Society*. Berkeley: University of California Press.

Okimoto, D. I. 1989. *Between MITI and the Market: Japanese Industrial Policy for High Technology*. Stanford: Stanford University Press.

Olson, M. 1982. *The Rise and Decline of Nations: Economic Growth, Stagflation, and Social Rigidities*. New Haven: Yale University Press.

Patrick, H., and H. Rosovsky, eds. 1976. *Asia's New Giant: How the Japanese Economy Works*. Washington, DC: Brookings Institution.

Pharr, S. J. 1990. *Losing Face: Status Politics in Japan*. Berkeley: University of California Press.

Richardson, B. M., and S. C. Flanagan. 1984. *Politics in Japan*. New York: Harper-Collins.

Rohlen, T. P. 1974. *For Harmony and Strength: Japanese White-Collar Organization in Comparative Perspective*. Berkeley: University of California Press.

Samuels, R. J. 1987. *The Business of the Japanese State: Energy Markets in Comparative and Historical Perspective*. Ithaca, NY: Cornell University Press.

———. 1989. "Consuming for Production: Japanese National Security, Nuclear Fuel Procurement and the Domestic Economy." *International Organization* 43 (4): 625–46.

Smith, R. J. 1978. *Kurusu: The Price of Progress in a Japanese Village, 1951–1975*. Stanford: Stanford University Press.

———. 1983. *Japanese Society: Tradition, Self and the Social Order*. Cambridge: Cambridge University Press.

Smitka, M. 1991. *Competitive Ties: Subcontracting in the Japanese Automotive Industry*. New York: Columbia University Press.

Steinhoff, P. 1984. "Student Conflict." In *Conflict in Japan*, edited by E. S. Krauss, T. P. Rohlen, and P. G. Steinhoff. Honolulu: University of Hawaii Press.

Upham, F. K. 1987. *Law and Social Change in Japan*. Cambridge: Harvard University Press.

———. 1988. Presentation at panel on "Postwar Japanese History: A Reassessment." Annual meeting of the Association for Asian Studies, Chicago, March 26.

Wakasugi, R. 1986. *Gijutsu Kakushin to Kenkyû Kaihatsu no Keizai Bunseki*. Tokyo: Tôyô Keizai Shinposha. Cited in Levy and Samuels 1989.

Yamamura, K., and J. Vandenberg. 1986. "Japan's Rapid-Growth Policy on Trial: The Television Case." In *Law and Trade Issues of the Japanese Economy*, edited by G. Saxonhouse and K. Yamamura, 238–83. Seattle: University of Washington Press.

Looking Forward: International Conflict in a Broader Perspective

Harold K. Jacobson and William Zimmerman

The outlines and character of international relations and international conflict in the remaining years of the twentieth century and the early years of the twenty-first are at best barely discernible. Revolutionary changes have been launched in the European states that had Communist governments and centrally planned economies. These changes have led to the demise of the alliance that united several of these states, the Warsaw Treaty Organization, and to the collapse of several of the states themselves, most notably the Soviet Union. The cold war, which could have brought forth nuclear Armageddon, has ended. The revolutionary changes, however, continue. Where they will lead cannot be foretold. What is clear is that the East-West conflict that dominated and structured international relations from the early post–World War II years until the late 1980s is a closed chapter. It could resurface, another pervasive dominating conflict could arise, or there could be multiple conflicts. Future conflicts could bring the world once more to the brink of massive violence. Perhaps, however, this could be forestalled.

The uncertainty about the nature of future international relations and conflict provides the occasion and the possibility for thinking about international conflict not in terms of particular historical circumstances, but more generally. If the ideas that Kenneth Waltz presented in *Theory of International Politics*[1] provided a guide to the future, one would expect that sooner or later the international system would be restructured along predictable lines; an expansionist state would challenge the territorial status quo, countervailing power would be amassed, and a new balance of power would be created, resulting in either a bipolar or multipolar configuration of international politics. For Waltz, international politics is an endless cycle of reconfigurations of balances of power.

This book suggests another vision, one that is more hopeful. It has drawn

---

1. K. W. Waltz, *Theory of International Politics* (Reading, MA: Addison-Wesley, 1979).

on different disciplines and cultures for insights that could contribute to broadening the understanding of international conflict and to developing alternative approaches for dealing with international conflict. It does not argue that theories developed in other fields or broad cultural understandings can be applied directly to international politics, but it does maintain that the insights gleaned from other disciplines and cultures are relevant and can contribute to reformulating thought about international conflict. This chapter will synthesize and highlight several of the more important points presented in the preceding chapters.

The most fundamental point concerns the inevitability and pervasiveness of conflict. On this point, the authors agree with Waltz. In the opening chapter, Bobbi Low showed how conflict occurs among all species, and she analyzed the biological and evolutionary roots of conflict among humans. Conflict among humans is especially dangerous because of the human capability to develop weapons with vast destructive power. For this reason, it is essential to control and manage conflict among humans and, to the extent possible, steer it toward constructive rather than destructive ends. All of the chapters in this book take conflict on all levels—interpersonal, interorganizational, intranational, and international—as a given. Conflict will occur.

A second point is that how societies think about and deal with conflict internally affects how they deal with international relations and international conflict. There are broad, general attitudes toward conflict that structure thinking within societies. There appear to be two polar positions: one sees conflict as inevitable, the other views conflict as an aberration that could be eliminated. Donald Munro described the traditional Chinese view that conflict was the result of a lack of unified thinking, a correctable flaw. Roman Szporluk described the similar, traditional Marxist view: that conflict would be eliminated when class divisions were. In both China and Russia, the assumption that conflict could be eliminated affected the political elite's views toward international relations as well as domestic issues.

All of the chapters in this volume make it evident that acceptance of the inevitability of conflict is a precondition to dealing with conflict other than through repression and suppression. Denying the existence and legitimacy of conflict within their societies affects the way elites and citizens think about international conflict. Societies that deny the legitimacy of domestic conflicts are likely to take a messianic approach to international conflict; they cannot deal with it as an ordinary phenomenon. Though they may, by force of circumstances, endure international conflict, there is always the underlying belief that conditions could be changed to eliminate the basis for conflict.

Accepting the inevitability of conflict means acknowledging that individuals and groups have different interests and that these differing interests can cause conflicts. Munro and Szporluk both indicated movement in China and

Russia toward acceptance of this view. Dealing with conflict effectively, however, requires more than acknowledging that conflict is inevitable; it requires adopting a morally neutral stance toward interest-based differences that result in conflict.

The argument that broad attitudes toward conflict affect the ways that political elites treat both domestic and international issues departs sharply from Kenneth Waltz's position that factors within countries have little effect on their international behavior. For Waltz, the key and the dominant factor shaping the international behavior of states, especially in the realm of conflict, is the international system and its structure.

The argument presented here reinforces the understanding built into the United Nations Charter that efforts to deal with international conflict must encompass concern for the nature of domestic regimes. The United Nations Charter mandates efforts to promote respect for human rights as a way of working toward international peace.[2] Human rights and democracy provide a structure for dealing with and managing interpersonal and intergroup conflict in nonviolent ways. The argument presented here also fits well with the emerging empirical evidence that democracies do not go to war with each other.[3]

Although the chapters in this volume are based on the assumption of the inevitability of interest-based conflicts, they also clearly acknowledge that conflicts and conflict processes contain elements that go beyond rationality. As Helen Weingarten put it, "people select means and goals primarily on the basis of their values, emotions, and social bonds." Eugene Burnstein, Mark Abboushi, and Shinobu Kitayama showed how normal mental processes result in magnifying the depth and extent of conflicts and perpetuating them.

This leads to a third insight. Managing conflicts involves dealing with the nonrational as well as with the rational bases for conflicts and utilizing other strategies for problem solving beyond those based on rationality alone. In Weingarten's terms, conflict management strategies must be designed "to fit a world that is considerably more complex than an iterated Prisoners' Dilemma game."

When conflict becomes so acute as to be classified as war in Weingarten's terms, sometimes the only possible strategy is the forcible prevention of aggression. Much theorizing about international conflict has focused precisely on this issue. Traditional balance-of-power theory and modern deterrence theory postulate that countering force with force will prevent aggression.

---

2. See United Nations Charter, Article 1, paragraphs 2 and 3; Article 55; Article 62; and Article 68.

3. See B. Russett, "Politics and Alternative Security: Toward a More Democratic, Therefore More Peaceful, World," *Alternative Security: Living without Nuclear Deterrence*, ed. B. H. Weston (Boulder: Westview Press, 1990), 107–36.

However, conventional theorizing about international conflict has seldom gone beyond this. In fact, some analysts such as Waltz explicitly argue that going beyond the power relations among states is irrelevant to issues of international conflict and conflict management. We take a different position. Weingarten argues that, in interpersonal conflicts involving intimate enemies, experience "suggests that agreements of nonaggression will only be sustained over the long run if the individual's sense of identity becomes invested in nonviolence and cooperation rather than if these behaviors are compelled by pressure from outside."

One, of course, cannot assume that generalizations drawn from analyses of interpersonal conflict apply automatically and without modification to international conflict. Nevertheless, several chapters in this volume reinforced and amplified Weingarten's point, even some that might not have been expected to do so.

Political science has traditionally focused on the role of power as a cause of international conflict and as a tool for dealing with it. J. David Singer's and A. F. K. Organski's chapters are both in this tradition, but they also departed from it in important and interesting ways. Singer's historical analyses intriguingly demonstrated that balance-of-power strategies have been, at best, only marginally effective in preventing the outbreak of war and aggression. Could it be that, in international relations as in interpersonal relations, deeper solutions are required? Organski argued that unipolarity, not bipolarity or multipolarity explains the relatively pacific character of international relations since World War II, and he projected a continuation of unipolarity into the distant future. But his explanation holds only because the dominant power has not had territorial ambitions and its goals have been widely perceived as being relatively benign. In addition, countries throughout the world emulate the dominant power's values and seek benefit from association with it. Both chapters clearly made the point that power and force alone do not create peace.

The fourth point then is that, although force may be required to stop conflict from turning violent or to prevent aggression, separating parties to a conflict by force or mobilizing counterforce to deter aggression cannot be the only component of a strategy for managing international conflict.

The basic point that John Cross made is related. Political science—and thus conventional theorizing about international conflicts—has tended to view conflicts as zero-sum games, as indeed is appropriate when the only or the central issue is sovereignty or control over territory. Cross argues that economists have never been comfortable with this approach, they are concerned with the creation of value as well as its distribution.

The fifth insight is that creative thinking about international conflict and its management requires that efforts should be made to view conflicts as potential positive-sum games, or that, as Weingarten argued, the principals see their interdependence and the opportunities that relationships offer for mutual gains through cooperation as well as the issues that divide them. International trade has been the conventional vehicle for realizing mutual benefits, and Richard Rosecrance, in his book *The Rise of the Trading State: Commerce and Conquest in the Modern World*, has demonstrated that as countries focus more and more of their attention on the benefits to be gained from interdependence, the threat of violence recedes.[4]

In the present volume, both John Cross and Robert Stern stressed the potential benefits of trade, and Stern showed the futility of trade wars. He also demonstrated the practical difficulties of efforts to use trade policies to obtain political goals or to gain economic benefits at the expense of others. According to his analysis, free, nondiscriminatory trade is the best formula for realizing many of the benefits of interdependence and international cooperation. Stern also recognized, though, that adjustment processes can be painful, and he urged cautious, deliberate steps toward free trade.

Interestingly, the United Nations Charter foresaw the connection between international trade and conflict management, and mandated the promotion of international trade as an approach to gaining and maintaining peace.[5] The founders of the United Nations felt that international trade was so important that before the U.N. came into being, specialized agencies had been created to facilitate international trade.[6]

But even if interdependence and international trade could work their benefits, there would, nevertheless, continue to be conflicts, and they could escalate. Beyond seeking to achieve the benefits of interdependence, a strategy for managing international conflicts must contain prescriptions for dealing with those that exist and will arise.

Singer argued for the importance of information and analyses in conflict management. He maintained that policies need to be based on the best knowledge, available. Burnstein and his colleagues demonstrated how, when individuals have minimal knowledge, they view issues stereotypically and simplistically, which can exacerbate conflict. Weingarten, on the other hand, showed how more knowledge may make adversaries more aware of the depth of their controversies.

Are these two, apparently contradictory positions reconcilable? In the long run, knowledge cannot be suppressed. Moreover, the benefits of cooper-

---

4. See R. Rosecrance, *The Rise of the Trading State: Commerce and Conquest in the Modern World* (New York: Basic Books, 1986).

5. See United Nations Charter, Article 1, paragraph 3; Article 55; and Article 62.

6. The International Monetary Fund and the International Bank for Reconstruction and Development were created at the Bretton Woods Conference in 1944. The General Agreement on Tariffs and Trade was created three years later.

ation and interdependence are frequently not immediately obvious; they must be pointed out. Knowledge is an inevitable and essential ingredient in the management of conflict, but, for the reasons that Weingarten pointed out, knowledge alone will not produce pacific outcomes. Knowledge can only work beneficially when there is trust among the principals and when there is a basic acceptance of the reality of interdependence.

Weingarten showed that, through the processes of conflict, the attitudes of the parties can shift from viewing the issues at stake in morally neutral terms to seeing them as involving fundamental principles. Don Herzog, in his chapter, demonstrated how easily and frequently this has happened in American political life. Conflict management at all levels involves controlling and reversing such processes. Herzog would plead for Americans to adopt more sophisticated and nuanced attitudes to international conflict and war, and he showed how traditional American political culture and theory provide bases for such shifts.

Weingarten described techniques that have been developed in dealing with interpersonal conflicts for freezing and gradually diminishing the level of tension among parties to conflicts. Other analyses in the book introduce other possibilities. John Campbell showed how prevalent conflict-moderation and resolution techniques are in Japanese political culture, and Robert Kahn showed how they have been developed in organizations. In short, there is a rich menu of techniques that have been used in interpersonal and intergroup conflicts that could be applied to international conflicts.

The sixth point then is that a variety of techniques exist for managing conflict. Information is important, and in any case cannot be suppressed, but information alone cannot be counted on to prevent conflicts from escalating or to diminish their intensity or resolve them.

The perspective of this book is optimistic. Conflict, though inevitable, can be dealt with. The cycle of World War I, World War II, and the cold war need not be repeated.

There is, however, one glimpse in the book of a possible darker future. Organski and Arbetman noted that China could, in a relatively short time, have the potential power to challenge the unipolar character of the international system. This possibility, combined with Munro's description of how ambivalent the Chinese political elite has been about accepting a pluralist view of conflict, could foreshadow an international conflict fraught with ideological and messianic overtones. The chapters in this book suggest strategies that could be employed in efforts to avoid the bleak possibility of a dangerous conflict involving China.

Many elements of the new thinking produced by this collection echo ways of thinking about international conflict that have a long lineage. The emphasis on human rights and economic growth through international trade found institutional expression in the United Nations Charter. Both prescriptions have deep roots in traditional political-economic theorizing, going back at least to Adam Smith and Immanuel Kant. That these prescriptions were deemphasized, neglected, or forgotten during the cold war should perhaps not be surprising. The cold war focused attention on the role of power in conflict. With the passing of the cold war, a broader approach is not only possible but mandatory. To focus exclusively on the role of power in the management of international conflict could be counterproductive, reproducing the same history that has plagued the twentieth century.

This book shows again the relevance of classical ideas about human rights, democracy, and trade to managing international conflict. It also adds new insights from the study of human behavior in the United States and other societies. The menu of techniques for dealing with international conflict is rich and varied. The task is to choose appropriately from this menu in the new, complex, and somewhat opaque international relations of the closing years of the twentieth century. The variety of techniques, many familiar and some new, gives cause for hope.

Contributors

Mark Abboushi has focused on researching the psychology of ethnic mobilization and has just completed an analysis of beliefs about the causes of group behavior. He is employed by the National Analyst in Philadelphia.

Marina Arbetman is Assistant Professor of Political Science at Tulane University and the Murphy Institute of Political Economy. Her current research interests include the development of measures of political capacity and the political economy of exchange-rate fluctuations.

Eugene Burnstein is Professor of Psychology and Research Scientist in the Research Center for Group Dynamics at the University of Michigan. He is currently studying the psychological processes involved in minority influence, intergroup conflict, and national identity.

John Creighton Campbell is Professor of Political Science and Director of the Japan Technology Management Program at the University of Michigan. His book *How Policies Change: The Japanese Government and Aging Society* was awarded the Masayoshi Ohira Memorial Prize for 1992.

John G. Cross is Professor of Economics and Associate Dean in the College of Literature, Science, and the Arts at the University of Michigan.

Don Herzog is Professor of Law and Associate Professor of Political Science at the University of Michigan.

Harold K. Jacobson is Jesse Siddal Reeves Professor of Political Science, Director of the Center for Political Studies, and Co-Director of the Program in International Peace and Security Research at the University of Michigan. He is the author of numerous works on international institutions and politics.

Robert L. Kahn is a social psychologist, now Professor Emeritus of Psychology and of Public Health and Research Scientist Emeritus in the Institute for Social Research at the University of Michigan. His research is concentrated on large-scale organizations—the factors that render them effective or ineffective, the quality of working life they provide, and their impact on employee health and well-being. He is currently a consultant to the MacArthur Foundation and a member of the Consortium for Productivity in the Schools.

Shinobu Kitayama, on leave from the University of Oregon, is carrying out cross-cultural experiments on emotions and group membership at Kyoto University, Japan.

321

Bobbi S. Low is Professor of Resource Ecology at the University of Michigan. Her research focuses on the behavioral ecology of resource use in humans.

Donald J. Munro is Professor of Philosophy and of Chinese at the University of Michigan. By training and research a classicist in Chinese studies, Munro also studies the perspective on contemporary China afforded by that experience.

A. F. K. Organski is Professor of Political Science and Program Director, Center for Political Studies, Institute for Social Research at the University of Michigan. He is the author, most recently, of *The $36 Billion Bargain*, and senior author of *The War Ledger* and *Births, Deaths, and Taxes*. The chapter in this volume is a sketch for a major work of the same title, in preparation.

J. David Singer is Professor of Political Science at the University of Michigan and founder and Director of the Correlates of War Project there.

Robert M. Stern is Professor of Economics and Public Policy in the Department of Economics and Institute of Public Policy Studies at the University of Michigan. He has published numerous books and articles over the past thirty-five years on a wide variety of topics, including international commodity problems, the determinants of comparative advantage, price behavior in international trade, balance-of-payments policies, and the computer modeling of international trade and trade policies.

Roman Szporluk is Professor of History at Harvard University and an associate of Harvard's Ukrainian Institute and of the Russian Research Center. He is the author of many publications. One of his recent works is "The National Question" in *After the Soviet Union*, edited by Timothy J. Colton and Robert Legvold. He is completing a book on the history of the Ukraine from the eighteenth century to the present.

Helen R. Weingarten is Associate Professor in the School of Social Work at the University of Michigan. She is a member of the Program in Conflict Management Alternatives—an interdisciplinary faculty program focused on advancing theory and research on the intersection of social justice, social change, and social conflict.

William Zimmerman is Professor of Political Science and Co-Director of the Program in International Peace and Security Research at the University of Michigan. The author of many works, his most recent book is an edited volume, *Beyond the Soviet Threat: Rethinking American Security Policy in a New Era*, also published by the University of Michigan Press.

Index